Expecting Pears from an Elm Tree

Expecting Pears from an Elm Tree

Franciscan Missions on the Chiriguano Frontier
in the Heart of South America, 1830–1949

ERICK D. LANGER

Duke University Press
Durham and London
2009

© 2009 Duke University Press
All rights reserved

Designed by Amy Ruth Buchanan
Typeset in Dante by
Tseng Information Systems, Inc.
Library of Congress Cataloging-in-
Publication Data appear on the last
printed page of this book.

Bautizar á un indio adulto que goza de salud completa, es lo mismo que pedir peras al olmo, solo pide el Sacramento cuando ve que no hay esperanza de vida y al principio de una Misión aún eso es dificultoso y muchísimos lo rechazan terminantemente.

To baptize an adult Indian who enjoys complete health is the same as to expect pears from an elm tree; [he] only asks for the sacrament when he sees that there is no hope for living, and at the beginning of a mission even that is difficult and many reject [baptism] peremptorily.

—Fr. Bernardino de Nino, OFM,
Etnografía chiriguana, 1912

CONTENTS

List of Illustrations and Tables ix
Acknowledgments xi
Introduction 1

1. The "Chiriguano Wars" 21
   Indian Warfare and the Establishment of the Missions
2. The Franciscans 61
3. Death and Migration 101
   The Population Decline of the Missions
4. Daily Life and the Development of Mission Culture 126
5. Conversion, Chiefs, and Rebellions 160
   Relationships of Power on the Missions
6. Missions and the Frontier Economy 196
7. Outside Relations and the Decline of the Missions 218
8. From the Chaco War to Secularization, 1932–1949 257
9. Comparisons 270

Appendix: The Inauguration of Tiguipa Church (1902) 284
Glossary 289
Notes 291
Bibliography 337
Index 355

LIST OF ILLUSTRATIONS AND TABLES

Illustrations

MAP. The Chiriguanía and environs. Created by Jerome Cookson. xiv

FIGURE 1. The Thouar expedition arrives in Mission Aguairenda on 18 July 1883. 81

FIGURE 2. Mandeponay of Macharetí, ca. 1920. 97

FIGURE 3. Macharetí mission. 130

FIGURE 4. Mission San Francisco Solano del Pilcomayo. 131

FIGURE 5. Chiriguanos from Mission San Pascual de Boicovo in traditional garb. 134

FIGURE 6. Chiriguano women from San Pascual de Boicovo. 135

FIGURE 7. Indian schoolgirls outside the San Francisco del Pilcomayo mission school playing *chocorore*. 142

FIGURE 8. The mission school at San Miguel Arcángel de Itau. 143

FIGURE 9. Unidentified mission church during services. 154

FIGURE 10. Chiriguano women converts on an unidentified mission. 155

FIGURE 11. Visit of Monseñor Hipólito Ulivelli and Franciscan delegation to Mission Macharetí around 1920. 181

FIGURE 12. View of Mission Macharetí from the central plaza. 193

Tables

TABLE 1. Franciscan missions of the Tarija convent. 52

TABLE 2. Franciscan missions of the Potosí convent. 53

TABLE 3. Number and type of Franciscans entering Tarija convent, 1835–1880. 64

TABLE 4. Epidemics and famines on the Franciscan missions, 1860–1922. 107

TABLE 5. Mortality and migration on Mission Aguairenda, 1878–1913. 110

TABLE 6. Percentage of population decline due to emigration in Mission Aguairenda, 1879–1912. 111

TABLE 7. Mortality and migration on Mission Macharetí, 1877–1913. 112

TABLE 8. Net migration in Mission Macharetí, 1879–1913. 113

TABLE 9. Males and females on Mission Macharetí, 1900. 113

TABLE 10. Typical school day for girls in the Tarija missions. 140

TABLE 11. School attendance in Tarairí mission, 1879–1913. 146

TABLE 12. School attendance in Mission Santa Rosa de Cuevo, 1889–1912. 146

TABLE 13. Adult baptisms in Mission Santa Rosa de Cuevo, 1889–1910. 163

TABLE 14. Children baptized in artículo mortis in Tarairí, 1855–1874. 165

TABLE 15. Converted versus unconverted Indians on Mission Santa Rosa de Cuevo, 1889–1909. 166

TABLE 16. Dates of mission establishment and convert majority. 167

TABLE 17. Income and expenditures compared to population on Mission Santa Rosa de Cuevo, 1887–1912. 210

TABLE 18. Franciscan mission population in 1930. 258

ACKNOWLEDGMENTS

I began this book project in 1988, confident that I would be able to finish it in a relatively short time. Almost two decades later, it is clear that my optimism was misplaced, though the project itself continued to give me much intellectual joy over the years. As a result of this long span I have accumulated a large number of personal debts to those who have helped me in completing this book.

The individuals in charge of the archives that I utilized were essential to the success of this project. They include foremost the late Fr. Gerardo Maldini, OFM, who kindly gave me access to the archives in the Franciscan convent in Tarija, Bolivia. I had met Fr. Maldini many years earlier, when he was parish priest in Cuevo, on the Chaco frontier and later he permitted me to travel with him in his intrepid Toyota Land Cruiser to visit his parishioners throughout the former mission territory. Since then, I have learned much from him about the Franciscans, the missions, and the Catholic Church as he kindly opened the Tarija convent archive to me and conversed with me about his order and its missionary enterprise. Fr. Lorenzo Calzavarini, OFM, his able successor, also helped me in every way possible and gave me the benefit of his knowledge in his office over hot cups of espresso.

My heartfelt thanks to the late Gunnar Mendoza, director for fifty years of the Archivo y Biblioteca Nacionales de Bolivia (ABNB), who not only provided support in the archives but shared with me a crucial aid, his first project at the ABNB, a listing of all official correspondence on the eastern frontiers. Subsequent directors at the ABNB, René Arze Aguirre, Josep Barnadas, Hugo Poppe E., and Marcela Inch, also provided important support.

In Potosí, Fr. Sergio Castelli, OFM helped me greatly in gaining access to the Franciscan convent's archive. Monsignor Juan Pellegrini, OFM opened the archives of the Apostolic Vicariate in Camiri; P. Francisco Foccardi, OFM let me work in Cuevo and provided lodging and a kerosene lamp after dark, just as Fathers Fulgencio and Simon Furletti, OFM did in Machareti.

José Barrancos, the secretary of the Sociedad de Agricultores y Ganaderos de Pequeños Propietarios de Macharetí, kindly facilitated the minutes of the organization to me. Prof. Alejandro Ortega Chávez and the Hon. Alcalde Municipal Guillermo Salazar Echart let me use the archives of the Delegación del Gran Chaco in Villamontes. Dr. Ricardo Ramos Prieto, Dr. Antonio Campero Segovia, and Dra. Trinidad Peña Aguero authorized the organization and use of the Juzgado de Partido y Instrucción de Entre Ríos, while Dra. Felicidad Castillo Ibáñez, Ingrid Rodríguez Flores, Dra. Doris Calderón, Delia Jaramillo Fernández, and Lidia Cruz helped organize the judicial archives there.

I also want to thank Eduardo Trigo O'Connor D'Arlach, who provided a copy of Francis Burdett O'Connor's diary, maps of Tarija, and his friendship; Zulema Bass Werner de Ruiz, Roberto Ruiz, and Guillermo Arancibia provided much other help in Tarija. Holger "Piti" Schütt provided friendship and housing in Potosí, as did my dear compadres Gonzalo and Mary Barrero in Sucre. Thanks to Jacqueline Bazoalto, who provided able research assistance in Tarija.

In the United States, Katherine McCann has been very helpful in getting me sources at the Library of Congress.

My thanks to two of my children, Rafael and Elizabeth, who accompanied me on that first research trip in 1988 to Tarija; Rafael also helped as research assistant on a subsequent trip in 1997. Jim and Naomi also suffered through many years of my writing this book.

Many organizations have provided financial aid for me to complete this research. They include the Fulbright Scholar Program, administered by the Council for International Exchange of Scholars; the American Philosophical Society; the American Historical Association through their Albert J. Beveridge Grant for Research in the History of the Western Hemisphere; and the Research Enablement Program, a grant program for mission scholarship supported by the Pew Charitable Trusts, Philadelphia, and administered by the Overseas Ministries Study Center in New Haven, Connecticut. My heartfelt thanks to all of these organizations; without their support, I would not have been able to start or finish this project.

I am also greatly indebted to Robert H. Jackson, who repeatedly read through the manuscript and made sure that I finished "the book I had begun in the last century" (as Robert put it), as well as Rick Maddox at Carnegie Mellon University. At Carnegie Mellon University, many students helped to collect or analyze data. I want to thank Cameron Brown, Thibaut de Barros Conti, Naci Can, Mirjana Lehane, Tania Scheer, and

John Thomas for their help with this book. Isabelle Combès has kindly provided extensive comments on chapter 1. I also want to thank the two anonymous reviewers for Duke University Press, and Valerie Millholland, who has also over the years encouraged the completion of the manuscript. A presentation of chapter 2 at St. Bonaventure University, at the invitation of Joel Horowitz, proved very useful. My colleagues at Georgetown, John McNeill, John Tutino, Bryan McCann, David Goldfrank, and Tommaso Astarita, and my student Marisabel Villagomez were kind enough to take some of their summer to read portions of the manuscript and give me valuable advice, which I have incorporated into the finished product. Of course, all errors of fact or interpretation are my own responsibility.

My thanks to Neal McTighe and Penelope Cray at Duke University Press, who took the manuscript through the production process and who improved it in many details.

The University of Nebraska Press kindly permitted me to reproduce in chapter 6 of this book portions of "Missions and the Frontier Economy: The Case of the Chiriguano Missions among the Chiriguanos, 1845–1930," which appeared in *The New Latin American Mission History*, edited by Erick D. Langer and Robert H. Jackson (Lincoln: University of Nebraska Press, 1995).

Most of all, I want to thank my wife, Yeris Urdaneta, who has been most important in encouraging me to finish this project. She also worked with me in Entre Ríos and has been a true companion and friend who has helped with this and many other endeavors, academic and otherwise. Her love has kept me going and I lovingly dedicate this book to her.

MAP. The Chiriguanía and environs. Created by Jerome Cookson.

INTRODUCTION

The frontier is ubiquitous in Latin American history; it is still important today. Many issues both in the past and the present are tied to the continued existence of these frontiers. We hear of the plight of the Yanomami Indians, who are dying of diseases for which they have no immunities and whose territory is being invaded and fouled by Brazilian gold miners.[1] As Warren Dean has shown and many people concerned with the environment have lamented, the destruction of the Amazon rainforest has been significant over time.[2] Similarly, the demographic decline of the indigenous population, to one extent or another, has been an important issue since the sixteenth century. In recent years Protestant missionary endeavors have received wide publicity, such as the controversial Summer Institute of Linguistics, which for decades now has been bringing numbers of small ethnic groups into mission settlements and presumably converting the indigenous population.[3]

The frontier looms large throughout Latin American history, from before the European conquest to the present. A study of frontiers is useful for understanding a host of issues, such as the role of state power and of the indigenous peoples, ecological concerns, and economic development. What initially appeared to be isolated regions in fact have had a major impact on world history, much as the rest of the world has impinged upon frontiers. Religious missions played a large part on the frontiers even after independence, but few scholars (other than anthropologists) have concerned themselves much with these missions. In fact, missions, whether Catholic or Protestant, played a vital role in frontier development throughout the nineteenth and twentieth centuries. Although missions were not tied as closely to the state as during the colonial period, they were key to the penetration of national societies into the regions and indigenous lands that the nascent republics claimed as their jurisdictions.

In this book I examine one of the most important Catholic mission systems in republican-era Latin America, the Franciscan missions among the Chiriguano Indians in southeastern Bolivia, as a model for the study of a postcolonial mission system. I have a number of interrelated purposes: to place mission history squarely in the center of the study of the Latin American frontier, to provide an analytical framework with which to examine Latin American missions and make possible effective comparisons between the various mission systems, to show the fruitfulness of studying the virtually ignored mission systems of the republican period, and to examine from an ethnohistorical perspective the struggle of the Chiriguano Indians to adapt to changing circumstances during the past 180 years. In addition, the book also is in a sense a history of Bolivia, Argentina, and (to a lesser extent) Paraguay, since all of the missions were located close to the borders of the latter two and all three countries had major effects on the missions and their inhabitants. The book is also, in a sense, a history of the modern world, for I show how modernity entered into the frontier and changed it as the frontier changed the world around it.[4] After all, to understand the missions we must examine not just the far corners of southeastern Bolivia, but also must take into account places as diverse as La Paz, Bolivia; Buenos Aires, Argentina; Berlin, Germany; and Florence and Rome in Italy.

The book involves a reconsideration of the frontier in Latin American history and the place of the mission in it. The frontier was (and is) a territory of interaction between at least two different cultures.[5] The mission was an important part of this frontier, for it was one of the principal institutions within which these interactions took place in much of Latin America, particularly the vast region encompassing two-thirds of the Hispanic territories that James Lockhart and Stuart Schwartz have called "the fringes."[6] (The question arises if in fact this vast region was a "fringe" in all but the Eurocentric viewpoint.) Herbert Bolton was one of the first historians to recognize the importance of the missions in Latin America when he published a seminal article in 1917, "The Mission as a Frontier Institution in the Spanish-American Colonies." He saw the missions as pivotal institutions that provided the Spanish Crown with control of the vast colonial frontiers and made possible the "civilizing" of the American natives. The missions, which led to the conquest of vast frontier areas in the Americas, were a powerful arm of the Spanish state. Although Bolton and his disciples examined the missions within a larger framework, that of Spanish imperial policy, they also emphasized the European side and interactions between the state, settlers, and missionaries. Bolton's argument in his article and in subsequent works had a defining impact on the study of Latin American missions by later historians.[7]

While extremely valuable in placing the mission in the center of the study of the Latin American frontier, the studies by Bolton and those influenced by him were problematic. For one thing, they tended to focus almost exclusively on the missionaries and their deeds. The Indians, when they appeared at all, were the acted-upon, those whom the missionaries molded. This focus on the missionary as agent and the Indians as instruments reached its apogee in Robert Ricard's important *Conquête Spirituelle du Méxique* (1933), translated into English in the 1960s.[8] Ricard described in vivid detail the heroic measures of the missionary friars and how they converted vast numbers of Indians during the initial period after colonization. This type of mission history was congruent with the studies written by clerics themselves, who believed it was part of their role to spread the word of their orders' successes, which were also apologia of the missionary endeavors. Many histories from the 1940s onward were institutional histories that examined the European side of the mission and frontier equation.[9]

The almost exclusive emphasis on the missionaries and, at times, their interactions with the colonial state was broken only in the 1960s, with the rise of social history and the use of new approaches and methodologies. Two critiques of the Boltonian approach of mission history crystallized during that period, both focusing on the Indian side of the mission picture. One was the new historical demography. Inspired in large part by the important but, until recently, rarely followed work of Sherburne F. Cook, scholars began to examine the demographic ramifications of the missions. Concentrating primarily on the California missions, on which Cook had done most of his work, the demographic historians documented a horrific population decline for the California Indians as a result of Franciscan mission policies. The change in culture implicit in the resettlement onto missions, the unhygienic living conditions, and the extensive contact with European diseases to which the Indians had no immunity brought about very high mortality rates among the mission Indians.[10] Suddenly the benign spirit of the missionaries as chronicled by Ricard and many others became the machinations of well-intentioned but thoughtless men who were responsible for the deaths of thousands of people and the disappearance of whole ethnic groups.[11] In this perspective, however, the Indians were still the acted-upon; rather than the beneficiaries of paternalistic missionary rule, the Indians were cast as the helpless victims of European expansion.

Because of the pro-European bias in much of the work by Boltonians and clerical apologists, the other critique, arising from ethnohistory, came a bit later and at first was a bit tentative. Nevertheless, in the 1970s it became clear that, with an imaginative approach, the sources from the missions could yield much ethnohistorical information. Instead of concentrating on the missionary, the new generation of mission historians saw the tremendous potential that the study of the missions had in the analysis of the clash of European and indigenous cultures. For the first time scholars saw this material as a means of giving voice to the voiceless and placing the Indians center stage, not as victims, but as actors in their own right, adapting to and creatively resisting European contact.[12]

Both the demographic and the ethnohistorical approaches alone, while illuminating new intellectual territories, also have certain drawbacks. Perhaps in reaction to the Boltonian approach, these new studies (with some notable exceptions) tended to downplay the role of the missions within the larger context of the Latin American frontier and society. In the close analysis of the Indian, often the larger context was lost. Ignored at times was the fact that while the missions were an extremely important part of the frontier, they represented only one part (though often the majority) of the frontier population. Thus the interactions with local officials, the role of the settlers, and the interactions with Indians not residing on the missions were ignored. As a result, the mission became divorced from a larger discussion of the frontier and became only an exercise in demographic or ethnohistorical method. Alistair Hennessy, in his important book of essays on the Latin American frontier, coined the term "mission frontier."[13] Was the study of the mission valuable only as one type of frontier? Given the ubiquity of the mission on the Latin American frontier and the importance of the indigenous populations it harbored, this marginalization in fact is unjustified.

Another problem has been that historical studies of missions have almost exclusively focused on the colonial period. This is the case because ethnohistorical methods and demographic analyses have been used mostly to analyze the initial contact between Europeans and Indians and its aftermath. Indeed, the colonial period was the time when most indigenous groups first encountered the Europeans and might have represented the high point of the mission in Latin America. Not only were larger numbers of Indians under the aegis of the religious orders during the colonial period than after independence, but the connection between the Spanish (and, I might add, the Portuguese) colonial state and the Church was very close.

Nevertheless, missions also were a significant factor in the postindependence period and, one could argue, are just as important for understanding Latin America, particularly its frontier, even for this era. Missions continued to play important roles in the republican period virtually everywhere frontiers continued to exist, in places as diverse as the Chaco region and the vast Amazon basin. In this sense the frontiers in Latin America are still inextricably intertwined with mission history even after independence.

How does one integrate the insights from the colonial period into a study of the republican-era missions? While many of the earlier colonial studies have their shortcomings, with their exclusive emphasis on the missionary's experience and the interaction with the colonial state, some of the newer works in turn ignore issues of the Church's relationship with the state and how the experiences of the missionaries formed the mission experience for the indigenous population. It is time to recapture some of the virtues of the earlier works, with their emphasis on the European side of the equation, and combine them with the valuable ethnohistorical and demographic perspectives. To do this, it is necessary to reconceptualize the mission and its history within the context of the Latin American frontier. This is especially important for the republican-era missions.

The historical circumstances of the postindependence period are different from those of the colonial era in certain fundamental ways. For one thing, the state was not so intimately tied to the Catholic Church as before; at times, in fact, governments opposed the Church and missionary endeavor when anticlerical liberals assumed control of the government. Also, the relationship of the state with the missionaries, while complex even in the colonial period, had a different tone in the republican era. Without being direct representatives of the state, republican-era missionaries could be more independent and attempt to fulfill their religious goals with less reverence for the goals of national or local officials.

Without the means openly to coerce, on the other hand, the missionaries were also in a weaker position vis-à-vis the Indians they were trying to convert. The Indians had more autonomy in their dealings with the priests, and the missions became places where the indigenous population had greater autonomy than in the colonial period. In demographic terms, the missions were less population sinks (where the mission inhabitants lost population) than in the colonial period, for most of the groups missionized had already been exposed to Eurasian diseases during the colonial period and thus epidemics were not so severe.[14] The case study of the Chiriguanos that follows will elucidate these points of difference.

Despite these variations, certain constants make the mission experience in the colonial and postindependence eras comparable over time. I define the mission as an institution that created fields of interaction under the protection of the missionaries, in which the Indians adapted and accommodated themselves to groups already integrated into national society. It is these interactions over time between the various actors that provide a fuller understanding of the mission system and the frontier as a whole. Five principal groups existed on the frontier and impinged in one way or another on the missions: the missionaries themselves, the Indians living on the mission, the Indians outside the missions, the European and mestizo settlers, and the groups that represented the state, both on the national and the local level. Local officials represented fellow settlers. There was no significant number of people of African descent in the region.

Each group had a self-interested position that often conflicted with that of other groups. Interests sometimes conflicted within groups as well. Moreover, these interests changed over time. To capture in sufficient detail the complexities of mission history, it is necessary to propose a rough model of change in mission systems. The most accurate metaphor for this model is the concept of the mission life cycle.[15] Both individual missions and mission systems are born, grow, and mature, and then wither away or are converted into something else, such as towns. To put this life cycle of missions in different terms, missions are established, reach a stage of consolidation, and then decline or are transformed. This happened to the Franciscan missions among the Chiriguanos and was common among most other mission systems in Latin America as well.

How does this metaphor of the mission life cycle help in achieving a more profound understanding of these institutions? Often scholars have examined only one part of the total mission life cycle or assumed that, essentially, the mission experience remained the same over time. This usually was not the case. By concentrating on one period or another, the historian is prone to privilege one group or process over another because usually different groups take on different importance during the distinct phases of a mission's life cycle. For example, in the initial phase, the missionaries' motives and the Indians' accommodations to mission life took on singular importance. Thus, Robert Ricard's treatise on the Mexican "spiritual conquest" privileged the Spanish missionaries and the apparently eager acceptance of Christian baptism by the Indians. However, as the mission went through its life cycle certain actors took on greater importance than others. Later on in the development of the missions, as Evelyn Hu-DeHart demonstrates in the case of the Jesuit missions among the Yaqui during the seventeenth and eighteenth centuries, the mining economy of northwestern New Spain created new conflicts between the Yaquis, the missionaries, and the miners who wanted to attain access to Indian labor.[16]

Moreover, each group behaved in different ways during the various phases of the life cycle. For example, in virtually all Latin American missions after the founding of the mission and a brief increase in population, the mission population tended to decline over the long run during the often lengthy period of consolidation. Even where the total population did not decrease, such as in the Franciscan Alta California missions, only the missionary policy of bringing in new native groups kept populations growing up to the 1820s.[17] The period of mission decline set in once the missions transformed the frontier and made possible the settlement of significant numbers of non-Indians. At this stage the state increased in importance, as it was usually able to assert its authority in the region, and began to restrict the activities of the missionaries. While Herbert Bolton saw this as an essentially benign process, the struggles over the missions could become quite violent, as in the case of the colonial Paraguayan Guaraní missions in the eighteenth century.[18] Likewise, Susan Deeds showed that Indian rebellions against the mission regime were different at the initial stage of mission foundation than those that occurred many years after the missions had been established. The first were messianic rebellions that tried to reestablish precontact social and cultural ties, whereas the later ones tried to redress the colonial pact between the Indians and the missionaries or the state.[19] Once historians become sensitive to these phases and the changes in the mission over time, we can properly evaluate each actor within the temporal context.

The life cycle metaphor makes possible different ways of looking at the mission within the larger context. During the life cycle of the mission various groups along the frontier took different positions vis-à-vis the missions, for the missions represented but one, though at certain times the most important, frontier institution. The changing role of the mission and the perceptions (by mission Indians, missionaries, local settlers, the government, etc.) of its desired role on the frontier led to the mission's eventual demise as more and more of the frontier population saw the mission as a hindrance.

Throughout Latin America religious orders usually established not just one mission, but a number of them. They formed an interacting system that either attempted to convert one large ethnic group or cover a coherent geographic unit. Examples abound; perhaps the most famous ones are the Jesuit missions in Paraguay among the Guaraní, the Franciscan Alta California missions, and the Jesuit missions in the Portuguese Amazon. Each mission system also had a life cycle that affected the success of the individual missions. Thus when considering the mission life cycle, we must consider not only each individual mission, but also when the mission was established in relation to the rest of the system. As more missions aged the whole mission system began to decline as well, and new missions often did not survive very long.

The mission life cycle was affected by a number of diverse and historically specific factors, making the history of each system unique. These histories in turn can be divided into internal dynamics and those that are essentially external to the mission system. The internal factors include the missionaries who went to the missions and their methods and goals; the aboriginal culture and the cultural impact that the establishment of missions had on those groups who settled in the missions; the demographic impact on the indigenous population of the settlement of the Indians into compact centers; missionary efforts at social control on the missions; and Indian resistance to acculturation.

Beyond these internal factors it is important to recognize that the missions were part of a larger society as well and must be seen within that context. The missions were not only institutions that changed indigenous culture; the existence of missions throughout their life cycle transformed the frontier itself. Thus these institutions affected indigenous groups who did not settle in the missions, as their frequent attacks on the missions attest. Moreover, the relationship between the missions and other actors along the frontier was vital to the mission life cycle. For example, the often complex and at times contradictory relationships between the missions and frontier settlers affected not only the development of the missions themselves, but also the way the frontier changed over time. Among the most important aspects in this regard was how the mission Indian labor was to be utilized within the frontier economy, although the mission must also be analyzed as a potential market for goods and as a producer. Then, after the missions transformed the frontier, the state asserted greater control over the region and a struggle between the missionaries and the state ensued over control of the indigenous populations and the former mission territory.

The missions thus greatly impacted the shape of the erstwhile frontier region. As some scholars have shown, missions created conditions that remained after their formal abolition. Not only did missions affect labor and settlement patterns after their secularization, but the missions created distinct conditions and cultures among the peoples who were missionized as well. David Block posited that the missions engendered a "mission culture" among the population of the former colonial mission settlements in the Beni region of Bolivia. This mission culture was an amalgam of native customs and adaptations of the Jesuit missionaries. As always, the Indians were creative in their accommodation to the system, and the Jesuits themselves adapted their ways to the Amazon savanna as best they could. Thus the former missions preserved certain aspects of mission life long after the expulsion of the Jesuits in 1767. Mission economic patterns, based on communal labor and on new, imported work rhythms, remained the basis of the settlements' existence. New hierarchies, blended from the eras before and after mission establishment, continued to dominate village life. Only the blows administered by the rubber boom were able to destroy the Upper Amazon mission culture after 1850.[20] In a similar vein, Susan Deeds describes the survival of missionized indigenous groups in colonial northern Mexico as the result of what she calls "mediated opportunism." She shows that certain groups, such as the Tarahumaras, used the missions as a means to mediate the influence of Spanish society. They used this institution more than others to maintain their ethnic identity as they changed according to new pressures and interactions with the wider world. Those groups that were successful in using the missions for their own ends survived, whereas those that were too weak disappeared into the mass of mestizo society, as most Creoles would have wanted.[21]

In sum, using the mission life cycle as an organizing principle is a valuable analytical tool. It emphasizes how the missions changed over time and highlights the indigenous population, the vast majority of people on the missions. Also, it places the missions into the larger contexts of the frontier and national policy. A number of scholars have implicitly used this model, but rarely explicitly.

Organization of the Book

Chapter 1 explores the early republican period and explains how the establishment of the missions, beginning in the 1840s, fundamentally changed the relationship between the Chiriguano villages and national society. Chapter 2 looks at the Franciscan missionaries' motives with an eye to nineteenth-century religious struggles in Europe, Italy in particular, and how they were applied to the reestablishment of the missions in the Cordillera. The European context was important, for all the Franciscan missionaries among the Chiriguanos were Europeans, predominantly from Italy.

In chapter 3 I examine the motives of the Indians and one of the most fundamental aspects of missions, namely, the demographic impact they had on the indigenous population that settled there. In chapter 4, the closely interrelated issues of Indian acculturation and the development of the mission economy receive scrutiny, particularly in light of the relatively high rates of Indian mortality and outmigration. In chapter 5 I show how the Chiriguanos resisted the imposition of alien ways and what means of repression the friars used. Here, I explore the Indians' lack of conversion to Catholicism and the implications of this.

Beginning in chapter 6 my focus changes from the internal dynamics of the missions to a broader point of view: the economic impact of the missions and the rest of frontier society in economic terms. Chapter 7 deals with the interactions between the missions and outside influences. These include the national state and local officials and non-Indian neighbors. I analyze the changing relationship between the relatively weak Bolivian state and the Church in the early nineteenth century. Both institutions initially saw a benefit in establishing missions along the frontier. As the Bolivian government grew stronger in the early twentieth century, it became increasingly anticlerical and attempted to control the power of the Church along the frontier and elsewhere in the nation. I trace the missions' history into the 1920s, when the missions entered into decline and the last part of their life cycle. In chapter 8 I discuss the demise of the missions, for during the Chaco War (1932–1935) many of the missions were overrun by the Paraguayan Army and many inhabitants fled or were taken prisoner. In the aftermath the invasion by non-Indians and the failure of certain Chiriguanos and Franciscans to re-create the missions led to their secularization in 1949. I analyze the persistence of the "mission culture" as well as the effects of the missions on the region.

An important purpose of this book is to connect the history of the republican-era missions to the vast mission historiography that deals almost exclusively with the colonial period. Thus in the concluding chapter I compare the Franciscan mission system among the Chiriguanos with colonial-era missions to show the differences and the continuities. One issue that is clearly distinct from the colonial period is the fact that nation-states such as Bolivia were, at least in theory, trying to create citizens rather than subjects. In practice, the role of the Catholic Church as transformer of indigenous peoples as well as racial and social ideas about Indians hampered these efforts. I show how effective the missions were in creating new citizens out of the native peoples the friars missionized. I also tie the missions back into the larger context of national and world history.

The study is restricted to the period 1830 to 1949 because this is when the Franciscan missions were active during the republican period. Around 1830, less than a decade after the colonial system had collapsed, the Franciscan convent in Tarija, Bolivia, began its push to remissionize the Chiriguanos. In 1949 the Bolivian government definitively secularized the remaining missions after the Chaco War had decimated their inhabitants. Although the study ranges beyond this time frame, my focus is on this intense period of missionization. But before I turn to these issues, it is necessary to place these missions within their geographic and historical contexts.

The Chiriguanos before Independence

Before we can enter the world of the nineteenth- and twentieth-century Chiriguano frontier and the Franciscan missions, it is necessary to describe briefly the history of the Chiriguanos and their relationship with the Europeans during the colonial period. Most historians who have studied this ethnic group have concentrated on the colonial Chiriguano. I will summarize the background relevant to the discussion of the Chiriguanos and the southeastern Bolivian frontier during the republican period: the origins of the Chiriguano, their conquest of the Chané (an Arawak-speaking people who lived in the Andean foothills), their political ideology, their relationship with the Spaniards and other ethnic groups, and the colonial missions.

A number of scholars have attempted to reconstruct the pre-Columbian history of the Chiriguanos. Although there is still some dispute about their origins, most conclude that the Chiriguano people emerged from a series of Guaraní migrations from what is now south-central Brazil into the eastern foothills of the Andes. While some suppose that the Chiriguanos arrived only with Alejo García, a shipwrecked Spanish sailor who in 1521 traveled from the Atlantic coast to the Andes mountains in search of gold and silver, the existence of a number of pre-Columbian fortresses along the eastern boundary of the Inca Empire in south-central Bolivia indicates that the Incas had contact with the warlike Chiriguano even before Columbus stumbled on the Americas. The currently accepted interpretation is based on Enrique de Gandia's assertion that the Chiriguanos were already in the Andean foothills by the 1470s. The Chiriguanos most likely came in a series of migrations over a hundred-year span from Paraguay and Brazil.[22]

The Cordillera, as the Andean foothills of southeastern Bolivia are called, was a frontier of the Inca Empire even before the European invasion. There a complex interplay among various ethnic groups took place. Not only did the Incas try to prevent the penetration of the Guaraní speakers into the Andean heartland, but when the Chiriguanos arrived in the Cordillera they encountered the Chané, who had previously migrated to the region and had absorbed many features of Andean civilization; they were defeated and became the slaves of the victors. As the Spanish delighted recounting in horrific tales, the Chiriguanos at times ate the Chanés they had captured. This is likely, given what we know about Tupí-Guaraní culture. In turn, the Guaraní warriors had children with Chané women and soon the population melded into one in which Chiriguano and Chané became indistinguishable. The conquest of the Chané was also linguistic, for the people who emerged from this intermixing spoke Guaraní rather than Arawak. There was also a cultural exchange. Isabelle Combès and Thierry Saignes argued that the name Chiriguano means *mestizo*, in homage to the ethnic mixing that resulted in Chiriguano society.[23] This is in fact the most likely explanation.

Only in certain parts of the region were isolated settlements able to maintain their Chané identity, although even there the lingua franca became Guaraní. Such was the case in the Caipipendi valley in Tarija, in Itiyuro along the Argentine border, and probably in the Izozog region along the eastern extension of the Parapetí River.[24] This historical experience, in which the Guaranís dominated another people militarily and absorbed them into their own society, shaped their attitudes toward other ethnic groups. The Chiriguanos were as ethnocentric and convinced of the superiority of their own culture as the Spaniards they would later meet.

In their migrations to the Andean foothills the Guaraní speakers came in search of Kandire, a mythical place where food grew plentifully and where the land was abundant in metals and contained houses of stone.[25] Perhaps the Chiriguano had heard of the Inca Empire; it is clear that they attempted to invade the Andean range a number of times, as the official Inca histories attest.[26] Regardless, within Guaraní culture generally a strong messianic impulse existed, as embodied in the Kandire myth.[27] It is difficult otherwise to explain why whole tribes made the arduous and dangerous trek across the vast Chaco regions into the Andean foothills to conquer a new land.

There is some truth to the foothills of the Andes being a kind of earthly paradise for an agricultural people. The foothills are ideal for growing food, particularly maize, the main staple of the Chiriguanos. No irrigation is necessary during normal years. There is a wet season from November to April and a dry season from May to October. Temperatures during the wet season are not as hot as in the tropical Amazon basin to the north nor the Gran Chaco to the east; constant breezes moderate the climate. During the dry season temperatures at times dip to freezing but usually become quite pleasant after a day or two. Kirtley F. Mather, a geographer who traveled through the region in the 1920s, described the climate as "genial and well-favored," likening it to New Mexico or southern Colorado. The landscape is rugged but beautiful. A parallel series of sharp crested ridges rising to altitudes of 1,500 to 2,500 feet above the valleys and running north-south are covered at all but the steepest places in a lush green subtropical vegetation. Long, narrow valleys contain streams that all but dry up during the cold season. Only the largest rivers, which eventually cut through the high ridges to form spectacularly steep cliffs, flow all year round.[28]

The landscape, with its high mountains separating one valley from another, also aided in the maintenance of a political ideology that Pierre Clastres has called a "society against the state."[29] That is, the Chiriguanos never developed a centralized state, but instead based their political organization on the village unit. Each village elected a chief, called a *tubicha*, who had sufficient charisma to lead the group and who was well respected. Usually, the tubicha was selected from the same lineage, though sons did not always inherit their father's position. Much emphasis was put on reaching consensus before acting, and thus the tubicha had to be a good orator and help convince the village assembly of his plans. When disputes came up that could not be resolved, the members of the lineages who disagreed with the tubicha left to form their own village.[30] There existed a regional chief, a *mburuvicha* or *tubicha rubicha*, who came from the most populous and resource-rich village and dominated a loose alliance of lesser villages in his area of influence. However, these alliances were often shaky and villages could and did change sides during disputes. In fact, as we shall see, the militaristic Chiriguanos were almost constantly at war, fighting other villages or outsiders.

In this context the Chiriguanos, who called themselves *ava*, or men, first made contact with the Spaniards. The Spaniards execrated the Chiriguanos, whom they regarded as cannibals (and thus were permitted to enslave, according to Spanish laws), but they also respected them for their military prowess. While there were extensive contacts between Chiriguanos and the Spanish, the latter failed ever to conquer more than segments of the former. Viceroy Toledo mounted a famous expedition to punish the Chiriguanos in 1574, but he had to retreat ignominiously when he fell ill at the beginning of the campaign. Thereafter the Spanish adopted a policy similar to that of their Inca predecessors, of creating town-fortresses along the frontier with the Chiriguanos to keep them from raiding. As a result, three militarized Spanish urban centers boxed in the Cordillera and the warlike Chiriguanos; in the north Santa Cruz de la Sierra, in the west Tomina, and to the south Tarija. Francisco Pifarré, who has written the best summary account of the Chiriguanos' colonial experience, asserts that in the sixteenth and seventeenth centuries most warfare between Spaniards and Chiriguanos boiled down to mutual raiding. The Spanish adopted a scorched-earth policy, seeking to destroy as many Chiriguano villages and corn depositories as possible. But because the Chiriguanos had no centralized government, unlike the Incas or the Aztecs, the Spanish found it impossible to conquer them.[31]

The almost continuous war with the Spanish and the Europeans' lack of permanent success against the ava did little to change the latter's attitudes toward outsiders. While the Chiriguanos contemptuously called most other indigenous ethnic groups *tapii*, or slaves, the Europeans received a more respectful title. They were called *karai*, the same name with which the Guaraní honored their powerful prophets who had led them to the Cordillera in the first place. Nevertheless, European culture apparently held little attraction for the Chiriguanos. At best, as Saignes asserts, they were desirous, like all Stone Age people, of acquiring metal objects such as needles, knives, and axes, which the Chiriguano recognized were superior to what their technology could produce.[32]

The Chiriguanos evolved new military strategies after contact with the Spanish. Rather than living in huge longhouses that housed a whole lineage, they switched to smaller houses in which only the nuclear family and perhaps old parents or unattached individuals lived.[33] Dispersed settlements made them less vulnerable to total devastation in a Spanish attack. They also made Chiriguano society less focused on larger kinship groups. The ava refined their war-making abilities with firearms, horses, and other novelties, like other indigenous groups such as the Indians of the Argentine pampas, the Apaches, and the Sioux. However, the ava conducted most warfare with knives, bows and arrows, and on foot; they were especially adept at guerrilla tactics such as the ambush and hit-and-run attacks. These tactics were ideal for the densely forested mountainous terrain of the Cordillera, where it was often impossible to use cavalry or see more than a few feet through the foliage.

The need for making war in their type of decentralized society gained even greater importance after contact with the Spaniards, and the Chiriguanos became essentially a society organized for war. Indeed, young men during late adolescence were expected to go to war to find honor on the battlefield or, more likely, in the many small skirmishes between their village and the Spaniards or opposing village alliances. These young men were called *queremba* and continually lobbied for war, hoping to gain glory in the process. The most adept warriors physically led the men into battle by engaging in particularly daring feats. They were sometimes different from the political leaders, who were mostly chosen from the existing chiefly lineages. Saignes asserts that the queremba, called *cunumi* in the sixteenth century, originated in the offspring of the Guaraní with Chané women and had to prove their military skills before being accepted as a full member into Chiriguano society.[34]

According to Pifarré, the Chiriguanos increased their population substantially after suffering from epidemics the first third of the seventeenth century and with slight variations into the eighteenth. The incorporation of the numerous Chanés into Chiriguano society, essentially the ethnogenesis of a new people, undoubtedly aided in the healthy increase in population. Pifarré estimates that by the 1770s, after a period of relative peace (that is to say, only minor intra-ethnic squabbling with no major conflagrations), the Chiriguanos reached a population of about 200,000. Although this figure appears somewhat high, it is clear that the Chiriguanos thrived during the colonial period, even under constant pressure by the Spanish on the fringes of the Cordillera. Afterward, demographic decline set in; this trend was reversed somewhat only in the twentieth century.[35]

It is not clear why at this point indigenous society became unable to reproduce itself, although a series of large-scale wars in the last decades of the eighteenth century and the influx of cattle into the Cordillera (a topic I address in chapter 1) were negative influences. Greater contact with colonial society in the late eighteenth century might also have spread diseases more readily than before. Perhaps most important in reversing the upward demographic trend were the drought, harvest failures, and subsequent famines that affected the Cordillera as well as much of the south-central Andes around the turn of the nineteenth century. In a pattern familiar to demographers, the severely weakened population succumbed to disease, further amplifying the effects of the drought.[36]

Up to this point, Spanish attempts to effect a spiritual conquest in the absence of a military conquest had proven unfruitful. The Jesuits had tried, and failed, to establish a mission system as they had done so successfully north of the Chiriguano territory, in Mojos and Chiquitos, and in Paraguay among the Chiriguanos' Guaraní-speaking cousins to the south. Whatever feeble accomplishments the Jesuits attained after the establishment of a missionary college in Tarija in 1690 were destroyed during the great wars in the Cordillera during the 1720s and 1730s in which the Chiriguanos burned down missions and martyred missionaries. In 1767, when the Jesuits were expelled from the Spanish Empire, they barely had one mission among the Chiriguanos, with only 268 Indians, in contrast to the tens of thousands contained in their mission systems among other ethnic groups. Other missionary orders, such as the Dominicans and Augustinians, had even less success among the Chiriguanos.[37]

Only the Franciscans, who had the good fortune to start their missionary enterprise during the late eighteenth-century crisis, succeeded in founding a viable mission system among the Chiriguanos. This paralleled the invigoration of the Franciscans as a missionary order, since they at the same time began to establish missions in the Californias. Altogether beginning in the 1780s the Franciscans founded twenty-two missions throughout the Cordillera. At their height in 1810 they included 24,000 Indians, or perhaps a fifth of the total Chiriguano population.[38] As virtually all authors assert, the Chiriguanos asked for missions not principally because they were desirous of converting to Christianity; rather, they saw the mission as an option to escape the pressures of frontier society and so maintain at least their lands.[39] Once the missions were established, the friars created two sections; one was for the converted and the other for the heathen. By 1810 many Chiriguanos appear to have converted; along the fringes of the Cordillera, where the missions had existed the longest, virtually all became converts. However, in the more recent missions a much smaller percentage converted. Be that as it may, P. Manuel Mingo, who wrote the most important history of the colonial Tarija missions, was not convinced that these conversions were very profound.[40]

The missions affected the Chiriguanos in many ways. The concentration of large numbers of people into a restricted space facilitated the spread of disease, and large numbers of mission Indians succumbed. Mission schools, which all the children from age seven to fifteen had to attend, separated parents from children and taught the latter new ways of dealing with the world, such as praying, the catechism, and sometimes reading and writing. This was at the expense of the old ways of doing things, learned at the parents' side during these formative years. When the parents were unruly the missionary did not hesitate to call the Spanish soldiers from the forts that were established near the missions.[41]

I agree with Saignes's view that the Franciscans' control over their charges should not be overemphasized. Saignes posits that the Chiriguanos remained on the missions and defended them against outsiders not so much because they were either desirous of hearing the Evangelium or even because the friars controlled the Indians' movement. Instead, the Indians stayed because they forced the friars to give them clothes, food, and other such items with minimal work in what became essentially a one-sided exchange. While the missionaries saw this as one way to attract the Indians to the Faith, the Chiriguanos in turn saw this as a dependent relationship in which they were the winners. It was the friars who had to maintain the group through their constant giving, for otherwise the Chiriguanos would abandon the mission. In this sense, the Indians controlled the mission from within, although the missionaries often did not perceive this.[42]

Viewed from the larger perspective of the colonial frontier, the actions of both Chiriguanos and missionaries become explicable and need not rest on the naiveté of either Chiriguano or Franciscan. The ava agreed to the mission regime when they saw this as their best option within the slowly constricting ethnic territory or when warfare with other villages made their military position untenable. The missionaries, in turn, had to provide certain benefits beyond protection to keep the Indians on the mission, for coercion was rarely sufficient given the sparse forces the colonial state commanded on the Chiriguano frontier. Conversion was a larger end, attainable over the long haul and only if the Indians remained in place long enough to be brought into the colonial system.

Part of Saignes's proof that the survival of the missions depended upon the missionaries' constant gift giving is the fact that, once the friars were taken prisoner and carted off to Buenos Aires during the wars for independence (1810–1825) the Indians themselves put the missions to flame and returned to their former villages without lamenting much the demise of the vast Franciscan mission system. Indeed, during the wars for independence the Chiriguanos fought on both sides, although the greatest leader of the time, the mburuvicha Cumbay from Ingre, aided the guerrillas on the patriot side and even met with the Argentine general Manuel Belgrano in 1813, when Argentine troops were occupying the silver mining center of Potosí.[43] However, nothing came of the meeting after the Argentines were forced to retreat, and the Cordillera became marginal to the great struggles between the patriots and the Spanish Crown. Thus by the early nineteenth century the mission system in the region had disappeared and most of the land that the Spaniards and the Franciscans had claimed had reverted to Chiriguano control by 1825. For non-Indians the region became again *la frontera*, a place where the Indians were in control and Europeans and mestizos entered at their peril. It is at this point in the story that chapter 1 begins.

Thus even in the colonial period the Cordillera was a place of complex interactions, with a multiplicity of frontiers. Different ethnic groups competed for the same territory. The Chiriguanos evolved from a fusion of two distinct cultures, the Guaraní and the Arawak-speaking Chanés. The Cordillera was also a frontier between the Andean cultural sphere and that of the lowland peoples, as well as a frontier between Spanish colonial society and indigenous groups largely outside European control. The Cordillera frontier was always permeable, both in a geographic and in a biological sense. Europeans, mestizos, and European diseases penetrated far into Chiriguano territory; much miscegenation also occurred between ethnic groups. Livestock penetrated the region as well, at the expense of the maize-growing Chiriguanos. The Franciscan missions briefly dominated the Cordillera at the turn of the nineteenth century, but even then the Spanish colonial state was unable to extend its control over the whole Cordillera as large numbers of Chiriguanos remained outside the missions. The colonial period is one of imposition of Spanish rule over part of the indigenous population, partial conversion, and reversion to independence from whites for most indigenous peoples on the frontier groups in the aftermath of the Creole rebellion against their Spanish overlords. Despite the Chiriguanos' newfound independence, the colonial heritage and the interactions that resulted shaped the region's indigenous inhabitants and provided continuities with the republican period.

Chiriguano Religion

These continuities can be seen in the religious sphere. By the nineteenth century the Chiriguanos' religion had become a hybrid belief system. Their experience with the Jesuit and Franciscan missions during the colonial period had exposed them to Christianity and biblical tales, some of which they transformed and incorporated as myths told around their village campfires after the destruction of the colonial missions. Anthropologists from Erland Nordenskiöld onward have tried to find the aboriginal religious ideas of the Chiriguanos, but that is not the point.[44] Rather than stripping Christian motifs from aboriginal beliefs to find the core ideas of the ava, one should accept that indigenous peoples, like everybody else, continuously added elements and transformed their ideas as they were exposed to new influences.[45] This is what happened among the Chiriguano villages after independence.

The evidence for systematic religious beliefs of the Chiriguanos begins only around the turn of the twentieth century and probably says as much about the anthropologists and missionaries who wrote of these beliefs as it does about the ava.[46] What can be gleaned from these sources is that the Chiriguano religion was highly personal and revolved around spirits and cultural heroes. It was an oral belief system, told through stories that varied from storyteller to storyteller and probably over time as well, as people embellished or changed elements of the account.

Nordenskiöld suspected that the missionaries promoted a foreign concept among the Chiriguanos, that of *Tunpaete vae*, which he translated as "the true God."[47] Be that as it may, this concept did not appear to hold much interest for the ava. Instead, the old men he interviewed talked about rival godlike creatures who competed against each other and thus created the world as the Chiriguano understood it. Christian elements were added and formed a mixture in these stories. Thus the story of Adam and Eve was reproduced in a longer story about the destruction of the Chiriguanos and their reconstitution, as well as the first man eating a forbidden fruit and the discovery of shame.[48] Tricksters such as Aguara-tunpa, a fox with godlike powers, figured in many of the tales. As did the Greek gods, he and others like him interacted with human beings, tricking them and having beautiful women bear his children.[49]

Fr. Bernardino de Nino attempted to fit the ideas he had heard from the Chiriguanos into Christian conceptions, but it is not clear that this interpretation is accurate. He believed the Chiriguano Tunparenda was equivalent to Heaven and Añarenda was Hell. However, the concept of the *tunpa* (or *tumpa*) was that of a benevolent spiritual being and *aña* was that of a malevolent one; both concepts derived from myths. *Renda* in Guaraní means "place of," but adding tunpa and aña to the term "place" was probably a conceptual addition the missionaries made. Nordenskiöld did not find these concepts in his compendium of myths and legends.

What is clear, however, is that there were both good and malevolent shamans, called *ipaye*, among the Chiriguano.[50] According to de Nino, Chiriguanos believed that death was caused only by violence or by ipayes' spiritual malevolence. Disease was understood not as a physical condition, but a spiritual one, in which somebody wanted to do damage to the ill person; disease was related to social control, jealousies, and interpersonal relations. The shamans played a significant role in mediating these relations through spiritual means. Shamans also were important in warding off diseases as well as causing them; thus they became central figures when epidemics threatened villages or missions.[51]

A strain of messianism, common in the Guaraní culture, appears to have been present as well. Messianic leaders were esteemed and charismatic figures who were able to speak well and articulate the problems and solutions of Chiriguano society. In certain circumstances, they took on superhuman qualities; the leaders who emerged periodically when Chiriguano society was under great stress promised a return to the old ways and a paradisiacal existence. Various such leaders during the Jesuit phase emerged in revolts against Spanish or Creole influence.[52] This messianism also manifested in the idea of Kandire, a kind of earthly paradise, as discussed earlier. The messianic leader, a tumpa, rose up at the end of the nineteenth century to defend his people; however, unlike in the eighteenth century, he failed to throw out the missionaries or the Creoles and reconstitute the Chiriguanía. The intersection of this frontier warfare with the missions finally destroyed Chiriguano independence.

CHAPTER ONE

The "Chiriguano Wars": Indian Warfare
and the Establishment of the Missions

A new conception of frontier history is necessary to understand the Chiriguano frontier in the nineteenth century. The wars for independence against the Spaniards resulted in the creation of various nation-states in the region, dominated by Creole elites. For most Chiriguanos, these conflicts also resulted in freedom from all oppressors, including the Creoles. Most of the space that the colonial state carved out of the Chiriguanía returned to the control of the indigenous villages. The reasons for this independence were multiple: the demographic weight and political culture of indigenous society, effective guerrilla warfare by the Indians and the types of weapons used, as well as the weakness of the ranching economic model and of the Bolivian state. These factors provided the majority of Chiriguanos with a period of effective independence that waned only in the second half of the nineteenth century.

In other words, frontier expansion was a variable process that did not inevitably lead to European or Creole domination. The frontier waxed and waned in different directions; at certain times indigenous groups retook territory, and at others the Creoles invaded successfully. The frontier created different possibilities for both indigenous and settler societies that changed over time as the power balance shifted from one side to the other. Groups within both indigenous and Creole societies allied with and against each other, so that an analysis based on a bifurcation between Indian and settler is simplistic. Rather, changing interethnic and intra-ethnic alliances (including between different indigenous ethnic groups) resulted in differing coalitions over time that made control of the frontier by the Bolivian state impossible until the very end of the nineteenth century.[1]

The Franciscan missions founded during the republican period helped slowly but surely to limit the Chiriguanos' independence by creating new alliance structures that, in the end, resulted in a frontier society in which the Indians were subordinated to local Creoles and, to a lesser extent, to the Bolivian state. Even here, resistance to domination changed over time and created different opportunities for different indigenous groups as they negotiated and continuously adapted to new circumstances.[2] During the first half of the nineteenth century it was not at all clear that either the Bolivian state or the colonists would overcome the powerful Chiriguanos. The establishment of missions was the result not of a deliberate and long-range strategy of frontier development, but rather a policy engendered by a weak state that found itself unable to protect its citizens despite its best military efforts. In the end, frontier conflict meant mainly Indian-on-Indian violence, and it was only after permanent alliances, fostered by the missions, were established between Creoles and indigenous groups that the Bolivian state was eventually able to claim a partial supremacy in the region. This chapter delineates this lengthy process and shows what role the missions played in the larger strategic, military, and political contexts of the frontier region.

The National Context

Before discussing the Chiriguano frontier, I need to provide the context of nineteenth-century Bolivian political development on the national level.[3] The Bolivian state did not control the Chiriguanía until about the turn of the twentieth century. Creole leaders in Sucre and La Paz arrogated for the Bolivian state possession of lands, including the Chiriguano territories, based on European (and colonial) ideas of statehood without any reference to the desires of the independent indigenous population. Bolivian national leaders (and their Paraguayan and Argentine counterparts) drew bright lines across maps that showed huge tracts of lands marked "unknown," believing that they thus had rights to the territory. The reality on the ground, as we shall see, was quite different. Indeed, the Chaco War in the 1930s and further into the twentieth century showed the Bolivian elites how little they actually controlled or knew about what they claimed to be national territory. Be that as it may, we still need to take into account Bolivian politics, since it impinged in myriad ways upon the frontier during the nineteenth century.

The independence wars (1810–1825) brought about the creation of

Bolivia based on the territory encompassed by the jurisdiction of the Audiencia de Charcas, an important colonial administrative and judicial body. The Alto Peruvian elites believed that they were better off alone rather than as a part of neighboring Peru or the Argentine Confederation. They persuaded second-in-command Antonio José de Sucre to join the cause for independence and, through flattery, were able to convince the independence leader Simón Bolívar to separate the country from Peru. After all, the great Liberator would now have a country named after him, and he diligently wrote a constitution (never implemented) for Bolivia. Sucre became Bolivia's first true president and, in his short administration, was able to implement liberal reforms. Although Bolivia later became known for its many revolutions and political instability, it emerged as one of the most powerful South American states in the first half of the nineteenth century. A series of strong and reform-minded leaders, such as Andrés de Santa Cruz (1829–1839) and José Ballivián (1841–1847), tried to improve the country's administration. A lack of fiscal resources, the threat of internal instability, and conflict with neighboring countries prevented much progress, though Bolivia was better off than all countries on the continent other than Chile and Brazil. Foreign involvement did not help, such as Santa Cruz's ill-fated Peru-Bolivian Confederation (1836–1839) or Agustín Gamarra's invasion of Bolivia at the head of Peruvian troops in 1841. Also, most national administrations, when they could, worried more about the status of Tarija (which had voted to join Bolivia rather than Argentina in 1826) or the Pacific coastal region of Atacama, under pressure from Chile and Peru. Only the Ballivián administration attempted to penetrate the eastern regions and establish state control, though it had little success, as we shall see later.

Political instability increased throughout the century. Factionalism increased and became more violent, with leaders whose political ideologies were diametrically opposed to each other. There were also personal enmities. Thus Manuel Isidoro Belzu (1848–1855) hated José Ballivián, who had seduced his wife, the famous writer Juana Manuela Gorriti. Belzu was also the declared enemy of José María Linares (1857–1861), as well as of Mariano Melgarejo (1864–1870), who in 1865 ended Belzu's life. Belzu, who had spent part of his military career on the Tarija frontier, represented a pro-artisan populism not seen before, while Linares represented the civilian, fervently pro-Catholic, but also free trade party. General Melgarejo also surrounded himself with laissez-faire liberals and imposed liberal policies, such as auctioning off Indian community land and taking advice from the free-trade Chilean ambassador. Melgarejo was forced to move from city to city, suffocating revolts against his regime, and finally was overthrown by an alliance between his Creole enemies and the Aymara Indians, who retook their usurped lands.

Melgarejo had signed away part of Bolivia's rights to its Pacific coast to the Chileans. The inability of the Bolivian state to impose control over the extremely arid but resource-rich Atacama coast (populated mostly by Chilean workers) led to further disputes with Chile. Bolivia tried to compensate for its weakness, signing a secret defense treaty with Peru, but a dispute over taxes on the coast led to the disastrous War of the Pacific (1879–1884), in which Bolivia lost its coastal territory to Chile. The war was a decisive turning point in Bolivian politics. As a result, the military was discredited and the newly wealthy silver mining elite of Sucre and Potosí took over the country after 1880. Allied with Chile through commercial and financial connections, they lobbied for railroad access to the Pacific and turned to consolidate control over the eastern frontier, including the Chiriguanía. They launched expeditions into the Chaco and into the rubber areas of the Beni region and created new land laws that made the legal taking of "vacant" (i.e., Indian-controlled) lands easier. The mining elites also tried to create new land markets by attempting to parcel out Indian communities to individuals and also open them up to sale. In the end, they lost out to another Aymara Indian rebellion, whose leaders allied themselves with the Liberal Party and La Paz regionalists. The Federalist War of 1898–1899 brought the Liberal Party to power and moved the executive and legislative branches to La Paz permanently, although the new government in the end repressed the Aymaras and intensified the Indian community land sales in the Andean highlands. In sum, the Bolivian state was able to concentrate its resources on the eastern frontier only at the end of the nineteenth century, though it did try to do so earlier as well, such as in the 1840s, under the Ballivián administration.

Political and Social Organizations on the Frontier

Given the weakness of the Bolivian national state during much of the nineteenth century, it is essential to focus on the local level for understanding the Chiriguano frontier, particularly the political and economic organizations of both the Chiriguanos and the settlers. Inter- and intra-ethnic relations created conditions that affected the struggle over the region's resources. During the first half of the nineteenth century the non-Indians on the frontier regions were difficult to define as "settlers." Most non-Indians were not agriculturalists but were cowhands, merchants, or ranch owners. The first two rarely stayed in one place. Although there were landowners who on paper owned huge tracts of land in this region, they usually lived in the Spanish towns distant from the frontier. This pattern was clearest in the southern portion of the frontier, where the heroes of the independence movement, Generals Bernardo Trigo and Francisco Burdett O'Connor (the latter an Irish aristocrat who fought with Bolivar's Colombian army and later married into the Tarija elites), were by far the largest landowners but lived in the town of Tarija, located 100 miles from the frontier. As one moved northward along the frontier, owners tended to live closer to their ranches, as in the case of Juan Agustín Terán, a resident of Sauces (today Monteagudo), who in 1833 received title to lands located in Sauces and in nearby Sapirangui cantones. Even here, the land grant contract made allowances for other individuals, called *piqueros*, to pasture up to twenty-five head of cattle without prejudice; the owner was to have four hundred head himself within the year.[4]

The economic basis of the frontier Creoles was ranching. Cattle thrived in the subtropical climate of the Andean foothills; they were used to the periodic droughts that scourged the region. Most important, the live animals or their hides could be transported to market in an area where roads were practically nonexistent. This type of ranching involved extensive rather than intensive use of the land and fostered only a very sparse settler population.[5] Moreover, in the first half of the nineteenth century, the frontier economy was poorly connected to the markets in the highlands. This meant that the settler economy remained relatively poor; although certain individuals owned huge amounts of land and hundreds if not thousands of cattle, there was little they could do with them and they had little incentive to expand production. The impetus for new lands came primarily from the exhaustion of old pastures, for cattle inevitably changed the ecology of the region where they grazed, leading eventually to erosion of the steep hillsides and the predominance of spiny plants that were unpalatable to the voracious bovine palate.

Despite a common dependence on cattle, the settlers were divided politically into often antagonistic camps. The most important divisions among the colonists corresponded to the administrative boundaries of the three departments, Santa Cruz, Chuquisaca, and Tarija, which claimed jurisdiction over portions of the Cordillera. Departmental boundaries could not be demarcated in the unconquered frontier. The three departmental administrations thus rarely cooperated in any consistent manner, since each political unit was afraid that aiding the other might lead to a diminution of its own territory. For this reason military efforts remained generally uncoordinated and ineffective. For example, in 1866 Sebastian Cainzo, the frontier commander of San Luis (Tarija), and General Francisco Burdett O'Connor tracked the attackers of a raid on a village of Indian allies into the jurisdiction of another militia commander. The commander prohibited the entry of the armed posse into his territory, and as a result the raiders, under the leadership of Buricanambi, the chief of Ingre (Chuquisaca), and some mestizos from Chuquisaca, were able to make off with the stolen cattle and the women and children taken as slaves.[6]

Moreover, policies toward the Chiriguanos also varied from department to department. In Tarija the colonization of the eastern frontier remained the highest priority. The departmental prefects frequently maintained relations with the Chiriguanos, as had been historically the case since the founding of the villa in 1574, when Luis de Fuentes beat off a host of Chiriguano armies before securing possession of the Guadalquivir valley. The Tarija settlers also had to deal with other Chaco tribes, such as the Tobas, Matacos, Tapietés, and Chorotis. Especially the Tobas were much-feared horsemen, and settlers had to consider their actions within the wider context of interethnic alliances and counteralliances.

In Chuquisaca there was much greater governmental neglect of the eastern frontier than in Tarija; officials of the departmental capital, Sucre, were usually much more concerned with national affairs because it was also the seat of the national government. If there was any help to be had from national military forces, it was most likely to come from Chuquisaca. Perhaps because the settlers were assured of military backing from the capital, settlers from Chuquisaca tended to be the most brutal group toward the ava and the least likely to seek alliances or compromises with the indigenous groups. However, the intense focus on national politics at times also brought about occasional ruptures between authorities appointed from Sucre and the settlers; in 1844, for example, the "principal *vecinos* [settlers] and landowners of Sauses" protested the Azero governor's request for weapons and men to combat "the invasions of the barbarians [*bárbaros*]," which, they said, was only "a pretext to oppress the inhabitants," not fight Indians.[7]

The settlers from Santa Cruz department were left largely to their own devices, though some of the colonists were also local officials, such as prefects and subprefects. The department in the nineteenth century contained unconquered indigenous groups on virtually all sides, though the Chiriguano threat was the most important concern. The number of whites in Cordillera province was minimal during the first half of the nineteenth century compared to other sections within Santa Cruz department and thus received correspondingly little attention. In 1839, for example, the vast province contained only 2,127 whites out of a total of 85,205 inhabitants in the department.[8] Nevertheless, the Cordilleranos were able to make do because of extensive race mixture with Chiriguanos and almost universal Spanish-Guaraní bilingualism and because of the care they took to ally themselves with other indigenous groups in the region as counterbalances to the Chiriguano military threat. Thus, although the bases of the settler economies were the same, each group related differently to the presence of the Indians. These relations were based upon the numbers of settlers relative to Chiriguanos, their military strength, the traditional manner of dealing with indigenous groups, and what they perceived to be their own interests.

Although some authors have spoken of a "Chiriguano nation," the ava were even less politically united than the settlers.[9] In many ways each village was independent, and even leadership among the great chiefs, the mburuvichas, was fragmented. Some chiefs were better known to Creole leaders, but whether they also wielded greater power within the Cordillera than other tubicha rubichas is not clear. After Cumbay, an important leader from the late eighteenth century and the early nineteenth, there was no overarching ava leader who appeared to be the first among equals, though Ayericuay in the 1830s might have come close. During the early republican period, there were probably about a dozen of these great men; by the end of the century, seven men could still claim that title.[10] Despite the small numbers of mburuvichas, as during the colonial period each chief on all levels maintained a great degree of independence and there was much conflict and jockeying for position between different groups and villages. This largely fits the Clastrian model, in which the political culture "against the state" does not permit the building of unitary alliances or the creation of a unified front. The lack of an overarching leader was due as much to internal disunity (and lack of a common sense of ethnic identity) as it was to the political culture that emphasized the independence of free warriors.[11]

Chiriguano politics and economy were intimately related to maize cultivation. The main staple of the ava economy was corn, although the women also cultivated other vegetables, such as squashes. Most villagers also owned some cattle and perhaps some horses. Particularly important was *cangui*, a type of corn beer that the women prepared. According to one acute observer, this beverage was "their coffee, their soup, their wine, their food, their drink, their everything."[12] Cangui also served as the lubricant in meetings to negotiate political and military alliances; when a chief wanted to gather together men for war or cement an alliance, he invited his guests to a feast in which all got drunk on corn beer. These feasts also served to show the resources of a particular chief; the more cangui he was able to provide, the more prestige he gained and the more he obligated his guests.[13]

The Period of Chiriguano Domination:
Alliances and Interethnic Relations

From approximately 1816 to 1860 the Chiriguanos held the upper hand along the vast frontier of the Andean foothills. Most historians and ethnographers have ignored this fact; perhaps the drama of the Chiriguanos' decline during the last quarter of the nineteenth century, the scarcity of published scholarly accounts for the period from 1810 to the 1870s, the uncritical reliance on the often self-serving accounts exclusively from the perspective of non-Chiriguanos, and the hindsight that appeared to make the Indians' defeat "inevitable" have hidden this important insight.[14] The fact that the ava dominated the frontier militarily during this period changes our understanding of the region's history over the whole republican period. This dominance defined interethnic relations even after the final military defeat of the Chiriguanos and helps to explain the crucial role the Franciscan missions played in the development of the frontier.

This dominance was based on three factors. First, the colonists and the military were important actors within the Cordillera during the first half of the nineteenth century but were primarily allies of more powerful Indian groups. Second, the colonists and the departmental governments themselves recognized Chiriguano dominance by paying tribute to the Indians and refusing to endorse the colonists' attempts to enter Indian territory. Third, even after the tributary relationship broke down in 1839, the military tactics of the Indian groups were superior to those of the militias and national troops and led to numerous defeats of Bolivian forces at the hands of the *queremba*, the ava warriors, or at least inconclusive victories by the military.

There is virtually no information on the Cordillera for the tumultuous period from 1816 to approximately 1830. Thus it is not possible to understand how the ava regained control over their territory.¹⁵ The organization of national administration in this region undoubtedly lagged behind that of the highlands, and probably the Indians took advantage of the power vacuum to eliminate the settlers from their homeland. Thus by the 1830s the independent Chiriguano villages controlled all the area between Cuyambuyo on the Bermejo River (today the border with Argentina), just east of Salinas mission, and in a virtually straight line to the Pilcomayo River into what is today Cinti province, to Huacareta, around the frontier outposts of Sauces and Sapirangui to the Guapay River. Only the new town of Gutiérrez, founded in 1830, and the sending of secular priests to the former missions as far south as Masavi prevented the complete reconquest of the northern territories by the ava.¹⁶

Instead of controlling their territory by virtue of their superior military strength, the colonists held on to their tiny settlements by forming alliances with powerful Chiriguano chiefs. Nevertheless, these alliances proved to be mostly temporary despite the settlers' efforts at placating powerful individuals through gifts and their intervention on the behalf of one group or another. Villages frequently shifted allegiances from one regional chief to another, so no one individual or group emerged as the undisputed leader. This was very similar to the "middle ground" in the Ohio territories in North America, where the villages of both indigenous peoples and mixed races formed temporary alliances with each other, without any one group being able to overcome the others.¹⁷ These temporary alignments were difficult to comprehend for the settlers, who in their ignorance of Chiriguano political culture asserted, "Those who are on our side actually are very perverse."¹⁸ The settlers failed to recognize that, rather than being traitorous, the Chiriguano villages tried to maintain a power equilibrium in which no one group could dominate the other. To the colonists, the fickleness of indigenous allegiances with Creole villagers smacked of treason rather than being part of a coherent strategy based on solid political principles.

An example of this pattern of shifting alliances can be seen in the case of the ava in the Ingre area. From 1836 to 1841 the ava in Ingre were one of the settlers' main opponents in the Cordillera. Their leader, the maximum chief (tubicha rubicha) Ayericuay, was described by frontier authorities as "an enemy who is the most powerful [leader] in this Cordillera." Ayericuay previously had been counted as one of the settlers' allies, but after the unprovoked burning and massacre of the village of Itacua by troops from Santa Cruz in 1836, he switched sides. In 1840, as befitted a mburuvicha who wanted to make war, Ayericuay "invited all of the Cordillera" to a feast of cangui drinking to convince other chiefs to join him in a campaign against the settlers. Two chiefs allied with the settlers had also been invited and saw "the feast and meeting of [the tubichas] of Guacaya and Cuevo" with Ayericuay, though they did not join. This did not stop Ayericuay; with Huacaya and Cuevo, two of the most important Chiriguano settlements, he began to attack the frontier ranches a short while later.[19]

Ayericuay's campaign against the Bolivian settlements did not last long. Ayericuay and his queremba changed sides again in 1841, when he lost a battle against a troop of 150 Bolivian soldiers and Aracua, the tubicha of Ñacamiri and descendant of Cumbay. Like his ancestor, Aracua had been a long-standing ally of the settlers and Ayericuay's rival, whom the tubicha rubicha from Ingre wanted to eliminate. Once he failed to do so, Ayericuay rejoined the settlers' and Aracua's cause. He remained on the settlers' side until 1848, when both he, Aracua, and the Chiriguanos living close to Sauces launched an attack on San Juan del Piray.[20] A local official warned in 1857, "[Ayericuay] with profound secrecy and caution is seducing the [Chiriguano] Captains allied with us so that they will not make difficulties in his projected invasion."[21]

Very few Chiriguano groups remained the settlers' allies throughout the nineteenth century other than in the north, where the Caipipendi Chiriguanos and the Izoceños were stout allies of the Santa Cruz prefecture in the second half of the nineteenth century.[22] Toward the south the ava villagers remained more independent. Only two Chiriguano villages remained bound to Creole society. These cases are instructive, for they show that there were powerful reasons for these exceptions. The Caraparirenda ava lived in a valley of that name close to the small town of Muyupampa. Caraparirenda was located between the area of influence of the settlers from Sauces, Azero province (Chuquisaca), and that of the Cordilleranos from Santa Cruz. To maintain their independence, the chiefs from Caraparirenda played off the colonists from both provinces against each other. For example, in 1859 a number of colonists from Vallegrande attempted to take ava village lands for themselves. The chiefs took their case to the governor of Tomina and Azero, who, because of the services rendered by the Caraparirenda Indians as allies, used his power to rid the valley of these interlopers. Similar attempts at land usurpation occurred in 1861, 1868, 1894, and even in the twentieth century, but each time the Chiriguanos won their case by playing off one authority against the other.[23]

The other exception was Caiza, located far to the east of the last

Andean foothills, on the border of the Chaco. The small group of Chiriguanos living there felt so threatened by the continuous raids by the Tobas, warlike hunting and gathering tribesmen who were superb horsemen, that they requested a mission and a fort to protect them. They were also threatened by settlers; in 1834 they complained about ranchers who tried to take their lands, "abundant in resources for all kinds of livestock."[24] Perhaps the Caiza ava felt that by having missionaries and local authorities settled there, they could minimize the land seizures. Although the efforts to establish a mission failed, in the 1840s the settlement did acquire a small fort with a complement of militia troops. By that time, of course, it was impossible to switch sides even if the Chiriguanos from Caiza had wanted to. Thus, as in the case of Caraparirenda, overwhelming pressure from outsiders forced these permanent alliances.

Warfare and Indian "Defeats"

Chiriguano allies played an essential role for the settlers' side in the conflict against other ava groups in the region. In most cases the victories that the Bolivian army or militia commanders ascribed to themselves were in fact won by the Indian allies who invariably accompanied any expedition into the Cordillera. Indian allies were the first ones to bring news of any potential attacks and served as reconnaissance troops to spy out enemy movements. One suspects that they also formed the bulk of the expeditions. Exact numbers are difficult to come by in the battle accounts in the nineteenth century, perhaps because the allied queremba always acted under their own chief and were not under the direct command of the Bolivian officers. It is also possible that the military commanders intentionally did not mention the number of ava allies because they wanted to highlight the actions of their own men.

In many cases the "invasions" (as the settlers liked to call the Indians' campaigns against them) resulted as much from the internal dynamics of the alliances and counteralliances within the Cordillera as from any actions on the settlers' part. It is more useful to think of the Bolivian military and the local militias as bit players in intra-ethnic conflicts rather than participating in a clear white-versus-Indian dynamic during the first half of the nineteenth century. At best, the ranchers took advantage of internal rivalries but were not the decisive actors. This was the case with Guiracota, the mburuvicha of Caipipendi (Cordillera province) and an ally of the settlers from Santa Cruz, who in the 1850s fell in love with the wife of

Yaveao, the mburuvicha of Cuevo. Yaveao found out about the adulterous affair, and Guiracota attacked him with the help of allied villages north of the Parapetí River. Yaveao counterattacked with the aid of the Tobas and defeated the interloper. Guiracota, fearing for his life, requested the help of the subprefect of Cordillera province, Colonel Manuel Ignacio Castedo. Castedo joined Guiracota and his allies and, through trickery, was able to defeat and wipe out a large number of Cuevo ava and capture many women and children.[25]

It was not only Chiriguano society that was often disunited. Conflict was endemic in national politics, and the ava took advantage of this. In 1841, for example, a faction headed by General José Ballivián moved the national army from Azero to fight for his cause in Potosí. With most of the troops gone and local authorities in disarray, the Chiriguanos exploited this weakness and attacked a number of strategic points.[26] It is not clear from the documentation available how much information the Chiriguano chiefs had on national politics, but since local governmental authorities had relatively good intelligence on Indian affairs it is extremely likely that the ava knew as much about the confused national situation as their settler counterparts.

Even more serious were these national political disputes when they devolved to the local level and some factions were even foolish enough to involve Chiriguano forces. In 1847 the governor of Azero sent thirty-five forced recruits from Sauces, culled from Indian allied villages, to Ballivián's army to put down a revolt in the highlands. The villages from whence the governor had taken the men rebelled, threatening to invade the town. As a result, the militia, or Guardia Nacional, had to be called up, "and all the people of the town sought refuge in the church." Finally, the Indians, under the tubicha Cuma, went to La Laguna (present-day Padilla) to recover the recruits.[27]

In the revolt of 1849 against President Belzu, led by General José Miguel de Velasco and José María Linares, the governor of Azero fled to help the revolutionaries. The governor of Tomina accused "the faction of Velasco and Linares which through their stupid and brutal ringleaders Barron and Padilla, stirred up the savage tribes."[28] Belzu had been a frontier commander in Tarija earlier in his career, and it is likely that he had made enemies among the Indians. The rebel generals used the fact to their advantage by allying with the Chiriguano chiefs against the hated Belzu. The Tobas also became involved, and it was necessary to bring an elite army battalion before the Indians agreed to make peace. Of course, once the

Chiriguanos and Tobas began their campaign they did not stop to find out to whose faction the settlers and the cowhands belonged. Indeed, when revolutionaries attempted to make trouble for local authorities by encouraging the Indians to campaign against the settlers, they did so only at their own peril, and what they began often had unintended dire consequences for the entire frontier area.

The pattern of alliances and counteralliances thus worked both ways. In an analysis of Indian-white relations it is often easy to forget that not only native, but also national societies contained many political fractures. This was especially the case in early nineteenth-century Bolivian society, where *caudillos* revolted with chronic regularity and created power vacuums.[29] The Indians were able to use these periodic lapses to further their own goals. Settler society was not monolithic, and neither was that of the Chiriguanos. The Indians were able to use national politics to their advantage and so remain independent.

Relationships among Government, Ranchers, and Indians

Despite the often fractured political landscape, both the Indians' and the settlers', it is clear that the Chiriguanos held the upper hand during much of the first half of the nineteenth century when confronting the Bolivian state and the settlers. Government correspondence shows that both landowners and government officials paid the Indians to prevent raids. This was a type of tribute and showed the military dominance of the ava over the settlers. In 1830, for example, the national government disallowed a settler's request to be given lands in Tariquia (Padcaya, Tarija). The government decided against the settler because the Indians claimed ownership over the land: "Because of this all the owners of livestock pay to the Indians the grazing fees [*yerbajes*] that corresponds [*sic*] to them for the time that they have them graze."[30]

The lands in Tariquia were former mission property and so the government sided with the Indians because it recognized their land rights. Where the Indians had never been part of the mission system, however, ava demanded recompense for the use of what they considered their land. In 1835 a local official reported, "The Indians of Ingre presented themselves in great numbers in the largest ranches of the frontier requiring that if the cowhands did not give them four steers from each ranch, that they would take all of the cattle, but they did not use force; only two of them titling themselves *capitanes* approached said cowhands, but they still took between eight or ten steers."³¹ One gets a clear picture of the superiority of Chiriguano military power from reports like these. In the end the ranchers paid or tried to dissuade the Indians from taking too many livestock.

The Indians' and settlers' different concepts of property undoubtedly contributed to this confused state of affairs. Although landowners often claimed huge tracts extending far into Indian territory, the ranchers were able to operate only at the sufferance of the indigenous population. Even the largest and most powerful ranchers, frequently military men who had gained distinction in the wars for independence, had to play by the Chiriguanos' rules. This was the case as reported in 1836 with Manuel Fernando Baca Flor and General Francisco Burdett O'Connor, large landowners in Tarija: "[They] possess through legal title huge estancias, whose dominions extend to the Pilcomayo river: these *Señores* however, who purchased these lands, provide gifts to the Indians every year so as not to receive damages, because they [the Indians?] allege property rights and have the land as theirs. The same occurs with others who in this form have their cattle in other estancias." According to the commander of frontier forces, armed force would be necessary to displace the Indians: "It would be inevitable that we would have to make war on them." This was a prospect neither the government nor the settlers were apparently willing to countenance.³²

During this period the nation had too few resources to prevent large-scale destruction if the Indians declared an all-out war on the settlers. Therefore the national government ordered the governor of Tarija province to prevent settlers from moving into Indian territory so as not to oblige "the government to take providential measures which by their nature cause infinite expenses to the public treasury." Moreover, the minister of war warned that he could be held responsible for protecting the ranchers only from unprovoked attacks by the Indians, but was not disposed to help when the frontiersmen "by ignoble means discomfort the Indians in their own territories."³³ The governor of Tarija even refused to carry out the measurement of land grants previously awarded because the Indians, who insisted that the territory was theirs, would have resisted. Instead, the governor limited himself to "warn[ing] all the commanders of the frontier [forces] about the care which they must have so that there not be the least injustice nor [should they] molest the Indians, procuring the conservation of the good intelligence and harmony that they are enjoying presently."³⁴

The national government in this period was also not above paying money and goods to the Chiriguanos so that the Indians would leave the settlers alone. For example, in 1843 the Tarija prefect presented gifts of ponchos of imported cloth, blankets, knives, tobacco, and jewelry "to all the Capitanes who have left [the Cordillera] to come see [him]," worth almost two hundred pesos, a large sum for that period. The diary of Francisco Burdett O'Connor records one of these trips that Capitán Guayupa made in 1850 to Tarija to meet the new departmental prefect. O'Connor personally accompanied Guayupa to the city and introduced him to the prefect. However, the prefect refused to pay the one hundred pesos that Guayupa said he received from the previous prefect for "defending all of the *Frontera* against the incursions of the other barbarians." O'Connor desperately argued for the stipend, but finally the prefect agreed to pay only sixteen pesos. The following day, when Guayupa passed through one of O'Connor's estates on the way home, the landowner heard that Guayupa had not received even the smaller amount the prefect had promised. O'Connor, not having any cash on hand, borrowed money from a friend and paid the Indian chief the sixteen pesos. Clearly it was in O'Connor's interest to keep as powerful an mburuvicha as Guayupa "gratified and content."[35]

The failure to give gifts to Chiriguano leaders who wanted them was foolish and a mistake that only a new prefect would make. Most prefects, such as Manuel Magariños in 1843, saw that "the investment of this small sum produces great advantages which do not need to be expounded upon. ... Never should one fail to invest in the interesting object for which [these sums] are destined."[36] Indeed, Thierry Saignes has published a list from the departmental treasury of Tarija of the expenditures paid to Chiriguano leaders. They range from 1830 to 1873, with sums as high as 215 pesos (1845) to much smaller sums in earlier and later years. The table also includes 43 pesos 6 reales for "lieutenant colonel" Guayupa in 1850; apparently the following year the Chiriguano chief was paid one hundred pesos. Of course, these sums did not include the money and gifts with which other authorities bought off the Chiriguano leaders.[37]

Crisis and Warfare, 1839–1841

Despite this effort to placate the ava, the relationship between the Indians and the settlers had worsened dramatically by the late 1830s. The Chiriguanos suffered from a severe drought that devastated the corn crops between 1839 and 1841. With famine threatening, the Indian villages resorted to eating cattle. Some of the villages had accepted the herds on their lands, but others had not; presumably the Chiriguano harvested those cattle from herds whose owners had not paid them. The ranchers were also at fault, for their herds were penetrating farther and farther into Indian territory as the drought-ridden pastures in the hinterland were unable to support the herds. Thus, according to José Manuel Sanchez, the military commander of Carapari district, in early 1839 the Chiriguanos of Caiza and their allies, the Chanés of Itiyuro, "almost . . . finished off the haciendas[,] robbing [them] secretly." The Chanés alone appropriated more than four hundred cattle and even took some to Orán, across the border in Argentina, to trade them for corn. Despite what the regional military authorities considered a clear provocation, the commander of frontier forces refused to move against the Indians; instead, Sanchez wrote, "[I was forced to] try to contain these Indians with kindness and pretending ignorance of their actions. . . . In this fashion I have avoided a general rebellion in these parts."[38]

Warfare was inevitable; as the famine continued the Indians continued to take the ranchers' livestock. The warriors organized into roving bands to capture herds of cattle and kill, if necessary, the armed cowhands. The ranchers could not countenance this, as they were losing their men and their fortunes. The battles between 1839 and 1841 were the most severe since the colonial period; although there had been numerous sorties earlier, the conflict during those three years affected the frontier for the first time since independence, especially in the south. Military actions occurred on a broad front, from Muyupampa, a village close to Sauces in Chuquisaca, to the former mission of Salinas, far to the south in Tarija.

The first battles took place in the south, where in March 1839 an army of national troops and militia sent from Tarija invaded the villages of Ipaguazo. The army was able to beat the Indians only after several attacks, when they killed Passani, the "principal Capitán who acted as General." Even after this defeat many warriors escaped into the forest, though troops slew up to 150 queremba and captured many women and children. In addition to 130 live cattle that were too thin to eat, the soldiers found hundreds of hides of butchered cows.[39]

Bolivian commanders ordered troops to hold the strategic Ipaguazo area. However, within a month the soldiers had to retreat after illness, lack of supplies, and constant harassment by the Indians made their position untenable. By April the Chiriguanos had taken back the initiative and attacked El Palmar in Cinti province. Moreover, national forces were severely handicapped due to a "fever epidemic," perhaps typhoid, that had already killed more than five thousand inhabitants. The following month Bernardo Trigo, the authority in charge of the campaign from Tarija, had to give up all the lands conquered in the campaign.[40]

Throughout 1840 and 1841 the Indians attacked virtually at will. Queremba from Choreti attacked Muyupampa as part of a vast alliance under tubicha rubicha Ayericuay that encompassed the important settlements of Huacaya, Cuevo, and Ingre. In one campaign the allies under Ayericuay captured more than five thousand cattle and two hundred horses. When national troops attempted to retrieve these herds they were badly beaten. In a panic, the inhabitants of the town of Sauces prepared themselves for an attack by creating an impromptu fort in the main plaza. The attack never came. Finally, national troops were able to disperse a band of Indians in Añimbo, but almost immediately afterward the Chiriguanos raided nearby San Juan del Piray.[41]

The only place where national forces were able to make inroads was near Chimeo, a Chiriguano village that had opposed the reestablishment of nearby Mission Itau. In 1840 the settlers of Zapatera, also located near Itau, sprang a trap on the Chiriguanos. Saying that they were tired of war, the militia brought presents to Caruruti, where they attracted a number of ava families from surrounding villages. When a large number of Indians had arrived by the third day, the militia from Zapatera took their arms out of hiding and massacred the Indian men, women, and children who had camped there. They then launched assaults on the villages in the area, killing and enslaving the unprepared Indians. As a result, the tubicha of Chimeo, Yaguareca, sued for peace and permitted a fort to be built in his settlement. Despite numerous attacks on the new fort and allied Chiriguano settlement by dissident queremba from Chimeo and the aid of the Chiriguano from Huacaya, the community remained, and in 1849 the Franciscans converted the settlement into a mission.[42]

This was war on a vaster scale than the usual skirmishes, and the settlers realized it. According to one observer, Luis Calvimontes, the Indians had not sown a single grain of corn and thus were forced to continue taking the settlers' cattle. In addition, Calvimontes noted a change in the Indians' attitude in war. He asserted:

> The obstinate War which today the Indians wage against us is not the same that they were accustomed to wage in previous years, in which we barely fired a gun when they all would flee fearfully to hide in the most rugged and isolated mountains. Through repeated reports which

I have received I know that these Indians have either advanced in the art of Warfare or they have somebody among them who animates them and directs their movements, in which case they will become a terrible threat because of the immensity of their numbers.[43]

The widespread war and the organization with which the Chiriguanos fought against the Creoles showed the latter that the balance of military power was on the side of the Indian alliance. The dedication to total warfare at the expense of agricultural disputes showed that the Indians did not behave as peasants, leaving fighting aside when the crops beckoned. Calvimontes's missive exposed the weak position of the Creoles and their lack of numbers and ability to bully the Chiriguanos. The Creoles were able to accomplish their military goals only if they could attract a substantial number of Indian villages to their side.

The war finally ended in April 1841, when a combined army of five hundred Chiriguano allies from Ñacamiri, under the leadership of Aracua, and 150 national troops beat the Ingre-Huacaya-Cuevo alliance in an all-day battle. The terms of peace effectively provided for a return to the status quo before 1839. The anti-Creole Indians agreed to return a few arms they had taken from the soldiers and any property and prisoners. Moreover, they agreed to be placed under the leadership of Aracua and attack any group that did not adhere to the treaty. Ayericuay consented to these terms, but, according to Luis Calvimontes, insinuated that one of his captains by the name of Chaverao would refuse to abide by the treaty. As the negotiations wore on, Chaverao was murdered, apparently by the militiamen.[44] Even this murderous act did not hide the fact that the settlers had lost much more than the Indians. According to one estimate, the ranchers had lost twenty thousand head of cattle. As a result, the prefect of Chuquisaca characterized the region as a place where "ruin has overcome almost totally its inhabitants because of the incursions and pillaging of the barbarians."[45]

The human casualties, while almost certainly not equal on both sides, were probably proportional relative to the number and ethnicities of people who lived in the region. The settlers probably had fewer casualties (we do not know how many cowhands lost their lives while riding herd), but they were a small minority in the region. Moreover, other than in the southern Tarija territory, there apparently were few raids on Indian villages with the subsequent killings and kidnapping of Indian women and children; most of the war had been fought on land settled by whites and mestizos. It is thus not surprising that the Chuquisaca prefecture, in line with the national government, after the end of the war in 1841 again recommended diplomacy to local authorities, saying, "The greatest prudence is to attract more and more the friendship and the good intelligence of those [allied Indians] and of the other Indians who remain."[46]

New Attempts by the Creoles at Frontier Dominance

The new frontier policy of remaining friendly to the Indians did not last long. In late 1841 a revolution brought to national power General José Ballivián. Ballivián was the first president to initiate an aggressive policy of expanding the frontier at the expense of the Indians.[47] The new administration's policies were put into effect first on the Chiriguano frontier, though with only limited results. In mid-1842 the commander general of Tomina, Manuel Carrasco, launched an expedition with national troops and his Indian allies Aracua and Aracua's sister, another important Chiriguano leader in her own right. They quickly invaded Ingre, Huacaya, and the upper Pilcomayo River. However, the allies were forced to return home after only a month in the field and finding little success; the Indians melted into the forest at the army's approach. Carrasco could only claim, "It is possible that the savage barbarians have received more than exemplary punishment." Because of "the lack in [the] canton of all foodstuffs" he had to send his cavalry back and cut the expedition short. He brought back eighty-eight Indian women and children; "the majority . . . perished . . . in a state of total poverty and malnourishment."[48] By December the troops who patrolled the ranchers' pastures had all retreated because of lack of pay and supplies and because tropical diseases were killing the soldiers.[49] The Indians returned to resettle the area and plant their corn crops, free again from Creole interference.

With the support of the Ballivián administration one prefect, Manuel Rodríguez Magariños of Tarija, attempted to invade Indian lands along the frontier in the early 1840s. To this end, he proposed exploring the Chaco and establishing a string of forts stretching from the Pilcomayo River all the way through Ingre and Santa Cruz to pacify the Chiriguanos and the Chaco tribes. A vigorous man of action, by 1842 he had established three forts and a military colony along the Pilcomayo and a year later led an ambitious expedition on boats down the river. However, instead of subduing the Indians along the frontier, his penetration into Toba and Mataco territory and the abuses his troops committed against the Indians only brought about violent resistance and a general uprising among the Chiriguanos, Tobas, and Matacos all along the frontier.⁵⁰

Within a year after Magariños's expensive efforts to create a line of defense against the Indians, only one of the five forts remained. This was the one in Caiza that antedated the Magariños project and remained because it enjoyed the protection of the Chiriguanos, who felt that the few soldiers with their rifles were preferable to continuous raids by their enemies, the Tobas. Thus a little over a year later the ava again were harassing the Indians of Ingre, at that moment allies of the ranchers, and the settlers of San Juan del Piray from Ipaguazo, Caruruti, and Cuevo, the same places as six years before.⁵¹ The settlers of Cinti province were able to contain the Chiriguano threat by building two forts in 1846, one in La Loma and the other in El Palmar, close to where the Pilaya and Pilcomayo Rivers meet. Since these colonists were mainly agriculturalists and so were willing to maintain control over a well-defined territory, their efforts proved more successful than those of the ranchers, whose cowhands roamed vast distances with their herds.⁵²

Otherwise, the frontier remained relatively stable until well into the 1850s. The only difference was that an alliance of Chiriguano villages joined with some Toba groups to form a formidable military force. As the ranchers in Caiza began encroaching on Toba hunting grounds, the Chaco ethnic group began to lay aside its traditional enmity with the Chiriguanos and formed occasional alliances with ava villages in the Cordillera to combat what both ethnic groups now saw as their more dangerous enemy. As mentioned earlier, the Chiriguanos fought largely (though not exclusively) on foot, whereas the Tobas preferred to fight on horseback. An indigenous army composed of both infantry and cavalry negated the frontier militia's advantage, which relied almost exclusively on cavalry. The results of this alliance can be seen in the new conflicts between 1848 and 1849, during which a force of Chiriguanos and their settler allies were soundly defeated in a battle in Sapirangui province. The Toba and Chiriguano force, half composed of cavalry, beat the Creole and Indian alliance, killing one allied Chiriguano chief, a settler, and wounding many others.⁵³ Only another pitched battle at Igue-catupire a few months later, where the elite Illimani battalion and their Indian allies faced three thousand queremba (the Tobas had already returned home), led to the dispersal of the Chiriguano forces. Even then the battle was not conclusive; the national army was able to capture only thirty women and retrieve one white captive with her three children.⁵⁴

Weaponry, Tactics, and War Aims: The "War of Resources"

What made it possible for the Chiriguanos to hold off national forces as effectively as they did? At first glance, it appears that the militia and especially the national army, with its horses, guns, and lances, would be far superior to the bows and arrows of the ava warriors. However, this was not the case. For one thing, the arms the militia possessed were old and in poor repair. The commanding officers were aware of this shortcoming; General Bernardo Trigo complained in 1839, "The armament which exists and which is mostly on the frontier, in addition to being insufficient [in number] for the enterprise, is destroyed, because it is of the antique kind from the time of General Olañeta [i.e., the wars for independence], which is more expensive to fix than it is worth."[55]

The humidity, dust, and extremes of heat of the subtropical Andean foothills were not conducive to the maintenance of firearms. The army did not provide the kind of care that was needed for the small arms stockpiles they had at hand. In 1840 one informant stated, "The hundred rifles destined for the security of the frontier are distributed between Pomabamba and Sauces [two towns in the region], and many of them [are] broken, as well as the ammunition lost and unserviceable because of the excessive humidity."[56] Two years later, when the national government took an arms inventory in the frontier region, the situation had not improved. The commander of national forces in Pomabamba, for example, reported that a third of his rifles and more than half of the *tercerolas*, short-barreled guns similar to carbines and the favorite weapon of frontier troops, were either in disrepair or completely unusable. Seventy-eight firearms were usable out of 108 in Pomabamba. Only the lances and bayonets were in satisfactory order.[57] Likewise, the governor of Cinti province complained in 1841, "When I took command, I encountered fifty old and out-of-order rifles and thirty packets of ammunition with useless powder, and one hundred lances without shafts or sockets."[58] Over and over, frontier officers complained of the lack of arms. In 1840 a Tomina officer commented that he could not make war on the "barbarians": "For that it is necessary that you aid me with firearms, ammunition, sables, lances, and cuirasses, since without these utensils everything, but everything is useless."[59]

Thus the differences between the weapons of the soldiers and those of the Indians were not always great. The lances, bayonets, and the few firearms (when they worked) were not greatly superior to the lances and bows and arrows of the queremba. The Chiriguanos carefully planned their campaigns and made sure that enough arms were available; one of the first signs of impending conflict was the reports of Indian villagers making arrows. Given the permeability of the frontier, war making on both sides was a public affair, known to the opposition some time in advance. Such was the case in 1833, when spies told the corregidor of Sauces that the Indians "were working continuously making arrows to go out to War."[60] According to Fr. Bernardino de Nino, before a campaign bows and arrows were manufactured in the main plaza of the village; the arrows were made with hooks that made them difficult to extract. Some arrows were fashioned out of a special kind of wood that tended to infect the wound even after the arrow had been extracted. The warriors who rode on horseback also carried a lance with a knife point or some sharp piece of iron tied to the tip.[61] All of these were formidable weapons against the poorly working Creole firearms.

The Chiriguanos usually employed better tactics in their campaigns than the military. As shown earlier, the Indians used the dense underbrush of the lush subtropical forest and the extremely rugged, hilly terrain to their best advantage. The queremba retreated in classic guerrilla style as well. Even after pitched battles the warriors escaped by melting into the forest, thus conserving their manpower and leaving the soldiers frustrated. At most, a few women who accompanied their men into the field to give them courage fell into the hands of the victors. Even in the battle of Igue-catupire in 1849, when the Illimani battalion, militia, and Indian allies attempted to encircle a force of three thousand queremba, the best they could do was to put the warriors "in complete dispersion and flight: and those who took the path to retreat, the fright and the terror precipitated them from the abysses of the mountain." Although this description sounds impressive, there were few casualties during the retreat (other than the queremba suffering from "the fright and the terror"), and the army was able to capture only thirty women. Earlier the commander of the battalion had been more honest when he admitted, "It is impossible for a battalion that can remain only a few days to acquire all possible advantages, because the inaccessible and mountainous territory and its immense jungles oppose themselves to the active pursuit of the quick *Cambas* [Chiriguanos]."[62] Even when the army was able to disperse the queremba formations, the Indians often re-formed into raiding parties and attacked elsewhere, as in 1841, when, after attacking Añimbo, the queremba regrouped close to San Juan del Piray, "where they put the houses to flame" until they were again driven off.[63]

The Indians virtually always chose the place of combat and used the topography to create a strong defensive position, letting the other side attack. Only when dealing with very small groups of settlers or cowhands did the Indians attack first. In the battle just described, the Chiriguano warriors awaited the troops "on the platform of a steep hill, defended by thick jungle and presenting only one entrance."[64] In 1839 the queremba occupied Ipaguazo, "a Castle of defense and inaccessible steep rocks." To get there the troops had to "overcome their trenches and rough trails."[65] In 1841 a colonel and his soldiers had to enter "the thickest parts of the forest in which the enemy had fortified himself." During this campaign, the decisive battle was joined when the soldiers met the six thousand warriors "in a narrow pass at the entrance of the Ingre canyon," an excellent defensive position where the troops could not use their cavalry, the major advantage they had over the Chiriguanos. The tide only turned when the soldiers broke through to the Ingre valley and used their cavalry to lethal effect. The tactical suggestion to do so came from Aracua, the Bolivians' Indian ally, making it possible for the Indian allies and Creole troops to gain the initiative.[66]

In contrast to the Chiriguanos, the militia's and regular army's tactic was usually a frontal charge on the enemy's positions. This foolish maneuver was probably based on the Creoles' sense of superiority of European over Indian tactics and their disdain for the Chiriguanos' martial discipline. Perhaps the soldiers' reliance on cavalry, firearms, and, occasionally, the small cannon that they hauled along the narrow trails also predicated this tactic. Once the Indians began to retreat, the troops tried to run them down, although this gave the warriors a chance to pick off soldiers with their arrows. The most effective tactic was for the soldiers to concentrate their fire on the war chiefs. Here the Bolivians used Chiriguano war customs to their advantage. It was a point of honor and sound tactics for the war leaders to lead the charge; as a result, mortality among them was high. Once the leaders had fallen, resistance usually ceased and the Indians retreated. Typical of this was the battle in 1839 in Ipaguazo, where the death of tubicha rubicha Passani decided the battle in favor of the soldiers and their Indian allies.[67]

These tactics also reveal the aims of the soldiers. Their main objective in war was to kill as many leaders and warriors as possible. Elimination of the warriors made it possible to take over the Chiriguano village lands and so let the cattle roam free. This was also one of the traditional ways European warfare determined victory or defeat. Given the almost incessant conflicts between the Chiriguanos and the ranchers, only the killing of the Indian warriors would assure that the villagers would not rise again to resist encroachment. A war of annihilation is the modern way of war.

For the Bolivian forces and especially the militia, women and children were considered the most desirable war booty. Chiriguano villages had little else to offer of value to the soldiers. Women and children could either be used as servants in the settler households or be sold in the towns in the hinterland. De facto slavery for Indian women and children was common on the frontier throughout the nineteenth century. An example was the aftermath of the battle of Ipaguazo: "Of the hundred-odd families of the Indians that have been taken, about half of them have been distributed among the frontier militia which has distinguished itself with its services, and the rest will arrive tomorrow to be distributed in the city [of Tarija]."[68]

In skirmishes with Chiriguanos, troop casualties were usually quite low. In any engagement there were normally only a handful of dead and many more wounded. In 1849 the casualty list at the settlers' defeat at Aratico was typical: "One Christian dead named Padilla but it is said that the Capitán Baraguari [an ally of the settlers] is also dead and there are many wounded." In the aftermath of this battle, instead of killing soldiers the Toba and ava warriors concentrated on retaking the cattle that the soldiers had captured.[69] The greatest casualties on the nationals' side usually came from among the cowhands and ranchers. Even there, the number of fatalities was not very large. The greatest number of dead from any single Indian attack during the first half of the nineteenth century was only ten cowhands, killed in 1844 at the Agua de Castilla ranch in eastern Cinti.[70] In this sense indigenous warfare was similar in the northern and southern hemispheres, as Indians in North America also did not claim large white casualties.

What, then, was the objective of the queremba when they declared war on the settlers? Clearly, the ava wanted to maintain their ancestral lands. But they did not try to kill off all interlopers, for certain non-Indians, such as traders, were welcome in the villages and not killed even during conflicts between Indians and national forces. That cowhands suffered the highest mortality during these conflicts points to the real goal of the Indians: to eliminate the cattle that invaded their lands.[71] As discussed earlier, the number of settlers, or *cristianos*, as they called themselves, along the frontier was minimal; the Indians by far outnumbered them. Although in 1842 "it [was] asserted that the Indians [were] infinite in number," one informed (though probably somewhat high) estimate placed the number of Chiriguanos at the beginning of the nineteenth century at 200,000; by the middle of the century perhaps 150,000 still remained.[72]

The incompatibility between the Chiriguanos and the Bolivian settlers came from the incompatibility of each group's different means of subsistence. The ranchers' cattle destroyed the Indians' corn crops, making it impossible for the Indian villagers to maintain their way of life. As one missionary exclaimed, "Instead of colonizing the frontier with men, it has been colonized with cows."[73] Thus most of the Indians' efforts during the campaigns against the Creoles in the first half of the nineteenth century were concentrated on eliminating or controlling the settlers' livestock. Eliminating cattle from Indian territory also got rid of the settlers, for without the herds, the ranchers had no reason to remain. This method was quite effective in the first decades after Bolivian independence. In 1836, for example, the Chiriguanos were effective in chasing a rancher away from the Parapetí River, since the only thing left on his *estancia* (ranch) was fifty steers, "among them many wounded by arrows."[74] Bolivian officials were also aware of this strategy. One old Indian fighter, General Bernardo Trigo, remarked that the ava had improved in this type of warfare since the colonial period: "In certain ways [the Chiriguanos] have advanced in the art of making war, especially [the art of making a war] of resources."[75] In 1840 the governor of Tomina exclaimed, "The Cordillera is threatened by an imminent invasion of the barbarian Indians, with the object of attacking the *estancia* owners and robbing their cattle."[76]

During the 1839–1841 famine, when their corn harvests failed, the Indians' objective was to eat the livestock, but even then they took many more animals than they could consume. Moreover, these robberies of cattle were a persistent feature of Indian warfare both before and after this three-year period. That the ranchers considered the taking of mostly unsupervised cattle grazing in the brush as "robbery" also points to differing conceptions of ownership. It is not clear how the Chiriguanos conceived of the invading bovines ranging free through the woods. The Chiriguanos themselves did some small-scale livestock ranching, but exclusively sheep.[77] Be that as it may, in 1848, in a prelude to the war of the following year, the Indians around Sauces reportedly were "already beginning to steal from the houses various things, to shoot horses and cattle; and consequently to eat some of the livestock." This the authorities interpreted (correctly) as a clear sign of an impending Chiriguano campaign.[78]

The ranchers were well aware that the ava were trying to drive them out by killing off their cattle, and they used this knowledge in their petitions for help. Writing to the government, they emphasized the importance of ranching to the Bolivian economy and the danger that the conflicts with the Indians represented for this enterprise. Typical of this was Manuel Sánchez de Velasco's appeal to the minister of war: "I do not doubt that Your Honor understands the importance of the frontier and of the vigilance which is necessary to keep the invaders [i.e., the Indians] from the wealth of the Department [of Chuquisaca], since the cattle that are raised and pastured there form the principal subsistence of two departments, [which are] confident only in the vigilance which merits the protection of the government." Sánchez de Velasco went on to ask for money to repair the many broken firearms on the Tomina frontier.[79]

Branislava Susnik has characterized the relations between settlers and the ava as a conflict between "cows and corn." According to this author, since the late eighteenth century the corn-cultivating Chiriguanos were clearly at a disadvantage against the ranchers, who slowly but surely drove off the indigenous population by herding their cattle onto the Indians' maize fields.[80] Susnik is essentially correct in her analysis, although she, like many others, has given too much credence to the settlers' claims, most of which come from the latter half of the century. Certainly there was a "war of resources," but the documents suggest that, in fact, the Indians held their own up to the 1860s. The Chiriguanos were able to do much more damage to the ranchers than the soldiers did to the villages. The Indians' guerrilla tactics minimized their casualties; the soldiers were unable to kill many queremba or capture many women and children. The battle at Ipaguazo in 1839 was an exception; there, the military used trickery to achieve an exceptionally high death toll.[81] The soldiers also were unable to occupy parts of the Chiriguanía for more than a few months at a time. Most important, however, the ava were successful in killing off vast numbers of cattle, effectively halting the advance into their territory or even pushing back the limits of the frontier. The extensive cattle grazing, in which a few cowhands supervised large numbers of livestock spread throughout a twisted maze of densely wooded, steep hills and narrow gorges, made resistance to the Indians' attacks on cattle impossible with the few resources the settlers and the Bolivian state had at their disposal.

One of the reasons the Chiriguano resistance was effective in the first decades after independence was the relatively low demand for cattle. There was little incentive to antagonize the Indians by expanding into virgin pastures. Expansion came about by the natural increase of the herds; the queremba could easily reverse this trend by eliminating the livestock along the margins of the Cordillera. They did this frequently during the first four decades of the republican period, and so reduced the threat to their livelihood.

The Franciscan Missions and the Decline of Chiriguano Independence

The situation changed significantly for the worse for the Chiriguanos beginning in the 1860s. In 1874 the ava villagers rose up in the greatest conflict since 1839, but this time were soundly defeated after more than three years of conflict. After the war, commonly called the Huacaya War, the government divided much of their land among the colonists. The last, desperate uprising took place in 1892, when Apiaguaiki Tumpa, a messianic leader, attempted to rally all Chiriguanos under his banner. However, this last rebellion failed. At least four factors played a role in the final defeat of Chiriguano power: the revitalization of the silver mining economy and the subsequent increase in the demand for cattle, an improvement in military tactics by the settlers, more effective military technology, and, most important, the reintroduction of Franciscan missions among the Chiriguanos.

The increase in Bolivian silver production began in the 1850s and accelerated until the turn of the century; because mining operations improved the surrounding roads, cattle production throughout southern Bolivia also increased. At last the ranchers of the frontier could export their cattle beyond the small urban markets of Tarija and Sucre into the lucrative highland mining markets. Although the relationship between ranching and the mining economy was a complex one, ranching became profitable in the second half of the nineteenth century. Growing demands and profits stimulated the expansion of livestock into the Cordillera and the Gran Chaco. This provided powerful incentives for the ranchers to invade Indian lands. The number of land grants in the region increased after 1860. Ranchers took a more aggressive stance toward the Indians by actively herding cattle onto their cornfields.[82] Without their major source of subsistence, the Chiriguanos were forced to move farther inland, into the heart of ava territory, around Cuevo and Huacaya, until the last independent villages were absorbed by the land grants and cattle ranches. By the time the silver mining economy collapsed in the last years of the nineteenth century, the Chiriguanos had been effectively conquered.[83]

It is not clear when more modern weaponry such as the repeating rifle was introduced into the frontier area. It is likely, however, and bears further investigation, that not only the type of weaponry improved, but the supply of arms and munitions became more regular as the Bolivian state consolidated beginning in the 1870s. The state had more revenue, at least in part because of the prosperity of the silver boom. The settlers also used new strategies to overcome the threat of Chiriguano resistance by constructing small fortresses. Thus between 1860 and 1900 the settlers built forts in Iguembe, Ingre, and Ñancaroinza and two near Cuevo. In contrast to the era before 1860, when the queremba were able to kill off ranchers living in isolated homesteads or lone cowhands watching their herds in the subtropical forest, the forts, even though they were often only primitive constructions of adobe and logs, proved to be sufficient defense. Such was the case of the famous fort in Iguembe, in which a handful of settlers held off thousands of queremba in 1866 and again in 1874. The Creole families had enough warning to flee or to hide in the fortress. The bows and arrows and guerrilla tactics were ineffective against a string of defensive positions.[84]

The change in military tactics also signaled a change in the attitudes of the military and the government toward the Indians. Unlike earlier in the century, when the government counseled restraint and even condemned actions such as the 1841 murder of Chief Chaverao, by the 1860s the prefects began authorizing land grants within the Cordillera at the expense of indigenous land rights. The granting of *tierras baldias* received its initial impetus during the Melgarejo regime to help remedy its perpetual fiscal crisis. The government's willingness to give away the Indians' land came at the right time for ranchers, as market forces made the costly colonization of prime pasture land a worthwhile endeavor. As the century wore on, the growth of positivism and social Darwinism, ideologies that exalted "white" races at the expense of non-Europeans, made the colonization of lands held by "savages" not only justifiable, but even beneficial.[85] Beginning in 1884 the government sold vast tracts of land at rock-bottom prices to claimants who asserted they were going to settle there. In the aftermath of the disastrous War of the Pacific (1879–1884), when it lost its coast to the Chileans, Bolivia encouraged the sale of fiscal lands on the frontier to settle territories there and avoid another debacle.

The settlers' attitudes also became harsher toward indigenous peoples, though for somewhat different reasons. The new intellectual currents of scientific racism and positivism probably played a role in this new outlook. More important was the conflict that began in the 1850s between the settlers and the Tobas, Matacos, and other Chaco groups. Unlike the Chiriguanos, who were agriculturalists and could be made to work on the haciendas, the Chaco peoples were hunters and gatherers who fought an all-out war with those who penetrated their territory. The war was one of mutual extermination. The Tobas saw the ranchers as enemies who attacked their villages and destroyed their hunting grounds. The settlers responded in kind; the Tobas and other Chaco peoples, according to the colonists, made very poor workers. The ranchers saw the Indians as impediments to the development of the ranching economy.[86]

The change in settlers' attitudes had a deleterious effect on the Chiriguanos as well. After the mid-nineteenth century, Bolivian soldiers saw few distinctions among the "savage barbarians" who impeded the settlement and progress of the region. For example, in 1859 the Chiriguanos of Cuevo and Caipipendi, at the time allies of the settlers, complained that troops sent out to combat the Tobas attacked them as well, killing eight of their men and taking their horses.[87] If these incidents occurred even among the allies of the settlers, there was no reason to think the soldiers would not massacre the populations of independent Chiriguano villages.

Although the first whole-scale massacre of the postindependence period occurred in 1839, after the battle of Ipaguazo, such hostilities became more frequent during the second half of the nineteenth century. Especially during the Huacaya War of 1874–1877 and the last rebellion of 1892, the executions of Indian prisoners of war and the sale of the surviving women and children now characterized warfare between the Chiriguanos and national forces. In 1875 eighty captive Chiriguanos were murdered in Yuqui by troops from Chuquisaca as they were being led to Sauces. In 1877 the whole Chiriguano settlement of Murucuyati was massacred while it was swollen in population with hungry Indians who had flocked to the village during a famine. During the 1892 rebellion more than two thousand ava men lost their lives, most not in combat but in subsequent massacres, and hundreds of women and children were either handed over to the Franciscan missionaries or taken to Bolivian cities and towns and sold to the highest bidder.[88] The massacres of the Indians in 1892 finally broke the back of Indian armed resistance; never again did the Chiriguanos engage in large-scale armed warfare with the settlers.

The Mission as a Factor in the Chiriguania

Although economic motivations, improved weaponry, and the increasing savagery with which the colonists attacked the Indians were significant, the most important factor in the loss of Chiriguano independence was the reestablishment of the Franciscan missions. After a long hiatus from the colonial period, the first mission was reestablished in 1845, but the missions among the Chiriguanos began to affect the balance of power only in the late 1850s. After the independence of Bolivia in 1825 the remnants of the Franciscan missions were in deplorable condition. To the north, in Cordillera province, a few of the former missions continued to exist as small mestizo settlements. All the missions in the central region of the Cordillera had been completely obliterated and were in the middle of what was now indisputably Indian territory. Only in the south, closest to the Tarija convent, were there any traces of the formerly flourishing mission system. In Tariquia, Salinas, and Itau the convent preserved its legal title, although in Tariquia only "a few Chiriguano apostates," perhaps sixty in number, resided in the former mission.[89]

After independence the Indians of Itau and Salinas also tried to free themselves from the domination of the Creoles, whom the Chiriguanos called karai, but their proximity to the settlers made this impossible. In 1834 the Chiriguanos of Itau rebelled against local authorities. General Francisco Burdett O'Connor used two companies of his crack Third Battalion to repress the uprising and took eighty-four men prisoner. Instead of executing them, he inducted the rebels as soldiers into his army. The wives and children of the Indian soldiers remained on the mission and periodically received food subventions from the government. The Itau Indians were forced to stay in the army and saw action against Argentine forces and even went all the way to Lima when the Peru-Bolivian Confederation was established (1836–1839) under President Andrés de Santa Cruz. The fate of the Salinas Indians was harsher. Salinas had remained a mission, though virtually only in name. In 1845, a year after the mission was secularized, the Salinas Indians rose up in rebellion. Again the rebels were inducted into the army. The fate of the women and children as well as the men not vigorous enough for army life was not as benign as in Itau; they were distributed among the landowners of the region to work as slaves. The landlords paid the state one peso per head for their upkeep.[90] The harsh treatment of the former mission Indians presented an object lesson that demonstrated the impossibility of the mission Indians ever breaking the alliance with the colonists.

The Franciscans reestablished Itau as a mission in 1845, more than a decade after the rebellion. Fr. Andrés Herrera, one of the few remaining members of the Tarija Franciscan convent, made several expeditions to Italy in the 1830s to recruit new friars. Others followed, mostly from Italy, providing a host of young friars for mission work. The Tarija convent was thus able to revive its missionary program in the Cordillera, and Itau was the first place to benefit from this influx of friars.[91]

Four years later the Franciscans founded the mission in nearby Chimeo. From there, with reinforcements from Italy, the Franciscan mission system expanded east and north. The Tarija convent established more missions in Aguairenda (1851), Tarairí (1854), Macharetí (1869), and Tiguipa (1872). The Tarija Franciscans also founded missions among the Tobas and Mataco-Noctenes (today called Weenhayek). The Franciscans "reduced" the Tobas to San Francisco Solano del Pilcomayo in 1860; however, only the addition of Chiriguanos from Tarairí in 1874 permitted the mission to survive because the friars did not trust the Tobas. In 1863 the Franciscans founded San Antonio de Padua for the Noctenes. This mission was less successful, as it was moved once and even shut down, from 1879 to 1884. (See table 1.)

In the 1870s the Franciscan convent of Potosí took the initiative. The missionary zeal of the Tarija convent had flagged by the late 1870s and the Tarija friars became increasingly bogged down administering their old missions and trying unsuccessfully to missionize the peoples in the Chaco. In contrast, the Potosí convent concentrated its efforts on the Chiriguanos in the northern sector, in Chuquisaca and Santa Cruz. They established Boicovo (1876), Santa Rosa de Cuevo (1887), and San Buenaventura de Ivo (1893). In addition, the Potosí friars founded three short-lived missions, San Francisco del Parapetí Grande in 1903, San Antonio del Parapetí in 1908, and Itatiqui in 1914. None lasted very long (see chapter 7). The government secularized San Francisco and San Antonio in 1912, whereas Itatiqui lasted only a year. (See table 2.)

Why did the Chiriguanos permit the establishment of missions? No overt coercion took place in the founding of the missions. Unlike in eighteenth-century Alta California, where the soldiers helped round up Indians to populate the missions, the Indians, or at least a faction, usually requested the missions themselves as refuges.[92] Since we do not have accounts writ-

TABLE 1. Franciscan missions of the Tarija convent

Year of establishment	Mission	Ethnic group(s)	Year of secularization
1845	Itau	Chiriguano	1905
1849	Chimeo	Chiriguano	1905
1851	Aguairenda	Chiriguano	1911
1854	Tarairí	Chiriguano	1949
1860	San Francisco del Pilcomayo	Toba, Chiriguano	1905
1863	San Antonio de Padua del Pilcomayo	Mataco (Weenhayek), Chiriguano	1905
1869	Macharetí	Chiriguano	1949
1872	Tiguipa	Chiriguano	1949

ten by the Indians themselves, we must infer their motives primarily from the evidence gathered by the missionaries and from indigenous behavior. Nevertheless, it is clear that the establishment of the missions among the Chiriguanos had little to do with a desire by the Indians to convert to Christianity or integrate themselves into national society. From the lack of interest in conversion, it appears that the Chiriguanos were generally content with maintaining their own religious beliefs (see chapter 4).

Although each case is somewhat different, three motives for requesting the establishment of a mission can be discerned, though in many cases the Chiriguanos wanted missions for a combination of reasons. One of the motives for inviting a missionary to the village arose from conflict between Indian groups. A Chiriguano chief requested a mission when another group threatened his village's existence. As one missionary put it in 1872, "All of our missions already founded have been put there because of 'war amongst themselves.'"[93] This was largely true for missions established before that date, such as Aguairenda, Tarairí, and Macharetí. In Tarairí, for example, according to Fr. Alejandro Corrado, groups to the north accused the settlement's leaders of being too friendly with the karai. When the Tarairí Indians insulted and killed a number of Tobas they had invited to a festival, the relatives of the dead sought revenge by allying themselves with the northern Chiriguano groups and attacked the village. Only the quick intervention of Fr. José Giannelli, who permitted the Tarairí Chiriguano to move their families to Mission Aguairenda, made possible the group's survival. Later the chiefs from Tarairí realized that the only way to return home was to permit the establishment of a mission. To that end, one Franciscan and a militia force from Salinas accompanied the refugees back to Tarairí. The Taraireños did not permit the troops to stay and did not allow Creole families to settle there.[94] Thus intra-indigenous conflict resulted in the establishment of many of the early missions. Up to the 1860s other indigenous enemies were more likely to be the Chiriguanos' main concern; the acceptance of missionaries appeared to be a lesser evil than succumbing to attack by other indigenous groups.

The relative lack of power along the frontier on the part of either the settlers or the government began to change in the late 1850s along the southern boundaries of the Cordillera. In this transitional period the militias delegated some of their duties to the mission Indians, who were militarily stronger than they. In 1858 the Chiriguanos from Aguairenda requested the head of the Tarija militia to authorize them to make war on the Tobas, their traditional enemies, and keep whatever unmarked cattle they captured. In return, the ava promised to return any stolen cattle with settlers' brands as well as turn over all Toba families they captured for "a modest gratification." Permission was granted for the expedition and a

TABLE 2. Franciscan missions of the Potosí convent

Year of establishment	Mission	Ethnic group(s)	Year of secularization
1876	San Pascual de Boicobo	Chiriguano	1949
1887	Santa Rosa de Cuevo	Chiriguano	1949
1893	San Buenaventura de Ivo	Chiriguano	1949
1903	San Francisco del Parapetí	Chiriguano (Izoceños?)	1912
1908	San Antonio del Parapetí	Chiriguano (Izoceños?)	1912
1914	Nuestra Señora de Lourdes de Itatiqui	Chiriguano	1915

year later led to a peace treaty between the Creoles and the Tobas that was very unfavorable for the latter.[95] While freelancing by mission Indians kept unfriendly indigenous groups at bay, it also meant that even these Chiriguanos remained effectively outside of government control.

Beginning in the 1870s, as the Indian-white frontier moved into the core region of the Cordillera, the Chiriguanos' motives for accepting missions related to the conflicts between Indians and settlers. The ava requested missions when they were unable to remove invading colonists and the cattle herds that consumed their cornfields. This was the principal reason for the founding of Tiguipa (1872), Santa Rosa de Cuevo (1887), San Antonio del Parapetí Grande (1903), and San Francisco Solano del Parapetí Grande (1903). Santa Rosa de Cuevo illustrates the changing motives best. Since the late 1870s, after Creole forces had beaten the Cuevo Chiriguano in the Huacaya War, certain Chiriguano factions within Cuevo had urged the Tarija Franciscans to establish a mission on their territory. In the aftermath of the war the settlers invaded the region and pastured their cattle in Cuevo Indian territory. For reasons discussed later, the Tarija convent proved incapable of establishing a mission. In desperation, the Cuevo ava built a huge fence around their cornfields, but even this measure was insufficient. Finally, the newly active Potosí convent agreed to build a mission, much to the chagrin of the settlers who wanted to take the land.[96] Thus reasons for the establishment of missions changed as the balance of power shifted from the Chiriguanos to the Creoles in the last third of the nineteenth century. The avas' main concern became the depredations of settlers rather than conflicts with other Indian villages.

The third motive for founding a mission rested on the initiative of the Franciscans rather than the Indians. The friars founded missions to attract Chiriguanos back to their ancestral lands after warfare had driven them away. This was the case with the missions of Itau and Chimeo, founded in 1845 and 1849 in the aftermath of the prolonged war and massacres of 1839–1841. Similarly, the Potosí convent founded Boicovo in 1876 near Huacaya, which during the war of 1874–1877 had been the center of Chiriguano resistance to settler invasions elsewhere. Missionaries from the same convent also founded San Buenaventura de Ivo in 1893 near the headquarters of the last messianic uprising of the Chiriguanos the year before. Unlike the other missions, for which the Indians requested the friars, these missions served as refuges and were designed to attract the Indians back to the area.

The establishment of the Franciscan missions had little to do with any desire on the Indians' part to convert to Christianity. Although the chiefs were the principal negotiators in bringing the friars to their settlements, none of the tubichas and only a few Indian adults converted to Christianity. Rather, the Franciscans were able to establish missions because the Chiriguanos saw the missions as their only option in a hostile frontier environment. Initially the Indians saw the missions as refuges against members of their own ethnic group, though this changed as the military balance of power shifted from the Indians to the settlers.[97]

By the mid-1860s and clearly by the 1870s Creole settlements had extended far into the Cordillera, and the new missions protected Indians from the depredations not of fellow Indians, but of Creoles. Although the threat of violence, as in the first case, was constant and real, the conflict between cows and corn became paramount. In Susnik's terms, the cows were winning. The missions now served as a refuge to maintain the economic basis of village life as well as avoid the abusive relationships that the settlers tried to impose upon the Indians, forcing them to work for little if any pay and taking their women and children.[98]

When the friars established the missions in the aftermath of wars or massacres they also held that these should serve as centers of refuge, for otherwise they felt that the Indians would not return. This occurred in Huacaya, where the Franciscans had to convince the ava, who had been the target of the 1874–1877 wars, to return to a new settlement near Huacaya, in Boicovo. The settlers had taken Huacaya and usurped all the land. According to Fr. Angélico Martarelli, the missionary convinced some of the Indians who desired to return of "the utility of the mission." In the end they agreed to move to the mission at nearby Boicovo because "they were motivated even more by the desire to settle, once and for all, in one spot to shelter their families and have a piece of land to cultivate to give them the necessary sustenance."[99] Boicovo had been part of the Huacaya Chiriguanos' territory, though few had lived there previously.

The influence of the missions on the frontier was profound because the missions transformed the frontier itself. They changed fundamentally the political and military equation of the Cordillera. For one thing, the missions provided the government with Indian labor to construct the forts that began to dot the region. Labor demands became particularly acute in the 1880s, when a number of government expeditions entered the Chaco. Officials taxed the capacity of the mission at Aguairenda to supply laborers, and it supplied hundreds of workers as builders of new trails and construction workers for new forts along the Pilcomayo River.[100] Because the queremba were unable to overcome even most small forts with their primitive weapons, the construction work of the Indians from Aguairenda and other missions made a significant difference.

The missions themselves were important fortresses as well. The church was always located on a strategic and easily defensible site and, in case of trouble, became the refuge of the mission population. Some, such as the missions in Santa Rosa and Macharetí, were walled, enclosing the missionary's quarters, the church, and the girls' school. In most cases, the mission buildings were much more impressive than the frontier forts and served very well as defensive positions. Although all missions were attacked at one time or another, not a single one fell to the invaders. The most dramatic case occurred in Santa Rosa de Cuevo in 1892. In addition to mission Indians, the whole mestizo population of the nearby town of Cuevo sought refuge there, as did other settlers living in the surrounding region. The rebel army, one thousand queremba on foot and three hundred on horseback, attempted to storm the mission. They were repulsed after suffering more than forty fatalities, whereas the battle left only fifteen defenders wounded.[101]

Most important, the missions destroyed the avas' ability to resist throughout the Cordillera because, for the first time since the colonial period, other than the rather small and marginal groups in Caraparirenda and Caiza the mission system permanently divided indigenous society. Unlike earlier, when alliances shifted continuously, once the Indians joined a mission they in effect entered into a permanent—and at times forced—alliance with the settlers. When the mission Indians tried to rebel, they were brutally repressed, as had occurred in Salinas and Chimeo. The rules of the political game thus changed once ava villages accepted the missionaries in their midst. The independent villages, which played by the old rules of switching sides and fighting among themselves, could not compete in the long term.[102]

The effect of the missions was cumulative; as the missionary project advanced, ever larger numbers of Indians could be used as combatants for warfare against the independent villages. This was important, for, as we have seen, the vast majority of combatants on both sides in the Cordillera were Chiriguano throughout the nineteenth century. Indeed, the mission Indians played a crucial role in the prolonged war of 1874–1877, providing warriors to the Creoles in their fight against the Huacaya and Cuevo Chiriguanos and their Toba allies. Usually the number of Indian fighters was overwhelming compared to that of the Creoles. In one of the few references to the ethnic composition of the Creoles, in 1875 the Creole forces in the campaign of the Caipipendi valley consisted of fifty militiamen and two hundred archers from the missions.[103]

The importance of the missions in the defeat of the independent ava was even greater in the war of 1892.[104] This occurred despite the fact that Apiaguaiki, the messianic leader of the rebel movement of 1892, tried to unite Chiriguano society by actively courting the mission Indian leaders and their followers. Messianic rebellions, led by tumpas (prophets) such as Apiaguaiki, had been effective in the early eighteenth century in rallying the Chiriguanos as a group against the karai and resulted in the destruction of the Jesuit missions. Nevertheless, even the strong messianic message this time failed to have its desired effect. Although small groups left the missions to fight for the tumpa, the tubichas of the missions, with few exceptions, remained loyal to the national side. In the last battle of Curuyuqui in January 1892, 50 army soldiers and 140 militiamen with guns accompanied 1,500 Indian archers mostly from the missions against a force of about 5,000 rebel queremba. The 1892 rebellion revealed the insurmountable divisions between Indians inside and outside the missions, dooming the movement to failure.[105] The Creole forces ultimately were able to win these wars because the missions provided their side with sufficient manpower to subdue the independent Chiriguanos.

In the end, the divisions in Chiriguano society that had made it impossible for the Spanish or the Creoles to conquer it turned from a strength to a weakness by the late nineteenth century. No ethnic solidarity had developed in a political culture that valued freedom from oppression from any source, including other tubichas. Chiriguanos fought against other Chiriguanos and helped in the takeover of the remaining independent villages. The missions thus made it possible for the Bolivian state to counteract the dynamics of the "tribal zone," in which ethnic chiefs maintained shifting alliances and levels of violence among villages that had hindered the region's final conquest.[106]

The missions also divided indigenous society in other ways. They complicated communication between the independent Chiriguano villages and unconquered tribal peoples from the Gran Chaco, making interethnic alliances more difficult. Fr. José Giannelli, the most dynamic founder of missions of the mid-nineteenth century, thought in these strategic terms and tried to found missions in places that would accomplish this goal. He founded missions along the eastern border of Chiriguano-held territory as springboards for further spiritual conquests in the Gran Chaco. While his plans were not as successful as he had envisioned, the Tarija missions of Tarairí, Macharetí, and Tiguipa did create an effective barrier between the independent Chiriguano villages to the west and the Tobas and other Chaco tribes to the east. In addition, Fr. Giannelli established two missions along the Pilcomayo River, San Francisco and San Antonio, dedicated to the conversion of the Chaco tribes. They served as barriers between the Creole frontier and the Chaco peoples as well as important barometers of Chaco peoples' intentions. Although the Pilcomayo missions were populated also by Chiriguanos, settled there to deter Toba and Mataco designs against the Creoles and to defend the friars, these missions provided unsurpassed intelligence on the plans and actions of the hostile Chaco ethnic groups. These missions continually received visitors from the Chaco interior, who provided information about the movements and intentions of Tobas, Matacos, and others.[107]

Warfare during the establishment phase of the missions also channeled the mission querembas' desire to distinguish themselves through combat as their fathers and grandfathers had done. It provided an outlet for the young men who were not obligated to convert and probably strengthened the tubichas' power, since the friars themselves did not organize campaigns or lead in warfare. The missionaries needed the war leaders and the young men for mission defense. The constant alerts on the missions and the war footing during the initial years also provided something for the queremba to do, thus fortifying solidarity with the mission enterprise that kept discontent among this group relatively low.

Beyond the military and political spheres, the string of missions on the eastern borders of the Cordillera by the 1880s had made direct communication between Tarija and Santa Cruz feasible for the first time. The missions also led to the establishment of a trade route between the Argentine border and the city of Santa Cruz. This trade route opened up the vast cattle resources of the Santa Cruz area, which began to export its cattle to Argentina. Suddenly cattle prices throughout the region increased, making the usurpation of Indian land more lucrative. In turn, Argentine and Tarija traders flooded the Cordillera and the Santa Cruz markets with manufactured goods from Argentina and Europe. Chiriguanos and Chaco tribesmen also used this trail to go to work in the northern Argentine sugarcane fields of Orán and Jujuy. By the early twentieth century the mission trail constituted the entry point that made most of the Bolivian portion of the circum-Chaco region an economic dependency of Argentina.[108] Economic and cultural change entered more from Argentina than from the Bolivian heartland. Ultimately, this also weakened the position of the Chiriguanos in the Cordillera.

Conclusion

To understand the Franciscan missions, it is necessary to examine the dynamics of the Cordillera frontier and the way Chiriguanos and Creoles interacted after independence. The ava exalted warfare, both interethnic and intraethnic, and after the turmoil of the independence struggles were largely able to rid the Cordillera of non-Indians. Indeed, until at least the middle of the century the Indians held the balance of power on the frontier, a fact recognized by government officials and landowners alike. Like indigenous society in the Cordillera, Creole frontier society in the early republican period was beset by serious internal differences, both ideological and regional in nature. In essence, the frontier zone resembled an area where each village, whether Indian or Creole, formed alliances with other villages, regardless of ethnicity. The Creoles usually were auxiliaries in these conflicts that revolved around disputes among the Chiriguano. Indeed, Creole political factions used Chiriguano military power at the peril of upsetting the precarious position of the settlers along the frontier.

It is best to understand the frequent conflicts along the frontier in the first decades after independence as interethnic alliances of villages (consisting of Chiriguanos, Creoles, and sometimes Tobas) that tried to gain the upper hand. Given the highly decentralized nature of Chiriguano society, the avas entered into a series of shifting alliances with groups both within and outside of the Cordillera, at times engaging the Bolivian militias as junior partners in their internecine struggles. However, Creoles generally tried to avoid conflict with Indians because they knew they were at a disadvantage. When large-scale interethnic warfare did break out, the querembas' methods were largely effective during the first half of the nineteenth century by targeting the landowners' poorly protected cattle herds.[109] Although Creole military commanders almost always claimed victory, a close examination of their presumed triumphs shows that these were rarely as complete as they claimed. The tactics of the militia and the poorly maintained weaponry into the 1860s were simply ineffective in the difficult conditions of the Cordillera. Even when the Creoles briefly gained the advantage, the lack of organization, resources, and adequate supply lines prevented the military from occupying hostile territory for any length of time.

A number of factors made the situation of the Chiriguanos difficult in the second half of the nineteenth century, but the reintroduction of the Franciscan missions was the primary reason for the military defeat of the Chiriguanos. It is important to note that in most cases the Indians themselves were interested in setting up missions, though never because of their desire to convert to Christianity. The most important reason for requesting a mission was to gain refuge from their enemies, initially from enemy Indian alliances and later from the depredations of Creole settlers. In the long term, however, the missions progressively restricted Chiriguano independence by making the mission Indians permanent allies of the Creoles and increasing the number of queremba who fought on the side of Bolivian frontier forces. The missions thus undermined the system of shifting alliances that previously permitted the ava to maintain their highly decentralized political structure. In the end, the missions created a system in which more and more of the Indian villages remained on the Creole side, whereas the independent villages kept fighting among themselves. This, in the end, weakened Chiriguano resistance and made their eventual surrender to national forces inevitable. Even the powerful messianic movement of 1892, which attempted to overcome divisions in Chiriguano society and mobilize against the karai, failed. With the mission system well in place, the last years of the nineteenth century witnessed the complete submission of the fiercely independent Chiriguanos and their integration into Bolivian frontier society.

CHAPTER TWO

The Franciscans

The historiography over the past few decades, during which ethnohistorical methods have become more popular, has put the primary emphasis on the indigenous population of the missions. This concern for the vast majority of the mission inhabitants is quite justified, especially since our knowledge of indigenous groups and their cultures is more deficient than that of the European missionaries. Nevertheless, it is important not to slight the missionaries when analyzing these institutions. This does not mean that the missionaries controlled everything, as we will see in subsequent chapters. Instead, we need to problematize the perceptions the missionaries brought to their enterprise, for their suppositions are not only crucial for understanding the missionary enterprise, but are not necessarily self-evident. After all, the missionaries, while in the vast majority Europeans and who thus presumably partook of the same culture as Europeans today, are distant from contemporary persons in time, place, and culture. We must first comprehend the missionaries to understand the missionary enterprise, for this provides the evidence necessary to see how well the missions succeeded and under what terms.

In the case of the Bolivian missions among the Chiriguanos, an analysis of the Franciscans is essential. When the missions were reestablished in the nineteenth century, the friars were mostly Italians from the Franciscan province of Tuscany, surrounding Florence. To better comprehend these intrepid men we must understand their background and the culture they brought with them to southeastern Bolivia. In the case of the nineteenth-century Chiriguano missions, these friars had passed their youth, the formative period in their lives, in a peculiar context of the Risorgimento, marked by the struggle between the Catholic Church and the republicans who wanted to unify the Italian peninsula into one country. The republican forces, one of the main groups, were generally anticlerical. They saw the existence of the papal states as one of the most serious impediments to their efforts to unify Italy. This struggle affected the friars who went to Bolivia, who took with them certain perceptions of their roles and that to their charges in the missions. Knowing how the Catholic Church was treated so poorly in their homeland inevitably also had an effect on how the missionaries perceived Latin American religiosity, the state, and the Indians they were to administer and convert.

The men who became Franciscans (rather than secular priests or, say, Jesuits) followed a special brand of Catholicism. Since its inception the Franciscan order has been a very special organization within the Catholic Church. St. Francis of Assisi founded the order in Italy during the early thirteenth century as a reform movement within the Church. The simplicity of Francis and his followers, their concern for the poor and disadvantaged, and their vows of poverty, giving everything they had to the Church and begging for alms, made them a popular religious movement in late medieval Europe. Francis was canonized only a few years after his death, and the Franciscans (or Friars Minor) became an important force within the Catholic Church, with branches in many places, including the Iberian Peninsula.[1] When the Spanish encountered the New World, the Franciscans, motivated by eschatological ideas, went in droves as missionaries to convert the Indians in Mexico and elsewhere. They became one of the most important orders in the Spanish possessions, especially as missionaries among indigenous peoples.[2]

The Franciscans of the nineteenth century and early twentieth were different from their medieval or even colonial-era predecessors, but, as we shall see, the renewed vitality of the order's missionary calling in the nineteenth century made these friars an exceptionally important and vibrant part of Catholic Christianity.

Both the personal experiences of the friars and their institutional context had an important effect on the way the missionaries perceived their duties and how they tried to run the missions. The missionaries who dedicated their lives to a new and strange environment and people were also profoundly affected by their new circumstances. Their experiences in the missions changed them. In some cases the missionaries changed more than the indigenous peoples they were trying to convert. It is these three dimensions that help define the mission enterprise: the personal life experiences of these overwhelmingly Italian Franciscans, the nineteenth-century methods and concerns of the Order of the Friars Minor, and the experiences that the friars had as they lived in the missions of the Andean foothills and the undulating plains of the Gran Chaco. First, let us turn to Europe, where the missionaries grew up.

Italian History and Its Effects on the Missionaries

By far the vast majority of the Franciscans in this second period (the colonial era is the first period) who staffed the missions among the Chiriguanos were Italian. After the independence struggles, the first attempt to bring the Franciscan convents up to strength came in 1834, when Fr. Andrés Herrera, a Spanish friar who had served in the jungles of Peru, returned to Europe to bring back some of his brethren. The pro-clerical Andrés de Santa Cruz, president of Bolivia (1829–1839), sponsored the expedition. After recruiting friars in Spain and Italy, Herrera returned with twelve Spanish and Italian Franciscans for both Peru and Bolivia. Of those twelve, Herrera sent two Italians, a Genoese and a Bolognese, to Tarija. A subsequent expedition in 1837 yielded another eleven friars for Tarija.[3] These men reestablished the convent and served the needs of the city and the surrounding countryside; only in the 1840s was it possible for the Tarija convent to extend its presence out into its former mission territory. (See table 3.)

Of the sixty-two friars who entered the Tarija convent between 1834 and 1864, at least fifty-one were Italian.[4] In the 1890s the convent contained twenty-two Italians, two Spaniards, two Bolivians, and one Frenchman among the priests and lay brothers.[5] The Italian Franciscans were most likely to end up in the missions, as the correspondence and the annual mission reports, available for a large segment of the life of the mission system, mention nary a friar who did not have an Italian last name. Given the predominance of the Italians, what intellectual and cultural baggage did they bring with them that might have affected the running of the missions?

A brief review of nineteenth-century Italian history, the period of the Risorgimento, suggests much of relevance. The nineteenth century was distinguished by an intense conflict between the Catholic Church and the liberals who wanted to unite Italy into one political unit. The liberals wanted to create a country in which individuals could distinguish themselves regardless of birth and according to merit. They rejected the rigid hierarchy of the Catholic Church, which they saw as repressive and medieval. They embraced rationalism over faith. Although many had monar-

TABLE 3. Number and type of Franciscans entering Tarija convent, 1835–1880

Year	Priests	Novices	Lay Brothers	Total
1835	2	0	0	2
1837	6	2	3	11
1844	9	0	0	9
1853	14	1	1	16
1860	5	3	0	8
1864	15	1	1	17
1872	9	8	2	19
1877	1	7	5	13

Source: Alejandro María Corrado, *El colegio franciscano de Tarija y sus misiones*, 2nd ed. ([1884] Tarija: Editorial Offset Franciscana, 1990), 2:316–17.

chical sympathies, especially for the progressive Savoy monarchy, liberals declared their allegiance to popular sovereignty rather than the divine right of kings. During this struggle the Catholic Church transformed itself to meet new challenges. It emerged more conservative theologically and politically, with greater centralization under Rome and the pope and emphatically opposed to the new liberal currents that were sweeping across Europe and other parts of the Western world. For example, Pope Gregory XVI's encyclical *Mirari vos* of 1832 denounced religious pluralism and was elaborated upon in Pope Pius IX's *Syllabus of Errors* (1864), which condemned the separation of Church and state, rationalism, and liberalism and also defended the rights of the papacy over the papal states.[6]

One of the principal reasons for the conflict between the Church and the nationalist forces was that the pope had inherited from medieval times a swath of land in the center of Italy as well as Rome, the cultural and historical capital of the peninsula. It included Ferrara and Bologna near the Po River in the northeast and crossed the Apennines to include a large area around Rome on the western side of the peninsula. The Italian nationalists, who wanted to unify the country, had to deal with this political fact. They did so by attacking the papacy's control over this territory. In addition, the intellectual climate of Europe, especially after the unleashing of the French Revolution and then the revolutions of 1848, led to greater emphasis on secularization, nationalism, and rationalism. As the struggle evolved the Church opposed all these new currents, isolating itself and bringing about the loss of the papal states in the 1860s, but at the same time consolidating its hold over its organization and spawning other manifestations of popular religiosity. This was the period of Vatican I (1869–1870), the council that codified a reactionary Catholicism that opposed all new intellectual currents of the day, such as liberalism, secularism, and socialism. The actions of three popes, Gregory XVI (1831–1846), Leo XIII (1878–1903), but most of all Pius IX (1846–1878), dominate this opposition to modern ideas.

For the purposes of this study, it is important to break down the history of Italy into periods that help define the life experiences that the missionaries brought to Bolivia. My hypothesis is that the Franciscans who came over from the Old World were profoundly marked by political conditions in their homeland and that they transferred the ideas current in Italy to the New World to a large extent. Once they came to Bolivia and worked as missionaries in the Chaco countryside, they were forced to modify their positions according to the reality that they had to deal with while working with the Indians, the surrounding settlers, and the Chaco environment. As they became involved in the missions, subsequent news from Italy, while it undoubtedly had an impact through letters and discussions of current events in the convent among people of their own nationality, had less importance than the situation in which they were living and working in South America.

Over the century of mission existence three generations of Italian Franciscans came, each marked in different ways by their upbringing and the political context of their birthplace. The first generation arrived between 1834 and 1844. In their youth they experienced the restoration of the papal states (1814) after the Napoleonic invasions in the beginning of the century. A revival of Catholicism among the educated appeared to bode well for the Roman Church. The papacy began to centralize power in its hands after the emasculation of national churches, such as the French Church, during the Napoleonic Wars. The Catholic Church became the bulwark of the conservative social order in Europe. A revitalized papacy revived the Jesuit order and the Church sent out missions into the French countryside to restore a sense of religiosity in the population. As a result the Catholic Church became one of the most reactionary forces in European society and a staunch supporter of the Holy Alliance, a union of Russia, Austria, and Prussia that in 1815 was to bring order back into Europe and push back revolutionary sentiment unleashed by the French Revolution. Until the 1840s the papacy remained close to the leadership of many of the Italian states, though afterward this relationship fell apart.[7]

The First Franciscan Generation
This generation of Franciscans grew up in the early nineteenth century, during the Romantic period. Certain strains of Catholicism picked up on Romanticism's "aesthetic and spiritual appeal as a source of inspiration to deal with the problems of the modern world."[8] Romanticism attenuated the rationalism of the Enlightenment with the ideals of the noble savage and the seemingly endless possibilities of children to learn, such as in Jean-Jacques Rousseau's *Emile*.[9] Rousseau (1712–1778), although dead before the nineteenth century, was one of the inspirations of this period. It is difficult to know what influence Romanticism had on the friars who came over to the New World, for the Franciscan order's asceticism (as opposed to the Romantic's sensualism) and the Catholic Church's explicit rejection of some postulates of the Romantic movement, such as its emphasis on individualism and secularism, went counter to Romanticism. In fact, one of the Franciscan promoters of the new missionary impulse to South America, Fr. José Matraya y Ricci, wrote a tract attacking Rousseau's *The Social Contract*, debating the postulates of one of the predecessors of the Romantic movement. Matraya y Ricci had lived in Peru and Bolivia during the colonial period but returned to his home in Lucca, Tuscany, in 1827, advising Pope Gregory XVI after his accession on the missionary enterprise and promoting Herrera's project to repopulate the missions in the New World.[10]

There is, for example, no evidence that the Franciscans subscribed to the notion of the noble savage; indeed, the one overarching test for the missionaries to distinguish between barbarism and civilization was whether the Indian was a Christian. Any Indians who were not converted to Catholicism could by definition not be noble or act "naturally" in a noble manner because they lacked the essential knowledge of the Christian God and were outside the fold of the Catholic Church. In Catholicism, including the Franciscan tradition, the priest as an intermediary between God and his people was absolutely crucial. Without the knowledge of God or acceptance of priests as the representatives of the Church, the Indians could not help but remain barbarians.

Despite the explicit rejection of Romantic ideas by one of the period's leading Franciscans, it was impossible to escape completely the spirit of the age. In certain ways the Franciscans also participated in this age, though selectively. The Franciscans who came over from Europe during this period were the pioneers of the missionary movement and acted as the intrepid heroes who went out into the wilderness to "conquer" the natives and establish missions among them. The dashing heroic figure was one of the staples of the Romantic period. Napoleon Bonaparte, Simón Bolívar, and others molded themselves into these figures and manipulated the Romantic notions of leadership to their benefit. In a sense some Franciscans also adopted this persona. In the case of the Franciscans, no one exemplified the heroic missionary zeal better than Fr. Giuseppe (José) Giannelli, born in 1823 in Lucca. Giannelli arrived in Tarija in 1845 and became the most active founder of missions during the second era of the Tarija convent in the Chaco region. He founded or cofounded the missions of Aguairenda (1851), Tarairí (1854), and San Antonio de Padua (1863). He spearheaded an expedition into the Chaco in 1863, exposing himself to death through disease, drowning, or attack.[11] Giannelli left the Tarija missions in 1870, when efforts at proselytizing the Tobas and other Chaco groups failed and the convent was unable to attract more friars to staff new missions. His promotion to administrative duties did not suit him and he moved to the Tarata convent.[12] Giannelli was fortunate to have come in this initial period, when heroic, larger-than-life men were needed. In this way, the Romantic notion of intrepid leadership and the founding phase of the missions fit well. The missionary pioneer was needed only during the first phase of the missionary cycle, the establishment phase, to enter new territories, persuade the natives to establish a mission, and heroically fend off attempts by the Indians to reconquer their land. When this type of figure lost importance, people like Fr. José had to move on.

A more obvious legacy of the Romantic period was the notion of educating the Indians. In *Émile* (1762) Rousseau argued that children were innocent beings who during their childhood were tabulae rasae, to be filled with either good or evil. Unlike adults, children were naturally good. The friars seem to have adopted this notion, for unlike in the colonial period, when all Indians living on the mission were required to convert, the Franciscans required only that children born on the mission were to be baptized and sent to school when they reached the age of seven. The missionaries did not try very hard to convert adults, who presumably were already contaminated by heathen practices. The Franciscans had focused on children during the colonial period as well; the new emphasis on children reinforced the friars' doctrinal priorities.[13]

In addition, the specific intellectual context of northern Italy in the

1830s and 1840s impacted the way the Franciscans set up the missionary enterprise. Carlo Cattaneo was an influential lay intellectual from Lombardy who steered between the rationalist Enlightenment doctrines and individualist Romanticism. Cattaneo advocated the application of experimental sciences and the scientific method to practical problems, which, he asserted, had had its origins in the city-states of Renaissance Italy. To the Italian nationalist author this was the genius of Western civilization and had rendered it superior to the East. The process of applying practical ideas to improve living conditions was the essence of *incivilimento*, the civilizing effect that emanated from Western Europe and Italy in particular. Thus Cattaneo linked the process of civilizing to economic progress and the practical arts.[14] He was not a friend of the Catholic Church, but certainly had picked up ideas linking European civilization to practical skills that the Franciscans had as well. In the colonial period the Franciscans created workshops and taught their charges on the missions practical arts. There was much continuity, as in the nineteenth century the friars systematically established schools and taught the Indian boys and girls "practical arts" as a way of civilizing their charges to integrate them into the national labor force.[15]

The Second Generation of Franciscans
The second generation of friars, those who arrived between 1852 and 1864, brought to the New World somewhat different experiences and viewpoints. In Italy the contest between the papacy and Italian liberals heated up, though new solutions appeared possible. This period included the second war for Italian independence (1859), in which French and Sardinian forces beat the Austrians and finally led to the abolition of the papal states. Vincenzo Gioberti fashioned a new influential political doctrine that tried to meld Italian nationhood and the Catholic Church. Gioberti argued that Catholicism was essential to Italian nationhood, that there could be an alliance between religion and progress. To that end he advocated an Italian confederation with the pope at its head. More directly relevant to the missionaries' role, he thought that a renovation of traditional forms of Catholicism would lead to this progress. After all, according to Gioberti, Christianity provided the discipline necessary for the good of society and institutional forms were more important than acts of individual faith.[16] As we shall see, this melding of faith and discipline is essential to understanding the missionary enterprise from the Franciscans' point of view.

Pius IX was elected pope in 1846, a little more than a year before the

1848 revolutions swept through western Europe and Italy. He had been elected as a liberal reformer, but the events of 1848 turned him against reformism. He had to flee Rome but was reinstated on the shoulders of the French Army sent by Louis Napoleon. Soon afterward reaction set in, turning the papacy against virtually all new currents of the nineteenth century. The major point of dispute was the papacy's temporal power and the disposition of the papal states. One of the milestones that profoundly affected the Franciscans in this period was the suppression of convents in some Italian states in 1855; surely this aided in recruitment for the foreign mission fields. In 1859 war broke out and the Piedmont state beat the Austrians and also conquered a large portion of the papal territories. These events brought on the wrath of Pius IX, who saw his role as being the preserver of the papacy's temporal power. During this period members of the Catholic Church, Franciscans included, saw their position threatened as it appeared that the Church was under threat from secular forces. The pope had to appeal to France to keep order. Only Napoleon III's troops in Rome helped maintain a semblance of restraint in the capital of the papacy.[17]

The most important Franciscan figure in Tarija who exemplified this new generation was Fr. Doroteo Giannecchini, who sailed from Italy in 1860. In many ways he represented his generation, both for his emphasis on the institutionalization of the missions and his conflicts with anticlerical officials in Bolivia. He was profoundly influenced by the situation he had left in Europe and the ideas of consolidation sweeping through the Catholic Church. Giannecchini was mission prefect through much of the second half of the nineteenth century, in charge of the missionaries and the missions in the Chaco. Rather than found new missions (despite his desire to do so in Cuevo and Ivo), Giannecchini became an important intermediary between the Bolivian military, the Chaco Indians, and the missions. This consolidated the importance of the Franciscan missions on the Chaco frontier. He twice accompanied military and scientific expeditions into the Chaco. He helped retrieve captives from the Tobas and was the primary negotiator in the important 1884 peace treaty between the Tobas and the Bolivian government. In addition, he helped improve the missions' infrastructure; during his tenure as prefect he had four churches completed, built residences for travelers on all the missions, built five cemeteries, built nine new school buildings, and generally emphasized the education of the Indian children, claiming that "the improvement of the neophytes depends essentially on the education of the children."[18]

Fr. Doroteo was also the champion of the Tarija Franciscans in an increasingly anticlerical world. In his participation in expeditions into the Chaco the friar defended the missions against what he saw as the depredations of liberal officials. The conflicts between the Franciscan and Daniel Campos, the leader of the 1883 expedition to Paraguay and named by the government general delegate of mission territories, were legendary. The anticlerical Campos saw the missions as resources for him to exploit, without regard to the mission system's economy, and continually required Chiriguano mission Indians as trailblazers, carriers, and messengers. Fr. Doroteo saw his role as defending the mission economy from unreasonable requests by Campos, asserting that the missions had higher goals than just providing men and materiel to Bolivian authorities. The conflict between Campos and the Italian friar became extremely acrimonious. In one letter to his superiors the latter blamed the problems of the missions on "the impious doctrines, the principles of liberty, synonymous with libertinage, which some officials have predicated and taught without any shame, through calumnies, satire, lies, and hate to the Fathers and all that is related to the true progress of Christian civilization."[19] Given the context, it is clear that Fr. Doroteo was referring to the anticlerical Campos, but the letter also gives us a taste of the kind of defense of Catholicism that the friar mounted against impious officials.

The anticlerical tide was rising throughout Latin America and indeed the Atlantic world during the late nineteenth century. This was also the case among local officials during Giannecchini's tenure (chapter 7 delineates the reasons for this). In fact, the Tarija missions reached their high point in the last decades of the nineteenth century. In the 1880s on the national level the relationship between the Catholic Church and the Bolivian government improved substantially. The Conservative Party that came to power in the 1880s and the silver mining oligarchs who became president were staunchly pro-clerical, especially during Mariano Baptista's administration (1892–1896).[20] The situation was starkly different in Italy, however, when the last generation of Franciscans left their birthplace in the 1870s to proselytize in South America. By 1870 the kingdom of Italy had been founded, at the expense of the papal states and the power of the papacy. Italian national troops had taken over Rome, confining the pope to the Vatican. Pius IX reacted to the attacks on the Church by acceding to ultramontane pressures to centralize the Church bureaucracy and becoming more dogmatic than ever before.

Pius IX's conservative reaction had started in the 1860s with the publication of the papal bull *Quanta Cura* in 1864 and the *Syllabus*, which together condemned the secular state, liberalism, rationalism, freemasonry, and a whole host of modern ideas. Vatican I (1869–1870) continued in this vein, consolidating Rome's control over the Catholic Church worldwide and stamping it with a conservative tendency it was to lose only with Vatican II in the 1960s. Out of Vatican I emerged the dogma of papal infallibility, frightening the European powers from supporting the ultramontanism of the pope. For the Franciscans the 1860s were a traumatic decade as well, as in 1866 throughout Italy all religious orders, including the Franciscans, were suppressed. Again many left for mission territories. In 1870 the invasion of Rome brought to an end the temporal power of the pope. Yet despite the pope's defeat by the Italian nationalists, the Catholic Church emerged more vigorous and combative than before on the theological level.[21]

The Third Generation of Franciscans
The third generation of Franciscans who arrived in Bolivia in 1872 and 1874 were refugees from the struggles between the forces of the Risorgimento and the Catholic Church. This was the case with Fr. Angélico Martarelli, who was the first mission historian of the Potosí convent's missions.[22] Unlike their predecessors, the friars who came from the 1870s onward were even more opposed to liberal influence and much more combative, at least in their publications, than previous generations. The best example of the new kind of Italian missionary came from the Potosí convent. The Tarija convent, which by the late nineteenth century received few recruits from Italy and had trouble staffing the missions it had already founded, was less vigorous. As we have seen, in the 1870s friars from Potosí began to expand into the northern ranges of the Chiriguano area, founding a number of missions between 1876 and 1913.

The archetypical missionary of this new generation was Fr. Bernardino de Nino. De Nino arrived in Potosí in 1891 and almost immediately got involved in the mission enterprise. He established new missions in Santa Cruz department, only to see them abolished a few years later by anticlerical authorities. He was an active publicist, haranguing against the secularization of missions in newspapers, letters, and audiences with national officials.[23] His combative style and highly public disputes with liberal forces everywhere denoted a new type of Franciscan, one who fearlessly took on national and local authorities (unlike Giannecchini, who had to deal with only one local anticlerical official). This Italian also had another side as a sensitive ethnographer. De Nino's *Etnografía Chiriguana* is the finest ethnography written on the Chiriguanos, still used as a basic source for cultural information on these peoples. As Fr. Doroteo had done before him, Fr. Bernardino sympathized with the Chiriguanos both on and off the missions and tried to defend them within the limits of his understanding and powers.[24] However, de Nino was also a realist and in 1919 had worked with the Bolivian and Roman churches and the national government to create an apostolic vicariate, which combined the Potosí and Tarija mission territories to consolidate the Franciscans' weakening control over their missions.[25]

To summarize, the Franciscans who came from Italy over the course of the nineteenth century were shaped by their experiences in their home country that led them to transfer many ideas to the New World. It is possible to discern many differences between individuals. After all, missionaries had extraordinary power to affect relations with the state and the lives of their charges on the missions; this also varied in part according to the individual personalities of each missionary. Nevertheless, seen as groups, three generations of those who made their way to Bolivia stand out. The first reestablished the missions, imbued in part with a heroic sense very much in tune with the Romantic proclivities of the first half of the nineteenth century. The second generation suffered some of the consequences of the rising liberal tide in Italy. The emphasis in Italy was the consolidation of the Catholic Church and centralizing it under the aegis of Rome. The friars who made it to Bolivia used the lessons learned in Italy, consolidating their hold over the missions and thus building on the previous generation's extraordinary efforts. The third generation had been most scarred by the conflict between Church and state, especially with the suppression of the Franciscan order in Italy. They saw with horror the increasing liberalization of Bolivia, their adopted country, and did everything in their power to combat liberalism and anticlericalism. The volume and the viciousness of the debate between the Franciscans and their opponents reached new heights during this period, only to abate somewhat in the 1920s. This aspect is discussed in greater depth in the last chapter.

Franciscan Religiosity

When discussing missionaries, one aspect that is often taken for granted is their faith. Those who study missions often see Catholicism in particular as monolithic and relatively unchanging. As should be clear from the previous discussion, this cannot be said of nineteenth-century Catholicism (if it can be said of any religion), especially in its Italian version. Some excellent studies have touched upon the religious background of the Catholic missionaries to Latin America, though all deal with the colonial period. It is important to distinguish the religiosity of the Franciscans of earlier periods from those of the nineteenth and twentieth centuries. To cite the two best known studies, the eschatology of the sixteenth-century Franciscans described by John L. Phelan in his superb *The Millennial Kingdom of the Franciscans in the New World* had long faded by the nineteenth century. In turn, Ramón Gutiérrez's provocative imposition of sexual perceptions in religious images for Baroque-era New Mexico Franciscans, if indeed it was true then, does not work well for the nineteenth- and twentieth-century missionaries.[26]

Across the barriers of time and in the absence of much written evidence of the missionaries' personal spirituality, it is impossible to probe into the personal faith of particular friars. However, it is possible to examine some general tendencies and influences. To analyze the sense of religiosity of the Franciscans who administered the missions in southeastern Bolivia we must distinguish between at least three different influences. First, as I have already argued, the secular influences and that of the struggle between Church and state in Italy had a profound effect on the missionaries. Second, the cultural context of Italy and its beliefs must be taken into account.[27] It is possible to examine Catholic doctrine and which portions of it the Franciscans attempted to enforce on the missions. Third, the influences of the Franciscan order, which emerged revitalized after the persecutions and abolition of the order in Italy during the nineteenth century. Of course, these influences affected individual missionaries in different ways, leading to some variety of religious expressions on the missions. Most important was the influence of the Franciscan order, for the administrative structure of the missions enforced the discipline of the friars on all missionaries.

There appears to have been some affinity between the Franciscan order and the Chiriguanos since colonial times. This was most notable in the eighteenth century, when the Jesuits, so successful among the Guaraní speakers in Paraguay and farther north in Mojos and Chiquitos, failed to pull the Chiriguanos into their missionary orbit for any length of time. The Franciscans, after a relatively short time, were spectacularly successful, boasting twenty-two missions among this ethnic group by 1810.[28] According to Thierry Saignes, it was not religion but the Franciscans' distribution of food and clothing as well as the less regimented work requirements (compared to the Jesuits) that made the Chiriguanos decide that the friars could establish missions among them.[29]

Indeed, in a comparison between the Franciscan order of the postindependence period with that of the colonial era, the similarities stand out. The fundamental characteristics of the order remained the same between the eighteenth and the twentieth centuries. The Franciscans were a communal organization that emphasized brotherhood, a sense of community, and vows of poverty. Unlike the Jesuits, for example, the Franciscans exalted manual labor not just for their charges, but for themselves as well. Their dedication to an ascetic way of life, like St. Francis, in which each friar lived simply and with a minimum of worldly goods, was an important tenet in their organization. Charity toward others and helping the poor (which by definition included indigenous peoples such as the Chiriguanos) were also central to the Franciscans' mission. This simplicity continued to attract the Chiriguanos, who, as we have seen, also emphasized the redistribution of goods (especially by leaders) in their culture.

The nineteenth-century Franciscans in Bolivia were weighed down by the history of strife between the Catholic Church and secular forces on the Italian peninsula. The Franciscan order (unlike the Jesuits, conceived in the sixteenth century as the personal shock troops of the pope) was not well suited or trained to act in the increasingly heated religiously partisan atmosphere that emerged in the events of the Risorgimento. In a sense Catholicism in Europe was being reinvigorated as an oppositional culture to modern trends. The Franciscans, often depending on good works and charity from the populace, must have found it increasingly difficult to act in such an environment. Also, the example of St. Francis, who avoided conflict and instead preached a doctrine of abnegation and patience, did not work well in this context.

The Jesuits, who were resuscitated in the early nineteenth century, thrived in the conflictual atmosphere of Risorgimento Italy. Indeed, to a large extent the Jesuits put their mark on the ever more conservative Catholic response in the raging debate over the role of the papacy and the Church as the Italian nation-state emerged from the painful debates and struggles of the mid-nineteenth century. Despite the different character of the Franciscan order, less designed to combat the new forces of nationalism and secularism, it too underwent revitalization in the mid-nineteenth century. Rather than joining the raging debates over the role of the Church in western Europe (after all, similar forces of nationalism and secularization were battering the Church throughout the continent), the Franciscans dedicated themselves anew to the missionary enterprise.

In the mission field the friars felt that, instead of losing in an increasingly secular western European world, they could make a difference by reaping new souls in the farthest corners of the New World. The friars who sailed across the Atlantic to South America wanted to leave the corrupt influences of the Old World behind. Unlike their brethren in the sixteenth century, the Franciscans of the nineteenth century were not very mystically inclined. What excited them were the very practical aspects of building missions, teaching the Indian children Catholic doctrine as well as a certain level of "civilization," and their relations with the other members of Bolivian society. Indeed, it is difficult to find much literature from this period that soared into mystical heights of devotion. Instead, religiosity was expressed through action, through the concrete everyday experiences that could bring about a more Christian world.

The surviving documents on the missions in Bolivia manifest strict adherence to Catholic doctrine. Whether this reflected the individual beliefs of every missionary is impossible to tell. The records show that orthodoxy was not only the norm, but was enforced in systematic ways. The structure of the missionary enterprise, elaborated and maintained from the sixteenth century onward, ensured this. On all missions (other than the small, dying ones of Itau and Chimeo in the late nineteenth century) missionaries occupied their posts in pairs. A mission prefect, elected by the members of the convent, exercised authority over the missionaries in the field and ruled on doctrinal and administrative matters. The missionaries and the prefect exchanged letters constantly, portions of which have survived in the convent archives. The copies of three prefects' circulars and decrees sent to the missionaries in the field also exist for the years 1851, 1870–1873, and 1879.[30] The circulars cover mundane administrative matters as well as how to regularize the prayers and establish confessionals in the churches, elections of Indian officials, and punishments. The 1851 circulars by Fr. Alfonso Corsetti are especially revealing. He even specified the attitudes that the friars were to have toward the Indians, exhorting that "the missionaries should be mild and humble of heart with all, joining the gentleness of the dove with the prudence of the snake; so that they be living examples of that gospel which they preach."[31] In addition, in the 1860s the prefects made annual inspections of all the missions, at which time a report had to be presented detailing the progress of the settlement and its population.

The structure of the missionary enterprise and the relatively tight control by the prefect was consistent with trends in the nineteenth-century Catholic Church. As the doctrine of papal infallibility, the result of Vatican I, shows, Rome began to assert great ecclesiastical control over the national churches and standardization of Church ritual and doctrine throughout the world. The Franciscans, revitalized in part through the persecutions of the order in Italy, also reflected this Church-wide tendency with their emphasis on hierarchy and on doctrinal conformity in the mission field.

This included conformity on some of the reigning social issues of the day. The Franciscans were vitally interested in the education of the Indian children. In Italy the state contested the Church's monopoly on education, but in the missions the friars held sway. Here was a chance to reproduce what had been lost in Italy: teaching the children Catholic ways so that they could become true Christians. The circulars emphasized the correct forms of prayers and other rituals, but also with some concern for the faith that was supposed to lie behind the repetition of the Catholic canon. Thus the 1851 circulars also admonished the friars to find out during Easter each convert's true beliefs as a way of seeing if he or she was ready to receive the sacraments of confession and communion.[32] These were important measuring sticks to find out the effectiveness of the mission schools.

Although the similarities in approach are most apparent, some subtle differences in religious sensibilities existed between the various generations. Again, the writings of the three friars who symbolized the three generations who worked as missionaries in nineteenth-century Bolivia are instructive. The writings of Fr. José Giannelli, the intrepid founder of missions during the first generation, reveal some of the religious attitudes of his peers. This is especially the case with his description of his expedition in 1863 into the Chaco, written to be seen only by his good friend and mission chronicler, Fr. Alejandro Corrado.[33] A missionary impulse played a large role in this manuscript, since Giannelli not only wanted to reach Paraguay, but also saw his role in the expedition as the "reconquest" of the Toba groups that had rebelled and left San Francisco mission that his friend Fr. Corrado had recently founded. The document shows Giannelli to be less reflective than action-oriented. He asserted to the Bolivian Army colonel who accompanied him that while the colonel wanted to make his flag wave on the eastern shore of the Pilcomayo River, the Franciscan wanted to "wave [the flag] of the Redemption of the world."[34] But what did Giannelli mean by that? In the account, his role as "pacifier" (*pacificador*) of the Tobas meant that the Indians would return to the missions. Even more so than the Chiriguanos, the adult Tobas did not convert, and, to a large extent, neither did the children. The spiritual side of the missionary experience figured very little in Giannelli's account; the "conquest" had few spiritual overtones, instead focusing on the presence of the Indians in the mission site. Giannelli was the one who founded the missions; others could then worry about converting the Indians.

The second generation, that of Fr. Doroteo Giannecchini, was more concerned with spiritual matters and the actual administration of the souls on the missions. Unfortunately we have few private documents for this important missionary; even the unpublished writings concern mainly administrative matters. His was the generation that expressed itself by requiring a much higher standard of religiosity of the Indians. One of the principal reasons Giannecchini closed the mission of San Antonio del Pilcomayo in 1879 (established by Fr. Giannelli in 1866) was that not a single adult Mataco Indian had asked for conversion in the thirteen years of its existence.[35] Spirituality did matter for this generation, a generation that saw its hopes of saving more Indians frustrated by the refusal of the Mataco and Toba Indians to convert or even stay on the missions created for them.[36]

Fr. Doroteo's writings show that the second generation was much more concerned with the internalization of Catholicism among their charges. They were more introspective themselves and searched for religious feelings among their fellow human beings. In his diary of the failed 1886 expedition to reach Paraguay, Fr. Doroteo was constantly evaluating the impact of Christianity on the natives and how that changed them. This idea of Christianity was deeply coupled with the mission to bring "civilization" to the Indians, with all its contradictory implications. He also tried to find a sense of religiosity among his fellow expedition members. The missionary was moved deeply enough to note in his diary when Arthur Thouar, the French leader of the expedition, stopped to take in a beautiful vista and pray in silence for the discoveries they had made. Fr. Doroteo admired Thouar's spirituality and wrote, "I sincerely confess that I was moved to compassion and edified and I asked the Lord with all my heart [for] His benediction, which I very much desire for him, as a true friend."[37]

The second generation saw spirituality emanating from the structure of the mission itself. It was this generation that emphasized education as a means of internalizing Christianity among the Indian children. These friars sought structure for their charges in a Catholic atmosphere that would dissipate the foreboding winds of secularism and other ills that were sweeping Europe and increasingly South America as well. This fit very well with the problems they had perceived in Italy, where it appeared that the Church was becoming increasingly helpless to overcome the modern anticlerical forces. The emphasis on internal discipline provided by outward structure was also a weapon the Church was using in the Old World as it became more conservative and demanded full allegiance from its faithful through the new rules laid down by Vatican I. The friars received the new dictates while in Bolivia, but Vatican I was really a culmination of a process that this generation had participated in both in Italy and in missionary territory. As such, the second-generation friars were excellent administrators and genuinely concerned with conversion, ideal for the continuation of the missions after the first generation had founded so many. Unfortunately for the former, their efforts at conversion largely failed, though their focus on administration brought about the flourishing of the mission system in the late nineteenth century, at least in its physical aspects.

The third generation of missionaries, those who arrived after 1864, were less introspective than the second. They were doers, like those of the first generation, but in a different mold. One of the few personal documents that exist of this generation is the unpublished diary of Fr. Bernardino de Nino, which spans the years 1903 to 1917.[38] Although it is possible that the Franciscan kept another, more personal diary, the extant one has few of his thoughts about the task of missionizing or about his religious beliefs. The period during which de Nino recorded his personal notes was the period during which he founded various missions (which ultimately failed) and was active in defending the order and the missions from the attacks of anticlerical local and national government officials. In the diary instrumentality reigns without much emphasis on the internal transformations that the missions required. When Fr. Bernardino exhorted the Indians at the founding of the new mission of San Antonio del Parapetí, he mentioned "the necessity of leaving the forest to live in society, the need to hear the Divine Word, that of receiving baptism and *do good works to gain the salvation of their souls.*"[39] External "good works," not internal transformations, were required. The whole diary is full of descriptions of places the friar visited, the actions he took on the missions to prevent epidemics or appoint Indian mission officials, and the political machinations of the Creoles opposed to the missions. As in the previous generation, administrative issues were at the forefront, but without the emphasis on internalizing religion. In all the years covered by the diary, no personal thoughts or religious exaltation appear. De Nino showed his faith through works rather than introspection. The way God showed himself to de Nino was in the number of Indian children converted, in the good fight against impious and wrongheaded officials, in the new missions built and the missions saved from the grasp of the anticlerical state. Although it is impossible to generalize from just one person, if this was the case with one of the most dynamic and thoughtful representatives of his generation, then it is likely that many other missionaries were cut of the same cloth.

Other factors beyond their childhood and early adult experiences also shaped the perceptions and thus the behavior of the missionaries in the field. These included the culture of the Franciscan order itself (which emphasized works over the showing of faith), the doctrinal predicates of the mid-nineteenth-century Catholic Church, and the missionary experience in the beautiful but alien environment of the Chaco and the Andean foothills. To understand the complex interplay of these factors it is best to examine the salient issues that emerge when studying the writings of the missionaries. They show how the Franciscans perceived the missions and their roles in them. In particular, crucial to the mission experience were the way the mission was set up, the way the friars measured their success, and their perceptions of the Indians they were supposed to convert to Catholicism.

Mission Organization

The Franciscans created an urban space that was foreign to how the Indians lived before coming to the mission. The mission was centered on a large central plaza, around which the houses of the Indians clustered. Large, rectangular spaces organized housing on a grid pattern. To one side or at the top of a hill sat the church as well as the missionaries' residences and the schools.

The mission grid pattern was inherited from the Renaissance ideal of a town, reproduced throughout Spanish America in the colonial-era and even republican-era town foundings. The cities of Tarija and Potosí, where the Franciscan convents were located, boasted the same grid pattern. The similarities exist because of the conception of what a "civilized" town should look like. After all, both Spanish and Italian cultures shared the idea that the center of civilization was the city, not the countryside. Although the conception that urban areas meant civilization can be traced in the Mediterranean to at least Greek and Roman times, the Spanish version was even stronger, given the characteristics of the Spanish Reconquest, in which the fortified town was the means by which Christian Spaniards expanded into the frontier and took land back from Muslim Spaniards. In the case of Italy, the Romantic movement, with its emphasis in art on countryscapes (with Italian motifs especially popular), attenuated the urban focus that the Hispanic Peninsula preserved. However, the idealization of the Italian countryside came mainly from foreigners from the north, who in this fashion pondered the tragic implications of Roman ruins scattered throughout the *campagna* [countryside].[40] Among Italians in the 1830s and beyond, Cattaneo's influential ideas about incivilimento reemphasized the importance of Italian cities and their connection to learning and other civilizing activities. It was an important component of the renascent sense of pride in being Italian.

The Franciscans thus transformed the nationalist impulse, pride in Italian cities as centers of civilization, by building urban missionary centers on the Bolivian frontier. The missions in fact were by far the largest urban settlements of the frontier, much larger than the mestizo towns that rarely had over a thousand inhabitants. It was a "mission frontier," as Alistair Hennessy defined it.[41] Implicitly at least, the creation of urban settlements reproduced, to the extent possible, the civilizing influence of the Italian example. On the Chaco frontier, however, the friars channeled the nationalist impulse into an attempt at transforming the Chiriguano Indians into Bolivian (rather than Italian) citizens. In the spirit of the times, only urban living could bring about a true civilizing influence. Here, however, the missionaries bound the attempts to create Bolivian citizens to the religious enterprise. As the strong reaction by the nineteenth-century Catholic Church in Italy suggests, to the friars civilization necessarily included a religious basis, which the Franciscans provided in their settlements.

The grid pattern not only followed familiar lines for the Italian friars and so suggested civilization, but in a very practical dimension provided a measure of control for the missionaries.[42] Unlike the medieval towns with twisted, narrow streets from whence the missionaries had come, the mission layout represented an ideal of the civilized town, where everyone could know each other's business. It was easy to look down a street in the mission and immediately know who was about or who was sitting on the doorstep or which children were playing in the dust of the street. This presumably was the framework for an ideal community, where true Catholics could make sure that each and all followed the regulations for the good life that the fathers had prescribed. Few could hide when the ringing of the church bells called the faithful to Mass. This layout was not new, of

FIGURE 1. The Thouar expedition arrives in Mission Aguairenda on 18 July 1883. The lineup of the mission Indians and local authorities is similar to that described for the inauguration of the new Tiguipa church in 1902. *Source*: Arthur Thouar, *Explorations dans l'Amerique du Sud* (Paris: Hachette, 1891), 31.

course; the colonial missions in Paraguay, the Californias, and elsewhere also followed this rectilinear pattern. In the nineteenth century, given the specific context of the times, the same pattern suggested in the minds of the Italian friars somewhat different meanings.

Most important, to the European eye the straight streets, the square corners, and the large central plaza imparted a sense of order, a key ingredient of the civilized life. Fr. Alejandro Corrado described with pride the mission in Tarairí: "[A wall] hems in on three sides this quadrangle [formed by the schools], the houses of the *neófitos*, perfectly aligned, and forming with it three very wide streets."[43] Since the missions were new towns, the missionaries could re-create the plans of an ideal community.

The vast plaza at the center of the mission served as the secular ceremonial center and place of parades and the like. When important visitors came the friars received them in the plaza, flanked by the mission band and rows of Chiriguano warriors. The explorer Arthur Thouar included a drawing of this scene in his book (see figure 1).[44] These plazas were usually as large as the plazas in major cities such as Sucre and Cochabamba and served as a place where virtually all the mission's population could meet. In Italy, central piazzas were also common and defined the importance of the town. In the case of the missions, the church looming on the hilltop over this setting symbolized the primacy of religion in the community.[45] Often the neophytes and the unconverted had different plazas, thus distinguishing one group from another symbolically and physically.

The center of the mission was reserved for those Indians who had converted to Catholicism. The friars separated the converts from the unconverted Indians; the latter were until late in the mission cycle the vast majority of the population. They did so because they wanted to keep the converts away from the bad habits of the unconverted, so that the former would not "leave and forget the customs that are contrary to Christianity or that can produce in them some unfortunate result, such as that attendance at the drinking of the heathen where they say and do things that are not convenient for a Christian to do, witness, or hear."[46] The new converts, called *neófitos*, lived in one-room adobe houses clustered around the plaza, often with roof tiles rather than straw. The extant photos of the missions show that virtually all houses had Spanish-style roof tiles, but the photos were taken in the 1890s, relatively late in the mission cycle. The impression from earlier in the mission life cycle was that only the converts and perhaps the chiefs (usually unconverted) lived in these houses. However, the missionaries tried to get everyone, whether chiefs, neophytes, or unconverted, into the European-style housing. In Tarairí mission, by 1880 even the 128 unconverted families lived around their own plaza, "all (as [in] the houses of the neófitos and the *catecúmenos*) preceded by comfortable galleries and exactly identical in all dimensions."[47] Getting the Indians to live in exactly the same houses was a triumph of the modern age, as in factory villages springing up in northern Italy and elsewhere in the nineteenth century.

The friars segregated different ethnic groups and the people obedient to different chiefs into different neighborhoods within the mission village. In the case of Santa Rosa de Cuevo, "the [mission] town [was] laid out in relation to the number of captains and of the families; the first are fifteen." As mentioned, there might be more than one plaza; in the case of Santa Rosa, the Chiriguanos of Ivo initially received their own plaza before they moved to their own mission.[48]

The missionaries went beyond the physical separation of ethnic groups and villages, and even entered into the private sphere of the individual family residence in their efforts to lay a physical framework for what they considered Christian living. They imported the idea of their sexual decency not just for the households of couples married within the Church, but also in the houses of what the friars considered consensual unions among the unconverted. According to one 1851 circular, in all dwellings partitions were to be built between the sleeping quarters of the adult couple and other relatives or older children as a way of keeping the couple's sexual acts hidden from the view of the other inhabitants.[49]

The physical infrastructure of the missions was important to the friars and became a measuring stick of their success in the wilderness. The enthusiasm for creating this regular urban space and its buildings reconfirmed the connection between city and civilization in the unordered and exuberant wilderness of the Chaco and the Andean foothills. In Itau, for example, Fr. Leonardo Delfante put so much energy and care into the reconstruction of the colonial-era church and other buildings that his work, often as a common laborer lifting stones and making tiles, left him so prostrated that he eventually had to return to the Tarija convent with broken health and only one eye.[50] The importance of the buildings as a measure of success of the missions is also apparent in the annual mission reports. For both the Tarija and Potosí missions, the annual reports emphasized improvements in the mission building stock. The friars described in loving detail the number of roof tiles that the Indians had made, the exact size of the buildings, and other specifics. This was also the case in the 1888 report of the San Antonio del Pilcomayo mission, where the new house for the missionaries was described as consisting "of a neat building twenty meters long by eight wide, with two floors, with three comfortable rooms on both, with an airy corridor in the front, sustained by beams and pillars, with only a whitewash and furniture missing."[51]

The most important measure of the success of the missions was the "spiritual administration." In annual reports the missionaries highlighted this activity by reporting on it right after the population statistics of each mission. These "spiritual statistics" measured the progress of the evangelization effort among the Indians. In both the Tarija and Potosí missions, the report listed the number of infants baptized, the number of confessions administered during the year, how many communions took place, and the number of marriages, confirmations, and ecclesiastical burials. These numbers were especially important since, unlike in colonial times, not all Indians who lived on the missions were formal converts. In the nineteenth century the missions themselves became a place for preaching and converting the Indians. Indeed, in the short summary narrative that followed the statistical survey of the religious and secular state of the mission, the missionaries highlighted their spiritual conquests of that year or lamented the apathy of their charges. They differed in this way from the statistics that were gathered elsewhere in the Catholic world.

In sum, the Franciscans' views of the mission reflected to a great degree their upbringing in Italy. They tried to reproduce a sense of civilization in the missions and imported the increasingly hierarchical and orthodox Catholicism that a reforming and conservative Catholic Church on the defensive in western Europe had created. Distinctive Franciscan traits were apparent, such as the emphasis on educating the Indian children (though not the adults) in practical learning, at which the Franciscans also excelled. These traits were also manifested in a kind of "bricks and souls" Catholicism, where the success of the mission enterprise was measured in the number of ecclesiastical activities, such as baptisms, confirmations, and marriage ceremonies, but also in the number of adobe bricks, roof tiles, and new structures built.

Conversion and the Idea of Civilization

Some might suppose that conversion to the Catholic Church was an attempt to affect only people's beliefs in the supernatural. In fact, nineteenth-century Catholicism (as indeed most conversion efforts throughout history and in all religions) implied a whole complex of beliefs and behaviors beyond the supernatural sphere that would change the converts' way of living in profound ways. Most religions—Christianity not excepted—incorporate a set of social prescriptions in addition to purely religious dictates. In Catholicism, for example, prohibition of polygamy, premarital sex, and divorce, to mention a few, are some of the religiously based dictates that have important social consequences.

Catholicism (especially prior to Vatican II in the 1960s) distinguishes itself from other Christian varieties through distinctive beliefs, some of which are shared by other Christian faiths. These include the special position that the bishop of Rome (also called the pope) has as the leader of the Church, the inheritor of the chair of the Apostle Peter in Rome. For Catholics ordained priests are necessary intercessors with God. The Church, which rests on the authority given to Peter, provides its flock with this intercession through the seven sacraments. For our purposes, the most important sacraments are baptism, confirmation, matrimony, confession, and unction. Baptism is the sacrament of initiation into the Church and is necessary for human beings to become eligible for entry into heaven. Only later does confirmation occur, which is, as the name implies, a confirmation of the mature person to be accepted into the Church. Generally, confirmation is preceded by some type of exam that shows that the person knows the basic rites of the Church and has some knowledge of the theological bases for Catholic beliefs. The sacrament of matrimony occurs only between one man and one woman (both believers), who thus create an eternal bond to procreate children and build up the Church. The sacrament of confession provides the believer with the ability to overcome his or her sins through the intermediation of an ordained priest; in Catholicism, if the believer is truly repentant the priest can provide absolution, in which the sins are washed away after penance. Unction provides a means for the priest to aid the believer to repent and, if deathly ill, improve the believer's chances of going to Heaven.

The Franciscans themselves freely admitted that they wanted to do more than convert the Indians to Catholicism. They also tried to integrate the Chiriguanos into national society. They were forging new citizens and, with their charges, trying to create a new nation-state that was profoundly Catholic. These two goals—converting Indians and creating national citizens—were interrelated in the friars' minds. They conceived of Bolivia as a Catholic society, where the profession of Catholicism was one of the fundamental characteristics of citizenship. Moreover, being Catholic implied a certain level of what the missionaries considered sufficient cultural development, needed to become a member of the flock and behave in acceptable ways. It is in this area, of course, where the cultural presuppositions of the European and, in this case, specifically Italian, mindset became part and parcel of the conversion effort. The Franciscans used the shorthand designation of "civilization" for the set of attitudes and behaviors they wanted to propagate among their Indian charges.[52]

The terminology that the non-Indians used for differentiating among Indians reveals the semantic structure that fostered this kind of thinking. Among the settlers, the Indians were called barbarians, *bárbaros*, implying a whole set of behaviors and justifying the often brutal treatment of indigenous peoples.[53] This attitude toward the Indians is clearly revealed in the documents requesting land grants, which thus despoiled the Indians of their territory. Illustrative of this terminology was the 1897 request by Juan Esteban Castillo, one of the colonizers given grants in the vicinity of

Mission Machareti. He asserted that he had rights to these lands because he had "sustained combat with the barbarians, who, without dedicating themselves to work, wander about, occupied in assaults and pillage."[54] The friars adopted the same terms; in their circulars they referred to Indians as "C" for converted, "B" (for bárbaro) for unconverted.[55]

Baptism, which was to lead to conversion, was the first step toward civilizing the Indian. But what did the friars understand by the term *civilization*? The word appears frequently in the friars' correspondence but is rarely defined. In an 1851 circular to the Tarija missions, the mission prefect, Fr. Alfonso Corsetti, urged the Franciscans:

> Assure that the Indians possess civilization, as this is the secondary goal of the missions. Teach them to obey the laws and to respect the authorities. Make them behave decently and [maintain] a reasonable etiquette in all their actions; in eating, in clothing, in sleeping, and in the treatment of their similars. Accustom them to be faithful and just in their labor agreements [*conchabos*] and sincere in their words and promises, and make sure that each has their clothes cleaned for the feast days. Get [?] some, at least those most able, to learn the first letters and create schools in the mechanical arts in conformity with their possibilities. Exile from the missions all types of shamans and do not permit ever that they [the Indians] be cured by them, though the most capable of them you might teach how to heal and bleed them, making sure that they [the shamans] do not do so without prior consultation.[56]

This interesting document reveals in rich detail how the Franciscans thought of civilization in four broad areas: obedience to laws, behaving in a decent manner, receiving certain types of education, and adhering to European religious and medical practices. Of course, at the base of all of these transformations was the Indian as a dependable laborer. Let us examine each category to understand how the friars thought of their mission.

First, Corsetti asserted that the Indians had to be taught to obey laws and Bolivian authorities. This was the major goal of the Bolivian state: to establish its authority over a docile population on the once dangerous frontier. Moreover, adherence to national laws distinguished what the state considered savages from a population integrated into the nation. This included also the idea that the Indians were to be faithful in their agreements, both individual labor contracts and treaties. In this way, the friars counteracted the Chiriguanos' previous strategy and political culture, which exalted individual freedom (or better said, the liberty of the queremba, free warriors and their households) and made possible the pattern of ever-shifting alliances into the late nineteenth century, which made the Creoles describe the Indians as untrustworthy. As we shall see, the Indians were to be integrated into the nation-state as manual laborers; thus faithfully adhering to their labor contracts was an essential part of creating a disciplined labor force.

The notions of decency and etiquette were important as well. To become a citizen, according to the friars, was to dress in European-style clothes. This had a number of practical implications, which will be explored in subsequent chapters. In terms of perceptions, dressing "decently" (i.e., not like savages) meant that the friars wanted to make the Indian population indistinguishable from the rest of the country's populace. Interestingly, in the photos from this period the clothes that the Franciscans had the schoolchildren wear approximate those of the *cholo* class, the large, partially urbanized lower class who stood between the highland Indians and the tiny Creole upper class (see figure 8).[57] The girls wore large skirts and long shawls, with short-sleeved blouses, while the boys wore an ensemble of European shirts and trousers.

The "etiquette . . . in sleeping" presumably referred to sexuality, at least indirectly. As we have seen, the friars had the Indians build partitions to keep the children from watching their parents' sexual activity. The restrictions on sexuality did not affect clothing, however, as might have been the case with other ethnic groups. In particular, the traditional woman's dress, the *tipoy*, covered women from their neck almost to their feet, with only their bare arms sticking out of holes on the sides. Chiriguano men had already adopted European-style clothing, so this was not an issue.[58] These clothing choices were not lascivious even by standards of the most conservative Italian friar.

Instead, civilization meant dressing like Europeans (or at least like urbanized working-class Bolivians). We have photos of the Chiriguanos on the missions only from the late nineteenth century, a period when Pope Leo XIII was concerned about maintaining the Catholic faith among the working classes. Perhaps the friars' emphasis on dressing the neófitos in working-class attire harked to the vision of integrating the Indians into Catholic working-class social organizations, the "modern" method of controlling spirituality used in western Europe.

The third aspect of civilization was education. As we have seen, the Franciscans from Italy stressed education, but with certain characteristics. The circular suggested that there was an educational hierarchy: not all Indian children were educable. "The most able" were to learn the rudiments of reading and writing, but also "mechanical arts." Civilization, as Cattaneo's concept of incivilimento suggests, favored the kinds of activities that had made Italy great during the Risorgimento. Not coincidentally, the mechanical arts, such as carpentry, shoemaking, and distilling, were extremely useful activities for the frontier economy where little labor specialization existed. Again, the friars conceived of the Indians as forming part of the laboring classes, with little hope for learning beyond the most primary schooling.

Finally, the exiling of shamans was consistent with the religious monopoly that Catholicism claimed for civilization and especially on a religious mission. It is curious that Corsetti took a pragmatic view of the shamans and acknowledged their capacity as healers. However, here the mission prefect expected the medical knowledge of Europe to replace that of the medicine men, though perhaps with their help. As the mention of bleeding patients suggests, nineteenth-century European medical practices were not necessarily more efficacious than those of the indigenous peoples. Nevertheless, practicing European medicine was part and parcel of what the friars considered to be civilization.

The concept of civilization changed over the history of the Franciscan missions. In the late nineteenth century and early twentieth, the racialist theories of social Darwinist thinkers and others had an impact among the friars. This was most clear among the Potosí Franciscans, who saw themselves as more modern and up to date than their colleagues from the Tarija convent. Even the most sensitive ethnographer of the Chiriguanos, Fr. Bernardino de Nino, felt that the "Chiriguano race" was facing rapid extinction, as predicated by racist theories that assumed the disappearance of weak, conquered races at the hands of the strong European race.[59] The changing racial discourse became a self-fulfilling prophecy, for de Nino asserted that the disappearance of the distinctiveness of the Chiriguanos was the object of the missions. He was proud to report that, thanks to the methods employed in the missions, "In a few years nobody will know that the Chiriguanos of the missions belonged to this race."[60] The extinction of the "Chiriguano race" also required its cultural obliteration. This was the true goal of civilizing the Indians, at least by the turn of the century.[61]

Images of Indians

Given the Franciscans' goals, how did they conceive of the Indians? After all, the conception of what the Indians were and what they needed to do to become Catholics and "civilized" human beings profoundly affected the way the missionaries tried to achieve these goals. The friars had opinions on virtually all aspects of the Indians, but I will concentrate on how the Franciscans conceived of the virtues and vices of the unconverted Chiriguanos, their potential to become Catholics and "civilized," and the Franciscans' views of the converts.

Most Franciscan authors agreed that the Chiriguanos in the past were a great people. Fr. Doroteo Giannecchini, for example, asserted in documents prepared for an exposition in Turin, Italy, in 1898 of Franciscan missions throughout the world, "The Chiriguano nation in the period of discovery of the New World was one of the most numerous, most savage, and strong ethnic groups [*naciones*]."[62] The friars emphasized in particular the Chiriguanos' martial abilities, superior to those of other Indian groups. Since Chiriguanos were agriculturists rather than nomadic peoples, they rated higher than the Chaco groups in the missionaries' estimation. According to Fr. Bernardino de Nino, an alliance with the Portuguese in the sixteenth century in Paraguay helped civilize them somewhat.[63] While their struggle with the Spanish and then the Bolivians lasted a long time, only the friars truly began to conquer them and bring them toward civilization. De Nino flatly asserted, "The unequal conflict lasted centuries and finally [the Chiriguanos] were conquered bit by bit by the missionaries." Likewise, Giannecchini affirmed, "The last remnants of advanced groups of this nation, once so numerous, we [the Tarija convent] and our brothers from Potosí have reduced . . . to missions," though he at least conceded that Bolivian arms also conquered other Indian villages: "[Thus,] speaking properly, the Chiriguano nation now does not exist in its most pure and genuine savagery."[64]

The missionaries saw the Chiriguanos as a fallen people who maintained their sense of independence but were impotent to maintain their autonomy in fact. The Franciscans realized full well that the reason the Indians permitted them to establish missions was not because they wanted to be converted but because they wanted to be saved them from the local ranchers who would oppress them.[65] The Franciscans refused to baptize adults who did not ask for conversion and first undergo intensive training in the faith. They viewed the adults as savages who would never be civilized and whose souls were lost except for occasional deathbed baptisms. While the friars admired the Indians' love of liberty, they found it appalling in other ways, for it limited the influence the missionaries could have over them. It meant that the Indians remained savages; submission to constituted authorities (and especially to the Catholic Church), not autonomy, was a characteristic of civilized men and women. Fr. Angélico Martarelli put the Franciscans' point of view best when he characterized the problems of colonial missionaries trying to convert the Indians: "The invincible obstinacy of the Chiriguanos, the disordered love for their savage independence, almost frustrated all the heroic efforts of the evangelical operatives."[66] The friars saw the Indians as pig-headed and, most of all, disorganized and unwilling to submit to the beneficent and civilizing influences of the padres. In other words, the Chiriguano political culture, which valued individual honor as free men and women and recognized no permanent authority in this face-to-face society, was a manifestation of their barbaric state.

Barbarism also meant being close to nature. Fr. Alejandro Corrado, in his book on the Tarija missions, used verbal imagery that equated the savage Indians with nature. His highly readable work used terms associated with wild animals to describe the actions of the Chiriguanos who resisted the missions. For example, in his narration of the establishment of Tarairí mission Corrado described Arayápui, the tubicha of Huacaya and enemy of the missionaries, as "roaring with courage" when he promised to avenge the death of his brother at the hands of mission Indians. The enemy warrior bands were likened to forces of nature; they charged the mission "creating a fierce thunderstorm." A year later "a fierce flood of Chiriguanos, Tobas and Tapietés inundated the surroundings of Tarairí." In turn, the missionaries "tamed" the Indians of the surrounding communities. The Tarairí chief who killed Arayápui's brother was "brave." However, when the Tarairí Indians started to build the first church, "because they were recently conquered [they] were very stupid and incapable."[67] More explicitly, Fr. Bernardino de Nino in 1914 still used many of the same metaphors. For him, the task of the mission was "to uproot the Indian from the forest, to make him leave barbarism and begin to teach him how to be a man, to consider himself more noble than a brute."[68]

Despite the rejection by the papacy of "modern" authors such as Jean-Jacques Rousseau, Corrado and other Franciscan authors used the same kind of discourse as the Romantics, though turned on its head. While the

Romantic authors might have asserted the inherent goodness of the natives uncorrupted by Western civilization, for the Franciscans the unconverted Indians were likened to nature or, in the case of Corrado, to destructive natural forces. In both cases, however, the Indians arose from nature and formed part of the natural habitat.[69]

The children were a different matter. As we have seen, the Franciscans' focus was on education and they put considerable effort into the mission schools, as the following chapters show. Fr. Alejandro Corrado saw the indoctrination of the children as "cultivating Christian seedlings destined to substitute little by little the brambles of barbarism and unbelief."[70] Despite this emphasis on education, according to the Italians, even the Indians educated since childhood shared the defects as adults that all Chiriguanos had. Fr. Doroteo wrote that, before puberty, the children "display an open intelligence and learn with facility to read, write, and do arithmetic, sing, [and] play [musical] instruments." After puberty, however, they "change ideas: vices, passions, life in the countryside make them stupid, slowly they lose interest in intellectual things and even more so in spiritual ones.... That is how they largely forget their moral and civil education that cost so much sweat from the missionary to teach."[71] It is clear that the Franciscans did not know much about hormonal changes in adolescents and had a hard time dealing with the boys and girls of that difficult age.

What irked the missionaries most was what they perceived to be the Indians' laziness and inconstancy. All the friars who characterized the Chiriguanos noted that the men in particular worked very little and did as little as possible. According to de Nino, "The missions... would progress more if the Chiriguano were not so inconsistent. Work is not lacking in their towns nor in the neighboring counties, mostly they are day laborers but they are not to be found."[72] To the Europeans, laziness was a characteristic shared by all the indigenous peoples of the region. The Chiriguanos were a little bit less lazy than the rest because they at least were farmers and sowed, weeded, and harvested, compared to the other ethnic groups that were hunters and gatherers.[73] Part of the implicit definition of civilization was to have constant work; the Italian Franciscans saw too much leisure as a vice. This was especially the case with this ethnic group, for the friars accused the Chiriguanos of passing their leisure time after the harvest with drinking and gambling, to which they claimed the Indians were much addicted.[74]

The friars recognized that, while the men were often idle, the women worked constantly. According to Fr. Angélico, "The women, in contrast, hardly ever rest. In addition to the ordinary domestic tasks and the making of chicha [beer made from corn], they are obligated to sow, harvest the crop, and bring it on their backs to the hut; sew, dye cloth, weave, bring clay, make clay pots, large earthen jars, and other receptacles for their use."[75] Chiriguano women also labored as domestics in the small towns that dotted the frontier.[76] Nevertheless, women's work apparently did not count toward making a people civilized.

According to the missionaries, the Chiriguanos did not have a true religion before they came in contact with the missionaries. Fr. Doroteo Giannecchini claimed that before the mission existed the Indians "[did] not profess publicly any religion and generally [did] not have temples or huts, nor idols, nor priests for religious practices." Instead, they believed in shamans, called *ipayes*, who were primarily healers and magicians rather than what the Franciscans considered to be true religious specialists. The missionaries did not worry much about other sects converting the Indians. They claimed that once the Indians left the mission and went to the towns or to Argentina, the former mission Indians simply forgot what they knew and did not practice the faith that the friars had taught them rather than join Protestant churches.[77]

To the Franciscans it appeared that the neophytes did not really care much about religion, and the friars worried about this apostasy. If indeed the path toward civilization led through conversion to Christianity in the Catholic missions, the Chiriguanos' lack of commitment to their new faith was deeply troubling. The friars saw only one solution: that the missions were a labor of generations, not just of conversion of the youth. Only as the Chiriguanos adopted most aspects of civilization and lost themselves in the mass of mestizos who increasingly settled the frontier regions could they be saved. Since the lack of concern about spiritual matters was inherent to the Indians, the missionaries' task was not finished until the Chiriguanos did not behave like Chiriguanos anymore. At least this is what missionaries such as Fr. Bernardino de Nino had concluded by the early twentieth century, but this goal was implicit even beforehand.

The only way to accomplish these goals was through a firm, paternalistic hand. Of course, the missionary enterprise by definition involves a hierarchical view of the world, where the missionary has superior knowledge that the neophytes are supposed to absorb. In the Catholic Church, with its emphasis on hierarchy and the vital role of the priest as an essential intermediary (and representative) of the Church and ultimately the Christian God, this paternalism was quite marked. The ultramontanism of the papacy and the Catholic Church in the nineteenth century, a process from which the overwhelmingly Italian Franciscans emerged, made this aspect of the missions even more marked. Fr. Bernardino de Nino spoke of the immorality of the increasingly secular world in Europe, where the pursuit of material goods was more important than spirituality. According to him and his fellow Franciscans, Catholicism brought morality and order out of this chaos, in which a recognizable hierarchy provided the structure to live a meaningful and ethical life.[78] The Franciscan order stressed humility and otherworldliness among its members, the perfect antidote to the impulses that corrupted the modern world.

The friars spoke openly of paternalism; the concept in the nineteenth century did not have the negative connotations of today. Fr. Angélico Martarelli boasted, "[The Chiriguano] understands that the only recourse that he has to live freely and independently is to enjoy the protection of the paternal government of the Missionary Fathers, the only ones who want his moral and material progress."[79] There are no references to the Chiriguanos in general as childlike. The missionaries ruled over the unconverted only indirectly, through their traditional chiefs, thus keeping them in what Fr. Alejandro Corrado described so vividly as a state of nature. In turn, the missionaries considered themselves the fathers of the children whom they educated and of the adult neophytes who eventually graduated from the mission schools. The adult converts remained children for the friars; their inconstancy and their frustrating capacity for refusing to civilize themselves in the way that the Franciscans wanted meant that it was necessary to maintain their tutelage over their charges. For the friars, the act of conversion was but one step in their progress toward civilization, which entailed numerous generations. It is perhaps for this reason that the Franciscans never considered training Chiriguano children to enter the priesthood. Being a priest or a Franciscan entailed much more than fervent belief; it required a whole complex of behaviors to which the Indians did not measure up. In the context of Vatican I and the increasingly restrictive theological views of the Catholic Church, making priests of Indians was simply too radical a concept.

Despite the missionaries' feeling of cultural superiority, some of the most sensitive friars who lived among the Indians began to adopt, probably unconsciously, some of the characteristics of their charges. It is by now a truism that the masters are profoundly affected by their subordinates, for the structure of the relationship between superior and subordinate forces accommodations not just on the part of the subordinate but also by the superior. As the abundant literature on slavery and the best works in subaltern studies have shown, the conditions of rule make necessary the acknowledgment on a number of levels of the humanity and the culture of the subordinate.[80] In the documents that have survived it is difficult to ascertain much of this, for the missionaries themselves continuously had to prove to themselves, their higher-ups, and outsiders the superiority of their position. However, sometimes the actions of the friars revealed this absorption of Chiriguano culture in unwitting ways. Fr. Doroteo Giannecchini, in a letter describing mission experiences among the Tobas, repeated Chiriguano sayings in Guaraní, claiming they were dirty and untrustworthy. The padre had assimilated the Chiriguano prejudices against the Tobas to such an extent that he employed the same words the Chiriguanos used to denigrate that ethnic group.[81] Given that the Franciscans lived for many years either in pairs or alone among the Chiriguanos on the missions, despite their generally high discipline and their religious dedication, they unwittingly assimilated other aspects of the culture of the people they were supposed to convert.

Thus, the Franciscans brought with them certain conceptions of the Indians, but their experiences in the missions also transformed them. They viewed the unconverted Indians as part of nature and believed it was their duty to transform them into beings who could enter civilized society. Conversion of beliefs was only one, albeit the most important, step in this process. The friars saw that, despite their best efforts, even the Chiriguanos who had grown up on the missions reverted to their "natural state," behaving much like their unconverted parents and relatives. For example, the school boys, as soon as they were able, participated in drunken feasts or, when they left for Argentina, did not go to Mass or apparently practice Catholicism while away. The mission enterprise thus became a long-term effort in which the Indians were to be remade into citizens without their ethnic heritage. This was at least the conclusion of some missionaries by the early twentieth century, such as Fr. Bernardino de Nino, who was a sensitive observer of Chiriguano culture but who also was imbued with the contemporary views of native peoples in the Americas. As such, we cannot separate the interesting mix of Italian background, views of the Catholic Church about the conversion of indigenous peoples, the cultural climate and how it changed over the years of mission work, as well as the experience these men had in dealing with the Indians on a daily basis.

The Inauguration of the New Church in Tiguipa in 1902

One way of understanding in concrete terms how the Franciscans viewed the mission Indians is to examine the public rituals that took place on the missions. Public rituals were important components of civic and religious life in Italy and throughout Latin America, including eastern Bolivia. Indeed, during the nineteenth and early twentieth centuries the Catholic Church used public spectacles to counteract rituals that the anticlerical liberals staged to gain the allegiance of the masses. Public displays formed important manifestations of the struggle between Church and state in modern Europe and in Latin America.[82] For the Bolivian missions, ritualized performances reflected in interesting ways an idealized notion of the mission community and how it was supposed to function. They built on models from the earliest colonial period, as the Catholic Church was expert in using shows to convert and awe crowds of believers and unbelievers alike. As in all public displays where many people were involved, not all of them in completely scripted fashion, it is also possible to discern the realities of mission life beyond the façade of the staged event.[83] This was the case for the inauguration of the rebuilt church in Mission Tiguipa in 1902, when the Franciscans organized a public spectacle lasting several days to celebrate the event. That year was also the high point of the Franciscan missions among the Chiriguanos, just before the secularization of the important missions of San Francisco del Pilcomayo and San Antonio as well as the imposition by President Ismael Montes of the stringent 1905 mission regulations.

As the description of the event by one of the friars present shows (see appendix), the inauguration of the mission featured a number of processions and rituals that presented the missions according to the Franciscans' priorities. All the processions (of which there were at least one per day) highlighted either children from the mission schools or religious statues. This showed the emphasis that the missionaries placed on the conversion and education of the children, for they were the main actors in these events. Indeed, only the neophytes and the schoolchildren were active participants; the unconverted Indians were only spectators at these events. This reflected in very real ways how the friars envisioned the mission: the unconverted adults lived on the missions, but it was the children on whom the missionary effort was concentrated.

It is important to note not only what groups the author of this description highlighted, but whom he left out. As we shall see, the friars had certain blind spots in their conception of the missions, especially when directed toward the national or international public. As the previous chapter makes clear, the traditional chiefs were absolutely crucial to the establishment of the missions and their subsequent functioning. None is mentioned here, though it is highly likely that the chiefs (not the corregidor's men) were the ones who enforced the peace during the celebrations. It is significant that the Indians who aided the Creoles sent by the corregidor were from Macharetí. Not only was it the largest mission, but Mandeponay, by far the most important Chiriguano chief and a powerful political personage in his own right, was the leader there. Though a supporter of the Franciscan enterprise, Mandeponay remained unconverted himself until 1922, when he converted on his deathbed; at the time of the celebration of 1902 he kept a harem of seven wives in direct contravention of missionary directives (see figure 2).

According to the missionary's account, the major themes of the church dedication were a celebration of religion foremost, but also of the degree of civilization that the natives had achieved. The first theme revealed itself in the various processions of the Virgin Mary and St. Joseph, the patron saint of the mission. Obviously, the aim of the festival was to dedicate a place of worship. However, intermixed with the religious message was a celebration of the integration of the Indians (at least of the converts and the children in the mission schools) into the Bolivian nation-state. This integration into the Bolivian nation was part and parcel of the missions' goals and reflected the differences with the "savage" Indians who ignored the rules and obligations of the nation-state.

On the first day, the ceremony involved having the schoolchildren approach the mission church with twenty-five national flags, a procession that must have looked impressive, given the Bolivian flags' highly colorful red, yellow, and green. The Franciscans also melded the idea of the nation with that of the missionaries. The image of the young friar, resplendent in his military uniform and towering above the Indian children of the marching band that surrounded him, was a powerful image of the juxtaposition of state and Church in the missions. That a Franciscan would lead these Indian children was important, but so was the fact that he was dressed not as a friar, but in the uniform of the Bolivian Army, symbol of secular authority on the frontier. Unlike in the colonial period, the Bolivian military did not overtly support the missionaries in their endeavors, but here the union was apparent. Perhaps the national military also presented a counterweight to the local settlers, who by this time were clamoring

FIGURE 2. Mandeponay of Macharetí, ca. 1920. Mandeponay was the most powerful Chiriguano leader of the nineteenth and early twentieth centuries. Note his large tembeta. He was likely in his eighties when this photo was taken. He died in 1922. *Source*: AFT, photographer unknown.

for the labor and the land of the missions. The group emerged from the neophyte part of the mission, symbolizing the union of nation-state and Catholic Church among the converted Indians. However, here the Franciscan represented secular authority, exactly what the Catholic Church had hoped for but failed to achieve in Italy.

This mix of integration of the Indian into the nation under the auspices of the Italian friars might appear contradictory, given the Catholic Church's resistance to nationalists in their home country. But the palpable mix of religion and the nation-state can be explained in at least two ways. First, by the early twentieth century the friars had accommodated themselves to the existence and perhaps even the necessity of the nation-state, especially on the frontier, where few other institutions could provide for the permanence of European-type civilization. Second, and a more central point, was the way the Franciscans envisioned the participation of the state. The rich symbolism of the rituals suggests that the friars used the rituals to show that the Church should have primacy, as even the symbolic representative of the state was in fact a man of the cloth. In a sense, the priests were re-creating in the celebration the Giobertian model, in which the Church had primacy and constituted the linchpin of the state.

The goal of civilizing the Indians also emanated from the great emphasis on music in the ceremonies. The ability to play European-style music was an important sign of civilization, and the Chiriguanos on the missions excelled in this. For Fr. Bernardino de Nino, music was an essential component of civilization, in which the soul, not just material needs, was addressed.[84] The mission bands, including those with the new wind instruments, were the pride of the friars. They showed that the Indians were adept at learning new skills, especially those that involved manual dexterity (as well as a sympathetic ear from the Creoles, who understood this type of music). After all, much of what the Franciscans tried to accomplish with the children, as we will see in subsequent chapters, was to integrate the mission converts into the regional economy as skilled and semiskilled laborers.

The emphasis on musical training in European-style music, both sacred and secular, also served to divert the Indians' talents from "savage" to civilized customs. As the Franciscans lamented, the Chiriguanos loved feasts and getting drunk, usually with native music, which incorporated flutes and drumming.[85] As Fr. Gervasio Costa, the author of the description of the Tiguipa ceremonies, suggests, "the melodious harmonies of the violins excited the soul" and "caused diverse effects of compassion," which the

Franciscans would describe as "civilized" sentiments. It is likely that the Franciscans imported the violin to the region, an instrument that since its introduction has become an important component of folkloric music in the Bolivian Chaco. Band instruments also included trumpets and other wind instruments. One friar, Fr. Domingo Regini, put Chiriguano melodies to band music as a way of entertaining the mission Indians but also distracting them from the music's original context.[86] The suggestion here is that the cliché "Music soothes the savage breast" perhaps was implicit in the mental framework of the Italians who administered the missions. In the festival described here, the Indians listened to music, but without the noxious influence of either chicha or brandy, which would have been the context of native music.

The description of the dedication of the Tiguipa mission church brings together a number of themes in this chapter. The Italian friars who arrived in the missions in southeastern Bolivia throughout the nineteenth century had visions of their tasks as missionaries and what the Indians they came to convert were like. They came with their own conceptions of what conversion meant; clearly, it meant more than just making the Chiriguanos believe in Catholic doctrine. These attitudes changed over the course of the century as different cohorts of Franciscans entered the missions. Also, the missionary experience itself and daily contact with the Indians provided for some modifications in outlook. Nevertheless, the public ceremonies surrounding the dedication presented an idealized view of the missions, thus showing in concrete ways the Franciscan perspective.

The Franciscan sense of religiosity comes through very nicely in these ceremonies. The bricks-and-souls Christianity is evident. The complex rites surrounding the church building demonstrate the Franciscans' emphasis on structures. Souls were even more important, as evidenced in the primacy of the children and neophytes (virtually all of them former students of the mission schools) in the ceremonies. But conversion in itself was not enough; the friars thought that the Indians had to be torn from their natural settings and educated to be truly civilized and what they considered to be "men."[87] Civilization in the case of these Indians meant also learning useful manual arts and the integration of the youth into the frontier (and thus national) labor market. Music was useful in this regard, both to improve dexterity and to provide some useful activity, but also to create civilized feelings by listening to the sublime music of the violins and other European instruments and melodies.

Civilization, at least for the friars, also meant a certain ordering of society that included both Church and state. For many of the Franciscans, who had been personally affected in their youth in the contentious atmosphere of the struggle between the papacy and the state in Risorgimento Italy, both had their roles to play. For missionaries such as Fr. Bernardino de Nino, civilization could not exist without a strong Church, for the Catholic Church provided the moral foundation of society. Thus the Church was paramount, as it served as the basis for the functioning of the state. So it was appropriate that the neophytes wave their flags but that a Franciscan play the role of the secular authority in his military uniform (often the most visible presence of the Bolivian state on the frontier). The Franciscan missions among the Chiriguanos reveal that the missionary enterprise, the friars' role therein and that of the Indians, was highly context-dependent. It was embedded in the rich and conflictual personal experiences of the missionaries, the changes they underwent on the missions, and their perceptions of the Indians they wanted to convert.

It is interesting to see also what these ceremonies failed to include. Women, though they must have been there, were left unmentioned. The friars tried to replace the (unconverted) mothers with their ceremonies. This is surprising, given that the missions were filled mostly with women and children when the men left for the sugarcane fields of Argentina or were required to work on some project outside the mission. The unconverted (still a majority on the Tiguipa mission in 1902) and the traditional chiefs were also nowhere mentioned in the description of the inauguration. They did not figure in the mission's religious enterprise and the friars did not attempt to convert the adults. The Chiriguano chiefs, to the last man unconverted, had no role to play in the staged drama of the church inauguration. However, as we shall see in the next chapters, the chiefly role was in fact essential for understanding the dynamics of the missions. Thus, while the rather absolute dichotomized vision of the conversion to civilization ruled the friars' rhetoric, their behavior and Chiriguano reality suggest a more interactive and contradictory adaptive process.

CHAPTER THREE

Death and Migration:
The Population Decline of the Missions

Understanding the issues of life, death, and migration are vital for understanding the Catholic missions among indigenous peoples in Latin America and elsewhere. More than any other factor, demographic issues determined the life of all missions. How many people resided on the missions, how long they remained alive, and how long they stayed had a profound impact on mission life. A determination of these factors informs all other issues, such as changes in culture, who ruled on the missions, and the economic impact of the missions.

The missions among the Chiriguanos suffered population decline in the long term, though over the short term some missions increased in population. Scholars examining other mission systems in Latin America have found this decline to be a virtually universal phenomenon, although so far the demographic information we have comes primarily from the colonial era. During that period death from disease outweighed any other cause for this population decline, though flight also was a major factor.[1] Few have examined whether this is the case for the republican period as well. As Robert Jackson and I have argued, most indigenous groups had some contact with Eurasian diseases by the nineteenth century, before their mission experience. For many populations the centuries-long contact with the Europeans meant that the mission populations were at least somewhat immune to disease and thus mortality rates were lower than in the extreme case of, for example, the Alta Californian missions.[2] The Franciscan missions among the Chiriguanos present an important case study to determine whether disease remained the primary factor in mission population decline.

Demographic factors also play an important role in understanding the missions. Population increases and decreases inevitably affected the missions. If the Indians died off so quickly that there was no chance to create a new, Christian religious consciousness among the residents (as likely occurred in California), then this affected the missionary goals. Likewise, the composition of the mission population affected the quality of life. If only women and children were present on the mission and if there were not enough able-bodied adults to sow and harvest the fields the very survival of the people on the mission could be compromised. Precipitous population decline, whether through flight or disease, could be disastrous for maintaining families, meeting the religious goals of the missionaries, and even building needed structures on the mission. On the other hand, Daniel Reff has argued that demographic catastrophes at times aided the Jesuits' conversion of mission populations, since the Indians sought refuge in the new religion when they lost their old cultural bearings.[3] It is clear that demographic factors provide a baseline by which to measure the success or failure of the missions.

Contact between the Chiriguanos and Europeans, as we have seen, was of long standing and had begun almost immediately after Europeans entered South America. Despite previous contacts, however, the Indian population on the Franciscan missions declined over the long term, with an especially marked diminution beginning in the late nineteenth century and accelerating during the early twentieth century. In 1877 the missions contained slightly more than thirteen thousand Indians. In 1900 the number had fallen to nine thousand, even with the addition of the important missions of Santa Rosa and Ivo, founded by the Potosí Franciscans after 1877. In 1924 the missions contained only forty-three hundred Indians. By this time the smallest missions—Aguairenda, Chimeo, Itau, San Francisco and San Antonio del Pilcomayo, San Francisco and San Antonio del Parapetí, and Itatiqui—had all been secularized.[4] Even without these secularizations, these missions followed the pattern of the colonial missions in their population decline.

Mission records are incomplete. Demographic data prior to 1877 are extremely sketchy. Beginning in that year we have systematic annual information on population movement in the missions. It is also not clear whether statistics on baptisms and burials are complete. The baptismal records of Tarairí, which are extant from the first two decades after the foundation of the mission (1854) onward, show that virtually only Indians on their deathbeds were baptized. The children, who according to regulations should have been baptized soon after birth, normally were not. Thus many children born on the mission were baptized well beyond their infant years. For example, in 1863, nine years after the establishment of Tarairí, Catalina Nandurai was baptized at age five because she was mortally ill with smallpox and the friars wanted to save her soul. The accuracy of baptismal and burial records improved greatly as the century wore on, making the use of the summary data in the annual mission reports possible from the late 1870s to 1913. The Tarairí data show that in the 1870s virtually all children were baptized within a short time after birth, healthy or not.[5]

Many Chiriguanos refused to be baptized even on their deathbed, and since the information in the *visitas* [inspections by mission prefects] were primarily for ecclesiastical purposes, it is not clear whether the deaths of the unbaptized were registered. In some missions, such as Chimeo and Santa Rosa, the only category listed is "ecclesiastical burials," making burial figures potentially unreliable for the total mission population, given that a significant portion of the mission Indians remained unconverted. Some missions appear to have more reliable information. Aguairenda had a special category for "heathens" (*infieles*), assuring that all deaths were recorded. In others, the term was simply *defunciones*, meaning "deaths," avoiding the ecclesiastical issue. In Boicovo the categories changed from "ecclesiastical burials" to "deaths" in 1894, signaling that all deaths were included after that point.

Despite some problems with the data, it is possible to find overall patterns. For example, in virtually all cases the Indian populations increased soon after the establishment of the missions.[6] All the missions experienced a period of turmoil after they were founded, during which Indian groups inimical to the missions attacked them. After the first few turbulent years, most Chiriguano groups felt safe enough to return and settle permanently in the missions. This process took longer in some missions than others. Some missions, such as Chimeo, Macharetí, Boicovo, and Ivo, were established in the aftermath of lengthy warfare. It took time for the missionaries to regain the trust of the indigenous groups and reunite formerly thriving communities that had been dispersed during the hostilities.

That populations increased soon after the missions were founded is most clearly evident in the case of Ivo, though Santa Rosa and San Antonio del Parapetí also followed this pattern. The increase of Ivo's population in the initial years can be attributed to the fact that this mission was founded in the aftermath of the 1892 rebellion, after which the missionaries attempted to bring back the Chiriguano population dispersed as a result of their defeat.[7] Ivo's population increased from 708 Indians in 1897 to over a thousand in 1900.[8] Although we do not have population figures for early periods for Chimeo (est. 1849) and Boicovo (est. 1876), these missions were both founded after wars and probably underwent similar population growth. It must be kept in mind, however, that while the Franciscans were largely successful in attracting many Indians, the deaths of many of the former indigenous inhabitants of the region during the struggles and the sale of captives afterward meant that a significant portion of the population had disappeared, thus making their numbers smaller than the original population prior to the mission period.

Population increases, in the short and medium term, occurred elsewhere as well. In those cases, the population increase was less marked, though attributable mainly to the immigration of dispersed Chiriguano households. In Santa Rosa, for example, the mission population increased slightly between 1887 and 1892 from 2,027 to 2,137 inhabitants, a 4 percent increase over five years. In San Antonio the mission contained only 1,150 Indians in 1903; two years later it had increased to almost 1,800. Over the rest of the mission's nine-year existence San Antonio never dipped below the 1903 figure. San Francisco del Parapetí, however, decreased in population in the early years, from 1,478 souls in 1907 to 680 in 1909.[9]

Thus we see a variety of patterns for the Franciscan missions from the late nineteenth century to the mid-twentieth century. First there was a long-term population decrease, punctuated by periods of recovery. Until approximately 1880 mission populations held steady or increased. Between 1877 and 1885, the total population on the Tarija missions increased from 12,860 souls to 17,338, or 34 percent.[10] After the middle of the 1880s most mission populations decreased. The three largest missions, Machareti, Tarairí, and Santa Rosa, held steady until 1890 or the turn of the century. In fact, San Buenaventura de Ivo increased in population until 1904. These developments were also related to another phenomenon: the older mission system from Tarija had lost steam by the late nineteenth century and the newer, more dynamic one from Potosí gained ground until the early twentieth century. Nevertheless, the pattern of eventual population decline, including on the Potosí missions, is apparent over the long term.

This pattern of population decline is notable despite high fertility rates.

In 1900 on Mission Machareti, for example, there were 4.6 children aged 0 to 4 years old for each woman aged 26 through 46. The population pyramids for Machareti and Boicovo missions during the early twentieth century show the typical preindustrial pattern, in which fertility and mortality was high. Large numbers of children were born, only to die during the first years of childhood. This pattern was probably very similar to that of mestizo settlers in the region.

The missionaries attributed multiple causes to this population decline, but highlighted emigration rather than excess mortality as the primary cause. The friars were correct, though their understanding of the causes was colored by their own religious views. Fr. Doroteo Giannecchini in 1883 mentioned "endemic epidemics" as factors in population drops but asserted that the lack of morals was more important. This supposed lack of morals led to the Chiriguanos' rejection of the missions and flight. However, for the friar the Indians' lack of morals came from outside the missions. The Franciscan faulted "the avarice of the hacendados [landlords] from within and without the republic" who seduced mission inhabitants to live away from the "fraternal care of the fathers who took them out of the forests." Giannecchini claimed that the ranchers taught the Indians all kinds of immoral behavior and worked against the friars, whose work was "related to the true progress of Christian civilization."[11] Thus outsiders with their worldly temptations worked against the ideals of the missions, just as liberalism and other modern ideologies had corrupted the world outside the Bolivian frontier.

The Tarija mission prefect, Rafael Paoli, declared two decades later that the three main causes for the decline of the missions were smallpox, the vagrancy of the mission population along the frontier, and seasonal migration to Argentina. Fr. Bernardino de Nino, one of the most sensitive Franciscan observers of the mission populations, made a similar assessment a decade later. He asserted in 1912, "The epidemics, vagrancy, and, more than anything emigration, moreover the lack of food, are destroying this race."[12] There are problems with the friars' analysis: they had a relatively unsophisticated understanding of demographic issues; they tried to present the missionary enterprise in the best light possible; and their emphasis was on spiritual and ritual aspects of birth, marriage, death, and the like, rather than demography per se. Were they correct in their assessment that out-migration rather than excess deaths over births brought about the decline of the missions? To examine these issues, let us first look at the role of disease.

The Role of Disease and Mortality on the Missions

The mission records show that epidemics were common. It is possible to pinpoint the most serious epidemics and famines that swept the missions. (See table 4.) By the turn of the century, however, famines, not diseases, were the main concerns. The appearance of famines was related to the ecological changes that had occurred as a result of the introduction of massive numbers of cattle into the Andean foothills and into the fragile Chaco Boreal environment in the 1880s. Widespread erosion in the foothills due to the extension of cattle ranching into the region after the defeat of Chiriguano forces in the 1870s pushed mestizo settlers out of the Huacaya, Ingre, and Abatire valleys. By the 1880s cattle ranchers had entered the Gran Chaco and begun to change the fragile Chaco ecological structure. Droughts became more common and spread over larger regions, culminating between 1897 and 1905, when drought persisted throughout the area for seven years.[13]

Some diseases were endemic on the missions. Tuberculosis, diarrhea, measles, whooping cough, cholera, syphilis, and others caused frequent deaths. In 1884 on Mission Boicovo, for example, of the 108 deaths whose causes are known, 37 were due to tuberculosis, 32 due to diarrhea or dysentery, and 28 to measles (including Chapuai, the ninety-year-old mburuvicha of the mission). Other diseases, such as colds, fevers, apoplexy, and whooping cough, also caused one death each. In 1886, of 126 deaths for which we have information, 43 were diagnosed as tuberculosis and 36 as "convulsive coughing." Smallpox also made a reappearance, with 12 dying of that illness. Only two Indians died of digestive system diseases. Apparently the missionaries were able to control the smallpox outbreak, for the following year only six individuals died from it. The friars tried to take appropriate measures with other diseases as well. In 1887 two individuals died of dysentery, and one was "interred in the countryside for fear of the mortal cholera plague."[14] Despite these temporary successes, epidemics continued. The missionaries singled out smallpox as the main cause of death. In 1895 the prefect of the Potosí missions claimed, "[Boicovo] is extinguishing itself because of that terrible and horrid disease of smallpox, which has spread in the mission various times."[15]

It is not clear when smallpox vaccinations began on the missions. The first reference comes from 1880, when the Indians received vaccinations from Fr. Doroteo Giannecchini in Mission San Francisco del Pilcomayo. The friar took the precaution when some migrants returned from Argen-

TABLE 4. Epidemics and famines on the Franciscan missions, 1860–1922

Year	Disease/famine (missions)
1863	smallpox (Tarairí)
1880	smallpox (Tarairí, San Francisco del Pilcomayo, Boicovo)
1886	smallpox (Boicovo, Macharetí); famine (Macharetí)
1891	whooping cough (Macharetí)
1893	smallpox (Santa Rosa, Boicovo)
1894	smallpox (Boicovo)
1896	smallpox (Macharetí)
1897	*peste* [?] (Boicovo); famine (Tarairí); smallpox (Aguairenda); famine [because of locusts] (Macharetí)
1898	famine (Aguairenda)
1901	famine (Macharetí)
1902	famine (Macharetí)
1903	*carestía* [famine?] (Santa Rosa, Ivo, Macharetí); famine (San Antonio del Pilcomayo)
1904	famine (Macharetí, San Antonio del Pilcomayo)
1905	*carestía, mortandad* [mortality?] (Ivo); *carestía* (San Antonio del Pilcomayo)
1922	smallpox (Tarija missions)

Sources: "Primer libro parroquial de bautismos y entierros de Tarairí," AVAChC; Angélico Martarelli, *El Colegio Franciscano de Potosí y sus misiones*, 2nd ed. (La Paz: Talleres Gráficos Marinoni, n.d.), 195; "Anales de este Colegio Franciscano de Tarija desde el año 1879: Libro primero," 8–9, AFT; Bernardino de Nino, *Etnografía chiriguana* (La Paz: Ismael Argote, 1912), 89; "Informe del Prefecto de las Misiones de la P.F.- de Potosí, Fr. Romualdo Dambrogi," in *Memoria del Ministro de Instrucción Pública y Colonización . . . de 1895* (Sucre: Tipografía Excelsior, 1895), 139-40, ANB; "Santas Visitas," AFT; Hernando Siles, *Memoria de Guerra y Colonización* (La Paz: N.p., 1922), 70.

tina with smallpox. The Swedish anthropologist Erland Nordenskiöld observed in 1909 that in Mission Ivo, Fr. Bernardino de Nino vaccinated all mission residents. In the nearby mestizo settlement of Cuevo, Nordenskiöld wrote that, in contrast, a number of settlers died due to their ignorance of the disease and a lack of preventive measures. In 1922 the Ministry of War and Colonization sent vaccines to the missions to prevent the outbreak of another smallpox epidemic.[16] The systematic vaccination of the missionary population might explain why famine, not epidemic disease, became the principal health concern of the missionaries after the turn of the century. Ironically, once the Franciscans had finally defeated most epidemic diseases, emigration sapped the missions of their populations.

The Importance of Migration

Migration played a more important role than disease in the population decline of the Franciscan missions among the Chiriguanos. Chiriguanos migrated for economic reasons and to quit the struggle over power between the friars and the Indians who felt their independence threatened by the mission regime. By the twentieth century the missions had become staging grounds for migration, a place where the Indians kept their women and children safe while they worked and cavorted in the sugar plantation labor camps.

Although over the long term out-migration was more important to the mission than immigration, the picture painted by an analysis of population data is one of constant movement back and forth. Indians moved between missions, and some escaped from the missions. Some Chiriguano families entered the missions, at least for a few seasons or perhaps a few years, only to go elsewhere. This was especially true among those who had not converted. The number of non-Christian families remained virtually stable, the prefect of the Potosí missions asserted in 1895, because "the deceased individuals [were] replaced with other Indians from the outside who join[ed] the missions."[17] While settlement of new Indians on the missions was not unusual, more Indians left the missions than entered them.

Despite the frequency of epidemics and the endemic nature of many other diseases, in certain crisis years, such as the smallpox epidemic in Aguairenda in 1897, mortality became more important than emigration. In that year 137 Indians died, whereas five more people entered the mission than left it. Generally it was the other way around, with migration playing a larger role than mortality or natality. In the early years of the twentieth century the population fluctuated greatly on this mission; for example, in 1903 160 Aguairenda Chiriguanos left the mission, leading to a net decrease in population despite nine more births than deaths recorded that year. Two years later 105 Indians returned to the mission and births exceeded deaths by five. Again, migration proved to be more important. The changes in population in the early twentieth century were due to the poor harvests suffered between 1896 and 1905, during which famine and epidemics led to widespread migration throughout the region. Even so, the population decline of Aguairenda from 706 Indians in 1878 to 160 in 1912 must be attributed to emigration. Aguairenda was also located next to the main road connecting Santa Cruz de la Sierra, the main eastern Bolivian town, and the Argentine border, making flight easy. If there had been no net emigration, the population of Aguairenda in 1912 should have stood at 711 Indians, or about the same level as in 1878. (See table 5.) This long-term trend was typical for the other Chiriguano missions as well.

In Aguairenda, the absolute numbers of net migrants diminished over the three decades for which we have data. Nevertheless, since the population of the mission diminished so rapidly, the proportion of population decline from migration increased, though slightly. (See table 6.) This pattern can be seen more clearly in the case of Santa Rosa de Cuevo, where during the 1890s the mission lost 23 Indians to emigration, while the following decade 419 Chiriguanos left the mission permanently.[18]

Similar trends can be detected on other missions. Machareti was the most vibrant, and most populous, mission, where indigenous authority remained strong under the leadership of Mandeponay until his death in 1922. If no one had migrated after 1877 and births and deaths had remained the same, the population would have increased by 1,493 individuals. However, migration left a net deficit of 2,844, reducing the population of the mission to approximately 1,500 individuals by 1913.[19] (See table 7.)

During the late 1870s more migrants entered Machareti than left it, but by the 1880s the situation had reversed. In the first two decades of the twentieth century departures increased dramatically; by the second decade more than 1,500 Chiriguanos had disappeared from the mission. (See table 8.) Although there is no detailed information for subsequent decades, the increasing laments of the missionaries and government officials suggest that emigration continued to worsen.

The manuscript for the 1900 census for Machareti also confirms the hypothesis that emigration was the most important factor in population decline. A population pyramid shows that young Chiriguano males between the ages of eleven and twenty, who were most likely to migrate, were absent from the mission in unusual numbers and in a higher proportion than young women of the same age. Whereas between the ages six and fifteen, there was a surplus of boys over girls, between the ages sixteen and thirty there were more women than men present at the mission.[20] (See table 9.) Disease also played a role, but to a lesser extent. The small numbers of boys and girls in the age group eleven to fifteen are probably due primarily to an unknown epidemic that hit Machareti in 1891. (The high

TABLE 5. Mortality and migration on Mission Aguairenda, 1878–1913

Year	Total	Change	Infant baptisms	Burials	Population increase/decrease	Immigration/emigration
1878	706		100	87	+13	
1879	624	−82	21	15	+6	−88
1880	660	+36	23	21	+2	+34
1882	698	+38	75	47	+28	+10
1883	645	−53	27	16	+11	−64
1885	579	−66	39	51	−12	−63
1886	550	−29	48	47	+1	−30
1887	548	−2	43	33	+10	−12
1889 Feb.	538	−10	37	51	−14	+4
1889 Nov.	520	−18	22	20	+2	−20
1891	439	−19	20	18	+2	−21
1892	435	−4	44	49	−5	−1
1894	440	+5	42	25	+17	−12
1896	382	−58	49	50	−1	−57
1897	270	−112	20	137	−117	+5
1898 Jan.	271	+1	19	7	+12	−11
1898 Dec.	274	+3	16	18	−2	+5
1899	223	−51	14	16	−2	−49
1901	260	+37	35	42	−7	+44
1903	109	−151	21	12	+9	−160
1904	103	−6	13	15	−2	−4
1905	213	+110	13	8	+5	+105
1906	178	−35	19	0	+19	−54
1908	168	−10	13	24	−11	+1
1909	176	+8	16	12	+4	+4
1910	147	−29	19	20	−1	−28
1912	160	+13	24	19	+5	+8
1913	120	−40	N/A	N/A		

Source: "Santas Visitas: Aguairenda, 1878–1913," AFT.

TABLE 6. Percentage of population decline due to emigration in Mission Aguairenda, 1879–1912

Years	Net migration	Percentage decline
1879–1889	−229	32
1890–1899	−147	33
1900–1912	−79	39

Source: "Santas Visitas: Aguairenda, 1878–1913," AFT.

number of burials in 1892 are in all likelihood from the deaths among warriors during the rebellion on both sides of the conflict.) In this age group the higher number of girls is due to the migration of the older boys from the mission. A similar pattern can be seen for the subsequent age group, the prime target group for labor contractors looking for healthy young males.

Where did the Chiriguanos go? The young men (principally) escaped the missions to go to work for landowners outside of the mission, wandered into the small towns of the Bolivian frontier, or left for the sugarcane fields of Jujuy province in northern Argentina. In the early twentieth century labor contractors also drafted some young men to work in the rubber regions of the Beni region to the north. It is difficult to quantify the importance of the different migration streams, though qualitative evidence suggests the overwhelming importance of northern Argentina by the late nineteenth century.

Migration to Argentina became more important over time. In 1873 the main concern of the missionaries was "vagrancy," which resulted in the missions losing population "day by day." The friar in charge of Chimeo mission proposed to remedy this by having "the fugitives who wander[ed] about various points of the province" brought back.[21] By the 1880s, however, the main concern was emigration to Argentina. Reflecting this concern, in 1886 the missionary of Macharetí prohibited migration to that country. The friars mentioned escape to other parts of Bolivia, though to a lesser extent. In 1896, for example, in Macharetí the missionary complained that many Indians refused to live permanently on the mission, "moving from one place to another" so as not to give up their children to the mission schools. The following year he lamented that converts went to live on haciendas and in independent Chiriguano villages. After 1900

TABLE 7. Mortality and migration on Mission Macharetí, 1877–1913

Year	Total population	Change	Infant baptisms	Burials	Increase/ decrease	Immigration/ emigration
1877	2,694		67	58	+9	
1879	2,948	+154	72	64	+8	+146
1881	3,114	+166	110	17	+93	+73
1882	4,116	+1,002	70	12	+58	+944
1883	3,499	−617	173	1	+172	−789
1885	3,689	+190	104	12	+82	+108
1886	3,957	+286	166	79	+87	+181
1887	3,526	−431	140	71	+69	−500
1888	3,500	−26	125	63	+62	−88
1890 Jan.	3,500	0	127	60	+67	−67
1890 Sept.	3,577	+77	31	24	+7	+70
1891	2,852	−725	181	128	+53	−778
1892	2,809	−41	111	176	−65	+24
1894 Jan.	2,729	−80	97	59	+38	−118
1894 Nov.	2,805	+76	30	28	+2	+74
1896 Jan.	2,388	−417	34	30	+4	−421
1896 Dec.	2,506	+118	50	33	+17	+101
1897	2,507	+1	56	55	+1	0
1899	2,488	−59	112	46	+66	−125
1900	2,580	+32	119	67	+52	−20
1901	3,137	+557	364	125	+239	+318
1903	2,045	−1,092	98	92	+6	−1,086
1904	1,405	−640	133	28	+105	−745
1905	1,598	+193	27	15	+12	+181
1906	1,635	+37	120	192	−72	+109
1907	1,413	−222	95	26	+69	−291
1909	1,380	−33	134	43	+91	−124
1910	1,450	+70	75	31	+44	+26
1912	1,300	−150	105	56	+49	−199
1913	1,500	+200	85	27	+58	+142

Source: "Santas Visitas: Macharetí, 1877–1913," AFT.

TABLE 8. Net migration in Mission Macharetí, 1879–1913

Years	Number of migrants
1877–1879	+146
1880–1889	−71
1890–1899	−1,240
1900–1913	−1,688

Source: "Santas Visitas: Macharetí, 1877–1913," AFT.

TABLE 9. Males and females on Mission Macharetí, 1900

Age	Males	Females	Male to female ratio
0–5	173	175	0.9886
6–10	180	153	1.1765
11–15	103	91	1.1319
16–20	64	85	0.7529
21–30	164	183	0.8962
31–40	126	118	1.0678
41–50	88	88	1.0000
51–60	74	67	1.1045
61–70	59	70	0.8429
71–80	5	15	0.3333
81+	2	3	0.6666

Source: "Padrón de la Misión de Macharetí Censo 1. formado por el P. Columbano Ma Puccetti 1900," APM.

migration to Argentina took on almost exclusive importance in the annual reports to the convent in Tarija. That year, after a great effort to return Chiriguano men from the towns of Caiza and Yacuiba, a number of married women in Machareti remained without their spouses, who had not returned from Argentina.[22]

Indian Labor and Economic Development in Northern Argentina

To understand how this demand for Chiriguano mission labor evolved, it is crucial to examine the development of the northern Argentine sugar industry and its labor demands.[23] Chiriguano laborers migrated almost exclusively to the sugarcane fields of Jujuy and Salta provinces in Argentina, located in the lush low valleys bordering the Argentine Chaco region. By the late colonial period the Spanish had taken these valleys from the Mataco and Toba ethnic groups. To consolidate their conquest, in 1794 they established the town of San Ramón de la Nueva Orán in the Zenta valley (Salta province). By the early nineteenth century the Zenta valley was producing sugarcane, though less than a thousand *arrobas* annually.[24] During the wars for independence and into the 1840s the valleys remained economically stagnant. The Argentine elites consolidated their hold over the state in the late nineteenth century. Three military expeditions into the Argentine Chaco, in 1872, 1884, and 1911, finally brought the region under state control.[25]

By the 1850s the sugar economy had grown. In the Zenta valley the estates produced three thousand arrobas of sugar and a similar amount of cane juice. Landowners turned most of the crop into cane alcohol for internal consumption within the region.[26] In the San Francisco valley (Jujuy province) Hacienda Ledesma (founded in 1830) produced six thousand arrobas of sugar in 1857, while Hacienda San Pedro (founded in 1844) produced one thousand. However, production remained restricted because of primitive machinery, transport difficulties, and weak tariff protection against foreign sugar imports.[27]

The most serious bottleneck was the continual lack of workers, particularly during the cane harvest season, when the plantations' labor demands shot up dramatically. During the late colonial period the landowners had considered importing large numbers of African slaves but were unable to acquire sufficient numbers. The highland Indians and Creoles from the Andean valleys to the west refused to descend to the low, hot valleys where sugarcane was grown. In the early nineteenth century, the few workers on the estates were largely Creole. By the 1840s the sugar planters had begun to use large numbers of Mataco and Chiriguano workers for seasonal labor. In 1841 Hacienda Misión de Zenta employed 140 Chaco Indians as well as 35 Creoles. Likewise, Ledesma used 50 Chiriguanos and 300 Matacos for its harvest in 1857.[28]

Because of the earlier experience with African slaves, Indians from Bolivia were bought and sold for work on the plantations (also called haciendas) in the first half of the nineteenth century. In 1844 the prefect of Tarija (Bolivia) claimed, "A considerable number of young Indians [*cambitas*] of both sexes are extracted for Orán, either through selling [them] or through other sinister means." He sent a military commander to the border with Orán to prevent this commerce in Indians, claiming, "This type of traffic is entirely contrary to the system of liberty."[29]

By the 1850s greater prosperity on the plantations and the ability to provide positive incentives had lessened coercion. In 1853 a delegation of Chiriguanos from Tartagal arrived in Orán asking for six square leagues of land in the Chaco in return for serving as allies to the settlers. Although the Creoles did not take them up on the offer, by this time some Chiriguanos had settled on some sugar estates and worked there during the harvest season. According to contemporary accounts, this migration was voluntary.[30]

By the 1850s the pattern of seasonal migration to the sugar plantations had begun to crystallize. According to one contemporary observer, in 1856 large numbers of Chiriguanos of their own accord came to work in the sugarcane harvest in Ledesma, San Lorenzo, and Campo Santo in Salta and Jujuy provinces. They especially enjoyed the *guarapo*, or sugar juice, produced on the primitive sugar mills. The other major Indian ethnic group to work in the fields was the Matacos.[31]

Thus all the components of the system that was to last into the early twentieth century were in place. Labor contractors, later called *enganchadores* as in the rest of Latin America, enticed the Indians from their villages to the haciendas, for which they received a reward per head. Rather than money, the plantations paid the Indians in goods. The *capitán* kept his people from leaving and maintained some semblance of labor discipline. The landlord was careful to pay the chief something extra at the end of his stay to provide him with an incentive to return the following season.

Labor statistics show the importance of the Indians and, in particular, of the Chiriguanos in the labor system of the sugar plantations.[32] In 1856 more than one thousand Indians worked in the sugarcane harvest, in addition to the Matacos and resident Chiriguanos who lived on the plantations as permanent workers. In 1900 approximately 40 percent of all Chiriguanos in Bolivia lived on the missions. Since mission Indians had fewer constraints placed on their leaving than those on Bolivian haciendas, it is likely that mission Indians constituted a larger proportion of the labor force, perhaps half, of the Chiriguanos on the *ingenios* (plantation complexes).

Labor demand for Indians increased after 1870, when the sugar estates began to modernize their machinery. Although machines usually substitute for labor in most industries, here the new machinery created more jobs because the new equipment created a much better product than more primitive methods. The modernization of the northern Argentine ingenios also inaugurated a vast expansion of the market for Argentine sugar. As in Tucumán province a little earlier, the sugar planters of Salta and Jujuy were responding to the introduction of railroads and the opening up of the vast markets of the Argentine Littoral for their products.[33] In what has been called the "age of the ingenio," the sugarcane fields expanded rapidly into the lush brush forest of the eastern valleys and so required more laborers to harvest the cane. In the case of Salta and Jujuy, this meant principally capturing workers over a larger region of the Chaco.[34]

Sugar cultivation has large seasonal swings in demand for labor. For about three to four months, the harvest season required many workers for cutting the cane, bringing it quickly to the ingenio, and processing it. The amount of sugar extracted depended on the ability of the planters to harvest in the weeks when the cane was the ripest. Also important was how fast the cane could be processed, for the amount of juice extracted after the cane was harvested diminished by the hour. As a result, the harvest season (in Argentina, from about May to October) was a period of intense work. Afterward labor demands dropped precipitously, to about a fifth to a quarter of that of the harvest season.

The ingenios met increased labor demand by augmenting their migratory workforce force of Indians. In 1904 on one of the largest ingenios, La Esperanza, between 800 and 1,000 Creoles were permanent workers on the estate, whereas only 400 Chiriguanos remained all year. During the harvest season, the number of Indians on La Esperanza increased to between 2,000 and 2,500. In turn, the number of Creoles increased by about 50 percent, to 1,500 workers.[35] The best data come from 1914; unfortunately, this was an exceptional year, when fewer Indians than usual found work because of the recession caused by the start of the First World War.

La Esperanza attracted 1,288 Indians, of whom almost 60 percent were Chiriguanos, 35 percent Matacos, and the rest Tobas and Andeans from the Jujuy highlands. Altogether, about 15,000 seasonal workers came for the sugarcane harvest in Jujuy province alone. Most were indigenous peoples from the Chaco or the Andean foothills. In 1916, 2,803 Indians arrived at Ledesma, consisting almost evenly of Matacos and Chiriguanos (almost 40 percent each), and about 20 percent peasants from the Andean highlands.[36] If these percentages correspond roughly to those of the region as a whole (which is very likely), a large majority of Indians, about evenly divided between Chiriguanos and Matacos, came to the ingenios as seasonal laborers.

The Chiriguano agriculturists were much more highly valued laborers than the hunting-and-gathering Chaco peoples such as the Matacos or Tobas. The planters valued them because they worked better at agricultural tasks and because they were perceived to be closer to nineteenth-century European ideas of civilized human beings. In 1856 Benjamín Villafañe asserted, "In one word, the Mataco is almost [a] savage in all aspects; the Chiriguano is almost civilized in the same measure." Likewise, in 1904 the Argentine labor inspector Juan Bialet y Massé claimed, "The Chiriguano is irreplaceable in digging work and in refining [*la labor*]."[37]

Chiriguanos also numbered among the permanent workers in the ingenios. Marcelo and Ana Lagos have shown that in 1914 out of the almost one thousand laborers working in the sugar mill itself, the only Indians working there, constituting 56 percent of the total, were the Chiriguanos.[38] Since they were agriculturists Chiriguanos were less likely to disappear into the Chaco and live off the land. This is why they worked in positions requiring greater skills. Until the conquest of the Argentine Chaco, the ethnic groups such as the Tobas and Matacos residing there, living in a hunting-and-gathering economy, contracted themselves out when the Chaco provided few food resources. Once the fruits of the Chaco could be gathered, the Indians left even when the sugar estates tried to keep them by not paying them the full amount owed. At the ingenios, members of most Chaco ethnic groups were not very diligent workers. According to one observer in 1908, Mataco men and women on Hacienda San Lorenzo, near La Esperanza, worked on average only twelve and a half and eleven and a half days a month, respectively. Labor discipline was a constant problem that was never completely resolved.[39]

Labor Migration: Voluntary or Coerced?

Migration specialists have analyzed population movements, particularly across international borders, for quite some time and have developed a specialized vocabulary to deal with why certain peoples migrated. One of the most important concepts is that of "push" or "pull." Specialists view migration as a dialectic between reasons for going someplace versus leaving the particular place migrants came from. In other words, migrants have complex rationales for migrating, in which either the attractiveness of the new place or the poor conditions of the old predominate.

Pull factors were more important for the Chiriguanos than push factors. Unlike the Chaco tribes such as the Matacos and the Tobas who were increasingly coerced to work by the Argentine army, the Chiriguanos migrated voluntarily. The slave-like conditions in Argentina in the 1840s had disappeared by the second half of that century. The Bolivian government tried to stop the emigration of Indians to the neighboring country. The government worried that Bolivian landowners (who did not generally treat the Chiriguanos well) would lose their labor force.

Both government officials and Franciscan missionaries accused each other of fostering Chiriguano emigration. In 1872, the missionaries refused the blandishments of an *enganchador* to pay one peso for each Indian sent to Argentina. The first governmental permission to let Chiriguanos go to Argentina comes from the Tarija prefect, Manuel Othon Jofré, who in 1875 felt that sending the mission Chiriguanos to the sugar plantations of Argentina would bring about "the habit of work." *Enganchadores* from Salta and Jujuy went to the Bolivian missions (and probably independent Chiriguano villages) to request workers for the harvest. By the mid-1880s, friars and officials alike had second thoughts and tried to curtail the traffic. They worried about the economic effect of losing so many laborers. The Franciscans also were concerned that the mission Indians would forget the lessons they had taught them.[40] Between 1905 and 1908 the Tarija prefect again permitted the export of Chiriguano mission workers for building the railroad to the Bolivian border, although this was exceptional in an era of increasing restrictions on emigration. The regulations of 1905 for the first time officially committed to paper that one of the missions' primary goals was to contain Indian emigration. Thereafter, the debate over the utility of the Franciscan missions among the Chiriguanos became intimately linked to the emigration issue. In the 1920s, as the problem of the loss of Chiriguano workers did not abate, the authorities hoped that jobs with Standard Oil Company, which was drilling for oil in the region, would keep the Indians home. However, Standard Oil employed mainly Argentines and apparently had little impact on the Chiriguano work force.[41]

The problem of Chiriguano emigration was very serious for the missions. Migration initially was seasonal, but became increasingly permanent as more Chiriguanos experienced life and work in Argentina. According to Fr. Santiago Romano, the mission prefect in 1907, "from age ten to fifty, seventy percent [of Chiriguanos] annually abandon their mission, to pass to the Argentine haciendas and of these, twenty percent do not return to the mission of their origin." This statement almost certainly exaggerated the extent of seasonal migration, though perhaps not the percentage of those who did not return. We have hard numbers for 1911, when 1,020 (out of about 4,500) Indians from the Tarija missions left for Argentina; only 450 returned the same year.[42] The large-scale emigration must have been disheartening to the friars, especially since they tried hard to prevent it. In 1923 the Tarija prefect lamented that Chaco and O'Connor provinces, the two provinces where the Indians resided, "find themselves abandoned to a large degree by the Chiriguano tribes that inhabit them."[43]

Why did the Chiriguanos leave the missions and go to Argentina if they had requested the missions as a refuge from the depredations of the settlers? There were important push factors. As discussed in chapter 5, the increasing restrictions on the missions drove many Indians to leave, a "secondary form of resistance," as Robert Jackson and Edward Castillo have called it.[44] Other factors were the locust plagues and droughts that afflicted the missions at the turn of the century. During these natural disasters, the Indians left their homes to scavenge elsewhere for food. The missionaries, especially during the long subsistence crisis at the turn of the century, let their Indians go to find food.[45] Many decided to go to Argentina instead where they could work and not suffer from hunger.

Although push factors were important, the predominance of northern Argentina as the destination of the Chiriguanos can be attributed primarily to pull factors. Despite the fact that in Argentina the Chiriguanos received lower wages than Creole workers and that they were probably often cheated given their illiteracy, the wages and benefits the Indians received there were still much higher than in Bolivia. The Indians received much of their wages in goods, not money. They also received daily food rations during their stay. As discussed above, the Indians also invariably received something at the end of their stay, whether it be a piece of cloth, a hat, a knife, a mule, or other such item.[46]

The enganchadores frequently requested mission Indians from the Franciscans, as many letters preserved in the mission archives attest.[47] When the missionaries did not accede to the enganchadores' requests, they went behind the friars' backs and obtained workers directly from the Indian chiefs (also called *capitanes*). By the late nineteenth century many capitanes had turned into enganchadores themselves. After traveling to the sugar estates the first few times, they made their deals directly with the owners. The best example was Mandeponay, the mburuvicha of Macharetí, and the most powerful chief among the Chiriguanos. The earliest mention of Mandeponay traveling to Argentina as capitán comes from 1884. The friars were scandalized by this development and attempted from 1889 to 1891 to depose Mandeponay from his position as traditional chief in Macharetí. However, they proved unsuccessful, in part due to the intervention of the administrator of the La Esperanza ingenio in Jujuy, who wrote Mandeponay a letter of recommendation and used his considerable weight with Bolivian authorities to support the chief. When the friars attempted to get rid of Mandeponay again in 1904, he and his son owed the La Esperanza ingenio, owned by the Leach brothers, 15,000 Bolivianos for anticipated *enganche* fees. The missionaries failed to oust Mandeponay, largely because local authorities backed the old chief as well.[48] His oldest son, José María Napoleón Tacu, also engaged in this traffic. According to a 1914 report, Tacu received cattle, fence wire, and money from the Leach Brothers estate. At one point the ingenio paid for Tacu's excursion to Buenos Aires.[49]

By this time Bolivian government authorities were also directly involved in the enganche of Indians, as the mission prefect, Fr. Gervacio Costa, asserted in 1902.[50] It is also not unlikely that the Bolivian consul in Jujuy also received money from the sugar estate owners; in 1905 an enganchador wrote to the mission prefect, claiming to have authorization from the consul to take some Indians.[51] The collusion of local Bolivian officials in labor recruitment for Argentina helps explain the support Mandeponay received from these men in his struggle with the friars.

It might be argued that once the capitanes and local authorities became enganchadores, migration to Argentina became less voluntary and more of an obligation for the majority of Chiriguanos. Be that as it may, it is clear that certain individuals, including the chiefs and enganchadores, profited much more than the common Indian from this traffic. However, the evidence contradicts any hypothesis of increasing coercion for the Chiriguanos. Most compelling in this respect were the attitudes of the Chiriguanos themselves. The Indians felt Argentina to be a place of wonder, with an abundance of highly desirable things not readily available on the Bolivian frontier. They brought back many wonderful things, such as knives, old uniforms, sugar, matches, and aniline dyes, among other items. In addition, they were able to do things not possible in their own country. For example, Maringay, the capitán of the Ingre Chiriguanos, asked Erland Nordenskiöld, the Swedish anthropologist, whether Argentina had stores where white women could be bought. He was referring to the houses of prostitution in the towns of northern Argentina. In Bolivia, Indian men were not permitted to enter brothels.[52]

The Chiriguanos had a special word for northern Argentina, *Mbaporenda*, "the place where there is work." The term implied not just the ability to get work, but also of a place where Chiriguanos received good treatment. Many Indians obtained new goods through their work on the ingenios, unlike on the debt peonage-based Bolivian haciendas. The idea of Mbaporenda had a unique hold on the Chiriguanos' imagination—one anthropologist has likened it to the idea of *Kandire*, or the mythical paradise of Guaraní culture where everything grew in abundance, where anything could be had, and where no one ever had to suffer from hunger.[53] One government official, General Carlos Villegas, in an effort to find out how to stop the flow of Indians, in 1914 asked the Chiriguanos on the Franciscan missions why they migrated to Argentina. Their response summarized neatly the idea of Mbaporenda and showed the voluntary nature of their migration: "Today for the Indian the supreme aspiration constitutes going to Argentine Republic, where he sees new things that calls his attention and which he calls *Baporenda* [sic], which means land of work, and to go there they escape their homes and no reason can keep them. They abandon their wives and children, as well as their fields and the few cattle they might possess."[54]

To counteract this powerful attraction, the friars on the missions tried to keep the young men home by marrying them off at an early age; nevertheless, according to Villegas, a friar told him that "there have been Indians who left for Argentina the day following the wedding, abandoning his [sic] bride."[55] Perhaps more than Kandire, northern Argentina represented for the Chiriguanos an alternative to what many Chiriguanos viewed as the oppressive conditions of the missions (or, indeed, of the haciendas). As the capitanes achieved greater power through their connection with the enganchadores or directly with the sugar estates, and as the missionaries consolidated their power on the missions as the Christian population increased, places where the Chiriguanos could attain a greater measure of freedom became more attractive. Abandoning an oppressive chief (or an increasingly oppressive missionary) was consonant with Guaraní political culture that valued individual liberty and consensual power. By migrating, the post-conquest Chiriguanos were acting upon their impulse to maintain, in Clastrian terms, a "society against the state."⁵⁶

Contemporary observers realized that going to northern Argentina was more than just an attempt to find higher wages. General Villegas grasped this when he reported:

> They say that they go to find better paid work, but my observations have made [me] see that the customs acquired in the Argentine Republic have brought about a desire to go there to enjoy the greatest liberty, to get drunk to their satisfaction, to frequent the prostitution houses and to work only when it pleases them, obtaining after a long period of work a horse or mare to mount, or firearms—rifle or shotgun—for which they have a predilection.⁵⁷

The missionaries understood the reason for migrating as well, but interpreted the Chiriguanos' behavior somewhat differently. As early as 1873 the Tarija mission prefect charged that "these Indians are too *bandoleros*, and their principal tendency is to wander." He proposed controlling his charges even more, which had just the opposite effect of what he desired.⁵⁸ Moreover, the missionaries complained bitterly and frequently about the behavior of the Indians once they returned from working in the sugar plantations. In 1871, for example, the same friar

> had seen with his own eyes that the Indian, who shows up [at the missions] with only his overflowing passions, as individuals born and raised in the middle of the woods, return always with double capacity for insubordination and evil, because of the bad examples that they see, and the wantonness that they observe in the men [who are] vagabonds, use bad language, and [do] nothing good to edify and help these unhappy [Indians], already by themselves so weak and inclined towards evil.⁵⁹

The friars maintained this opinion about migration's negative impact over the years.⁶⁰ These complaints indicate the contradictory motives of the friars and the Indians. Whereas the missionaries attempted to "civilize" the Chiriguanos by teaching them docility and obedience as the increasingly hierarchical Catholic Church dictated, the Chiriguanos migrated when the friars became too restrictive. When the Indians returned to the mission, they refused to submit to the Franciscans' highly paternalistic regime. In many cases what the friars termed insubordination was probably the Chiriguanos' insistence on being treated as equals rather than as weak-willed yet temperamental children. The friars maintained their paternalistic image in order to justify the mission's enterprise.[61]

Effects of Migration

The effects of migration to Argentina for the indigenous population on the missions were both good and bad, though this depended on the observer's perspective. The young Chiriguano men were delighted to see another part of the world and finally earn money that provided them access to goods that they could only dream of acquiring on the missions. In the labor camps of the ingenios of Jujuy the men had much greater freedom and could spend their time the way they wanted to, without the missionaries' constant interference in their personal affairs. Those who escaped from the mission schools were especially relieved to get away from the isolation and drudgery of the weekday, in which the children at times worked more as servants of the missionaries than at learning basic skills or crafts. During the subsistence crises of the turn of the century and in subsequent decades, the Chiriguanos were glad to find a place where they could eat regularly. The missionaries themselves conceded that going to Argentina saved their flock from extinction and provided them with work not available in Bolivia.[62]

Other than during these occasional crises, the friars assumed that the effects of migrating to Argentina were uniformly bad for the mission Indians. The Chiriguanos' choice to switch to drinking sugarcane alcohol (*aguardiente*) on the ingenios, a much more potent drink than the traditional *chicha*, which was made from corn or other crops, was not a very healthy one. Beyond its physical effects, using cane alcohol instead of chicha profoundly altered the indigenous culture. For example, one of the primary functions of women in Chiriguano society was the production of chicha. The quality and the quantity of chicha produced for festivals determined to a large degree the social prestige of the women and their households. Most capitanes among the Chiriguano had many wives so that their households could produce many kettles of chicha for the festivals and other events they sponsored. As the Chiriguano chiefs became enganchadores, however, they also began to use aguardiente in their festivals (did the estate owners perhaps pay them in aguardiente?), and thus diminished women's roles in society.[63]

Women suffered the most as a result of migration to Argentina. The Chiriguanos usually left their women and children at home. This meant that during certain seasons many missions contained mainly old men, women, and children. Most younger men were off to the sugarcane harvest. The Franciscans were largely blind to this seasonal gender imbalance on the mission; at least they did not write about it in those terms. But the ability to keep their families relatively safe on the missions while they were in Argentina must have made establishing residence on the missions attractive to the male migrants, at least in the short term.

In the long term, the absence of the men often presented serious problems for the women, especially in the years when the harvest at home was poor. The lack of men to find food farther afield meant that the families left behind during famine years suffered greatly from hunger. It also made kidnapping of children from female-headed households more likely by labor-hungry Bolivian landowners. Migration also prompted the breakup of family units. Long absences, at times lasting years, made adultery a common problem for both spouses. Wife beating, mutual distrust, and fighting between men upon their return were often the consequences of these illicit unions. Concerned with what they considered affronts to Christian morality, the friars continually complained about these problems.[64]

For the missionaries, emigration to Argentina was frustrating. The young men of the missions left, leaving few to do the daily work of the settlement. The traditional chiefs, such as Mandeponay, who had permitted the establishment of the missions and who in many ways proved to be firm allies (though rarely subordinates of the missionaries, as the friars had hoped), were the worst culprits and actually led their charges to Argentina or at least profited from selling their men's labor.

Most troubling was the disappearance of the school children. The friars attempted to "civilize" them by teaching them Spanish, reading and writing, only to see their charges take off for the border as soon as they were old enough to work. The missionaries saw that they were training the Indians not for a life of Christian compliance and selfless work for the economic and spiritual betterment of the Bolivian nation, but for the debauchery of the Argentine ingenios. In the long term, migration did more to undermine the mission system than disease. Even those Indians who returned eventually threatened the underpinnings of obedience and the sense of strict Catholic morality that the friars had tried to instill in them. The Franciscans created the need for goods (such as European-style clothes) when they "civilized" the Indians. In creating these needs that could be satisfied with migration, the friars were reaping what they were sowing in the decline of their missions, though in ways they had not expected.

Conclusion

The Franciscan missions among the Chiriguanos in the republican period differed substantially from colonial missions. The mission populations of southeastern Bolivia exhibited a typical preindustrial pattern of high mortality combined with sufficient fertility to offset the endemic diseases that preyed especially on the young. Periodic outbreaks of epidemic disease did occur and led to high death rates. However, by the early twentieth century one of the deadliest diseases, smallpox, had been brought under at least partial control by periodically vaccinating the mission population. Indeed, beginning at the turn of the century, other types of disasters such as drought and locust plagues that brought about famine had greater impact on the mission Indian population. Famine did not so much kill the Indians, as push them out of the region and into the sugarcane fields of northern Argentina. Thus, these natural disasters brought about migration to Argentina, exacerbating a trend that had begun by the middle of the nineteenth century.

Migration weakened the missions. Able-bodied men were most likely to leave, depriving the missions of prime laborers. The returning migrants brought problems back with them, such as alcoholism, new perspectives on mission life, and an unwillingness to follow the rules set by the friars. Absenteeism exacerbated problems among spouses and split families. Much of what the friars had so laboriously taught the children in the schools appeared to be for naught. As time went on, the missions began to resemble in large part reservoirs of women, children, and old men who remained after many of the younger men had left. For the Franciscans, migration meant mission failure.

Conversely, the Chiriguano men enjoyed their time in a foreign land and felt better compensated for their work. They gained access to goods, experiences, and knowledge not available on the Bolivian frontier. Their women and children were relatively safe on the missions, certainly safer than in independent villages. In the long term, migration weakened the Chiriguano family and created problems over authority with the missionaries and also probably with the traditional chiefs. As with many other things on the missions, the issues of cultural and economic survival were complex. Demographic patterns and migration provide some insight into these complexities.

CHAPTER FOUR

Daily Life and the Development of Mission Culture

In 1883 José Manuel Yandori, a mission Indian from Aguairenda, was a man in much demand. He had learned the art of making mud bricks during his youth in the mission school. His skill came in handy that year. He worked for wages and was constantly busy building and repairing houses in the neófito section of the mission, where the friars had him and his companions construct new houses in neat rows for the growing number of recently married neophyte couples. He also worked off the mission. The newly appointed national delegate, Dr. Daniel Campos, had in mind launching an expedition into the interior of the Chaco. He needed skilled workmen such as Yandori to construct forts and barracks at Colonia Crevaux. It was a location well known to Yandori, even if only in name. He, like the other Aguairenda Chiriguanos, knew the place as Teyu, one of the principal settlements of the Toba Indians on the Pilcomayo River. The fiery Italian missionary in charge of Aguairenda, Fr. Doroteo Giannecchini, had already sent Yandori various times to do Campos's bidding, though Yandori had to complain to the Franciscan to get the delegate to pay the pesos he had been promised by the government. By September of that year Yandori had had enough of that kind of work and left the mission for Caraparí, an old Creole settlement. Perhaps, after a suitable rest, he could work a bit in town and for higher pay before returning to his family in Aguairenda. This did not sit well with the missionary. With skilled laborers such as Yandori scarce, Giannecchini tracked the Indian down. After he found him, he asked local officials to arrest him and send him back to the frontier fort. By this time Yandori had fallen ill and so was not required to work under the strenuous conditions of the frontier.[1]

Almost a generation later, in early 1907, Zoila, a Chiriguano teenager in Machareti, was unhappy. She was tired of the excessive regimentation of the mission school, which she attended with about 150 other girls. Not only did she have to get up at five o'clock in the morning and prepare food for her teacher and the missionaries, and then go to classes, punctuated by devotions to the saints, but the female teachers in charge of the school never let her and her classmates out of sight. Zoila was interested in boys, but the friars frowned on her even speaking to the young men who took classes in the neighboring building. One night she stole the keys from the schoolmistress and let some Chiriguano boys into the girls' dormitory. One of the teachers discovered the boys and sent them packing. The teachers punished Zoila and she began to hate even more being cooped up in the mission school.

Later that year famine threatened. To ease the burden of feeding so many people the missionaries decided to let any children with relatives elsewhere leave the mission. Zoila took this opportunity to move in with Amerani, her godfather, and his family in Carandaiti, a Creole frontier outpost. She fell in love with a young Creole settler and briefly moved into his shack, but her godfather found out and sent her back to Machareti, appalled that she would take up with a karai. After getting a taste of the wider world Zoila could no longer stand the mission school and attempted to escape. The missionary found her, whipped her, cut off her beautiful long dark hair, and put her in the stocks. Finally she escaped to the town of Villamontes and denounced her mistreatment to local authorities.[2]

These stories show that daily life on the Franciscan missions in southeastern Bolivia varied across time and space and affected different mission Indians differently. Each mission had its own patterns of daily life based on the location and ethnic composition of its population. Women experienced the missions differently from men, as did children in contrast to adults. Moreover, economic activity and demographic behavior varied according to the phases of the mission cycle. Life during the rapid building of the mission church in the foundation of the mission and the frequent war parties sent out to attack villages opposing the new missions in the establishment phase was very different from life during the consolidation period, when the mission's primary concerns were the migrants to the sugar harvest in the plantations of Jujuy and the maintenance of the houses where the converted Indians lived. Space and time constitute two dimensions that differentiated the daily mission experience; after all, Yandori's experiences were rather different from Zoila's.

To show the multiplicity of mission experiences, I have broken down the mission population into unconverted Indians, schoolchildren, adult neófitos, and Indian women. The last category, of course, encompasses members of some of the other groups, but because of their importance and their unique position women on the missions must be treated as a separate category. Of course, there were also other individuals who inhabited the Franciscan missions at one time or another, such as small numbers of mestizo settlers, petty merchants, government officials, and soldiers. These nonnatives are treated in other parts of the book.

Unconverted Indians

As we have seen, over the life of most missions the unconverted population constituted by far the largest segment of mission residents. Other than in Machareti, they lived in a separate section of the mission, in houses they built themselves in a traditional wattle and daub style, with the four corners anchored by large branches and walls made of wooden branches pushed into the earth and then covered with mud. The Indians also placed a few central posts for the gable, then covered the roof beams with straw or grass, protecting the inhabitants from everything but the hardest rains.[3]

In most cases, the nuclear family formed the basic kinship unit within the house. Most families consisted of two adults, one of each sex, with their respective children. Some young couples did not have children but still lived in their own house. Some older couples lived alone since their children had paired off and left their parents' home. This was the case in Machareti, where the census from 1900 reveals that out of 527 households of unconverted Chiriguanos, a bit less than 10 percent, or 44, consisted of a couple without children. Of that number, 10 were young couples who had recently married or whose children had died; these couples tended to be in their early twenties or late teens. Twenty-three households consisted of couples over the age of fifty who probably had married children who had moved into separate houses. Only 7 households consisted of childless couples whose ages fluctuated between thirty and forty-nine.[4] In other words, most households contained mother, father, and children. No one lived alone. In many cases, the households contained members of the nuclear family. This was so in 116 households, less than a quarter of the total. Widowed parents (most frequently women) often lived with their children. Dislocations due to wars and famines brought other relatives to the household, such as sisters, brothers, uncles, and aunts.

Some households in Machareti were polygynous; in seven families the male head of household had what the friars referred to as "concubines." Female-headed households were virtually nonexistent. Where this occurred the woman of the household was almost certainly one of the multiple wives of a great chief. Mandeponay, for example, had six wives living outside of his principal household, of whom five lived in separate houses with their children by the mburuvicha. Only one of Mandeponay's wives, a woman of forty-five, lived with other mission Indians; she shared a house with a couple and their three children. Two other chiefs had their second wives live in separate houses as well.[5] In all, the census records only ten men who had more than one wife. This is probably a low estimate, since it is likely that the Indians tried to hide this arrangement from the friars. After all, the friars frowned on polygyny even among the unconverted and tried to wipe out this practice.

The unconverted Indians lived in "streets" or *alcaldías* controlled by different tubichas, probably based upon political structures that reflected the divisions into villages or subdivisions within villages prior to the establishment of the missions. Thus in Machareti the unconverted had at least three subdivisions: Mandeponay's Street, Alcaldía III, and Cundeye's Street. Cundeye was the brother of Mandeponay. We have other sources to confirm this system of spatial organization based on chiefly lineages. Slightly less than a decade earlier, Manuel Jofré's report claimed, "The neófitos and the heathen are separated by streets, and these [latter] in sections of the soldados of the Capitán Mandeponai and others of those of the second chiefs Güirangay and Guaruyu."[6] As we will see in subsequent chapters, this residential division mirrored to a large extent the political structure of the mission, for the friars ruled only indirectly, through the traditional chiefs, in the unconverted section of the mission.

In all missions the houses were organized in long rows, with the streets reflecting the European emphasis on a grid plan favored in urban planning. The photographic evidence we have from the largest missions, such as Machareti, Santa Rosa, Tarairí, Ivo, and San Antonio, suggest this type of organization. (See figures 3, 4.) In other, older missions, such as Itau and Chimeo, the houses were arranged in less orderly fashion. In all cases, the settlements usually centered on plazas, which in Chiriguano, other missions such as the colonial Chiquitos missions, and Mediterranean cultures were the social centers of the settlements.

Unlike Chiriguano custom, most missions contained two plazas, one in the center of the section where the unconverted Indians lived and one for the neophytes. There were only two exceptions. In Machareti, where

FIGURE 3. Macharetí mission, the largest of all the Franciscan missions and home of Mandeponay and Cundeye. It was located at the margins of the Chaco and was an important meeting place between Chiriguanos and Chaco peoples. Note the regular spacing of the houses and the organization into streets. Also note the large central plaza. This view is from the hillock upon which the parish house, church, and schools were located. *Source*: Doroteo Giannecchini and Vincenzo Mascio, *Album fotográfico de las Misiones Franciscanas en la República de Bolivia a cargo de los Colegios Apostólicos de Tarija y Potosí 1898* (La Paz: Banco Central de Bolivia and Archivo y Biblioteca Nacionales de Bolivia, 1995).

Mandeponay's great power prevented the division between converted and unconverted, there was only one large central plaza for both converted and unconverted. In Tarairí the Indians lived in houses surrounding three plazas: one for the unconverted, one for those learning Christian rites, and one for the neófitos.

Thus most unconverted Indians lived segregated from their neophyte relatives. The section reserved for those who had not converted consisted mainly of adults. Once the missionaries were able to assert their control over the mission population (which varied widely from mission to mission; see chapter 5), children older than seven spent most of the day in school. Both boys and girls went home for lunch and for dinner. Girls slept in the mission schools; only boys were permitted to live at home.[7] Among the unconverted, a visitor would likely have heard only the cries of infants

FIGURE 4. Mission San Francisco Solano del Pilcomayo. This was a mission for the Tobas and Chiriguanos, located on the Pilcomayo River. Note the regular spacing of the houses, with their porches toward the "streets." The large building in the middle is the church and the school. *Source*: Doroteo Giannecchini and Vincenzo Mascio, *Album fotográfico de las Misiones Franciscanas en la República de Bolivia a cargo de los Colegios Apostólicos de Tarija y Potosí 1898* (La Paz: Banco Central de Bolivia and Archivo y Biblioteca Nacionales de Bolivia, 1995).

and the squeals of small children, except at lunchtime, when their older brothers and sisters added to the cacophony of voices along the long and dusty streets of the mission.[8]

In the nineteenth century unconverted adults wore traditional dress. Men wore a cloth around their middle and, in cold weather, blankets and a thick cloth thrown over their torsos. Men also wore a *tembeta*, a small plug of wood or metal inserted into a hole in the chin made during a coming-of-age ritual. They also wore their hair long, kept under a scarf tied on the head. Unconverted men claimed that those who refused to adorn their chin with a tembeta "looked like women." (See figure 5.) However, by the late nineteenth century at least, most Indian men, even the unconverted, wore European clothing. Only while working in the fields did they return to wearing the more practical loincloth around their genitals.[9] Women's dress changed more slowly. Most unconverted women on the missions wore brightly colored *tirus*, a piece of cloth with armholes that covered their body from the shoulders down to their feet. (See figure 6.)

The men and women of the unconverted section could hear the mission bells at various intervals, calling the neophytes and the schoolchildren to Mass, but they ignored these interruptions. After all, they did not have to go to church or participate in any of the other religious rituals. Only occasionally, during one of the great Christian feasts such as Easter, was it necessary to obey the call of their chiefs to meet in the plaza and listen to the harangues of the friars. Likewise, when an important government functionary happened to pass through the missions, such as Dr. Manuel O. Jofré on his inspection tour in 1893, the unconverted had to line up behind their chiefs at the mission entrance and give the official a proper welcome. In normal times, only on their deathbed or when a new child had to be baptized did the common mission Indian have to bother much with the missionary. Instead, the people living in the unconverted section dealt primarily with their chief and not with the Franciscans who lived in the big house on the top of the hill. The activities in the converted section did not much alter the everyday lives of the unconverted, who were the great majority of the population throughout much of the history of the republican-era missions.

As is natural among farming peoples such as the Chiriguanos, the agricultural cycle, especially for maize, largely determined the way the unconverted Indians spent their time. Although they were primarily corn farmers, the Chiriguanos living at the missions were mindful of the cycles of other crops as well. The Indians on the missions also followed their own agricultural rhythms. Most important was the maize cycle. In November, after a few good, hard rains had softened the earth, the Indian men began to plant their main staple. Although they planted only a few types in great quantities, Fr. Bernardino de Nino counted eleven varieties of corn, having different taste and uses; some matured later than the main varieties to provide staggered harvests. In addition, the Indians planted a variety of beans and squashes (the latter primarily by women) to supplement their diet. On the missions the friars ordered the small fields to be sowed first. After that, the Indians sowed their own fields and then those of the individuals who had no children to help them. For this they used teams of oxen, which the missionaries supplied.[10]

All able-bodied Indians on the mission, men, women, and even children, participated in the corn harvest, which began about three months later, in February, but reached its peak between May and June. The different climate zones of the rugged terrain and different maize types prolonged the harvest for about three months. The corn not eaten immediately was stored in huts built into treetops and used until the following harvest. In the meantime, beans, squashes, and other produce supplemented the mission diet. Chiriguanos were not great hunters or fishermen, unlike other ethnic groups of the Chaco. Instead, the natives developed a taste for beef.[11]

Harvest time was also festival time, as has been the case for millennia among most agricultural peoples. The ava held a fiesta after the harvest, socializing with members of other missions and surrounding Indian villages. The *mbaepiro*, or dry season, was the time for the *arete*, the feast in which the village invited surrounding Chiriguano communities to reaffirm old friendships, discuss alliances, and show off the abilities of the women to make *cangui*, also called chicha or corn beer. The chief first put a large container in front of his house and then exhorted the rest of the village to produce sufficient corn beer for the festival. This action affirmed the tubicha's position within the settlement, since the chief was also obligated, through the female members of the household, to provide large quantities of the beer. While the women ground up the corn, the men went into the forest to cut firewood and hunt game. Within twenty days the women would produce enough cangui for the feast, putting up to three large clay vessels full of corn beer in front of their houses. After sleeping outside the village the night before, the guests, both men and women, entered the village at daybreak, adorned with face paint and wearing their finest clothes. After the youngest jumped over the tubicha's chicha vessel, the drinking began. The older and more respected men of the community sat on benches, while those with little prestige stood or sat on the ground. Women stood apart, keeping very quiet, undoubtedly examining very carefully the participants in the feast.

When most of the guests had arrived, the dancing and singing began. The feast did not end until all the cangui and the food was gone, which usually took a week or more of drinking. Both men and women participated in the drinking, though cooking and cleaning remained the responsibility of the women. For the Chiriguano, the state of drunkenness was good, a heightened state of sociability in which people of different villages became more or less equal and friendly with one another. Other, smaller

FIGURE 5. Chiriguanos from Mission San Pascual de Boicovo in traditional garb and with traditional work tools. Note the tembetas in their chins. They were from Huacaya, the most important center of Chiriguano resistance in the nineteenth century. The original caption claims that they were resting laborers. *Source*: Doroteo Giannecchini and Vincenzo Mascio, *Album fotográfico de las Misiones Franciscanas en la República de Bolivia a cargo de los Colegios Apostólicos de Tarija y Potosí 1898* (La Paz: Banco Central de Bolivia and Archivo y Biblioteca Nacionales de Bolivia, 1995).

FIGURE 6. Chiriguano women from San Pascual de Boicovo. They are wearing traditional tirus and ornamentation. *Source*: Doroteo Giannecchini and Vincenzo Mascio, *Album fotográfico de las Misiones Franciscanas en la República de Bolivia a cargo de los Colegios Apostólicos de Tarija y Potosí 1898* (La Paz: Banco Central de Bolivia and Archivo y Biblioteca Nacionales de Bolivia, 1995).

feasts followed the harvest festival; the principle of reciprocity guaranteed that the guests of one feast would try to surpass the amount of food and corn beer available at the next arete.[12]

The friars could do little to change this custom among the unconverted since it was so important to social intercourse among villages and mission sections, as well as for maintaining the authority of the tubicha. This did not mean that they did not try. For one thing, they prohibited, with uneven success, converts from participating in these feasts. Erland Nordenskiöld noted that people tended to be friendlier in the unconverted sections of the missions, undoubtedly because the periodic feasts facilitated social relations among the Indians, making a greater openness possible among those who had drunk together.[13]

The missionaries' attempts to suppress the festivals were unsuccessful even as the nature of the feasts changed in character. Alcohol consumption patterns changed on the missions, in large part because of the Indians' contact with the sugar plantations of northern Argentina. There, instead of cangui, the workers learned to drink cane alcohol, a much more potent drink without the nutritional qualities of the former. They brought home the custom of drinking cane alcohol and imbibed the home-brew available from neighboring mestizos. Cane alcohol consumption had become a severe problem by the early twentieth century, fostered by some chiefs, such as Mandeponay. According to Fr. Bernardino de Nino, this and the consumption of coca leaves led to degeneracy among the Chiriguanos. According to the friar, "Many youth disappear with the abuse of these substances and usually in the missions the best disappear, [in other words] those who know a skill or have some wealth; [because] everything that they earn, after buying their clothes (though not always) they invest in liquors and coca and so shorten their life."[14] Even as friendly an observer of the Indians as Nordenskiöld lamented the increasing use of cane alcohol and its effects on the Chiriguanos' health, morals, and heightened belligerence during feasts.[15]

In other words, there were significant changes in the lives of the vast majority of adults who agreed to join the mission but did not convert, but much of their day-to-day lives remained the same. Although the missionaries preached to the unconverted, they had little success in persuading adults to become Christians. The same chiefs remained at the head of their section of the missions, maintaining the same authority among the unconverted that had existed before the establishment of the mission. Among chiefs, as before, polygyny remained common. Agricultural cycles did not change, and feasts continued, although with some restrictions. Although in theory Indians needed permission to leave the mission grounds, in practice the unconverted came and went as they pleased. There were changes as well, though it is difficult to measure completely their impact. The missionaries physically divided the residents into different sections, spatially demarcating the divisions in beliefs between the converts and the unconverted. Different building materials and a somewhat greater regulation of life was reflected in the grid design and the presence of the missionary on the hill above the settlement. Some extra labor was required for the mission fields and to build or maintain mission buildings, but the fields were generally small and building needs abated after the missionaries organized the settlement. In turn, mission residents gained a sense of security on the missions that was lacking in independent villages. On the whole, after the initial hardscrabble years after the mission's founding and the wars of 1874–1877 and 1892, the Indians did not need to worry about attacks from fellow Indians. The friars also protected the Indians quite effectively from attacks and abuses of surrounding settlers. Thus the unconverted lived relatively comfortably, which explains why the chiefs, with the consent of the assembly of village men, had agreed to permit the establishment of missions.

While the situation did not change substantially for unconverted adults living on the mission, this was not the case for their children. I turn next to this segment of the mission population and their daily routines.

Mission Schools

Given the resistance of the adults to Christianity and their recalcitrance in having their children baptized except under extreme circumstances, the friars turned to converting the younger generations. As was the case in North America, mission schools became prime agents of conversion, control, and what the friars called "civilizing" the younger generations of Chiriguanos. In theory at least, all Indian children were supposed to enter the mission school at age seven. They were to remain until they married or reached the age of twenty. The children learned to read and write as well as vocations the friars considered appropriate to their sex.[16]

The missionaries themselves taught only the boys. Women from the surrounding mestizo settlements taught the girls. These women received salaries of between eighty and one hundred Bolivianos a year. We do not have the names of many of the teachers; the only ones for which there is some information are the six del Castillo sisters, who were teachers on the missions in the late nineteenth century and early twentieth.

Control over the girls of the mission was much stricter than over the boys. In both the Tarija and Potosí missions, the boys were students during the day but went home for lunch and at night. The girls, however, boarded at the school, though they were sent home daily for less than an hour to eat lunch. The missionaries boasted that the female teachers assigned to the girls were with them always, in the school, attending Mass, and even at night. In the case of the Potosí missions, the teachers slept in a room adjacent to the girls' dormitory, whereas in the Tarija missions, the girls had beds in the same room as their instructors.[17]

In this fashion the missionaries attempted to control the sexuality of the girls. This was extremely important to what the friars conceived of as their civilizing mission; indeed, for the Franciscans, control of female sexuality was the key to making the Chiriguanos into civilized beings. According to the missionaries, the Indians' principal failing and the major reason they were savages was that they were dedicated to libertinage. Bernardino de Nino excoriated them for encouraging premarital sexual relations. The adults, he asserted, were proud of their children's first extramarital sexual experiences and claimed that their children were thus transformed into men and women.[18] Coming from a southern European background that emphasized the preservation of women's virtue, the friars attempted to restrain male access to the girls under their charge. Young men did not have to live under these restrictions, for, in the friars' conception, they did not have to be protected in the same way that young, fertile women had to be.

The restriction of sexual access among the unmarried members of the mission community was a weapon that the missionaries tried to use to control the behavior of the Indians and impose different standards of morality. The missionaries used sexual access quite deliberately; in the early twentieth century they also attempted to marry off the Indians as young as possible to prevent so many young men from leaving for Argentina. This policy did not work; some young men even disappeared the day after their wedding.[19]

One of the problems with understanding the natives' behavior from missionary sources is the biases the friars brought to issues such as sexuality that were both doctrinally defined and derived from their own cultural preconceptions. Nordenskiöld, who visited the missions in the late nineteenth century and early twentieth, painted a very different picture of the Indians' sexuality. He claimed that the Franciscans unjustifiably assumed the worst of the Indians in this regard. According to Nordenskiöld, the very restrictions that the friars attempted to enforce on the missions brought about just the opposite behavior. He contrasted the morality in the independent village of Maringay in the Ingre valley with that of the missions and found the latter wanting. Whereas in Maringay's village no woman offered herself for money to the expeditionaries with whom the anthropologist traveled, this occurred frequently on the missions. Nordenskiöld found that, in general, the unconverted women and the independent villages were much more restrained in their sexual behavior than the converts.[20] Among the unconverted, the mothers played a very strong role in the control of her daughters, whereas surely the female teachers on the mission schools, with the dozens of girls under their care, could not provide the same kind of supervision.

For both boys and girls on the mission schools, their days were busy from dawn to dusk. This was a deliberate policy, for the friars thought that in this way they could keep the children out of trouble. It also combined well with the Franciscans' own concerns about schedules for devotions at certain set times of the day. As Thierry Saignes has pointed out for the colonial-era missions among the Chiriguanos, the missionaries divided up the day into discrete and precise segments punctuated by the mission bells, very unlike the agricultural rhythms of the independent villages.[21] The children, over whom the missionaries exerted the greatest control, were the ones most affected by the Franciscans' affinity for rigid schedules. The schoolchildren had a full schedule to keep every day of the week, as table 10 makes clear.

The boys' schedule was similar to the girls, though there was more free time and less control by the missionaries. For example, the boys had free time between Mass and the beginning of school. They were exempt from serving the friars and teachers, and only on Saturdays were they required to sweep the school. Moreover, they had summer vacation from mid-December to mid-January, during which time they only had to go to Mass every day and one hour of classes in the mornings and afternoons. On Thursdays and Saturdays during the summer no classes took place at all.[22] Another important difference was that the boys slept at home, whereas the girls were forced to spend the night on the school grounds.

For the first five years in school the children learned prayers, to read, to write, arithmetic, and to sing. After that the missionaries sent them to

TABLE 10. Typical school day for girls in the Tarija missions

5:00–5:30 a.m.	Dress and eat breakfast.
5:30–6:30	Mass (except Sundays and holidays)
6:30–7:30	Serve breakfast to friars and teachers;
	Bring water to missionaries' and teachers' residences;
	Clean missionaries' and teachers' residences, and mission church (Sundays and holidays)
7:30–8:00	Personal hygiene
8:00–9:30	Classes
9:30–10:00	Recess
10:00–10:45	Classes (catechism class Tuesdays, Thursdays, and Saturdays)
10:45–11:00	Devotion to saint (in mission church)
11:00–12:00 p.m.	Serve lunch to friars and teachers;
	Lunch at home
12:00–12:30	Return to school
12:30–2:00	Siesta (at school)
2:00–3:30	Classes
3:30–4:00	Recess
4:00–5:00	Classes
5:00–6:30	Dinner at home
6:30–8:00	Return to school;
	Serve dinner to friars and teachers
8:00	Turn in for the night (in school dormitory)

Source: "Reglamento para la escuela de niñas, Cuevo, Ene 1°, 1928, de P. César Vigiani," APC, APM.

learn a trade. The boys learned gardening, bricklaying, blacksmithing, tile making, and carpentry. The boys with musical talent also joined a band, which played at religious festivals and which the Franciscans hired out. These mission bands were famous throughout the region and even appeared in a novel by Adolfo Costa du Rels, who spent part of his life as an oil prospector in the region.[23] The girls learned to wash and dye clothes, iron, sew, and weave. As we will see, the missionaries farmed out many children to a select number of surrounding settler families, who were to provide examples as good Christians and teach them in the ways of "civilization."[24]

As elsewhere, the primary purpose of the mission schools was to transform the Indian children from "savages" into what the friars considered to be civilized human beings. First and foremost, that meant that the Indians become Christians. Catholicism emphasized ritual and the belief system imbedded in it. The friars spent much time on these daily and weekly routines. The prayers several times a day, both at the beginning of class and at the end, the twice-weekly catechism classes, the daily Masses, all were designed to transform the boys and girls into faithful Catholics in clearly demonstrable ways, that is, by knowing the various prayers, credos, and rituals. The rituals and prayers were primarily in Latin; thus the missionaries, while they also taught Spanish, did not see this as their most important priority. Only on the Potosí missions, founded between 1876 and 1909, did the friars forbid the students to speak anything but Spanish. Whether this policy was adhered to is hard to say, although by the second decade of the twentieth century the anticlerical accusations included the fact that few mission Indians actually spoke the national language.[25]

Only after saving souls did the missionaries consider their goal the civilizing of the children. The term *civilization*, so frequently used by the friars and loaded with considerable ethnocentric baggage, meant essentially two things. In addition to the control of sexuality, it meant, first, abolishing most indigenous customs (or "superstitions," as the friars would have put it), and second, transforming the Chiriguanos into productive members of the national economy. Thus the children and all neófitos were forbidden to consume alcohol, since this was seen as prejudicial to productivity, an incentive to illicit sexual behavior, and an opportunity to backslide into superstitious practices. For the same reasons they were prohibited from participating in festivals that included the unconverted. Instead, the Franciscans used the schools as a means to provide a whole new cultural underpinning. This included the physical separation of the children from their parents and other unconverted adults as a means to prevent contamination of the neophytes by their "savage" relatives and parents.

The mission schools also served in other ways as a civilizing influence. The friars obligated the children to dress in European-style clothing, which the teachers provided to the schoolchildren several times a year. Instead of their traditional dress, the boys wore shirts and pants and the girls blouses and pleated skirts called *polleras*. The missionaries prohibited the practice of cutting tembeta holes into the boys and made sure that they had their

FIGURE 7. Indian schoolgirls outside the San Francisco del Pilcomayo mission school playing *chocorore*. Note the mestizo machine-made dresses, flowered blouses, and long pigtails. *Source*: Doroteo Giannecchini and Vincenzo Mascio, *Album fotográfico de las Misiones Franciscanas en la República de Bolivia a cargo de los Colegios Apostólicos de Tarija y Potosí 1898* (La Paz: Banco Central de Bolivia and Archivo y Biblioteca Nacionales de Bolivia, 1995).

hair cut short, European-style, for school. Interestingly, the Franciscans did not attempt to dress the boys and girls in styles of the Latin American elites or of the Italian middle classes. Instead, they wore the clothes of the people the friars had converted them into: the mestizo, or cholo, group. This type of dress was a marker of class and of town living that obliterated any marker of ethnic origin.[26] (See figures 7 and 8.)

Not only did the new dress distinguish the converts from the unconverted, but it also created new demand for manufactured goods. Among Chiriguano men, dressing in European-style clothing was very common even in independent villages and, to a certain extent, a mark of prestige. Commerce and exchange between merchants and government officials, on the one hand, and the Indians, on the other, throughout the nineteenth century included the exchange of European textiles.[27] Saignes posited that the eighteenth-century Franciscan missions among the Chiriguanos sur-

FIGURE 8. The mission school at San Miguel Arcángel de Itau. On the right are the Chiriguano girls, all dressed in mestizo (chola) clothes, with their female teacher. In the center left are the mestizo boys who also attended the school. To the left of the friar are the Chiriguano boys in their ponchos. *Source*: Doroteo Giannecchini and Vincenzo Mascio, *Album fotográfico de las Misiones Franciscanas en la República de Bolivia a cargo de los Colegios Apostólicos de Tarija y Potosí 1898* (La Paz: Banco Central de Bolivia and Archivo y Biblioteca Nacionales de Bolivia, 1995).

vived in large part because the Indians saw the missions as ways of gaining access to cloth and other goods, which the missionaries distributed frequently among the resident Indians.[28] Be that as it may, the dynamics of the missions before 1810 included more coercion by Spanish soldiers, combined with much less pressure on Chiriguano territory by landlords. Nevertheless, the distribution of clothing to schoolchildren in republican times was an attractive feature for the Chiriguanos living on the missions. Most important, it created new needs from a large part of the mission population. Once the missions were established in the frontier the already notable merchant presence grew even more and made access to cloth much easier than during the colonial period. Moreover, the wearing of European-style clothes became a marker that distinguished the neófitos from the Indians living in independent villages. Once a sufficient number of converts lived on the missions, a new culture developed in which mestizo-style (cholo/chola) dress, as well as short hair and no tembeta for males, became markers of differentiation.

Many unconverted parents saw many advantages to living on the mission and even in the training of their children for the new life on the frontier. However, as we have seen, many also were highly ambivalent about having their children wrenched from them and brought up in ways alien and even in opposition to their own way of life. Consequently, many parents resisted sending their children to school. After all, what the historian recognizes as a new, hybrid culture emerging from the experience of mission schools, attempts at Franciscan social engineering, transformations in ever-changing Chiriguano customs, and the effects of market forces and mestizo influence, was an often painful process that affected each household in varying degrees over the life of the missions. Its long-term effect was to pit the younger generation of Chiriguanos, the converted schoolchildren, against their unconverted parents, uncles and aunts, and grandparents. It is thus not surprising that the adults tried to halt or at least postpone the process by which they would lose control over the younger generation.[29]

Indeed, the missionaries complained continually that the parents often kept their children from the schools. In the first decades after the establishment of the missions, births often were hidden from the friars or the parents refused to have their children baptized unless they were deathly ill. As the missionaries gained more knowledge of the Indian population and were able to baptize most newborns, resistance to the schools slowly ended. Fr. Alejandro Corrado estimated that five years after the establishment of Tarairí only about a tenth of all children went to the mission school.[30] Once the friars were able to assert control over the mission settlements, some parents took their children out of the settlement and, as one of the Franciscans complained, "If they can hide them, they make no excuses, but have [the children] grow up in the woods." In Macharetí in 1891, rather than handing their children over to the friars, some families simply left the mission. Three years later, even after the brutal repression during the 1892 rebellion had eliminated all possibility of a Chiriguano resurgence, Doroteo Giannecchini complained, "[The] infidels, after so many years of enjoying the presence and exhortations of the Apostolic Missionary still deny us [*mezquinar*] their children for their respective schools." A few years later the missionaries complained that there existed still "a multitude of Indians, who do not live permanently on the mission, moving from one place to another, many so as to not have to hand over their children [for schooling]." Macharetí, because of its size and the powerful position of its chief, was somewhat unusual, but still one presumes that the friars should have been able to resolve many of these problems almost three decades after the establishment of the mission. In Aguairenda, a much smaller mission established years before Machareti, children who were supposed to be in school often did not appear either.[31]

Schools did not always function well, which suggests that the tight control implied by the highly regimented school schedule was less real than the missionaries would have liked. Besides the problem of parents keeping their children away (this was especially endemic among the children of the traditional chiefs), the schools were not always open, nor were the missionaries always able to accommodate all the children in the school buildings. Although the friars publicly asserted, "All [children] go to school from the age indicated until [they] get married,"[32] the reality was different, as evidenced in the unpublished annual inspections.

The problems of absenteeism, poor schooling, and lack of infrastructure were related to the different phases in the mission life cycle. During the initial establishment phase, as heroic as the Franciscans might have been in setting up the mission, their lack of control over the mission population made getting the parents to give up their children difficult. Only once the mission had survived the first few decades, when the missionaries had the power to insist on the terms of the bargain they had struck with the adults, did the mission schools flourish. Yet even then the pupils were often truant. In other cases, the infrastructure simply did not exist to put all the children into mission schools. Fr. José Cardús noted in 1886 that in Machareti the school had room for only one hundred pupils of each sex, which meant that the vast majority of the children (about six hundred) received only minimal instruction. This state of affairs continued for years; even in 1888, at the height of missionary power, the school continued to have insufficient teachers for the large number of students. After 1890 the friars accommodated larger numbers of pupils, quintupling the number of students by the turn of the century.[33]

School attendance varied over time. In terms of percentages of total mission population, attendance went up steadily from the late 1870s (the earliest figures we have) to the first decade of the twentieth century. Thereafter attendance tended to decline. A comparison of two of the most dynamic missions from each of the two Franciscan convents is instructive. In the case of the Tarija-run Mission Tarairí, school attendance was only 8 percent of the total mission population in 1879, indicating that more than two decades after the foundation of the mission parents were still rela-

TABLE 11. School attendance in Tarairí mission, 1879–1913 (Ten-year averages)

Year	Number of schoolchildren	Total mission population
1879	128	1,528
1880–1889	216	1,305
1890–1899	344	1,321
1900–1909	272	882
1910–1913	125	770

Source: "Santas Visitas: Tarairí," 1879–1913, AFT.

TABLE 12. School attendance in Mission Santa Rosa de Cuevo, 1889–1912 (Ten-year averages)

Year	Number of schoolchildren	Total mission population
1889	218	2,027
1890–1899	450	1,983
1900–1909	340	1,577
1910–1912	239	1,317

Source: "Santas Visitas: Santa Rosa de Cuevo," 1889–1912, AFT.

tively effective in keeping their children from going to school.[34] During the 1880s attendance doubled in terms of the total mission population; the two decades between 1890 and 1909 saw the largest proportion of the mission population go to school. After 1909, attendance fell again to the levels of the 1880s. (See table 11.) Mission Santa Rosa, staffed by missionaries from the Potosí convent, exhibited a similar pattern. Founded more than three decades later, in its first years it also showed low attendance. The two decades surrounding the turn of the century, as in the case of Tarairí, saw the highest enrollment in Santa Rosa, though not as high as in the case of the Tarija-run mission. As in Tarairí, attendance dropped after 1909. (See table 12.)

These figures are quite impressive compared to the general Bolivian population during the same period. I have no information about any schools for the settlers in the surrounding villages along the frontier. Presumably the families that were well off sent their children to Sucre or Santa Cruz for schooling. On the national level, Manuel Contreras estimates that in 1900 2 percent of the total population was in primary school, a much lower level than on the missions. By 1930 the proportion had almost doubled, to 3.9 percent, but was still much lower than among the mission Indians.[35]

School attendance and the care missionaries exhibited in schooling dipped in conjunction with the mission life cycle. Nowhere was this more evident than in Itau and Chimeo, the two oldest missions. Established in 1840 and 1849, respectively, by the late nineteenth century they had already undergone a long process of decline; the Indian population had fallen and mestizos began to predominate even on mission lands. In 1877 the friars were already complaining of "the desertion of almost all youth who do not want to have impediments to the venting of their unruly passions." In 1886 the friars noted, "Schoolchildren do nothing but come and go [as they please]"; three years later the mission prefect asserted, "The boys and girls of the mission are veritable bandits. They frequently do not attend classes, which is why they only know the minimum." By that time only about twenty Indian neophyte families remained on the mission lands. In 1892 the few boys had forgotten most of their prayers, whereas cloistering the girls with their teachers day and night brought satisfactory academic results. This situation continued until the annual records cease in 1912.[36] Apparently the Tarija Franciscans had lost interest in schooling the few children there and only perfunctorily covered these two missions. Few wanted to live there since the region where Itau and Chimeo were located had the reputation of being an unhealthy place where the water quality was poor.[37]

By the first decade of the twentieth century many missionaries had become disheartened, and the school system, their hope for the future, suffered as well. The tide of anticlericalism seemed overwhelming, especially when Bolivian authorities, most notably the delegate of the Gran Chaco territories from 1905 to 1911, Julio Trigo Raña, began to restrict the authority of the missionaries. The new mission laws, passed by a Congress dominated by the largely anticlerical Liberal Party, did not permit the Franciscans to use corporal and other punishments long used on the missions, such as jail and the stocks. While it is highly unlikely that missionaries used these types of discipline frequently (the chiefs, not the missionaries, had jurisdiction over the unconverted), cases such as Zoila's in which local officials interfered with what the friars claimed to be an internal mission matter made it appear to the friars that they had little if any effective authority left. This in turn diverted attention from the running of the schools, since it appeared that the government at any minute might abolish the missions.

Unfortunately the annual mission reports, so useful for our understanding of mission life, cease after 1914, so we have little information on how well the schools functioned from then to 1949. However, decadence was already apparent in the early decades of the twentieth century, though more so in the missions founded by the Tarija convent. In 1913 the Potosí missions of Ivo and Boicovo were doing well; construction of new schools continued in both. However, in Santa Rosa de Cuevo, the oldest Potosí mission, although the boys were still doing well on their exams, the girls' educational level had fallen because of poorly trained teachers. In Aguairenda the government quartered a regiment of soldiers at the schoolhouse in 1910, leaving the children without a building. In Tiguipa poor instruction meant that the children barely knew the Holy Sacraments, one of the most basic goals of the mission schools. In Macharetí most children could understand Spanish and recite prayers, but many had migrated to Argentina. In Tarairí the children were progressing only very slowly in learning Spanish. By 1914 the missionaries were not teaching at all, but had left instruction to former pupils, whose work the territorial delegate found substandard.[38]

The Franciscans were aware of their failings on the educational front. After the two mission systems combined in 1919 as an apostolic vicariate, the convents renewed their efforts in education. The new school regulations of 1928, which carefully planned the boys' and girls' days and nights, were an attempt to reimpose the rigor that previously characterized the mission schools. However, it is difficult to judge how well these regulations worked in an environment where migration to Argentina and an inability to discipline their charges weakened the friars' authority.

In sum, teaching the next generation to become Christians, one of the essential premises of the missionary enterprise, had begun to fail by the twentieth century. Since our concern here is primarily the daily life experiences of the children, the slackening of school discipline in the early twentieth century (a phenomenon that was apparent beforehand in some of the most decadent missions, such as Ivo and Chimeo) probably meant that boys and girls were able to spend more time with their parents than was the case in the nineteenth century. Since many also went with their parents or, if they were old enough, alone to Argentina, the children's horizons were considerably broadened beyond the missions by the early twentieth century. It also meant that the Franciscans' indoctrination campaign to "civilize" their charges weakened just as neophytes became the majority of the mission population, leaving future generations to maintain more of their indigenous culture than the missionaries had planned. The last part of the educational system to be weakened was the devotional practices and the teaching of the articles of Catholic faith. This meant that the mission culture that emerged after the abolition of the missions remained deeply devotional, but with a strong influence of Chiriguano notions of reciprocity and hereditary chiefly authority and a tradition of maximum individual independence within a community structure.

Adult Neophytes

The goal of the mission schools was to create devout Catholics with some manual skills who settled down and married between the ages of sixteen and twenty, which permitted them to leave school and set up their own household within the mission. These new families would transform the missions into vibrant urban settlements that would provide the bulwark of national society in the former frontier regions. To a certain extent the missionaries accomplished their goals for, as in the case of José Manuel Yandori, those who had passed through the mission schools and had learned a craft contributed to the frontier economy.

However, the case of Yandori brings to the forefront another important issue: that many adult neophytes spent considerable time away from the mission, either in the surrounding towns or as the most sought-after workers for the sugar plantations in Jujuy. In addition, the labor requirements of frontier authorities, which were especially great when an expedition was planned into the uncharted wilderness of the Chaco, meant that many neophytes labored far from the missions as contract workers building forts, opening up roads, and the like. It is also likely that Yandori, as was the case with other older schoolboys, spent some time outside the mission, working in the homes of surrounding settlers. The missionaries encouraged the contracting out of their older students to selected colonists as a way to keep the boys occupied and out of trouble.[39] This made neophyte men rather mobile, with often extensive knowledge of life outside the missions and connections with local mestizos.

Neophytes also acquired important connections to local settlers through godparent ties. Almost invariably the mission Indians received as godparents (*compadres*) settlers from surrounding communities. Out of thirty-four godparents for the sacrament of confirmation on Mission Boicovo between 1879 and 1891, only five had Chiriguano last names. With names such as Chindari and Baringay, it is likely that they came from chiefly families. The rest, the vast majority, were local settlers who thus tied their names to members of the mission community. The same happened in Mission Tarairí, where the few children baptized who were not on their deathbed had as godparents local settlers, mostly from the neighboring mestizo village of Caiza. In one case Francisco Carmona, the *jefe politico* of the frontier headquartered in Salinas, stood as godfather to an infant Chiriguano from Tarairí.[40]

Although we have no direct evidence to argue that local settlers used *compadrazgo* as a means of obtaining labor from the mission Indians, it is very likely. As in the rest of Latin America, compadrazgo ties were not just a welter of religious obligations, but important social links between individuals of high and low status. Through these vertical ties rural folk tried to mitigate the problems that their low status brought them by allying themselves with people of greater power. In an ideal compadrazgo relationship, those of high status protected those with whom they had these ties, as well as helping them in times of need or providing employment more readily or on more favorable terms than others. In turn, the low-status compadre or *ahijado* worked for his benefactor and provided him, if necessary, with political or other support. In the labor-scarce eastern lowland frontier, compadrazgo ties were probably important in providing settlers with workers. It is also likely that the converted youths eventually ended up working in the households of their godparents. This the friars could scarcely have denied, for godparents were to educate their godchildren in Christian ways.

Thus the number of ties the mission Indians had with settlers probably helped determine the labor resources of the settlers and also the potential clout an individual Indian might have in settler society. What immediately stands out is that converts often had the same godparent. For example, Rafael Rios, a neighboring landlord, obtained in just one year, 1891, sixteen ahijados from Mission Boicovo. Most impressive were the numbers of converts who were tied to the del Castillo family, the largest landholding family in the region and fast friends of the Franciscans. For just the 1879, 1880, 1883, and 1891 confirmation registers, six members of the del Castillo family had a total of ninety-six godchildren! The del Castillo women (who were the teachers in the girls' mission school) were the godmothers to girls, whereas the men became godfathers of the boys. In this way the friars created fictive kinship ties between the Indians and settlers that made possible access to mission labor in informal settings. These ties did not exist solely with converted Indians of Boicovo, but also with Chiriguanos from elsewhere. In 1904, for example, eighty-one godchildren were from Boicovo, but eleven children from Macharetí and a smattering from seven other missions and communities also had as godparents settlers from the Huacaya area.[41]

As was the case with the schoolchildren, the lives of the neophytes were much more structured than those of their unconverted relatives. Since most of the neophytes were alumni of the mission schools (since so few adults converted) they were accustomed to this type of life. In many ways their lives were freer in the neophyte section than in the schools. Other than in Macharetí, all neophytes lived in a section of the mission separated from the unconverted. The houses of the converted clustered around a central plaza, usually the same size as the central plaza of the much larger unconverted quarter. Each couple had a separate one-room adobe house built on a grid and with a tile roof. This generous amount of space was quite a change for the recently married, especially for the women, who as schoolgirls had lived in the cramped dormitory with their teachers. Around the house there was a little room to grow some plants and perhaps a few orange trees to provide shade in the back. The front doors opened up to a patio, where many of the neophytes stayed during the heat of the day.

Manuel O. Jofré, in his inspection of 1893, described the interior of the neophyte houses in Aguairenda, giving us a rare glimpse into the material culture of the mission Indians. According to the inspector, the houses were clean and the walls had foodstuffs hanging from hooks, such as pieces of beef and sacks of maize. In addition, most houses contained a string of candles, some clothes, assorted domestic utensils, and agricultural implements and saddles. An altar graced one corner, with its saints and fresh flowers. All the members of the family slept on wooden bedsteads or hammocks, and when the children got older the parents slept in a small room apart from their offspring.[42] The patio gave way to a long straight dirt street or, in the case of Aguairenda, where all the houses were built along the edges of the urban center, on to the central public area or plaza. As elsewhere in the subtropics, the heat drove most people outside during the day and made it necessary for the neophytes to leave the doors of their houses open. Many neophytes had rough wooden chairs or cowhides on the front porch, on which they sat, watched their neighbors, and chatted during times of leisure.[43] With the design of the grid plan and the wide open public spaces and because people left their doors open, in the neophyte village social control was relatively easy for the friars and the neophyte officials. A word spoken here or furtive behavior there did not go unnoticed and could quickly be dealt with by the authorities.

Social control in the neophyte section was also made easy because the majority of the mission populations remained resolutely unconverted until the turn of the century. In most cases it took many decades for the missionaries to achieve a neophyte majority (see chapter 5). By the time the majority had converted, the total mission population had diminished significantly, keeping the neophyte section small in comparison to the previous size of the mission. For example, in Mission Machareti, where it had taken the missionaries thirty-five years to bring about a majority of neophytes, the mission population had dropped from a high of 4,116 inhabitants in 1882 to 1,405 in 1904, the year when neophytes became the majority. Of this number, a total of 955 Indians lived in the convert section. Only in missions such as Boicovo where the friars had greater success in converting the Chiriguanos' offspring did the neophyte section grow relatively large compared to the rest of the mission. Even then, continued emigration depleted the number of residents. The neophyte population of Boicovo reached the majority in 1893, with 533 converts out of a total of 969 residents. But a decade later only 210 neophytes and catecúmenos remained out of a total of 390 adults.[44]

Once the schoolchildren had married and settled into the neophyte section, they came under the jurisdiction of neophyte authorities. These were elected by the neophytes themselves, though it appears that the missionaries selected the candidates from those neófitos "who are most apparent for this purpose." Once elected, the *alcalde* of the neophytes were "careful that the *conumis* [children] and the women attend[ed] prayers, the schools, and the other functions of the Church and . . . [worked hard] to avoid all disorder and public scandal and [did] as much as they [could] to conserve common peace and maintain order."[45] In other words, the alcaldes were to take the place of the traditional chiefs in the neophyte sections. However, in the end the friar had the final say in any matters pertaining to the neophytes. It appears that no members of the chiefly families became neophyte alcaldes. This meant that these officials had little real power and that the other Indians usually saw the traditional chiefs and their lineage as the authority on the missions.

The neophyte officials were in charge of supervising the daily routines. Other than the tasks of the agricultural cycle, which were the same for the unconverted, the principal difference in routine was attendance at Mass. While some neophytes attended every day with the schoolchildren, many appeared only at the obligatory Mass on Sunday afternoon. Within the church a strict hierarchy prevailed, which impressed visitors to the mission. Even the entrance into the church for Mass followed strict patterns, providing visual confirmation of the ideal social order on the missions. All went dressed in their best Sunday finery of European-style clothes, reflecting their level of cultural integration or, as the friars would have termed it, their level of "civilization." After the ringing of the bells, the Chiriguano men entered first, standing in perfect lines along the left side of the nave, their hats at their feet. In the front, next to the altar, went the schoolboys organized in straight lines. Women entered next and stood on the right, with the girls in neat rows in the front. When the mission had a band, the musicians lined up on the men's side with their drums and fiddles. (See figure 9.) The distribution in the church recognized the division of the population by age and by sex. The separation of the children from the adults showed that the friars were in charge of the children and that, at least in religious matters, the Church had priority over the family grouping. The separation of men and women represented the ideal state of civilization, where men and women did not intermingle promiscuously at social occasions, which the missionaries believed had led to the decadence of the European society they had left behind. The boys left first, by twos, then the men, the girls, and last, the women.

The authorities insisted that the neophytes wear European-style dress. Tembetas were prohibited, and adult men sported short hair rather than the full-length hair wrapped under a brightly-colored bandanna of their unconverted brethren. Otherwise, dress style was not much different in the two sections, given that most Chiriguano men admired European-style clothing and wore it for most day-to-day use even outside the missions. Female dress changed much more dramatically. Women continued to wear the types of dresses they received during the school years, appearing very much like lower-class women elsewhere in Bolivia. That meant long-sleeved blouses that covered the torso up to the neck and long skirts that covered their legs. In addition, women wore their long hair in

FIGURE 9. Unidentified mission church during services. Note how the men, women, and children are separated. On the left, under the pulpit, is the mission band, composed of Chiriguano men. *Source*: AFT.

two severe braids. (See figure 10.) Thus the selection of clothing that the Franciscans believed the Indians should wear followed the dictates of class and marked the Indians as members of the laboring classes of the country. In this case, dress codes reinforced the grim realities of the frontier, where the Chiriguanos, especially those who lived in the missions, constituted the most important agricultural labor force of the region.

The Development of Mission Culture

The word *neófito* was used to describe converts living on the missions regardless of how many generations ago the family had converted and implied a certain recent and perhaps incomplete acceptance of Christianity; it also conferred a certain spiritual inferiority. Ironically, Indian converts were likely to have been educated into the mysteries of the Catholic faith to a much greater degree than the surrounding mestizo settlers, who were commonly known as *cristianos*. As shown in chapter 2, the friars during the mission period were always skeptical of the commitment the Chiriguanos had to Christianity; indeed, they trained not a single mission Indian to follow in their footsteps and become a Franciscan or a priest of any kind. This, however, did not deter the converts. According to all reports they got along very well with their unconverted relatives living with them on the missions, but the fairly rigorous training in school, their lengthy separation from their parents during childhood, their married lives in separate sections of the mission villages, and the typically Chiriguano sense of pride brought about a distinctive identity in which they relished their role as neófitos. They themselves adopted the rhetoric of the missions, in which their relatives were termed *infieles* who lived in the dirty and less organized section of the mission in a more savage state. This contempt was greater for those unconverted who lived on other missions and most of all for those who were forced to live as peons on surrounding estates and in the rapidly shrinking number of independent villages. While neophytes also called the settlers cristianos or perhaps the older term karai, they knew they were superior to most of these men and women in schooling and in their knowledge of Christianity. As a result, the neófitos developed a separate culture that mixed elements of Chiriguano customs and the lessons

FIGURE 10. Chiriguano women converts on an unidentified mission. Note their European-style dresses and mestizo hairstyles. Compare to figure 2. *Source*: AFT.

imparted by the Franciscans, the culture of surrounding colonists, and, much more than the friars liked, their experiences in the sugarcane fields of Argentina.

Those things learned in the country to the south were perhaps least important to their new culture. After all, if the reports about increasing and predominantly male migration to the sugar plantations is correct, during much of the year the missions consisted mainly of women. Unfortunately the few mission censuses do not show this, either because absent men were counted or because the censuses were taken when most men had returned from Jujuy. Nevertheless, it appears likely that it was the women, who had undergone a much more intense schooling in greater isolation from the unconverted population, who were the main propagators of this new mission culture.[46]

It is difficult to document the development of this mission culture, for the documents record mainly the deeds of the missionaries and those of the major chiefs. Daily life on the missions slowly but surely changed the Indians living there until, by the early twentieth century, new cultural patterns had emerged that distinguished the Chiriguanos living on the missions from their brethren elsewhere. Although the friars professed to integrate the Indians into national life, this did not mean that they became just like the settlers in the surrounding communities or, increasingly, those who lived on the mission grounds themselves. In other words, despite the setbacks of the twentieth century and the lack of enthusiasm on the part of the missionaries in the waning phase of the mission cycle, an extraordinary culture had emerged from the day-to-day experiences over a number of generations lived in the missions.

Among the most important characteristics was the mission political culture. A blend of hierarchy and democracy created a strange hybrid that was neither fully Chiriguano nor Creole. On the one hand, the strict authority structure implicit in the Catholic hierarchy took root. The missionary was the paramount figure on the mission, and disobedience (at least of the overt style) was not to be tolerated. The teachers in school (in the case of the boys, the missionaries themselves) pounded—sometimes literally—this principle into the children. In turn, among the mission Chiriguanos, even the unconverted, the authority principle was strong because the missionaries' alliance with the traditional chiefs bolstered the influence of the latter. Certainly the alcaldes also had the support of the friars.

Political culture among the Chiriguanos was, however, also relatively egalitarian, with great individual freedom among adult men. As in the days before the missions, men in particular left their settlement at their leisure. With the mission regime, they abandoned their homes for the sugarcane fields of Argentina, as in earlier times they had set up their own settlement if they did not agree with their leader. The tubicha's authority was based primarily on his charisma and his strength of persuasion in public meetings rather than raw, naked power. Moreover, the chief had the obligation to occasionally distribute some of his goods to his followers to keep them content. This could be in the form of the arete, in which all enjoyed the chicha brewed by the chief's wives, or in booty gained in warfare or by redistributing tribute payments (mainly in textiles) that the frontier authorities and local landlords provided to powerful Chiriguano chiefs. While modified in important ways, these types of interactions continued in the mission, where the friar in his sermon took on the role of the chief persuading his flock (often not very successfully) to remain or follow other dictates. Obviously the situation was different, for the whole Catholic ritual attempted to highlight the role of the priest as an intermediary between God and his believers, in which the priest became the spokesman for the highest authority on earth and in heaven. Unlike the lengthy meetings with the tubichas, where all warriors had a right to speak their mind and where it was the chief's job to achieve some kind of consensus, the very hierarchical nature of the interaction between missionary and the converted made this kind of dialogue virtually impossible. Nevertheless, some forms of egalitarianism remained, for the friars had the converted population elect its alcaldes themselves. Unfortunately we don't have any evidence that documents the relationship between alcaldes and converts, but my suspicion is that they acted in ways similar to that of the traditional chiefs. Moreover, the friars also took on the role of the chiefs by distributing clothes to their acolytes, especially in the schools. Thus in 1875 the friars spent ten *cargas* of corn "to feed the sick," and in 1879 paid 23 pesos 7 reales "for goods passed on to the Indians."[47]

The redistribution of goods, not just between chiefs and their people but among people of the same lineage, was an essential part of Chiriguano manners. This remained an important characteristic of even the converts. The Franciscans, given their own vows of poverty and their centuries-long tradition of charitable acts, were sympathetic to the sharing of resources. The great missionary order, the Jesuits, had failed to establish missions among the Chiriguanos during the colonial period. In contrast, the Franciscans had succeeded, at least partly because the Indians felt that the men from the Order of St. Francis acted more in line with their own traditions of chiefly redistribution than did the men in the black robes. The Franciscans redistributed goods they received rather than trying to profit from the mission enterprise.[48] Despite this affinity, the friars were not always pleased with the survival in the missions of the obligation of sharing among kinfolk and others. Fr. Bernardino de Nino complained that the Indians who went to Argentina often returned with many clothes and even a mule or donkey, but that they soon sold or used up their new wealth.[49] But rather than being spendthrifts, as the friar thought, the Indians were following Chiriguano codes of conduct in which the goods one man had were also available to his relatives and friends. Indeed, as we will see in the next chapter, some chiefly sons did engage in accumulating rather than sharing goods, but in the end this did not benefit them much. Be that as it may, the vast majority of Indians remained committed to previous patterns of sharing. This made the accumulation of goods by individuals very difficult and shows that the Indians remained interested more in investing in good relations with their relatives than engaging in possessive individualism characteristic of their Creole neighbors.

As a result of their experience with the schools, the mission Indians also developed a sense of pride in their education. Given the absolute lack of a public school system on the frontier, the mission children received an education superior to what was available to the children living in the mestizo settlements. Although we have no figures on literacy, the ability to read must have been much higher among the mission Indians than in surrounding frontier communities. In the 1900 census, Machareti boasted a student population of 370, whereas in neighboring Ñancaroinza, a *cantón* and town founded and run by the del Castillo family, there were no students at all.[50] The mission Indians developed a sense of intellectual superiority that also distinguished them from their brethren in independent communities and from the resident peons on the haciendas, where going to school was simply unthinkable. In addition, the training the missionaries gave the children in the various trades made those who graduated into specialized workers with highly coveted skills that were probably even more important along the rough frontier than literacy. Thus being neófito meant something special to those who had this training, of which those who had made it through school were perfectly aware. These skills, in conjunction with their knowledge of Catholic ritual, distinguished the growing number of neófitos from both the surrounding settlers and members of their ethnic group living beyond the missions. This is not to say that there were not unfavorable characteristics that came along with this sense of superiority. Most notable to the anthropologist Nordenskiöld was that the children in the mission schools looked "gloomy and reserved." Nordenskiöld believed this was because they received a European-style education in which they were told what they could and could not do, whereas the children in independent villages were permitted to explore more freely and imitate their parents.[51]

To summarize, daily life on the mission varied widely depending on which group the inhabitants belonged to. Although there were some constraints on the unconverted, relatively little changed for them. As migration to Argentina increased, women began to predominate in the mission settlement to a degree that probably did not exist in independent villages. The mission schools imposed a harsh regime upon the children, from which many fled. However, as the unconverted population dropped and the convert population expanded from the alumni of these schools, a new type of individual emerged from the mission school who had an interesting combination of characteristics. The converts were proud of being neophytes and felt superior to the unconverted and members of independent villages, even more so compared to the oppressed Indian peon population of the neighboring estates. The neophytes also maintained some characteristics of their forebears, such as the imperative to share resources. The creation of this new indigenous population, generally pious and more highly educated on average than the settlers and skilled at various professions, led to a sense that they did not belong to the surrounding mestizo population either. Thus, while the missionaries had accomplished their goal of eliminating the Chiriguanos as a barbarian force that could disrupt the frontier, daily life on the missions did not bring about an integration of the neophyte population into the laboring masses. Instead, the neophytes began to identify themselves as unique and even superior, although, because of the majority's unwillingness to become possessive individualists, they never accumulated many goods, as did their mestizo neighbors. To understand more deeply the dynamics of mission life and the development of mission culture, we must now turn to the question of power.

CHAPTER FIVE

Conversion, Chiefs, and Rebellions:
Relationships of Power on the Missions

Scholars have generally focused on the changes that the missionaries imposed on the Indians who lived in the missions. The Franciscans in Bolivia, because of their experiences growing up in Italy and their perceptions of the indigenous population that they had sworn to convert, attempted to create a Christian community in opposition to the increasingly liberal and anticlerical world. The images that official historians, all Franciscan missionaries themselves, presented to the outside world reflected these concerns and presented the Catholic world as a justification for their labors. However, there were few missionaries and many Indians. The friars reshaped the Chiriguano world on the missions in many ways, but the Indians did as well, by ignoring or adapting the missions to their own purposes. Rather than thinking of the missions as institutions where the missionaries changed the indigenous population at will, it is more accurate to think of the missions as points of permanent negotiation between the Indians and the friars, the terms of which varied as power shifted over the course of the missions' trajectory. As each party made new demands, refused to play by the rules, or simply gave up, the contours of the culture on the missions changed. These processes of negotiation, during which a new mission culture eventually emerged, can be seen in two crucial but interrelated facets of mission life: the conversion process and the role of the traditional chiefs. These processes led to new fault lines of power, as exemplified by the great messianic rebellion of 1892, in which the missions played an important role.

The unreliability of ecclesiastical information, particularly baptisms, burials, and marriages, for demographic analysis discussed in the previous chapter demonstrates the limits of the friars' control on the missions. Unlike in the colonial period, when the indigenous peoples living on the missions had no choice but to be baptized, the missionaries in the republican era did not have that power. In the postindependence period the Catholic Church did not reign supreme, nor was it allied with the military power of the state, as in the colonial period. In the case of the Chiriguano missions, the Franciscans did not have the ability or the will to convert people against their will. According to José Cardús, "The Indians admitted the Fathers into their settlements under the condition that they were not to be molested in anything, and much less their beliefs; that they could live with complete liberty and according to their old customs, agreeing only to give up their children to be educated the way the Padres thought best."[1] This meant that the Chiriguano adults did not have to convert, but the children born on the mission and all children going to the mission schools were to be baptized.[2] Baptism was a spiritual rebirth, but it also had very practical consequences. It presumed that the Indians came under the direct jurisdiction of the missionaries and the Indian authorities they selected rather than the traditional chiefs. However, the realities of mission life meant that the conversion process was more complicated than the simple rules that presumably led to conversion. As elsewhere in the world, those who had power could and did determine which part of the bargain would be enforced. Only as the missionaries asserted their control over their charges were they able to hold the Indians to the original bargain. The conversion process is one means through which it is possible to discern the shifts of power from the traditional chiefs to the missionaries.

The Chiriguanos did not permit the establishment of missions because of their desire not to abandon their own indigenous beliefs. We have seen that the Chiriguanos welcomed the Franciscans primarily for secular reasons, particularly the preservation of their communities and to maintain some independence from land- and labor-hungry Creole landlords. Indeed, Bernardino de Nino's phrase about asking for pears from an elm tree, the title of this work, refers to the recalcitrance of healthy Chiriguano adults to become Catholics. Only adult Indians on their deathbed, de Nino asserted, consented to be baptized. This fact was echoed by all the other official contemporary historians of the Franciscans in republican-era Bolivia. Indeed, the friars expected only to baptize ill Indians in the beginning to save their souls and as a first step toward making sure all children were baptized at birth sometime later.[3]

This was also the case on the missions. For example, in Santa Rosa between 1889 and 1912 adult baptisms never exceeded 150 a year and there were usually considerably fewer. Adult baptisms increased only in years when there was high mortality or other stresses on mission life. For example, the highest number of adult baptisms occurred in 1892 as a consequence of the rebellion of that year. It is not clear whether Indians converted because the defeat of the messianic movement destroyed their hopes of ever being free of the Christian yoke or because the many warriors from the mission who were wounded as a result of the fierce battle of Curuyuqui or other skirmishes of that year lingered on death's doorstep. Other increases in adult baptisms at Santa Rosa were related to mortality crises, such as the smallpox epidemic of 1894, when 115 received baptism, or in 1904, when famine stalked the missions.[4] (See table 13.)

Despite the missionaries' best efforts, not all Indian adults converted when they became ill. The missionaries saw the epidemics as an opportunity to reap a rich harvest of souls before death claimed the earthly existence of the Indian adults. However, even under the extreme circumstances of so many people dying in a short period, few adults converted. The friars' partial success at conversion during epidemics shows vividly the lack of power that the Franciscans had in spiritual matters. Often the Indians' resistance to becoming Christian remained vigorous even on their deathbed. A poignant example of this occurred in 1880, as recorded by the chronicler of the Tarija convent, Fr. Alejandro Corrado. That year smallpox attacked populations in the adjacent missions of San Francisco del Pilcomayo and Tarairí. As soon as the missionaries discovered the disease, they called all the inhabitants in Tarairí to the main plaza. They preached that the Indians should confide in God and not believe in the superstitious practices of the ipayes, the native medicine men. The missionaries argued that if the Indians followed the ipayes' directions they would surely fall ill as a mark of God's displeasure. According to Corrado, the Indians refused to listen and went to the medicine men anyway. Despite the rebuff, the friars aided the sick as the epidemic spread. Apparently this lessened some of the Indians' resistance, and before the epidemic was over the Franciscans had baptized 107 Indians, almost all on their deathbed.[5]

Not all the friars' efforts to convert the sick worked. One Indian, who had as wives a mother and daughter, refused baptism even on his deathbed. He asserted that he preferred to be in hell with his older wife, who had passed away the day before, than go to heaven. After he died the missionary approached the surviving wife, who was by this time also deathly ill. When the friar began to speak of baptism and repenting her sins, she

TABLE 13. Adult baptisms in Mission
Santa Rosa de Cuevo, 1889–1910

Year	Adult baptisms	Total population
1889	38	2,027
1892	150	2,137
1893	70	1,905
1894	115	1,908
1895	87	2,050
1897	140	1,984
1898	80	1,917
1903	41	2,065
1904	135	1,614
1905	82	1,467
1907	91	1,589
1909	90	1,225
1910	11	1,218

Source: "Santas Visitas: Santa Rosa, 1887–1912," AFP.

became angry and screamed, "I do not want baptism, I don't want God to have pity on me, I don't want God to pardon me for my sins, I don't want to go with God; I want the devil to take me, I want to go to the place of fire and of torments together with my mother and my husband." Soon afterward she died as well.[6] How common was resistance to deathbed conversion is not known, but it appears to have been widespread. As Bernardino de Nino remarked, even deathbed conversion was difficult during the first years after the establishment of a mission.[7]

The resistance of adult Chiriguanos to baptism can also be seen in the figures for the baptism of children, who, according to regulations, were to be baptized at birth or certainly by the time they entered school. The Indians were able to avoid infant baptism, at least at the beginning of the mission; the baptismal records of Tarairí from 1854 to 1874 make this clear. In the first years there were few baptisms recorded for infants in proportion to the Indian population, which probably numbered around fifteen hundred at the time of the establishment of the mission. The records also show that the friars succeeded in baptizing only children in danger of dying rather than at birth. For example, in 1858, four years after the establishment of the mission, ten of the thirteen infants (defined as less than one year of age) baptized were on their deathbed. Even among children twelve and under, ten of the thirteen baptized were dying or sick. A decade later the situation had not changed much. In 1868, of 65 infants baptized, 45 were on death's doorstep. Of 34 children from the age of one to twelve who were baptized, 29 received baptism *in articulo mortis*. (See table 14.) Indeed, as happened in other places where Christian missionaries insisted on baptizing the dying, this religious act became associated with death. Many Indians refused baptism for their children because they believed that christening the infants actually caused death.[8]

The pattern of baptism at death changed only after 1869, when the proportion of healthy infants baptized increased to more than half of all those baptized. The date is significant, for in that year a mission was established in Machareti, thus eliminating the greatest focus of resistance to the mission at Tarairí and permitting the friars to establish greater control over their charges.[9] Thus, while baptismal data for the initial period of the missions do not serve for demographic analysis, they do show limitations in control and conversion.

The Conversion Process

Analysis of conversion patterns shows that baptism and conversion proved more difficult than the Franciscans admitted. Given the preindustrial demographic pattern in which the population was overwhelmingly young, the conversion process should have gone relatively quickly, at least once the missionaries gained a modicum of control over their charges. However, figures on baptism show that this process took much longer than it should have had the program the Franciscans implemented on the missions functioned as they had hoped.

The only mission for which there is a complete record of religious affiliation from the beginning is Santa Rosa, one of the better administered missions and one where for years the Chiriguanos pleaded for the establishment of a mission before it was finally granted in 1887.[10] Because of the late foundation of the mission, the vigorous leadership of the Potosí missionaries, and the fact that the Indians themselves had repeatedly requested its establishment, this mission should have experienced rapid conversion. However, this proved not to have been the case, as table 15

TABLE 14. Children baptized in artículo mortis in Tarairí, 1855–1874

Year	Total infants baptized[1]	Sick infants	Percentage sick	Total children baptized[2]	Sick children	Percentage sick
1855	4	4	100	1	1	100
1856	3	2	67	0	0	
1857	6	3	50	8	3	38
1858	13	11	85	13	10	77
1859	6	5	83	5	3	60
1860	44	20	45	31	13	42
1861	15	12	80	24	15	63
1862	30	30	100	36	35	97
1863	13	13	100	30	28	93
1864	10	9	90	5	5	100
1865	25	23	92	13	11	85
1866	24	19	79	14	7	50
1867	30	25	83	43	40	93
1868	65	45	69	34	29	85
1869	30	16	53	8	5	63
1870	49	25	51	22	6	27
1871	45	15	33	20	9	45
1872	39	6	15	5	4	80
1873	25	9	36	2	2	100
1874	59	15	25	54	7	13

[1]Infants are defined as children one year old or less.
[2]Children are defined as older than one but no older than twelve.
Source: "Primer Libro Parroquial de bautismos y entierros de Tarairí," AVACHC.

TABLE 15. Converted versus unconverted Indians on Mission Santa Rosa de Cuevo, 1889–1909

Year	Total population	Converts	Percentage converts
1889	2,027	50	2
1892	2,137	243	11
1893	1,905	269	14
1894	1,908	356	19
1895	2,050	454	22
1897	1,984	586	30
1901	2,065	849	41
1903	1,614	852	53
1905	1,589	547	34
1907	1,503	578	38
1909	1,225	564	46

Source: "Santas Visitas: Santa Rosa," AFP.

demonstrates. In the whole period for which we have information, 1889 to 1909, the majority of Indians remained unconverted. Only in 1903 were the converts briefly in the majority, only to fall back to about a third of the population in 1905. The year 1912, twenty-five years after the foundation of the mission, marks when the friars could claim that over half of the families on the mission were converts.[11]

The length of time before a majority of mission residents were converts varied significantly between missions. In San Antonio and San Francisco del Parapetí, the short-lived missions reestablished at the beginning of the twentieth century, the majority of the Indians were already baptized at foundation. Boicovo was the most successful mission spiritually for the Franciscans; there, after only seventeen years, baptized neophytes predominated. Achieving a majority of baptized Indians within a generation was possible because Boicovo was the Potosí convent's first mission and it was able to put large-scale personnel and material resources into the mission. Most important, Boicovo brought together Indians dispersed during the lengthy 1874–1877 Huacaya War. The missionaries founded the mission to gather the refugees of the war, in particular the former residents of Huacaya, a settlement that had been taken over by Creoles. Apparently the formerly dispersed Chiriguano families were less able to resist the enticements to convert, at least in name, to Catholicism. It is also possible that disease played a large role, killing off or driving away many of the unconverted.[12] Likewise, San Buenaventura de Ivo became majority baptized after only nineteen years. The mission was founded after the brief but extremely bloody messianic uprising of 1892, when it became clear that the possibility of Chiriguano independence had finally disappeared. The missions founded among the Indians recently conquered in major warfare were more likely to accept baptism. (See table 16.)

An important issue is what baptism meant for the Indians. Did it mean that they accepted all the tenets of the Catholic faith and became devout Christians? It is difficult to tell from the evidence that the Franciscans left because, as previous chapters note, the main emphasis of the friars was on spiritual statistics, in other words on the number of baptisms, confirmations, and marriages that took place on the missions. Whether the

TABLE 16. Dates of mission establishment and convert majority

Mission	Date of foundation	Date of Neófito majority	Years to establish majority
Itau	1845	1877	32
Aguairenda	1851	1879	28
Tarairí	1854	1896	42
Macharetí	1869	1904	35
Tiguipa	1872	after 1900	>28
Boicovo	1876	1893	17
Santa Rosa	1887	1912	25
Ivo	1893	1912	19

Note: Chimeo, Itatiqui, San Francisco, and San Antonio del Parapetí are not included; the first two because of lack of data, whereas the latter two already had a majority of converts at their foundation.

Sources: "Santas Visitas," AFP, AFT; "Memoria que en ocación de las elecciones capitulares del Colegio de Tarija presenta al M.R.P. comisarios General de Colegios de Propaganda Fide en Bolivia a su Venerable Discretorio y los R.R.P.P. Conversores de las mismas," AFT; Bolivia, *Censo de la población de la República de Bolivia según el empadronamiento de 1 de septiembre de 1900*, 2nd ed. (Cochabamba: Editorial Inca, 1973).

neophytes truly believed in the doctrines of the Roman Catholic faith or whether they in fact knew these doctrines is difficult to tell. It is likely that the adults who were baptized (other than on their sickbed) became knowledgeable in the faith they had accepted, as the missionaries kept them as catecúmenos for a relatively long time, until they could show that they knew essential doctrines. However, the faith of the baptized children and the adults who accepted baptism when they were extremely ill is less certain. In the case of the children, the length they remained in the mission schools probably is strongly correlated with the depth of their faith in Catholic doctrine. On the other hand, as we have seen, many were eager to leave as soon as possible for the sugarcane plantations of Argentina once they were old enough to make the trek to *Mbaporenda*. Be that as it may, the number of baptized is relevant in terms of the relations of power, because the converted came under the direct supervision of the Indian officials elected by the baptized community and thus under the jurisdiction of the missionaries in ways the unconverted, who remained under the authority of the traditional chiefs, did not. Thus the role of conversion, given the paucity of information about the beliefs of the baptized, can be used as a proxy for understanding changes in power relations on the missions rather than the nature of personal beliefs by the Indians.

The missions founded by the Tarija convent took considerably more time to become majority baptized; the shortest period for conversion was twenty-eight years for Aguairenda. As in the case of Boicovo, Aguairenda was one of the Tarija convent's first missions and thus the recipient of much evangelical enthusiasm and convent resources.[13] Moreover, the mission was relatively small and thus it was easier to subvert traditional indigenous structures. Itau followed with thirty-two years, which constituted more than one generational turnover. Unfortunately we do not have information on Chimeo, a mission founded on the burning embers of a Chiriguano village in which much of the population had been massacred.[14] In all likelihood it followed patterns for Boicovo and Ivo, with a relatively rapid conversion rate, since it was established after a military defeat, as were the other two.

The three missions of Macharetí, Tarairí, and Tiguipa were among the largest missions, and their populations took the longest to convert. Size probably was an important factor, since the maintenance of indigenous beliefs, even under the constant barrage of Franciscan conversion efforts and in the presence of surrounding settlers, was easier when large communities remained in place. In addition, these three missions served as important gateways to the peoples of the Chaco and so maintained greater contacts with ethnic groups relatively untouched by Creole society. Macharetí was traditionally the meeting place between the Chaco ethnic groups and the Chiriguanos.[15] The other missions were almost adjacent to each other, thus forming almost a single unit; the back-and-forth of mission Indians between the settlements must have occurred daily. This meant that it was difficult for the friars to control the unconverted and, under the leadership of Mandeponay, the chief of Macharetí, go against the power of the traditional chiefs on these missions.

The Role of the Traditional Chiefs

Another, closely related factor making conversion a long drawn-out affair was the power of the traditional chiefs. These men played an ambiguous role; on the one hand, they or their fathers had invited the friars to establish the missions among their folk and were the guardians of order on the missions, while on the other hand, they were the representatives of the old order and of the unconverted, for none of the old chiefs converted to Catholicism except on their deathbed. Moreover, they kept up their old social practices that were antithetical to Franciscan morality, such as polygyny and the sponsorship of drinking feasts, many of them vital to maintaining power in the mission and beyond.

Traditional chiefs played a role not unlike that of the highland Andean *kurakas*, or ethnic lords, described by Karen Spalding and others for the colonial period.[16] They acted as intermediaries between the missionary and the outside world and their own folk, both the converted and unconverted. However, unlike their highland colonial counterparts, the first generation of Chiriguano chiefs did not seek acceptance among the European social elite on the frontier, nor did they try to accumulate goods or land privately in an effort to distinguish themselves from their fellow Indians. Rather, the considerable goods and power some chiefs accumulated were directed toward improving their status among fellow Indians as well as in their struggle for power with the missionaries.

Unlike on many other missions, such as the colonial missions in the Paraguayan Chaco or in northern Mexico, there appears to have been little struggle between the old ceremonial and religious specialists (shamans), called ipayes among the Chiriguanos, and the new ones, the Franciscans.[17] Chiriguano religiosity in the nineteenth century included the concept of a universal God (perhaps adopted or modified from their previous mission experience in the colonial period), but it appears that the shamans had few formal functions that directly conflicted with the role the missionaries assigned themselves. The ipayes appear in missionary reports only during epidemics, when Indians and settlers alike often preferred to go to the time-honored medicine men rather than experiment with the European remedies the friars dispensed with a heavy dose of religious paternalism.[18]

The power of the traditional chiefs was the main impediment to the friars' plans to establish Christian communities under their exclusive rule. Through tactical and strategic alliances with other members of frontier society (and sometimes at the national level) the chiefs held on to their influence on the missions or even augmented it. As had occurred before the missions were established, the chiefs used their links to other groups to fortify their positions as independent actors. These groups included other ethnic groups from the surrounding areas, settlers, and government officials. As a result of this complex interplay of alliances, the chiefs were able to determine the outcome of the contours of the missions to a much greater extent than the friars were willing to admit or than had been the case in most of the colonial missions.

The role of the chiefs varied over the life cycle of the missions. In the establishment phase the Franciscans desperately needed the influence and the military expertise of the traditional chiefs and their ability to hold their communities together. Here, tubichas such as the young Mandeponay, who took over Machareti after his father's assassination by the Cuevo Chiriguanos in 1868, and Guaripa in Chimeo were essential in defending the new missions from the attacks of the neighboring nonmission Chiriguano villages.[19] The tubichas who had accepted the missions were crucial to the settlements' survival, since neither the regular army nor frontier militias were able to defend the missions. In the case of Tarairí, in 1860, five years after the foundation of the mission, General Francisco Carmona, the head of Bolivian frontier forces, gave the mission Indians and their Toba allies a license to launch expeditions against other Tobas who had taken cattle from the settlers at Caiza. Carmona's need to give the mission Indians free rein, "without subjection to any [Creole] authority," during which time "all plunder obtained [were] to be the property of those who acquire[d] it," showed the weakness of national authorities on the frontier.[20] Such weakness also meant that the missionaries had to rely on traditional chiefs, since there was no other authority to back them up on the missions.

Indeed, the Tarairí Chiriguanos were so powerful that they were able to pressure the Franciscans to retire the military escort of settler militia that Fr. Gentili brought to defend the mission and, presumably, impose discipline on the mission inhabitants.[21] Military force thus remained in the hands of the mission Indians. This was unlike the colonial mission experiences, where the military *presidio*, or fort, often followed the missionaries. The lack of soldiers to support the missionaries also meant that Tarairí native authorities had veto power over policies proposed by the Franciscans.

In Tarairí the establishment of the mission in 1854 exposed not only the disunity among the local Chiriguano chiefs, but also opposition to the mission by Creole factions. As occurred in a number of missions, such as Aguairenda and Chimeo, Tarairí mission was a conglomerate of separate settlements brought together into one central location. As a result, a number of tubichas vied for supreme authority there. The joining of various communities and the resulting conflicts made it possible for outsiders to interfere in the mission. Bayandari, one of the chiefs of nearby Camatindi, conspired with Cornelio Ríos, leader of the frontier militia and a prominent settler in Caiza, the closest mestizo frontier town to the south, to eliminate the new mission. Bayandari also schemed with Arayápuy, the tubicha of Huacaya and one of the main opponents of the missionary enterprise, to attack the mission. Ríos bankrolled the enterprise, offering to pay an indemnity for any warrior who was killed in the operation. Arayápuy set up various ambushes, killing a number of mission Indians. An alliance of independent Chiriguanos, Tobas, and Tapietés attacked the mission, but without success. The intervention in favor of the pro-missionary tubichas by Juan Manuel Chituri, one of the major Chiriguano chiefs of a former colonial mission on the Parapetí River, was instrumental in counterbalancing the efforts of Ríos and Bayandari, and the mission survived.[22]

It is not clear why the head of the settler militia would conspire with malcontents on the new mission and, most of all, with their archenemies, the Indians from Huacaya. This incident shows well the constantly shifting alliances on the Chiriguano frontier, where personal liberty and the ability to remain independent often made for strange bedfellows in war. Ríos's opposition to the missions probably arose because he felt he would maintain greater power on the frontier without a strong Franciscan presence. Perhaps he also felt that, without the missionaries, he could more easily manipulate the Tarairí Indians to obtain their labor for his estates or take over their land.

Opposition to new missions was a normal occurrence, often based on personal animosities, factionalism, and alliances in frontier society that existed before the foundation of the mission. In Chimeo in 1849 two tubichas left the newly established mission because they were opposed to its foundation. In the case of Machareti, the personal rivalry between Guariyu, who favored a mission as a way to cut down on the depredations by Creole settlers, and Taruncunti, who had opposed the Franciscans, hindered the establishment of the mission until the latter's death. Even then, Taruncunti's son, Mandeponay, made life difficult for Guariyu, his father's rival. In the end the missionaries heeded Mandeponay and settled Guariyu's people in nearby San Francisco mission. Not only did this eliminate a source of constant friction on the mission, but the resettlement helped protect the friars from the always unreliable Tobas settled in San Francisco.[23]

What were the objectives of the chiefs who invited the missionaries into their villages? Foremost on the chiefs' minds was the preservation of land, indigenous culture, and the village's social and political structures. Accepting the missions was also the only way that they could remain leaders of their communities. Friars and chiefs shared the first objective, the preservation of village lands; without sufficient land, the Indians would have left. Conflict was bound to occur over the second set of objectives, since the missionaries hoped to remake the Chiriguanos into Christians and "civilize" them. In turn, the chiefs kept as many people as possible in their camp—best if unconverted—to maintain culture and preserve longstanding social and political structures. Thus the establishment of the missions created inherently contradictory motives between the missionaries and the village chiefs even when the Indians had accepted the missions voluntarily. As shown by the slowness of the conversion process, the tubichas were, at least in the medium term, relatively successful.

To foster the "civilization" process, the friars split the missions into two different sections, separating the converted from the unconverted Indians. In theory, the missionaries were in control of the whole mission and could punish the unconverted, including the chiefs. In practice, however, things were a bit different. In the neófito section, the traditional chiefs had little power. The missionaries had the neophytes elect their own authorities, who were relatively independent of the traditional chiefs. These authorities, called alcaldes, were under the direct supervision of the Franciscans, and all converts had to obey both the alcaldes and the friars. In the unconverted section the Indians also elected their own authorities, who happened to be the traditional chiefs or members of the chiefly families. This was the case when in Tarairí the old chief Cuarenda died in 1872. Fr. Alejandro Ercole supervised the elections, in which Guirasavai won. In turn, the newly elected chief suggested that the friar appoint Caitume as his alcalde, which the friar did. Both were members of the chiefly families that ruled in Tarairí. The chiefs, with the help of appointed alcaldes, kept public order in their sections, made sure the settlement remained clean, and, presumably, informed the missionaries of any disorder.[24] In other words, the chiefs were able to continue ruling the unconverted as they had before, with only certain restrictions regarding the running of the mission and relations with outsiders.

The friars were aware that the unconverted adult Chiriguanos would make poor Catholics. Fr. Corrado, one of the most experienced missionaries from the Tarija convent, asserted in a rather brutal manner, "The missionaries, to not throw their pearls to those dirty swine, abstain from teaching [the adults] the mysteries of the Faith, except *in articulo mortis*." Instead the Franciscans concentrated on the young, who, Corrado claimed, were "Christian saplings destined to substitute little by little the brambles of barbarism and paganism."[25] The chiefs realized this, and, as Ramón Gutiérrez has described so well for the colonial New Mexican missions, the struggle over power in the mission focused largely on the younger generation.[26]

That is not to say that the struggle over conversion did not also involve adults. Corrado records one incident, when the capitán Yanera in Aguairenda tried to prevent the baptism of a man on his deathbed. Yanera grabbed the hand of the missionary to prevent the baptism, but a few drops of holy water reached the dying man and the friar thus concluded that he had saved his soul.[27] The chiefs also realized the implications of the missionaries' effects on the children and it is likely that the chiefs actively collaborated in keeping the children from the mission schools.

The struggle between chiefs and missionaries over school-age children manifested in different ways. As the decades wore on, the friars gained sufficient information and control over the Indians to baptize most newborns and so eventually augment the population of schoolchildren. In turn, it was in the chiefs' interest that as few as possible go to school and thus eventually move from the unconverted to the neophyte section of town. While the traditional chiefs wanted the missions to preserve their land and not fall into the hands of the landlords who would turn their people into abject debt peons, they did not want their people on the missions to become Christian. Perhaps it is for this reason that the chiefs promoted migration to northern Argentina, for the young males, just at the age when they would be confirmed and move from catechumen status to that of neophyte, were also prime laborers for the sugarcane fields of Jujuy. Consequently the chiefs took the young men on the expeditions to the ingenios and so achieved various objectives. The young men were usually under the orders of the old chief, thus reaffirming traditional ties to rival those the friars had established with the youths in school. And the chiefs received money for each worker they could bring to the sugarcane fields.

As far as I can tell, the chiefs did not use this money for hoarding material goods. Instead, they invested the money in cane alcohol (*aguardiente*), purchased in the same ingenios, or in maintaining a large number of wives. Both were extremely important for maintaining what, on the frontier, constituted real power: the control over labor. The traditional chiefs achieved this through frequent fiestas, in which chicha and aguardiente flowed freely. Women (especially wives) were absolutely necessary for the preparation of chicha, a tedious and very labor-intensive task. This brew provided virtually complete nutritional requirements for the Indians.[28] Those who came to these feasts and drinking bouts were in turn obligated to recognize the largesse of the host and were more likely to follow his lead when he requested that they go with him to the sugarcane fields in the marvelous land of mbaporenda, "the land where there is work."

The tactic seems to have worked and the chiefs used this method more and more as the missions matured. The friars despaired over the increasing number of drunken feasts in the early twentieth century. While red wine is an essential ingredient in Catholic ritual and surely the Franciscans themselves were not averse to drinking in moderation, they were very much against these drinking bouts. Getting drunk on ritual occasions went against their definition of what "civilized" people did. Moreover, drinking often led to fights and attacks with knives,[29] as those who went to Argentina imitated the gauchos and began to use this deadly weapon. The friars also feared that the Indians would revert to their pagan practices during these bouts, beat their wives, and generally cause public disorder.[30]

As migration to Argentina increased, the use of potent distilled aguardiente instead of the low-alcohol fermented chicha became more common. According to the Franciscans, this was detrimental to the Indians' health and pocketbooks; in fact, Fr. de Nino blamed high adult mortality on the ill effects of liquor and also the general poverty of the Indians who were left with little after spending their money on clothes, alcohol, and coca leaves.[31] What the friars apparently did not perceive was that increasing cane alcohol consumption fostered by the tubichas was part of the power struggle between Franciscans and the chiefs. Despite their best efforts, the missionaries were never able to prevent widespread drinking or the sale of spirits. At least in the medium term, this favored the tubichas. It might have diminished the status of women, however, since they prepared the chicha. Moreover, the rationale for polygyny also declined for the tubichas, since cane alcohol eliminated the need for many wives to prepare alcoholic beverages for the feasts. As we will see in the case of Mandeponay, it also did not favor the chiefs in the long run.

To understand the dynamics of the complex struggle for power on the missions between the tubichas and the Franciscans, let us examine the case of Mandeponay, the great chief of Macharetí and arguably the most important Chiriguano leader and the most powerful individual along the whole southeastern frontier.[32] While not typical of tubichas in general because of his longevity and his great power, his history nonetheless reveals the possibilities of the cacique's role but also its limitations.

I have already briefly discussed Mandeponay's role in preserving the newly established mission under attack from an alliance of the Huacaya and Cuevo Chiriguanos to the north. Mandeponay had very personal reasons for defending his settlement against attack from the Chiriguano alliance. When his father, Taruncunti, began to make overtures to the missionaries in the 1860s, his former allies from Huacaya and Cuevo assaulted his camp and cut his throat from ear to ear, shouting, "Only the one who betrays his relatives has such an ugly mouth!" Mandeponay aided in the establishment of the mission to avenge his father's dishonorable death.

Mandeponay's power derived from the large population of Macharetí and also from its strategic position. Macharetí was by far the largest Chiriguano mission throughout the existence of the mission system. It was in fact the largest settlement along the whole frontier, at one point numbering over four thousand inhabitants.[33] Not even mestizo settlements could rival the mission in size. Thus its chief had control over the largest number of workers in the region, an extremely valuable resource along the frontier, where labor was always scarce. Since 1882 Mandeponay had supplied mission Indians to the sugarcane fields of Jujuy, receiving for each man a fixed sum of money, thus augmenting his resources even more. Thus, labor was doubly valuable for the Macharetí chief. He controlled both a large portion of labor for the surrounding region and also received premiums for exporting labor to the neighboring country.[34]

Also, Macharetí was the traditional meeting point between the Chiriguanos and the Chaco ethnic groups. Tobas, Matacos, and Choretes came to hunt near the settlement and also exchanged goods from the Chaco and their labor in return for corn, which they, as hunters and gatherers, did not produce themselves.[35] Mandeponay controlled access to the Chaco interior, making the mission an obligatory stop for expeditions to the frontier. As a result, we have a number of brief descriptions of the Chiriguano mburuvicha written by foreign travelers. According to Arthur Thouar, in 1886 Mandeponay was "one of the most influential chiefs of the Chiriguanos [who] resides in the mission [Macharetí]. In his struggles against the Tobas, he has shown talent and courage, he also enjoys as much among the [Creole] nationals as among the Indians of the interior a justly deserved reputation." When Erland Nordenskiöld visited Macharetí twenty years later, he described Mandeponay as being one of the three most powerful Chiriguano chiefs.[36]

The establishment of a mission at Macharetí was the greatest victory of the Tarija Franciscans' evangelization campaign. More than any other mission, Macharetí secured the frontier and constituted the bulwark for Creole society against the settlements of the central Chiriguano territory (Huacaya, Ingre, Cuevo, and Ivo) to the north and the Chaco peoples to the east. The new mission also opened up vast and productive ranchland. The Franciscan policy of securing land grants from the national government for sympathetic landlords (most notably the del Castillo family) shows the importance of the cattle economy in the region.[37] Manuel Mariano Gómez, the military leader of the Chaco forts, relied closely on Mandeponay. Indeed, in 1886 Gómez arranged for Mandeponay to receive a land grant of one square league (2,500 hectares) close to the Taringuite fort, apt for cattle grazing. Normally Gómez handed out these lands to settlers willing to reside in the forts. In this case, the Macharetí mburuvicha justified the receipt of the grant, asserting, "[I have] cooperated in the foundation of this fort [Taringuite] . . . with part of my *soldados* and I am always resolved to help in the defense of the interests of this province against the attacks of the savage Tobas." Having the Macharetí Indians as permanent allies proved essential for the establishment of the three forts in the Carandaití area and the government's push into the center of the Chaco.[38]

Mandeponay was also the linchpin of the Franciscan mission policy, and he knew it. Unlike on any other mission, where the neophytes were sectioned off from the unconverted, with separate plazas and streets, in Macharetí only one plaza existed and all Indians, converted and unconverted, were dispersed throughout the mission. This gave Mandeponay greater control over the Indian population than the traditional chiefs in other missions. Mandeponay weakened the missionaries' evangelization efforts since the friars were unable to control converts as in the villages exclusively for neophytes. Only in 1888 did the neophytes begin to build their own settlement. As we have seen, Mandeponay's strategy was successful, for it took until 1904, fully thirty-five years after Macharetí's foundation, for the friars to achieve a majority of converts on the mission.

Mandeponay was able to make his own rules, with little interference from the friars. For example, he remained polygynous, in direct opposition to mission rules. In 1890 the mission prefect complained that he continued to have six "concubines" more than twenty years after the mission was established.[39] This annoyed the Franciscans to no end, and as a new generation of missionaries arrived on the frontier, they began to see the old chief as a bad example and a vestige of the old ways to be eliminated. By 1889 Mandeponay had sensed that the missionaries wanted to get rid of him. However, support from the manager of the La Esperanza plantation in Jujuy and, most important, a threatened uprising by the Tobas that year kept the Franciscans from acting. Mandeponay was simply too important to be shunted aside.

Two years later, after the Toba threat had abated, the friars, who thought that Mandeponay was "isolated from the Fathers, scorned by many of his *soldados*, and afraid of punishment," decided to depose him as supreme chief of the mission. They badly miscalculated, for many unconverted left the mission to settle among the still unconquered villages near Huacaya or simply disappeared into the bush. Those who remained often refused to talk to the friars, in exactly the same way the friars refused to talk to Mandeponay. The mission became ungovernable and the missionaries had to back down. They asked Mandeponay to bring back the Indians and exile one Indian, Mandecui, who refused to follow their dictates. Mandeponay had won the power struggle by showing how essential he was to keeping the mission under control.[40]

The Franciscans had acted just in time. Soon after the reconciliation between Mandeponay and the friars, the Chiriguanía exploded in revolt under the leadership of Apiaguaiki, a young leader who wanted to rid the Chiriguano territory of all whites.[41] The friars' refusal to speak with Mandeponay may have created a situation in which such a rebellion was possible. Certainly Mandeponay's interview with Apiaguaiki prior to the revolt and the former's equivocal opposition to the messianic leader in the crisis before the outbreak of violence created a power vacuum that the Chiriguanos opposed to the Creoles utilized for their own ends. In the end Mandeponay aided the government forces sent against the rebels and helped maintain the mission system. The old leader probably realized that violent resistance was futile so many years after the resounding defeat of Chiriguano forces in the Huacaya War of 1874–1877 and that he would lose much of his power if the missions were destroyed.

The return to power of Mandeponay did not please the friars for long. As before, Mandeponay insisted on holding many feasts lubricated by cane brandy. In 1896 it appeared that his power was at its apex. Not only had he helped suppress the uprising, putting many local officials and settlers in his debt, but his orders were supreme even over those of the missionaries, who complained bitterly that the Indians obeyed only their old chief and virtually ignored them. This was also due to Mandeponay's natural talents as a leader. The French explorer Thouar commented that Mandeponay's oratorical skills, so vital for Guaraní political culture, were far superior to those of the Franciscans: "The facility of expression and the vigor of his logic [is] such that all the Padres' arguments are often demolished."[42]

Moreover, the friars gave up trying to prohibit polygyny because of "the bad example of their *capitán* Mandeponay" and his sons, who had three wives each. Yaguaracu, most commonly known by his Christian name, Simón María Napoleón Tacu (or Tacu, for short) and Atucuna aided their father, despite having been baptized and thus presumably under the guidance of the missionaries. The friars' impotence against the chief was most clear when that year Mandeponay took so many of his people to Argentina—without permission from the missionary—that the friars were unable to finish their building program on the mission. Even the schoolchildren left. The Franciscans were unable to stop them.[43]

Eventually Mandeponay's strategy of taking his workers to the plantations and his ample use of aguardiente for his feasts backfired. For many, the continual seasonal migrations to Jujuy turned into permanent residence near the ingenios; other workers on the long journey between the missions and the plantations never made it back. Many women who remained on the mission lost their spouses when they didn't return. Drunkenness became endemic on the missions. Unlike fermented chicha, which has many nutritive properties—proteins and complex carbohydrates—and a low alcohol content, the high percentage of alcohol in distilled brandy and its deficiencies as a food source created many problems on the missions. Many of the unconverted, and neophytes as well, became habitual drunkards, leading to an explosion of alcoholism on the missions, with all its social pathologies. In addition, a combination of locust plagues, droughts, and famine at the turn of the century made life on the missions even less attractive. In 1903 alone, ninety families of unconverted Indians left Macharetí with their children, whom the missionaries had to let go from school because they were unable to feed them. Another forty-four neophyte families left, though many settled in other missions. Thus Mandeponay's prime source of power, his control over abundant labor, began to disappear. During these difficult years even the many Chanés and Tobas who were semipermanent residents of Macharetí disappeared beyond the frontier, diminishing Mandeponay's role as intermediary with the Chaco peoples.[44]

The old chief realized he was losing his power. In 1902 he went to Monteagudo, the administrative capital of Azero province, and complained to the prosecutor that the friars were harassing him and his son Tacu. This apparently helped briefly, for the following year he had to compromise with the missionaries. In the friars' words, he promised that he would "rule with greater sensitivity and govern his own [the unconverted] with more prudence and moderation." Mandeponay's assertions did not assuage the friars for long. With many of the unconverted disappearing from the mission and the balance shifting toward the neophytes, the Franciscans deposed Mandeponay as supreme chief of the mission in 1904. Again a flood of petitions from members of frontier society arrived to defend Mandeponay. Germán del Castillo, erstwhile ally of the Franciscans and at that point the judge of Ñancaroinza, a nearby mestizo settlement, admonished the friars for harassing the old chief. Manuel Mariano Gómez, the founder of private military forts in the Chaco and one of the most powerful men and largest landowners on the frontier, also defended him. The Argentine plantation owners, to whom, according to the friars, the mburuvicha owed large amounts of money, chimed in with their support. Despite this strong opposition, the friars formally eliminated his position as *capitán grande*.[45]

But the Franciscans had acted too late. New mission regulations in 1905 imposed by the new national government of anticlerical liberals severely restricted the missionaries' power on the missions. Mandeponay continued to extract laborers from the mission, receiving a price for each one he could deliver. In 1906 the mburuvicha supplied forty-two married neophytes to the labor contractors; in 1910 fifty left for the sugarcane fields, as well as forty unconverted adults and sixty schoolchildren.[46]

By 1911 Mandeponay had returned to the Franciscans' good graces. He sided with them when the Bolivian government tried to recruit mission Indians over the friars' objections to serve on an expedition into the Chaco. Interestingly, his favorite son, Tacu, aided the expeditionaries, defying his father. Was Mandeponay playing a double game, publicly opposing the government authorities while his son made deals that made it possible for the expedition to proceed?[47]

Mandeponay's role after the first decade of the twentieth century is not clear. In retrospect his policy of measured independence from the Franciscans while maintaining the mission system had been largely successful during his long life. The contradictions of this policy came to a head at the turn of the century, when Mandeponay's need to keep control over his people by sending them to Argentina conflicted with the resulting depopulation of the mission and increasing drunkenness. Nevertheless, in a photograph probably taken in 1920, Mandeponay is seated in front of the mission school next to Fr. Hipólito Ulivelli, the bishop of the newly created Chaco bishopric and head of the combined missions from Tarija and Potosí. He is the only native present among a sea of Franciscan robes. (See figure 11.) Clearly he remained the *éminence grise* among all the mission chiefs and an important power broker along the frontier. Only on his deathbed, on 18 January 1922, did he permit himself to be baptized.[48] Thus the most important Chiriguano chief, who had influenced events over more than half a century and had contributed both to the power of the missions and their decline, died a converted man. Only his death eliminated his power over the unconverted.

While it is possible to document the twists and turns of the relationships between Mandeponay and the Franciscans, much less is known about Chiriguano chiefs from other missions and even less about lower level chiefs. In the missionary accounts it is the friars who have names, and few Indians other than exceptional leaders such as Mandeponay are mentioned. This is typical even in a large mission such as Tarairí, where at the foundation the population was even greater than at Machareti.

Cuarenda stands out as one of the founders of the Tarairí mission, but little is known about him. He was from the nearby village of Caigua-mi. After haranguing the Tobas for their cattle raiding at one of the periodic feasts at his settlement, a fight broke out and four Toba warriors died. As a result Cuarenda sought the aid of the missionaries in Aguairenda and remained there with his people as a refugee. He returned with the foundation of the mission at nearby Tarairí. His skills as war leader were crucial to the survival of the mission from attacks in the early years. He

FIGURE 11. Visit of Monseñor Hipólito Ulivelli and a Franciscan delegation to Mission Macharetí around 1920. To the right is Mandeponay, the only Indian seated on a chair. Behind him are the mission schoolboys, next to the boys' school. *Source*: AFT, photographer unknown.

also led the fight against the conspiracy of Bayandari and Cornelio Ríos, killing the brother of Arayápui, the mburuvicha of Huacaya, during the latter's assault on the mission in 1855.⁴⁹ It is not clear who became chief of the unconverted on the mission after Cuarenda's death.⁵⁰

By the 1880s Araguiyu had emerged as the new leader of the unconverted. He did not please the Franciscans. Araguiyu was an ipaye, or medicine man, a rival to the missionaries' claims for religious leadership. Apparently the friars had deposed Araguiyu earlier as mburuvicha. The reason for his demotion was his open opposition to the missionaries. In 1883, when the anticlerical Daniel Campos, whom the Bolivian government of General Narciso Campero had named delegate of the frontier, launched his expedition into the Chaco, Araguiyu, "who desiring his old liberty and the bad habits of the neighboring settlers [cristianos]," tried to remove the Franciscans from Tarairí. The friars faulted Campos for aiding Araguiyu. The Franciscans did not budge. When the dislocations that the expeditionary forces had caused subsided the following year, the mburuvicha, according to the missionaries, "remained isolated and [had] fallen into disrepute to the point that nobody [paid] him any attention."⁵¹

Despite the friars' judgment of the mburuvicha's unpopularity, Araguiyu continued to influence many Indians on the mission. This suggests that in the 1880s a kind of parallel government emerged on the mission. Indians disaffected with the Franciscans banded around Araguiyu. The struggle for power over the mission manifested itself in many ways. In 1891 Araguiyu tried to reassert his claims as supreme leader of the community, causing various "disturbances, animosities, hatred, and sentiments." Four years later he appealed to the national authorities, over the heads of the missionaries. He traveled to the Bolivian capital, Sucre, with eighty of his men to have President Mariano Baptista designate him capitán over Tarairí. However, Araguiyu had the misfortune of petitioning the most proclerical president of the late nineteenth century. President Baptista, relying on the advice of his Franciscan friends, denied the Tarairí chief's petition. The missionaries then had the old chief exiled from the mission. The friars noted that the habitual disorders between neophytes, catechumens, and unconverted diminished significantly with Araguiyu's departure.[52] In the end, Araguiyu's attempts at regaining his former position failed, but only after decades of struggle in which he countered the influence of the missionaries. It was also because of individuals like Araguiyu that Tarairí's unconverted population gained the reputation among the friars of being the most resistent to conversion among all the missions.

Power struggles on the missions were common, and the disputes with chiefs were not only manifestations of opposition to the friars' project of "civilizing" the natives. Settlers tried to exert their influence in the missions by pitting one chief against another. Macharetí provides a telling example. In 1884 Cundeye, Mandeponay's brother, wanted to take some of the Macharetí Indians to work on Aniceto Arce's haciendas near Sucre, in the western highlands. Mandeponay, on the way to the Argentine plantations, told the Macharetí Indians that if anyone went to Sucre with his brother he would exile them from the mission. Despite this prohibition—surely because Mandeponay did not want his brother to empty the mission of all workers—a settler, David Pacheco, finally convinced Cundeye to go to Sucre with thirty mission Indians. Cundeye made it only as far as nearby Cuevo, to Pacheco's house, before the Indians turned back. At Pacheco's house Cundeye demurred, telling the settler over and over again that he was not chief. According to Cundeye, Pacheco forced him, under pain of receiving two hundred lashes, to travel to Sucre with a letter requesting that his cousin, Bolivian president Gregorio Pacheco, appoint him capitán grande and chief of Macharetí. The president did so, but the friars did not accept the document. It appears that Cundeye did not have the same rhetorical gifts or the charisma of his brother, and Pacheco's efforts to put into place a chief beholden to him did not succeed.[53]

The Indians who most presented problems for the missionaries were the sons of the old tubichas. Many became what the missionaries considered troublemakers. This is not surprising, given the interstitial position these young men occupied in the mission. After all, the Franciscans' aim was to convert the population. The authorities over the converted population, the alcaldes, were selected not for their membership in chiefly families but because they were the most avid converts and considered the most pliable to the missionaries' demands. If converted, the chiefly sons came under the direct supervision of the friars and were supposed to live in the neófito section of the mission. If the sons did not accept baptism by the time their father had given over authority to them, they ruled over a greatly diminished unconverted population. The deal struck between the Chiriguanos and the missionaries, that the converted come under the direct jurisdiction of the padres, left these individuals with a bleak future compared to their powerful fathers.

The difficult position of the chiefly son was apparent in Tarairí. Chanchi, the son of Cuarenda, founder of the mission, had little hope of achieving his father's status. Nevertheless, he tried to assert his authority in the mission. In 1870, when the head teacher of the mission school for girls left for the neighboring mission, he tried to scare the pupils by sacrificing sheep behind the school building at night. The screams of the animals and the view of the decapitated corpses the following morning frightened the girls. They told the friar, who the following night put an armed guard at the school. The guard scared the Indians away when he fired his gun into the air. Annoyed at his failure, the next night Chanchi organized an attack party of about thirty Indian boys. When the raiding party broke down the door of the school, the guard shot and killed the first to enter, one of the boys in Chanchi's group. The shotgun blast dispersed the rest of the crowd. Chanchi and the other surviving members of the attack party fled to Argentina. The incident ended any chance he might have had of succeeding his father.[54]

Part of the sons' problem also involved the lack of access that young Chiriguano men had to young women due to the restrictions placed upon the schoolgirls. This hindered the natural courtship process that occurred in nonmission villages, where the girls and boys could meet and court under their parents' watchful eyes. Other aspects, such as the animal sacrifices, are not clear in this incident. Be that as it may, it is significant that the chief's son was the leader of the protest. Chanchi was stuck between two worlds: the mission world and the world of his forefathers, life as a Catholic and life as the inheritor of a powerful chieftainship. In the end he had to flee the mission and live in exile.

The most important example of the problematic nature of chiefly sons was Mandeponay's son, Simón María Napoleón Tacu. Tacu made the best of the situation by becoming an entrepreneur, protected by his father. He combined modern practices of commerce with the traditional prestige accorded to the chiefly family. Like Chanchi and other chiefly sons, he had few hopes of being elected tubicha of Macharetí. After all, he had been baptized, lived in the neophyte section of the mission, and thus was ineligible to rule over the unconverted, as his father had since 1869. Moreover, by the time his long-lived father gave up the chieftainship there were few unconverted Indians left. Becoming leader of the converts was also out of the question. Even had the friars permitted this, Tacu himself would have been a mere spokesman for the missionaries, a position that this proud man would not have accepted. In any case, the Franciscans abhorred Tacu, but they felt powerless to expel him from the mission.

There were many reasons for the friars' disgust with Tacu. For one, he refused to live like a Christian, as he had numerous wives. The missionaries also felt that he worked actively against them, conspiring with other Chiriguanos and outsiders to corrupt the neophytes and keep the unconverted beholden to his family and not the Franciscans. Fr. Gervasio Costa, the mission prefect of Tarija in 1902, called Tacu "an old labor contractor of Indians, despicable seller of aguardiente and backsliding mission Indian: man of depraved habits, without any idea of morality, religion or honor, but cunning and egotistical without doubt; vile and abusive seducer, kidnapper, and hypocritical rustler, calloused in depravity, cruel and inhuman with those who cross [him], even if they are his own children."[55]

Why did Tacu receive this vituperation from the Franciscans, who presumably were level-headed men of God? Tacu's behavior challenged much of what the Franciscans preached. He was one of the most important *enganchadores* [contractor] for labor to the Argentine sugar plantations on Macharetí and perhaps on other missions as well. He also provided liquor to the mission Indians, fueling drunkenness that threatened the friars' control. He allied himself with government authorities, thus sidestepping the padres' discipline, much as his father and the most successful chiefs had done.

Perhaps most damning in the friars' eyes, Tacu was an entrepreneur, selling aguardiente to all comers; even at his fiestas he sold alcohol, rather than distributing it for free, as traditional leaders did.[56] Tacu was an important transitional figure in other ways as well. Nordenskiöld used Mandeponay's son as an example of a "rich Indian," who, according to the anthropologist, lived like the white man and had Chiriguano servants, a new practice among Chiriguano chiefs. Nordenskiöld also characterized Tacu as one of the "most civilized" Indians.[57] This sobriquet was not a compliment: unlike other Indians, Tacu did not share his earnings, but kept them to assume a Creole lifestyle.

Tacu's entrepreneurship went against everything the missionaries had tried to impart to their charges. After all, the Franciscans themselves had given up earthly goods and had taken vows of poverty. In the Chaco they were trying to recreate a religious world that had been lost in anticlerical Europe. The traditions of chiefly redistribution of goods, of the relative poverty of the chiefs (other than in women and prestige, outside of the European calculus of wealth), had attracted the Franciscans to the Chiriguanos. Likewise, the Chiriguanos probably accepted the Franciscans, both in the eighteenth and again in the nineteenth century, precisely because the friars, like their own chiefs, distributed goods to their charges and, unlike other white men, did not try to accumulate goods or cheat the Indians.[58] Tacu had absorbed the lessons of capital accumulation in a selfish way that smacked of exploitation of his fellow Indians. He did not listen to the friars and behaved not like a pious convert, but rather combined what the friars saw as the worst traits of both cultures: polygyny, drunkenness, avarice, and disobedience.

So bad did relations between the friars and Tacu become that they tried to banish him from the mission in 1904, the year his father briefly fell from power. The Franciscans complained to the foreign minister (also in charge of religious matters) in La Paz, asking him for help in banishing Tacu from the mission. Two years earlier the friars had pointed to Tacu's efforts at contracting laborers for Argentina as the prime reason for the mission's decline. In 1904, although they attacked his father, they saw Tacu as the real culprit behind the problems on the mission. However, strong support from local authorities for both Tacu and his father (in all likelihood local officials also benefited economically from the labor exports and the sale of liquor on the missions) stymied the friars. In 1907 new complaints surfaced regarding Tacu's activities; still he did not leave the mission. In 1913, protected by his father, Tacu continued to sell liquor. Because the sugar economy in Argentina was in crisis that year, few Indians had migrated to Argentina and instead worked locally, so the chief's son concentrated on his liquor-selling business.[59]

Despite Tacu's attempts at becoming a "rich Indian," he failed. He died in 1915, leaving behind very few material goods. The probate records show that he owned some household goods, two horses, three donkeys, two small sugarcane fields, and two small cornfields. He owed local settlers 917 Bolivianos, an amount that probably exceeded his total worth.[60]

In sum, conversion rates, the crucial role of the traditional chiefs in maintaining order within the mission villages, and the ability of the chiefs' sons to subvert missionary authority all point to a much more complex field of power within the missions than the Franciscans were willing to admit in their public writings. The internal mission documents show that communities were riven by constant struggles between the missionaries and indigenous authorities. Rather than the establishment of missions immediately leading to Indian acquiescence, the friars were able to impose some of their ideas and methods on the mission population only over many decades. The power struggles were sometimes accompanied by violence, but most of the time the indigenous authorities, such as Mandeponay, were in constant peaceful negotiation with the friars. Outsiders to the mission were involved as well, though outside influence waxed and waned over time (see chapter 7).

When the missionaries left the indigenous authorities alone things usually went relatively smoothly, though the mission functioned very far from the ideals that the friars wanted to implant among the "savages." When the Franciscans tried to impose their own will against that of the unconverted chiefs, the missions became ungovernable. This was not new; when missionaries in the colonial period treated mission Indians as children, they fought back. To make the case even clearer and show the lines of power that ran through the missions, it is useful to turn to a specific case study, the 1892 rebellion.

The 1892 Rebellion

In 1892 the missions contained over eleven thousand Chiriguanos, of whom about a third had been baptized as Christians. The missions with the highest proportion of unconverted were Santa Rosa de Cuevo, founded in 1887, and Macharetí, founded in 1869.[61] Numerous children went to the mission schools, and while Mandeponay and other tubichas struggled to remain independent, the government remained squarely behind the missionary endeavor. Migration to Argentina created some problems but did not reach the high levels of the first decades of the twentieth century. Power had begun to shift from the Indians to the missionaries as cattle barons and their herds penetrated ever more deeply into the Chaco, pushing back other tribes, most notably the Tobas, who had been on-and-off allies of the Chiriguanos in their wars against Bolivian forces.

After the Huacaya War of 1874–1877, in which the centers of resistance to Bolivian hegemony in Huacaya had been given to the cattle barons as land grants (and for good measure that of the settlers' allies, the territories of the Chiriguano chief Buricanambi in Ingre), it appeared that the Chiriguanos had finally been beaten. The Potosí Franciscans, eager to establish missions and help the waning Tarija convent, collected the defeated Indians of Huacaya in nearby Boicovo. Only the territories of the Chiriguanos of the Cuevo-Ivo area and the Caipipendi valley to the north maintained some semblance of independence. In the Cuevo-Ivo area settlers pressured the Chiriguanos, and in particular destroyed cornfields with their cattle. Since the 1870s the Indians of the area had repeatedly requested the establishment of a mission, but the Tarija Franciscans, exhausted from their efforts to convert the Tobas and other tribes in the Gran Chaco, had inadequate manpower and resources to do so. In 1887 the more vigorous Potosí Franciscans created a mission in Cuevo. In the Caipipendi region the chiefly Aireyu family had made an uneasy peace with the settlers, preferring to send laborers to the estates and provide local government officials with servants rather than challenge Creole hegemony. Most other Chiriguanos were under settler control, working on the estates carved out of former native lands.[62]

The Chiriguano settlement of Ivo, adjacent to Santa Rosa, was unable to fend off the depredations of the settlers. In 1891 the Chiriguanos of Ivo feared a complete takeover by ranchers. At this moment a young man appeared, named Chapiaguasu. He claimed to be a god come to earth (*tumpa*) to save the Chiriguanos from the karai. He called himself Apiaguaiki, or "eunuch of god," suggesting he was equivalent to the Franciscan priests.[63] His mother was a domestic on a number of estancias in the Chiriguanía, and during the twenty-eight years of his life Chapiaguasu had considerable exposure to Creoles. It is likely that he witnessed the massacre of Chiriguano families in Murucuyati in 1877, one of the last battles of the

Huacaya War. He also briefly lived on Mission Santa Rosa as a child, and thus presumably knew some rudiments of the Catholic faith, such as the belief in Christ's second coming.

A number of Chiriguano leaders recognized Chapiaguasu's intelligence and taught him ava culture. We know that he spent some time with Machirope, the mburuvicha of the Huacaya region. The boy's mother probably died during the Murucuyati massacre, and Machirope, one of the important ava chiefs who refused to settle in Mission Boicovo, adopted him and other orphans from the massacre, as behooved a good Chiriguano chief. These incidents and his experiences as a member of the household of the fiercely independent Machirope probably engendered Chapiaguasu's hatred toward the ranchers, his rejection of the missions, and his desire to rid his ancestral lands of the karai.

More important, Guariju, an old ipaye from Sipotendi, also recognized Chapiaguasu's talents and eventually took him on as an apprentice. Thus Chapiaguasu learned the healing arts and perhaps an antipathy for the missionaries, rivals of traditional shamans such as Guariju. The region's Chiriguanos appreciated Chapiaguasu, who gained a following by healing an Indian from Santa Rosa mission. In this way he set himself up as a rival to the powers of the Franciscans, who, as we have seen, claimed (but did not have) a monopoly over the medical arts. In late 1891 the Indians of Ivo elected Chapiaguasu tumpa. It was then that he changed his name to Apiaguaiki. The young man sequestered himself in a house in Curuyuqui, a settlement on the outskirts of Ivo. To reinforce his claim as prophet, his followers decorated his abode with colorful textiles and stationed young warriors as guards. Anyone wishing to speak with the tumpa first had to follow certain prescribed ceremonies and then speak to him on his knees through intermediaries. The creation of an aura of mystery and semidivinity, the speaking through intermediaries, and the separation of the prophet from the ordinary Indians were reminiscent of the Speaking Crosses during the Caste Wars of the Yucatán. As in Yucatán, these effects surely increased the authority of Apiaguaiki's prophetic pronouncements and created messianic fervor for the movement.[64]

Apiaguaiki consciously set himself up as a rival of the friars. He sent a message to all the tubichas throughout the Chiriguanía, telling them to visit him and, according to one friar, put themselves under his authority. When Fr. Santiago D'Ambrogi from nearby Santa Rosa mission went with other local authorities to visit the tumpa, Apiaguaiki challenged the Franciscan while trying to sound conciliatory toward the secular authorities. Apiaguaiki claimed, in the words of Angélico Martarelli, that, "as the Christians say their prayers to God and to the Saints so that the drought ceases . . . , they did the same according to their own customs."[65] In other words, his authority was more authentically Chiriguano and merited greater consideration than that of the Franciscans.

While Apiaguaiki could not convince any mburuvicha to join his cause, a number of tubichas and their men, women, and children joined the settlement at Curuyuqui. One missionary estimated that the new settlement contained five thousand warriors, as well as women and children. Tubichas and their followers from all over the region joined the messianic leader's cause, both those attached to estates as well as the independent villages. It included Indians from Carandaití, on the fringes of the Chaco, and those living along the Parapetí River, farther to the north.[66]

The threat to the missions was great. While virtually no Indians from Boicovo—the remnants of the powerful Huacaya Chiriguanos crushed in the war of 1874–1877—joined the movement, in the largest missions sizable contingents of warriors disappeared from their homes to join the growing Curuyuqui settlement outside of Ivo. These included Indians from Santa Rosa and Macharetí. Guariyu, Mandeponay's rival and the leader of the ava living in the Toba mission of San Francisco, pledged his men to Apiaguaiki, but demurred when he realized that bloodshed was inevitable.[67]

Mandeponay, as usual, played a double game. At first he went to Apiaguaiki and asserted that he was ready for war. Immediately after his visit with the tumpa he left the region to visit the Tobas, ostensibly to purchase horses. It is not clear whether, as had been the case in various instances over the nineteenth century, he attempted to forge a multiethnic alliance with the Tobas against the Creoles. When the officials in Ñancaroinza sent a small force of militia accompanied by seventy Indians from Tarairí into the Chaco to prevent a coordination of the Ivo Chiriguanos and the Tobas in the first few days of the revolt, Mandeponay reappeared. He claimed that the Tobas would not join the messianic leader. He took over leadership of the mission Indians arrayed against the rebel movement and marched with his people and mission Indians from Tarairí against the tumpa's forces.[68]

Mandeponay's actions were not as unequivocal as might appear at first glance. His favorite son and frequent collaborator, Tacu, joined Apiaguaiki, only to reappear in the mission after the war.[69] In this way, the old chief kept his hand in both camps. Also, we do not know what happened in Toba territory, where Mandeponay visited the messianic leader's potential allies. Did the old chief's fervor decline when he realized that the Tobas were unwilling to join the rebels against the Creoles? Did the appearance of the militia and the Tarairí Indians as he was meeting with the Tobas foil his plans? Did he wait a few days in the interior of the Chaco to see how well the Iveños were doing before declaring for one side or another? Or was Tacu indeed freelancing, working against his father, given the former's well-known antipathy for the missionaries?

The rebellion was massive when it broke out in early January of 1892. The Indians concentrated at Curuyuqui had intended on giving a devastating blow to the karai the very first day, which they had fixed for carnival, when many settlers were bound to be drunk and partying, despite the heightened tensions between Chiriguanos and Creoles. However, it was not to be. The revolt began weeks earlier, precipitated by the rape and murder of a young Chiriguano woman, a relative of Azucari, the tubicha of Ivo, by Fermín Saldías, the corregidor of Ñumbicte (Cuevo). When Azucari and the warriors of the rapidly growing settlement around Ivo found out about the rape-murder, they deployed on 6 January. The following day, after ambushing a column of militia and settlers near Cuevo, the Indians attacked and then sacked the town of Cuevo. Most of the settler families had already fled to the nearby Santa Rosa mission. Other assaults followed in which the Chiriguanos destroyed many hacienda houses, killed a number of settlers, and took herds of cattle back to the rebel base at Curuyuqui.[70]

The surviving settlers from as far away as Ingre left the countryside in a panic, taking refuge either in the towns far from the rebellion or in the missions. Santa Rosa, near the main rebel base of Curuyuqui, became the military headquarters of the settlers and their allies. As was customary, the majority of combatants on both sides were Indians. While some mission Indians had gone over to the messianic leader's side, most remained loyal to the friars. Moreover, some settlers brought their own Indian allies with whom they had extensive ties, such as the Chiriguanos recruited from the outskirts of Monteagudo, brought to Santa Rosa by Colonel Tomás Frías.

The rebel Chiriguanos attacked Santa Rosa on 21 January with one thousand warriors on foot and three hundred on horseback, commanded by the tumpa himself. Mandeponay tried to warn Frías of the assault, but the friar messenger from Macharetí to Santa Rosa failed to arrive in time. The death of Baririqui, one of the most important war leaders, in the assault brought about a retreat to Ivo. The people of Santa Rosa had a close call. They had nearly exhausted their supply of ammunition when the tumpa's men broke off the attack.⁷¹

While Chiriguano tactics always included attacking the missions, victory in this case would have had special meaning. It would have shown the tumpa's superiority over both the settlers who had fled to the mission and the religion represented by the hated mission that had divided Chiriguano society into mission Indians and independent villages and into unconverted Indians and neófitos. The confusion caused by all the refugees who had fled to Santa Rosa made the attack on the mission easier, and without the military veteran Frías's desperate rallying of his forces to defend the mission, Apiaguaiki's men would probably have succeeded. However, unlike in earlier Chiriguano wars, Apiaguaiki tried to imitate Creole military tactics through massive assaults and defining battles rather than the more traditional Chiriguano guerrilla tactics of hit and run by relatively small forces. The use of European methods of warfare with the inferior technology of bows and arrows doomed the uprising and brought about a quick but bloody end to the conflict.

The Creole-led forces counterattacked six days later with reinforcements from surrounding towns. The hastily assembled force consisted of fifteen hundred Indians, the majority from the missions of Machareti and Boicovo, who were armed with bows and arrows and knives.⁷² Fifty regular soldiers from the Bolivian Army joined 140 Creole militiamen, 100 of whom possessed repeating rifles. They marched to Curuyuqui, where they found the Indians dug in behind two long trenches. The Creole-led forces attacked the approximately five thousand Chiriguanos, who fought to the death. The tumpa had told them that those who believed in the cause could not be hurt by bullets. While this proved untrue, the defenders at Curuyuqui also knew that their lives and that of their families were on the line and were willing to die for their cause. By the end of the day, the Creole-led troops had broken through the second trench in hand-to-hand combat, but the tumpa's warriors continued to resist. Colonel Frías called his men to retreat when the ammunition began running out.

The following day Frías's scouts found an empty settlement. Apiaguaiki's men had abandoned Curuyuqui, fleeing during the night into the dense chaparral. Over six hundred warriors had died. Only four mission Indians had been killed in the battle and thirty wounded. The Creole soldiers suffered five wounded. Many rebel Indians gave themselves up, but once they were conducted as prisoners to Santa Rosa, the settlers who had sought refuge there massacred them. One hundred prisoners died at the hands of the Creoles in the mission. In the aftermath the settlers and militiamen distributed the surviving women and children to sell as slaves. Eventually the Creoles were able to capture the tumpa and other military chiefs and executed them.[73] Thus ended the last and one of the most violent Chiriguano wars.

The missions had again proved their usefulness. Despite concerted attempts by Apiaguaiki to bring the mission Indians to his side, the majority remained loyal to their traditional chiefs, few of whom went over to the rebel side. Apiaguaiki's attempts at winning over the mission chiefs might have actually proved detrimental to his cause, for this intelligence provided the Creoles with information on enemy movements.

As in earlier times, when the missions were right on the edge of the frontier, they also served as places of refuge for the surrounding settlers. Santa Rosa played this vital role. By the end of the brief war the mission contained about three thousand Creole refugees, in addition to the approximately two thousand mission Indians.[74] Missions such as Santa Rosa had been built in easily defensible positions (see figure 12), where the church and the school complex dominated the highest hill in the area. From the church towers lookouts could spot an approaching mass of warriors. (Indeed, it is almost possible to see Ivo itself from Santa Rosa's church.) The fortresslike mission buildings on the hilltop could have served as a makeshift last refuge, though the failure of the Iveños to capture the town below made this unnecessary.

The permanent alliance between Creoles and Chiriguano groups that the mission system created largely held. As was usually the case in these frontier wars, the Chiriguanos constituted by far the vast majority of combatants on both sides. While Winchester rifles made up for the numerical disadvantage of the Creoles, the casualty figures show that in all likelihood the mission Indians engaged in most of the hand-to-hand fighting in the trenches. The missions, especially Santa Rosa, proved indispensable as sources of manpower and as bases from which to counterattack.

This permanent alliance, despite the cracks that Apiaguaiki's messianic message revealed, was particularly important for keeping the involvement of other ethnic groups to a minimum. Unlike the 1874–1877 Huacaya War, when the Tobas fought alongside the Chiriguanos and, in the later phases, offered them refuge in the interior of the Chaco from which to launch guerrilla raids, the Chiriguanos fought on their own against the Creoles. This was in large part due to the fact that the main intermediary between Chiriguanos and Tobas, Machareti's Mandeponay, supported the Creoles.

FIGURE 12. View of Mission Machareti from the central plaza toward the hill with the church and parish house (center), as well as the girls' and boys' schools (right and left). The walled establishments on the hill provided protection from raids if necessary. *Source*: Doroteo Giannecchini and Vincenzo Mascio, *Album fotográfico de las Misiones Franciscanas en la República de Bolivia a cargo de los Colegios Apostólicos de Tarija y Potosí 1898* (La Paz: Banco Central de Bolivia and Archivo y Biblioteca Nacionales de Bolivia, 1995).

The prestige of the tumpa and of the chiefs in Ivo could not equal that of the old chief and thus prevented the creation of a multiethnic indigenous alliance that might have brought about a longer war with much higher Creole casualties.

Despite Mandeponay's decisive but somewhat belated help in putting down the rebellion, military authorities distrusted all Chiriguano chiefs, showing their ignorance of the realities of Chiriguano power relations. Creole authorities suspected Mandeponay as one of the major instigators of the rebellion. About a month after the revolt fifty fully armed Bolivian Army soldiers showed up in Machareti to arrest and execute Mandeponay. Luckily for the old chief, the prefect of the Tarija missions was present when the soldiers marched in and the old Franciscan was able to prevent his seizure. A similar incident had apparently occurred in 1877, in the aftermath of the Huacaya War, when the missionaries also saved Mandeponay's life.[75]

Perhaps Mandeponay's tribulations were related to the Machareti Indians' attempts to save the rebel prisoners' lives. As the militia and the army rounded up suspected rebels, the Macharetí Indians took those Indian prisoners who passed through their mission and, with the support of Fr. Santiago Romano, the Franciscan in charge of the mission, refused to let them leave mission territory. After the massacre of helpless Chiriguano prisoners in Santa Rosa, the friar and the Indians feared that new prisoners sent to the settlers' headquarters in Ñancaroinza might also be summarily executed. Fr. Santiago permitted the transport of the prisoners to Tarairí, next door to Ñancaroinza, but only after entrusting them to regular army troops, who were less likely to take vengeance on them.[76] Later these Indian warriors and their families were the first to be resettled in Ivo, where the Potosí Franciscans established a mission in 1893.

What does the 1892 rebellion tell us about the changing lines of power on the missions? If the behavior of Tacu is any indication, those convinced by Apiaguaiki's messianic message were not only the old unconverted Indians, but members of younger generations who were anxious to reconstitute Chiriguano independence and eliminate the Creole presence in their homelands. The actions of those from the missions who joined the rebellion also showed that the Franciscans' control over their charges was at best imperfect. Nevertheless, it is clear that, in general, the majority of the mission population did not repudiate the Franciscans. We have seen that the role of the traditional chiefs such as Mandeponay was essential to the missions' preservation, for it was personal loyalty to Indian mission leaders that prevented the wholesale abandonment of the missions, not the exhortations of the friars. Indeed, from Franciscans' letters written during the rebellion one gets the sense of how important the chiefs were in controlling the mission population. These letters focused on assessing the loyalty of the traditional chiefs at each of the missions rather than on the alcaldes elected from among the converted. It is for this reason that, despite the somewhat equivocal behavior of Mandeponay and his recent transgressions, the friars came out in his defense.

While it appears that the chiefs in many ways had the upper hand during a large part of the missions' existence, the rebellion and the attempted execution of Mandeponay show that the chiefs and the friars needed each other. Without their base on the missions protected by the Franciscans, Mandeponay and the other chiefs would have had much less autonomy than in land-poor independent communities or under the rule of the local landowners. On the missions, however, as more and more Indians converted, even the great chiefs slowly but surely lost their power. At best, the most astute, such as Tacu, turned into entrepreneurs who commercialized the labor power of the dwindling number of workers under their command as a means of holding on to some shreds of ascendancy. Indeed, in the end, this was to be the fate of the traditional chiefs in the first decades of the twentieth century; they became increasingly irrelevant as migration took the unconverted and the converted majority came under the direct authority of the friars. But the friars' authority was also declining as a result of the rising anticlericalism in Bolivian politics. Nevertheless, the change in power relations was a lengthy process in which traditional chiefs had held on longer than the friars initially supposed. Only at the very end of mission life, with the smaller depopulated missions and under constant attack from the settlers and the anticlerical government, did the friars attain the kind of power that their apologetic treatises ascribed to them at an earlier date.

CHAPTER SIX

Missions and the Frontier Economy

The recent current of mission history has attempted to counteract the overwhelmingly apologetic historiography by examining old evidence more critically and unearthing new ways to get at the realities of the mission experience itself.[1] Rather than describe the motives of the missionaries or their views of the mission populations, the revisionists have concentrated on the effects the missions had on the Indians. Relying heavily on demographic data found in parish records, the new mission historians have emphasized the exploitation and rapid depopulation due to epidemic diseases that mission populations suffered. These scholars have seen the mission essentially as an arm of the state, with horrifyingly high costs to the indigenous peoples that fell into the clutches of the Europeans. They found that Indians were often forced to work and constituted the economic support both in terms of labor supply and food production for the settlers and the soldiers of the frontier forts.

While much more sensitive to economic issues than the traditional and apologetic view, the "new mission history" arguments about the economic role have until now played a subsidiary role in a framework that emphasizes the destructive relations between missions and indigenous peoples. A reason for this emphasis is related to the higher levels of coercion that existed on colonial missions than in the republican period.[2] Since most historians continue to focus on the missions during the period of Hispanic domination, the stress on coercion is an important corrective to earlier, often self-interested versions of mission history. Nevertheless, the debate over the relative benevolence of the mission system prevents an explicit comparative discussion about other important issues, such as the economic importance of the missions in the frontier economy. We must go back all the way to Herbert E. Bolton's pathbreaking, and in many ways very Eurocentric, article of 1917 to get a sense of the mission as an essential part of the Hispanic frontier.[3]

How do we take into account the economic importance of the mission in Latin America? Was it a hindrance or an asset to the liberal economic development of the frontier? How do we take into account, as social history and ethnohistory have rightfully rejoined us, not only the European side but also that of the Indians? To do this we must examine a number of closely related issues. What intensity of economic interaction did missions foster? Did missions aim at self-sufficiency, or did they represent important economic enterprises that had repercussions within the frontier region? What level of exploitation of the indigenous population did the missions permit? How was this related to the survival of the mission population and the way the Indians were integrated into the European economy? And last, how were missions similar to and how were they different from other frontier institutions, such as haciendas and military posts?

Analysis of the Franciscan missions among the Chiriguanos can help us answer these complex questions. First, the economy of the missions needs to be broken into its constituent parts: the mission as a labor resource, as a developer of infrastructure, as a place of production, and as a market for goods. Second, I will compare the relative efficacy of the missions to other frontier institutions. Throughout, we must keep in mind that the mission's interactions in the frontier economy in each rubric also depended to a large extent on the particular point in the life cycle of the mission.

The Mission Life Cycle and Economic Interaction

Two major factors were involved in the changing economic significance of the missions. First, the mission itself matured. Indigenous peoples who survived the diseases adapted to their new circumstances living on premises profoundly influenced by European models. They tended to speak European languages, adopted some imported customs (though often in creative ways), dressed differently, and adapted a different daily routine. The Indian population decreased while members of other ethnic groups moved in. Second, the frontier itself changed as non-Indian settlers moved in: the frontier became more secure for the settlers, the economic basis of the region changed, and the state asserted more of its power in the region. Both factors not only impinged on economic activities of the missions, but also created great changes all along the frontier. Thus a sophisticated analysis must take into account these changes over time when analyzing the economic impact of the missions. To do so, I will concentrate on three major issues: labor demands, mission production, and the mission as a market for goods.

The Mission as a Source of Labor

The issue of labor usage of the mission population has been one of the most frequently examined points, for it fits into the debate over the demographic impact of the mission in Latin America. Settlers often saw the missions primarily as a source of labor (at least at a certain point in the life of a mission), and much documentation has survived on the numerous debates over labor between settlers, missionaries, and the government. Thus many of the classic mission histories make mention of this issue, although it is usually treated by emphasizing the fight between missionaries and settlers over this resource.[4]

To examine this issue in more depth it is necessary to bring into play the idea that labor demands and the mission's ability to add to the settlers' labor resources depended heavily on, among other things, the particular point in the life cycle of the mission. Labor demands for work within the mission, for example, tended to be higher in the period right after the mission's establishment. Indian men built the various structures contained within the missions and, as warriors, protected the mission from attacks by neighboring groups that were opposed to the existence of the mission. This was the case in Santa Rosa. Two years after the foundation of the mission the Franciscans boasted of a town with two plazas, one for the neophytes and the other for the unconverted, with neat rows of houses for all the families. In addition, the Indians built a parish house, with "a spacious parlor, two comfortable apartments, two hallways on each side, and four rooms," plus a separate kitchen, a pantry, and a tool shed. The new mission church, 30 meters long and 8 wide, was already half built by that time. In addition, the Indians had built a school for the girls with two large classrooms with hallways, measuring 20 by 6 meters and 17 by 6 meters, as well as two rooms for the female teachers. In 1892, fully five years after the establishment of the mission, the church was completed.[5] The establishment of the mission thus represented a major outlay in Indian labor, setting up the town itself and building such indispensable edifices as the church and the schools. The missionaries did pay the Indians for their labors, but minimal sums. After the Indians fulfilled the labor demands in setting up the mission, the mission population began to work outside of the new settlement with regularity.

Important changes occurred in the indigenous labor economy after the establishment of the mission. For one thing, the labor demands for male workers went up. In the case of the Chiriguanos, women in the premission villages did most of the agricultural labor; men were responsible only for clearing, sowing, and weeding the fields. In the missions men did more farm labor, also harvesting the fields.[6] Building construction, for which the missionaries used exclusively male labor, was a new activity that meant that Indian men had less leisure time than before. It is important not to belabor this point, for even before the establishment of the missions the Chiriguano men worked in agricultural tasks on the settlers' haciendas, harvesting corn and other products. Apparently they did not do so in their own villages, where it was considered women's work. Whether men considered harvest labor on haciendas demeaning is not known. It is clear, however, that these labor demands outside of the village economy and nontraditional labor for men existed before the establishment of the missions. In fact, many of the Chiriguano groups asked for missions because, among other problems, the settlers demanded excessive labor from the native villagers without sufficient compensation.

Once the mission was established, invariably the indigenous population had to defend itself from incursions by neighboring groups that considered the mission a threat to their existence. Thus in the first few years, until the mission was at least tolerated by those who refused to join, the men also engaged in much warfare. Acceptance was often a long process and depended much on the relative strength of those opposed to the missions. The earliest missions established in the middle of the nineteenth century suffered from more warfare and attacks by other groups than later ones. This meant that the men were frequently fighting and away from the mission; until the 1860s the missionaries and frontier authorities had no choice but to permit the mission Indians to conduct their own raids on their enemies. Such was the case with the Tarairí Chiriguanos, who received permission in 1858 from the military commander of Salinas to make war on the Toba Indians, another ethnic group from the Chaco that traditionally preyed on both settlers and Chiriguanos.[7] Warfare was a traditional activity among the Chiriguano men and in that sense did not interrupt previous patterns.

The rhythm of warfare changed, however, once a Chiriguano group permitted the establishment of a mission. Before they were incorporated into a mission, Chiriguano settlements allied themselves with various groups (either Creole, Chiriguano, or another ethnic group), and often broke their alliances when it was in their best interests. This proved impossible once a mission was established, for then they effectively entered into a permanent alliance with the settlers. As a result, the manpower requirements for warfare rose dramatically because the government saw the mission Indians as a permanent source of auxiliaries for expeditions of exploration and the many campaigns against other indigenous groups. In 1832 the Bolivian Army dragooned 180 Indians from Mission Itau to combat an Argentine invasion.[8] The Daniel Campos expedition of 1883, which explored the Pilcomayo River to find a route to Paraguay, was also notorious (and caused much ill will among the missionaries and their charges) for its demands of manpower. Although Campos paid the Chiriguanos who worked as sappers, transporters of cargo, and cowhands, the hundreds he requested severely strained mission resources. A number of neófitos died or sickened under the dangerous conditions and heavy workload; the continuous requests for more laborers during the planting season also created problems for the mission. During this period, the subprefect required the Indians of Mission Aguairenda to hunt down ten deserters from the militia of a frontier battalion.[9] In fact, the conflict between Bolivian forces and autonomous indigenous groups was waged largely by Indians on both sides; the "national" frontier forces were largely composed of mission Indians. In many ways the process of frontier expansion by Bolivian forces was more a civil war among indigenous groups than a conquest by Creoles.[10]

After the initial phases of the mission life cycle, labor demands and work patterns changed significantly. As a new generation grew up on the mission and the demands of war lessened somewhat, the Indians began to use new agricultural techniques learned from the missionaries, and some became specialized in nonagricultural skills. The mission Indians abandoned the practice of planting corn with a digging stick and successfully adopted European technology such as the use of teams of oxen and the plow. According to Fr. Bernardino de Nino, by the early twentieth century the successful adoption of European technology had occurred on the missions run by the Franciscans from Potosí, where the neófitos "[were] competitive with and even outperform[ed] many mestizo workers."[11] The mission Indians also adopted the cultivation of plants that Europeans had introduced. In the late nineteenth century a visitor to Mission Tarairí found that the Chiriguanos had their own groves of banana, lime, fig, and orange trees, as well as fields of sugarcane, rice, and cotton.[12]

Changes in agricultural practices were only one facet of the changing work patterns on the mission. At the turn of the century Erland Nordenskiöld, a Swedish adventurer and pioneering anthropologist, decried the loss of old skills, such as designing pots and making traditional clothing.[13] Instead, the missionaries from the Tarija monastery taught the schoolboys "tailoring, hat-making, carpentry, weaving, masonry, leather-working, ranching, mule-driving, pottery, [and] saddlery," although the vast majority practiced only agriculture and ranching.[14] In Santa Rosa de Cuevo, under the jurisdiction of the Potosí Franciscans, in 1901 some young Chiriguanos were working as shoemakers, tailors, and leatherworkers.[15] The girls in the mission schools also learned European arts, such as "embroidery, trimming, weaving, and other tasks suited to their sex," which, as one missionary boasted, "[could] compete with those of the schools in the cities."[16] However, the girls did not use their newly acquired skills once they left the mission schools. According to Nordenskiöld, the Chiriguano girls found the flowers and other European patterns "too strange for their fancy" and refused to wear the ornaments they had learned to embroider.[17] Possibly the mission school experience led to a net diminution in traditional women's skills, such as pottery, tool making, and herbal lore. These skills were passed on from mother to daughter; since the girls spent most of their time in school, they might not have had the opportunity to learn them from their mothers.

The frontier also changed as the missions provided security to the ever-increasing number of settlers. This included labor demands on the indigenous population. While Indian men learned certain new skills beyond hunting and traditional agriculture and used them in the mission, the settlers in the vicinity of the missions were interested primarily in securing agricultural laborers. After the role that the Indian warriors played in defending the missions (and the settlers nearby) during the early days of the mission, the use of neófito labor was of paramount economic importance to the Bolivian landlords on the frontier. In the case of the Chiriguanos this was particularly significant because the Indians tended to retreat from areas newly taken by the colonists, leaving them with too few workers for agriculture. Thus by the late nineteenth century the hacendados perceived the missions primarily as labor pools, to be utilized when cash advances and coercion proved insufficient for recruiting enough peons.[18]

Some evidence remains to measure the significance of neófito labor. For example, in 1883 an expeditionary leader to the Chaco requested two hundred men from the Aguairenda mission. The friar could not fill this order, since "many found themselves occupied by Mr. Arce and J. Abenabar and by other Christians [i.e., landlords]." A few written requests for mission labor also survive, documenting the demand for Chiriguano labor. In some, even the wage rates are specified; in 1883 one hacendado was willing to pay three Indians three reales and food to build a house; three others were offered two reales and food to excavate earth for the foundation for a term of four or five days.[19]

The Franciscans regulated wage rates, apparently quite successfully, and prevented abuses of their charges.[20] This led to numerous conflicts between missionaries and settlers and much ambivalence from the latter over this issue. The hacendados wanted unrestricted power over the Indians, but they saw the necessity of keeping the missions if they wanted access to enough workers. Since the Franciscans controlled between 25 and 40 percent of the total Chiriguano population when the labor crisis became acute in the late nineteenth century and early twentieth, their contribution to the agriculture of the frontier region was considerable.[21] Most of the land had been divided up into huge estates and there were few mestizo frontiersmen (and even fewer landlords) who were willing to dismount from their horses and work the land with their own hands. Moreover, the other ethnic groups of the region, the Tobas, Matacos, and Choretis, were hunters and gatherers and made poor agricultural workers. As one Franciscan asserted, throughout the frontier region "the only *jornalero* [i.e., agricultural day laborer] . . . [was] the Chiriguano."[22]

The major problem with this arrangement was that the Franciscans of republican Bolivia did not dispose of, nor were they inclined to use, the degree of physical coercion that many of their brethren had employed during the colonial period. This meant that, at least initially, the missionaries had to rule through the traditional chiefs. Only after many years did the Franciscans have a large enough number of converted Indians (most adults never converted) to assert much authority over labor recruitment. Even then, the friars did not permit any forced labor. Unfortunately for the missionaries and the settlers, it was precisely then that the Indians began to emigrate in large numbers to neighboring Argentina to work in the sugarcane plantations of Jujuy. Neófitos as well as the unconverted were equally prone to leave; in fact, it appeared that the young men of the mission schools, the future population of the mission, were most willing to go. Since the Franciscans possessed no means to keep their charges from leaving, the region lost many of its prime Indian workers. According to one source, in the early twentieth century migrants averaged about twenty percent of the able-bodied male population.[23] (See chapter 3.)

The contribution of laborers from the missions to the frontier economy was thus substantial, though it changed over the life cycle of the missions. The Chiriguanos in the missions were vital as agricultural laborers within the region and also as warriors who fought their brethren and helped extend the national economy farther into the frontier. The establishment of the missions also resulted in substantial changes in indigenous labor patterns, as was the case in the colonial period as well. The mission entailed new and greater labor requirements, as in the construction of permanent and substantial European-style buildings such as churches, the cultivation of new crops, and the tending both of mission and private plots. Some neófitos became specialized in certain tasks that previously had not existed among the Chiriguanos. New technologies also brought about different labor requirements and different rhythms in the labor regime, as well as a transformation in the division of labor between the sexes. These labor demands changed as the missions went through the different stages of their life cycle, probably easing up somewhat after the initial years of mission life.

Production

The establishment of a mission brought about a change in production patterns as well. In the case of southeastern Bolivia, this meant a reversal of the trend of diminishing agriculture in favor of the expansion of the cattle economy. Branislava Susnik has characterized the conflict between Chiriguanos and settlers as a struggle between corn and cattle.[24] Although this observation is more applicable to certain periods than others, especially in the nineteenth century much of the frontier expansion took place when cowhands drove their cattle herds onto the Indians' cornfields, thus forcing them to retreat away from the herds. As the Franciscans recognized, the Chiriguanos requested missions not because of the presumed benefits of Christianity, but because the missions permitted the Indians to escape the exploitation of the settlers and to get the settlers' cattle off the Indians' fields.[25]

When the Franciscans founded a mission they also reasserted the Indians' rights to their land and thus made it possible for the Chiriguanos to again cultivate their corn unmolested. The missionaries aggressively rounded up cattle on mission lands and forced their owners to take their animals elsewhere.[26] After the establishment of a mission one of the first concerns was to make it self-sufficient in food production, and so agriculture was encouraged. It is difficult to estimate either food production or the amount of land given over to agriculture. In the only figures of land under production, which we have for the Tarija missions for 1883, it appears that approximately seventy-two acres were cultivated in the whole mission system.[27] If we divide this figure by the seven missions, this amount of land was clearly incapable of sustaining the more than ten thousand Indians who lived on the missions. Presumably these figures referred only to the land cultivated for the personal needs of the Franciscans or for distribution to widows and orphans and did not take into account the much more numerous private plots that each Indian family farmed.

The visita of Manuel Jofré of 1893 provides a more detailed picture, which helps to close some of the gaps in our knowledge of the extent of agricultural production on the missions. Jofré implied that the Indians cultivated lands apart from the fields for the benefit of the mission as a whole. In the case of Aguairenda, the vast majority of the cultivated lands on the mission were in the hands of the Chiriguanos: "Other than the three small kitchen gardens of the mission the Indians have 30 banana plantations, 34 sugarcane fields, and 36 orange orchards, other than plantings of less consideration, and their plantings of corn."[28] Although we have no good information on types of agricultural production in the Indian villages before the establishment of the missions (other than a list of "traditional" crops — but did the Chiriguanos also cultivate "nontraditional" plant species?), it is nevertheless logical to assume that the mission Indians cultivated certain European crops, such as sugarcane, more intensively once the missions were established.

On the missions of Tarairí, Tiguipa, and Aguairenda the extent of cultivated land varied between one-fifth and one-sixth of the total area, with the rest used as pasture. Because most of Machareti's land was not fertile enough for agriculture, only a few fields "of little consideration" existed. In all, on the three missions for which figures are available, it can be estimated that in 1893 the missions and the Indians cultivated approximately 1,290 hectares, or 3,680 acres, a substantial amount in the largely cattle economy of the frontier. This land had to feed the 3,344 mission inhabitants.[29]

It is likely that initially the missionaries stressed agricultural production, since the mission had to be self-sufficient in food and all missions among the Chiriguanos were founded on the sites of already existing villages. One might assume that as the missions began to lose population to disease and emigration (the latter being more serious, given the fact that able-bodied males tended to predominate among migrants) agricultural production declined. This was not the case. Cadastral surveys provide spotty but nevertheless suggestive information. In 1900 on Mission Santa Rosa de Cuevo the population of approximately two thousand souls worked 336 of the 50,625 hectares and produced 6,000 cargas of corn. In the same year on San Pascual de Ivo approximately one thousand inhabitants worked 225 of the 40,000 hectares and produced 1,600 cargas. We lack production figures for 1906, but the proportion between population and acreage under cultivation is suggestive. Although the population on Santa Rosa dropped by a quarter, to 1,500, the acreage under production increased by almost 18 percent, to 395 hectares. On Ivo a similar pattern can be discerned: in the same year the population had dropped by more than a quarter, to about 700 Indians, while the area under cultivation increased by one hectare, to 225.[30] The increase in productivity in the face of population decline (if area under cultivation can in this case be assumed to be an indication of productivity, given the lack of production data for 1906) was probably due primarily to the increasing use of the plow and draft animals over the traditional digging stick.

It is not clear how much of the harvest was sold to outsiders and how much was consumed on the mission itself. For one thing, mission account books contain few production figures for agricultural products (in contrast to the yearly livestock inventories), and those that we have are inadequate; for example, what else and how much did the Santa Rosa and Ivo missions produce in 1900 besides corn? The unusually detailed description of the Tarija missions by Jofré asserts for the mission at Aguairenda, "One sees that the principal sources of income for the mission are the sale of some cattle, hides, animal fat, cheeses, and fruits, such as oranges and bananas."[31]

This statement frustratingly ignores the mission Indians' participation in the agricultural market. Depending on the efficiency and productivity of agriculture (about which we have no quantitative data), there was probably a substantial surplus that was sold to sustain the rest of the region. Clearly, as the cadastral data show, the missions farmed much vaster areas than any other properties along the frontier. Given the fact that most of the mission fields were farmed by the families living there, to dispose as they saw fit, it is very likely that the mission Indians helped feed much of the frontier population.

As is clear from the Franciscan records, cattle thrived on the mission lands; the missions maintained their own herds and other livestock as well. The few extant mission account books show that, outside of clerical fees, the sale of cattle was by far the largest source of mission income. Unfortunately the notation system of the account books, in which the name of the buyer rather than the product sold is most commonly given, makes it impossible to provide accurate statistics on the sale of cattle. The only concrete numbers on the sale of mission cattle are available for the years 1877 to 1885, in which the Tarija missions sold a total of 2,801 head. Internal consumption on the mission ran another 1,114 head, while theft and natural death took 1,563 cattle. In the late 1920s, after a number of missions had been secularized, one expert estimated that the missions sold more than 3,000 head of cattle a year; the primary source of livestock was Machareti.[32]

Given the importance of this source of income it is surprising that, unlike in agriculture, the Franciscans apparently did nothing either to improve the breeding stock of the animals that roamed the mission lands or to introduce more efficient ranching methods. The missionaries' numerous complaints about cattle rustling, committed initially primarily by unconquered Chaco tribes and later by the mission Indians themselves or settlers, attest to the fact that there was very little control over the herds. Losses sometimes mounted into the hundreds of cattle, but the missionaries felt powerless to stop this theft.[33]

The neófitos also maintained their own cattle, although in this case they collectively owned fewer animals than the mission did. To cite again the Jofré report, the Chiriguanos owned about half as many head as the mission herd; for example, on Tarairí the mission herd included 1,007 head, whereas the Indians owned only 660. Even on Mission Machareti, where there was little agriculture, the Franciscans controlled almost 2,000 head, while the Indians collectively possessed 705. Overall, on the four active Chiriguano missions of the Tarija convent, the mission owned 4,509 head of cattle, the Indians 1,715. However, as was typical, the Chiriguanos had more horses than the Franciscans, 626 versus 136. The relatively small numbers and the predominance of stallions suggest that in both cases horses were not bred primarily for sale, but to provide animal power for agricultural tasks, and, above all, transportation for their owners.[34] Both mission animals and those owned by the resident families, however, suffered about equally from theft.

The cattle herds increased on mission lands from the late nineteenth century to the early twentieth, paralleling the upward trend in cattle raising throughout the region.[35] The figures are suggestive: on the Tarija missions, cattle increased from 2,819 in 1883 to 3,997 only two years later, although some of this increase probably resulted from more systematic cattle roundups (*rodeos*). By 1893, despite the severe problems with cattle rustling, the herds on the Tarija missions had nevertheless increased to 5,897 head.[36] Beginning in 1887 the missions founded by the Potosí Franciscans exhibited the same trend. In 1893 mission lands contained only 1,405 head of cattle, which after four years increased to over 2,000 head. By 1909 the mission herds had multiplied to 4,093.[37]

This increase in cattle did not come at the expense of agriculture. One might have assumed that as the population on the missions declined, the remaining inhabitants would have substituted cattle ranching for agriculture, a much less labor-intensive activity. Instead, there appears to have been an intensification of productive activity throughout the missions, offsetting the loss of workers, at least on the missions themselves. No wonder the settlers were much more vociferous than the Franciscans in complaining about the emigration of Chiriguanos to Argentina, as the former suffered much more severely than the latter, at least in economic terms.

As noted earlier, the missions also trained the Chiriguano children in artisanal crafts, thus changing indigenous labor patterns but also introducing greater specialization (and so presumably greater productivity for the national market) among the Indian population. It is not possible to quantify the effects of this artisanal activity on the frontier economy because we lack sufficiently detailed information. For example, virtually all missions made roof tiles, but the records suggest that all of this production went to covering the houses in which the Indian families lived, as well as the miscellaneous other buildings on the missions. Likewise, it is not clear whether the boys were in fact competent enough or willing to use the skills in carpentry, shoe repair, tailoring, and the like that the Franciscans boasted they taught the boys in the mission schools. Since what the frontier landowners (and for that matter the sugar plantation owners in Argentina) wanted most from the Chiriguano men was work in the fields, most mission Indians probably did not use the skills acquired on the missions extensively.

Only two principal products found a ready market outside the missions, although in both cases they were secondary in importance to the sale of cattle as the main source of mission income. These were distilled sugarcane for making brandy (aguardiente) and weaving. The former trade employed exclusively boys and was primarily exercised on Mission Tarairí. It is not clear when the distillery was established, but the Jofré report mentions it as a source of income in 1893. Apparently other Tarija missions also began distilling sugarcane, but had to cease doing so in 1905, when the convent authorities forbade it "to silence the grumblings against the Missionaries for the retailing of liquors." Only the distillery in Tarairí was permitted to function, and in 1908 new machinery was inaugurated. In 1912 the distillery was repaired again; in 1913 the sugarcane fields yielded one thousand Bolivianos (presumably from the sale of aguardiente).[38]

Information on the sale of weavings manufactured in the girls' mission schools is even more dispersed and is difficult to quantify. In all missions the sale of these items is mentioned occasionally in the reports as a means of income for the mission itself. Given the skill level needed to create these weavings, it is likely that only the schools (and therefore the missions) that had been established for some time could manage to produce a significant amount of weavings. The number of girls available to do this work was substantial; however, a lack of information on both the breakdown of the ages of the girls and the age at which they performed these tasks makes it difficult to provide accurate estimates. In 1901, at the height of the missions among the Chiriguanos, the Franciscans had 1,037 girls in their schools.[39] Even if only a third were capable of making weavings, this was a substantial number of weavers. However, since this activity remained very much on an artisanal level, with no attempts made to systematize the weaving process, production probably remained very low compared to the *obrajes* [primitive textile factories] of the Andean highlands.

One way to measure the economic impact of the missions on the frontier is to look at the mission income and expenditures. Unlike the Jesuits during the colonial period, the Franciscans did not attempt to create commercial enterprises (other than selling some heads of cattle); instead, they aimed at subsistence. Their accounts reflect this goal, although they did not take into account the economic activity of the mission Indians, which, as we have seen, was probably substantial. Thus the figures we have from the mission accounts represent only a portion of the total circulation of money on the mission. The relative importance of these accounts in the total mission economy probably shrank as the mission reached maturity, since the participation of the Indians on the missions in all likelihood increased as they participated in greater numbers in the monetary economy. In any case, the injection of money into the frontier economy after the organization of the mission was substantial. Unfortunately the account books for the Tarija missions, which were founded earlier in the nineteenth century when the frontier area was much larger (and the economic impact of the missions more important), are not extant. The oldest records come from Mission San Pascual de Boicovo (est. 1876), where the Potosí Franciscans in the first twelve years spent 53,634 Bolivianos and earned 54,009.[40]

One might hypothesize that as the missions matured, income increased, reflecting greater efficiency and the socialization of the mission Indians into European work patterns, while expenses decreased since costs for infrastructure presumably went down. This hypothesis is not borne out by the figures. Because the Franciscans attempted to sell only an amount sufficient to cover their costs, income and expenditures, both total amounts and per capita, fluctuated widely, without any discernable pattern. Mission Santa Rosa de Cuevo presents a typical case study. (See table 17.) Expenses and income were thus not directly related to how long the mission had been established, the educational levels achieved by the younger generations, or the gradual loss of population.

Table 17 shows that mission expenditures and income appeared to be largely immune from either agricultural crises, inflation, or other economic or climatic changes. For example, during the last years of the nineteenth century and the early years of the twentieth, when a series of droughts caused great hardship among the inhabitants of southeastern Bolivia, per capita expenditures did not go up consistently. Perhaps the high expenditures of 1904–1905 were related to this drought, but by then a normal crop year had improved conditions substantially. There is little accounting for inflation either, which was relatively high in the early twentieth century, for the friars had reached levels of expenditure and income in the last years of the nineteenth century as high as during the subsequent period, when inflation began to be a problem elsewhere in Bolivia.

These mission accounts show that as the population declined it became more difficult to provide a small surplus. However, this trend is not clear. For example, between 1907 and 1909 the friars were still able to earn almost 23,000 Bolivianos, a huge sum for the area, despite the drastic population loss in the first years of the twentieth century. This also helps explain the relative lack of concern over the theft of livestock. Since the mission possessed more cattle than the friars would sell in any year, theft was not an important issue. Only in the twentieth century, when overall mission

TABLE 17. Income and expenditures compared to population on Mission Santa Rosa de Cuevo, 1887–1912

Years	Population	Annual income	Annual income per capita	Expenditures	Expenditures per capita
1887–1889	2,027	3,188.96	.79	3,018.96	.74
1889–1892	2,137	8,450.50	1.32	6,550.20	1.02
1892–1893	1,905	5,833.09	3.06	5,154.17	2.71
1893–1894	1,908	2,003.65	1.05	2,041.90	1.07
1894–1895	2,050	4,365.75	2.13	2,556.65	1.25
1895–1897	1,984	12,911.05	3.25	9,479.75	2.38
1897–1898	1,917	10,267.55	5.36	4,334.35	2.26
1898–1901	2,065	23,578.35	3.81	20,076.10	3.24
1901–1903	1,614	8,485.30	2.62	8,617.90	2.67
1903–1904	1,467	4,052.25	2.76	5,955.65	4.06
1904–1905	1,589	12,200.70	7.68	16,072.24	10.11
1905–1907	1,503	10,262.42	3.41	8,801.83	2.93
1907–1909	1,225	22,852.70	9.33	21,561.04	8.80
1909–1910	1,218	2,034.70	1.67	2,274.05	1.87
1910–1912	1,416	10,147.91	3.58	9,191.44	3.25

Note: Figures are in Bolivianos.
Source: "Santa Visita: Santa Rosa de Cuevo, 1889–1912," AFP.

resources were dwindling, did the missionaries begin to complain consistently about the loss of their herds.

The loss of livestock might have been related to the increasing number of outsiders in the missions as they matured. The missionaries rented land to neighboring landowners or landless mestizos beginning in the 1920s, when the population decline left some mission lands underutilized. Since the missions controlled not only large numbers of workers who could be employed in the missions, but also some of the few sources of water, the rental of mission property was potentially lucrative. However, according to the generally anticlerical Gran Chaco national delegates, the national authorities directly responsible for the frontier, the Franciscans did not promote rental of mission lands and by 1927 had stopped this practice (though by the 1930s they appear to have started up again—see chapter 7). By this time the government saw the missions as hindering the economic and social progress of the region.[41] To a certain extent this was true, for unlike the Jesuits during the colonial era the Franciscans in republican-era southeastern Bolivia never tried to make efficient economic units of their missions or to provide much more than subsistence for their charges.

The Mission as a Market

As is the case with most studies on Latin American institutions in the countryside, we have much better information on production than we have on the consumption of goods not produced by the economic unit, in this case the missions. I have suggested elsewhere that the Chiriguanos on the missions were very important consumers and it was in large part due to their market participation that the seasonal fairs of the Azero region were able to thrive in the second half of the nineteenth century.[42] The evidence for this argument is unfortunately only circumstantial: the fairs increased in importance when the missions were established and declined when the missions lost their population due to emigration to Argentina. Another point of reference is that coca, a stimulant grown on the eastern foothills farther north, was an important trade item in these fairs. Chiriguanos today are known to be avid consumers of these leaves, and it is reasonable to assume that these consumption patterns were established during the period under question.[43]

There were many merchants who lived near the missions, as this was one of the main markets for goods. According to the census of 1900, in Cuevo, for example, next door to Mission Santa Rosa, twenty-nine merchants were resident. In Ñancaroinza, a tiny settlement on the eastern limits of the Chaco frontier but close to the mission at Macharetí, twelve merchants plied their trade. Carandaití, another frontier outpost, contained nine merchants.[44]

One product that the missions required was clothes. The Franciscans spent considerable sums to provide the mission schoolchildren with European-style clothes. In Mission Boicovo alone the annual cost of providing clothes in the 1890s for the two hundred children was one thousand Bolivianos.[45] Apparently the friars' efforts at changing the clothing styles were successful, as the photos of the missions at different stages of their life cycle show the Indians increasingly in Western dress (see figures 7, 8, 9, 10).[46] This was part of the campaign to "civilize" the neophytes. As one friar from the Potosí missions explained, "It is necessary that the [Indian] forgets all that had to do with their savage and superstitious state. . . . With this goal in mind, it has been determined to have all the school boys and girls adopt the clothing of the Christians: the boys wear shirt, pants, poncho and hat, and the girls use blouses, skirts, and *mantillas* just like the Christians of those regions."[47]

Moreover, the Chiriguanos purchased Western clothing when they went for the sugarcane harvest in northern Argentina. The missionaries complained that those who returned to the missions had spent all their hard-earned money on new clothes and had also acquired a number of unsavory habits, such as a propensity for hard liquor, wife beating, and knife fights.[48]

Western clothing was common by the early twentieth century among all Chiriguano men; according to Erland Nordenskiöld, "The Chiriguano and Chané men of the present day wear European clothes which they buy at the stores, get at the missions, or more often still, when working at the sugar factories in northern Argentina."[49] It is highly likely that the mission experience among the Chiriguanos helped create the demand for ready-made clothing, although the seasonal migration to Argentina, where the Indians received part of their payment in clothing, must also have been important. It appears that, for men at least, Western-style clothing was more practical than the traditional clothing, which consisted of a cloth around the waist and blankets around the rest of the body, if necessary. In the dense woods of the Chiriguanía pants and shirts provided better protection for the skin from thorns and the sun. Western clothing was also more prestigious for men. The Chiriguanos had been able to acquire it easily by the nineteenth century, either as payment for work or in exchange relationships. By the late nineteenth century all men wore Western-style clothing, though those off the mission continued to wear their hair long and draped into a red or blue band. Women in independent villages and in haciendas continued to wear their practical and beautiful tiru.[50]

In any case, the missions presented the largest market (at least in terms of the number of customers) for clothing along the frontier. This was mitigated, however, by the fact that many Chiriguanos acquired their European clothes in Argentina. By the twentieth century the Franciscans believed that the promise of receiving clothing was a powerful incentive to remain on the mission. In 1908 the missionaries used the distribution of coveted Western clothes as an incentive for children to attend school; for example, the missionary in Tarairí promised that after Easter he would give "one pair of pants and one shirt to those who frequent[ed] the school daily."⁵¹

The Chiriguanos on the missions became important consumers for local merchants of goods from the national and international markets, particularly clothing and coca. This phenomenon was not confined to those who converted; in most missions throughout the republican period the unconverted outnumbered the converted. It is likely, however, that converts, most raised in the mission schools, were the most avid consumers of Western goods. They distinguished themselves through clothing from their "savage" and "heathen" neighbors, demonstrating their allegiance to the missions and "civilization." As the mission system matured, more and more Indians began to participate in the market as consumers of these types of products.

Chiriguano culture laid great importance on the sharing of goods, for in this way the gift giver would receive added prestige. When the Chiriguanos returned from Argentina with clothes, horses, and donkeys, the rules of hospitality made it difficult, even if they had wanted to, to hold on to the goods acquired while working in the plantations.⁵² From the Franciscans' point of view, the Chiriguanos quickly spent all they earned and had little to show for it. From the Chiriguanos' point of view, the giving away of their goods fortified social bonds and thus had an important purpose.

Comparisons with Other Frontier Institutions

The missions were superior to all other Chaco frontier institutions in economic importance, including the small villages that surrounded the small forts (*fortines*) scattered throughout the region. Only the haciendas competed in economic importance, with their cattle ranching. How important were the ranch herds compared to those of the missions? The few inventories found suggest that ranchers' cattle roamed the land mostly unattended and the land was worth little in comparison to the livestock it contained. This was a common pattern throughout Latin America and elsewhere in the world. A thousand or more head per ranch was probably not uncommon, such as in the case of the Partiñanca ranch, close to Yacuiba, whose 1899 inventory claimed 1,225 head of cattle.⁵³ The cadastral data for the same time period notoriously underestimated the number of cattle, but the data are still suggestive. As a case in point, in 1906 the cadastre for Yacuiba canton (where Partiñanca was located) counted 893 head of cattle. Keeping in mind perennial undercounting, the cadastres of 1906 for the provinces in which the missions were located estimated that there were a total of 61,406 head of cattle. The missions owned a relatively insignificant number of the total cattle population in the region, especially when considered on a per capita basis.[54]

The ranches held back the agricultural economy on the frontier. Land grant petitioners attempted to gain legal possession over land that included Indian villages because these could then be forced to provide labor for the new landowner. Settlers exploited the hapless Indians who remained on these tracts and refused to pay them competitive wages. As we have seen, this encouraged outmigration to Argentina and elsewhere. The settlers caused much of the labor shortage. Instead of paying higher wages, landowners kept the Indians in debt so that they had legal grounds to retrieve any peons who fled. But in the poorly controlled conditions of the frontier, coercion such as debt peonage was not effective. Many peons left the haciendas and went to the towns or crossed the border to Argentina. Moreover, the hacienda peons could not afford the higher consumption patterns on the missions, for the landowners permitted them to maintain only a few plots to meet bare subsistence needs. Settlers rightly feared that if they permitted any more than that, their peons might buy themselves out of their debts and leave to work in better conditions.[55]

The fortines were not much better in terms of labor conditions. In the early 1840s Manuel Rodríguez Magariños, the dynamic prefect of Tarija, established a number of small forts along the Pilcomayo River. Presumably the forts would be staffed temporarily by soldiers and later, when the area had been colonized, would be turned over to the local settlers. However, events turned out differently. The soldiers refused to work as laborers in the small fields established next to their fortifications and began killing Indians in an indiscriminate manner.[56] They were afraid that the Indians would steal their livestock. Other than a few exceptions, the forts were abandoned within a short period. Even in the 1880s, when the state gained resources and was able to mount a more sustained effort in maintaining forts, the forts proved ineffective in providing the security necessary to promote much economic activity. The soldiers were chronically underpaid and often went hungry; as a result, many deserted. Out of thirty troops in Crevaux in 1893 almost half deserted their posts.[57]

The only fortines that were effective were those established in the 1860s in the Ingre-Iguembe area and in the 1870s near Cuevo. However, colonists had built these forts; they contained no regular soldiers, only frontier militia. The forts served as refuges for the settlers during periods of warfare with the Chiriguanos, as in the war in 1874–1877. Later, traders and some ranchers settled next to the forts of Ingre and Iguembe and formed small towns by the same names. Similarly, the grandly named forts of Bolívar and Sucre became the centers around which Cuevo was formed. In the late nineteenth century these towns briefly became important trading entrepôts in the commerce between Argentina and eastern Bolivia when the road between these points passed through town.

The push farther into the Chaco soon thereafter depleted the towns of population as the settlers continued to move eastward when overgrazing destroyed the pastures surrounding the towns. Thus most of these towns did not have the same long-term economic importance as the missions. None became as large as the most important missions, rarely exceeding even briefly a population of a thousand. These towns often relied on the labor of neighboring missions. This was the case with Huacaya, located next to Mission Boicovo; with Cuevo, a few miles north of Santa Rosa; and with Camatindi, sandwiched between the missions at Tiguipa and Tarairí.[58] The towns had some economic significance as centers of commerce and as extensions of Creole influence. They were also vital parts of the frontier hinterland, for they represented permanent links to the national government and the national economy. Nevertheless, they depended to a large degree on the missions as sources of both labor and consumers to buy the town traders' merchandise.

Conclusion

What was the economic importance of the mission in the frontier economy? What does the specific case of the Chiriguanos tell about mission systems in general? Some trends and tendencies might help to answer these questions when compared to other mission systems. Two conclusions are readily apparent. One deals with the life cycle of the mission and other with the importance of mission Indian labor.

For one thing, the role of the mission in the frontier economy changed as the mission matured and the frontier moved farther outward. At first the mission was vital in permitting the establishment of colonists' settlements in the frontier. The mission Indians were crucial auxiliaries in the fight against unconquered groups, and the settlement of the colonists reflected this, since most clustered as closely as possible to the mission grounds. However, initially the Indians were occupied in establishing the mission economy, constructing often imposing buildings, cultivating communal fields, and caring for mission cattle, as well as reorganizing their own production once the threat of land usurpation diminished. This meant that relatively little labor was available for the settlers.

Once the mission was firmly established and the military threat from other indigenous groups had faded, the missionaries were able to fulfill some of the labor demands of the surrounding haciendas as well as devote their charges' time to the development of infrastructure such as forts and roads. They trained a whole generation of workers in the mission schools who, for the most part, were relatively highly skilled (possibly much more so than the vast majority of the settlers) and who were beginning to value the acquisition of Western goods. Whether or not the Franciscans succeeded in imbuing a European work ethic is less clear, for many Chiriguano traits, such as the emphasis on sharing to gain prestige and the disregard for accumulating material goods, persisted.

As the mission matured and the frontier area was integrated more fully into the national economy, certain restrictions precluded the full development of the economic potential of the mission. This was noticeable in the spheres of labor, production, and consumption. These restrictions were inherent in the goals of the mission and eventually created serious friction with settlers and local government officials. First, the missionaries mediated in the relationship between workers and hacendados and so prevented the whole-scale exploitation of the Indians at the hands of the settlers. The colonists saw this as a serious drawback, especially because the missions represented the largest pool of indigenous labor in the region. Second, the missionaries did not foster much production beyond subsistence. The mission account books are eloquent testimony to this phenomenon, although they capture only one aspect of the mission economy. The mission kept out of circulation a large part of its resources and did not require the Indians to participate fully in the nascent frontier economy. Although evidence suggests that the Indians themselves began to produce for the market, this was not done in a systematic fashion. Third, the mission did not become a free market for any and all traders, despite the large number of human beings assembled there. The Franciscans abhorred the crass materialism of the traders, mostly located in adjacent towns, and tried to shield their charges from many of the worst abuses. Thus the role of the mission as a refuge for the frontier indigenous population, although it probably kept many more Indians in the area than if there had been no missions, in the long term also prevented the full utilization (and severe exploitation) of the indigenous population that otherwise might have occurred. The missions mediated the integration of the Indians into the market.

As was the case with virtually all mission systems in the history of Latin America, as the Chiriguano missions matured the mission population decreased. Although in the case of these institutions this was related largely to outmigration rather than high mortality, it put the missions in a position similar to that of missions in other locations in Latin America. The missions grew in economic importance as the Indian population dwindled because they represented the last labor reserves in an area that was losing its indigenous workers. This created great problems for the missionaries. The settlers became vociferous opponents of the missions because the Franciscans refused to let go of their protective role. The missionaries themselves were acutely aware of the population drop and became even more resistant to permitting the exploitation of their charges at the same time that they themselves were becoming demoralized by the exodus of their charges.

Thus the missions played a crucial role, especially at the beginning of the colonization process. They radically altered the indigenous economy and, after the first few years, made a large number of indigenous workers available to the settlers. Once the frontier had moved past the missions, the importance of Indian labor increased but the restrictions of the missionaries severely limited the usefulness of the missions to the national economy. As both the colonial and later national governments throughout Latin America recognized, there came a point when the missions had outgrown their usefulness in the region. It is a tribute to the political skill of the Franciscan missionaries in the twentieth century and their dedication to the protection of the Chiriguanos that most of the missions in southeastern Bolivia were not secularized until as late as 1949.

CHAPTER SEVEN

Outside Relations and the Decline of the Missions

Frontier missions do not exist in a vacuum; the Franciscan missions in southeastern Bolivia were connected in multiple ways to the region and the nation. Indeed, even during the colonial period the missions were not autonomous units. After independence the missions became more intertwined with frontier and national affairs. The formation of nation-states made missions integral parts of the new Latin American countries, subject to the vagaries of national and local politics. The mission residents also interacted with local settlers and outside indigenous groups. This chapter deals with the missions' relations with outsiders and how the mission inhabitants related to the outside world, especially in terms of politics.[1]

The principal outsiders who had dealings with the missions fall into four major categories: Indians, settlers, local officials (often also settlers), and national authorities. The complex interplay of these relations varied over time, as the interests of the various groups changed over the course of mission development from outposts on a relatively uncontrolled frontier to established urban centers that represented the largest sources of labor and centers of production and consumption.

It is possible to discern five different phases in the relationship between the missions and outside forces. In the first phase, from Bolivia's independence to about the middle of the century, the Franciscan convent in Tarija had to define its relations with the national government and the Creoles who were already on the frontier. During the second phase, from the 1840s to the 1890s, the mission system achieved its smoothest relationship with local Creoles, as well as local officials and the national government, though there were temporary conflicts, especially with anticlerical liberal outsiders sent by the national government. In the third phase, from about

1900 to 1932, the relationship between the Franciscans, the settlers, and the national as well as local governments soured. Despite some improvement after 1914, in the 1920s the missionaries found themselves with few supporters at the local or national level. The Chaco War (1932–1935), when most of the missions were destroyed or severely damaged, weakened the Franciscans' position even more. The missions limped along until 1949, when the government secularized them and turned them into agricultural cooperatives.

The first phase was a period of reconstituting missions that had existed during the colonial period. As described in chapter 1, only two missions survived the independence wars, but in a debilitated state. The anticlerical Sucre government (1826–1828) had little use for religious institutions and especially the mendicant orders such as the Franciscans, for the liberal theory of the time assumed that friars and nuns were unproductive members of society, parasites who lived off the generosity of the government and civil society. Worse, the male orders were staffed by Spaniards, who did not merit much sympathy from the patriot fighters. There was no massive expulsion of Spaniards as in Mexico after independence, but the European friars had been forced to leave the missions during the independence struggles. After independence the more important issue that affected the religious orders was anticlericalism. Throughout Bolivia Sucre consolidated the members of several convents into one and suppressed others.[2] The Tarija convent barely survived. In the 1820s the Franciscans found themselves unable to maintain the missions in Cuyambuyo and Tariquea. By 1827 they had only a nominal presence in the former missions of Salinas and Itau. President Sucre, who had little sympathy for the Franciscans, donated the mission lands of Salinas to Francis Burdett O'Connor, the Irish aristocrat and colonel in the patriot army who had married into the Tarija landed elite and was a key ally of Sucre in the dispute between Bolivia and Argentina over Tarija. O'Connor used the pretext of an insurrection in Itau to impress eighty-four Chiriguano Indians from the mission into the army. Although O'Connor lauded the Indians' performance in the skirmishes that followed, only six men eventually returned to the mission.[3] However, the Franciscan convent maintained some claims over the land, making the settlers leery of investing their time and effort in disputed territory.[4]

When Fr. Andrés Herrera began to revitalize the Tarija convent with new friars in the 1830s the Franciscans found themselves involved in a host of land disputes as they recovered old missions and established new ones. O'Connor, who by then had become the largest landlord on the frontier, opposed the expansion of the missions. He felt that the friars were encroaching on the land that the Sucre government had given him. After extensive litigation, which dragged on into the 1830s, the Irish general and other beneficiaries of Sucre's largesse gave up their claims to the mission lands.[5] Even after this legal victory the friars had to defend the lands they had regained. In 1836 an ambitious settler in nearby San Luís proposed to the government that he be given the rich agricultural lands of Itau and Salinas to organize a settlement of colonists from Tarija.[6] As long as the Franciscans lacked the personnel to pursue actively the evangelization of the Indians, mission lands were open to usurpation.

One solution was to rent out former mission lands to which the Tarija convent had legal rights. Renting lands to outsiders was dangerous, but the Franciscans needed revenue. In 1836 they leased the pastures of Salinas mission to Creole ranchers; presumably there were not enough mission Indians to exploit fully the lands on the mission tract. Indeed, Andrés Mealla, the rancher renting the pastures, had trouble getting other cattle owners on the land to pay their grazing fees because they assumed that the state would declare the tracts vacant and grant them the land instead.[7] The weakness of the Tarija convent was palpable on the frontier. The Creoles were circling the mission territories in the 1830s like buzzards, ready to pick them off when the Tarija convent appeared too weak to defend its interests.

Just as all appeared to have been lost, a European recruiting expedition by Fr. Alfonso Corsetti in 1842 revitalized the convent, and the injection of nine young Franciscans in 1844 made it possible to maintain the old missions and expand into new territories.[8] As part of a project to renew their commitment to establish new missions the Franciscans consolidated their holdings. The Tarija convent gave up Salinas mission in 1844. Already in 1832 O'Connor had claimed that missionaries were unnecessary there, reasoning, "The Indians of this mission [Salinas] are converted and live in the village next to the mission building."[9] By the mid-1840s the Franciscans were willing to move on to concentrate their efforts farther east, where the government, settlers, and local authorities wanted them to pacify the Chiriguanos. After reestablishing a small mission at Itau in 1845 they moved on into new regions on the frontier.

Thus the first two decades after independence were a period of retrenchment and reorganization for the Tarija convent. Threats from the outside diminished as the friars gained new members from Europe and consolidated their legal position. The government had also changed; the Sucre administration's anticlerical stance in the 1820s was replaced by President Andrés de Santa Cruz's (1829–1839) favorable attitude toward the mission enterprise. By the 1840s the Franciscans had repositioned themselves to reach out toward the frontier. This made it possible for the Tarija convent to begin its missionary enterprise again.

Positive Relations with Outsiders, 1845–1890s

The foundations of Chimeo (1849), Aguairenda (1851), Tarairí (1854), Macharetí (1869), and Tiguipa (1872) corresponded to the high point of the Tarija mission enterprise among the Chiriguanos. The national government supported the missions with small stipends of three hundred pesos annually per mission, as the Spanish Crown had done in its possessions during the colonial period. In 1830 President Andrés de Santa Cruz authorized the Franciscan order to establish new missions in Bolivian territory and assigned frontier territories to the convents of La Paz, Cochabamba, Tarata, Potosí, and Tarija. The reasons for establishing the missions were both religious and secular. According to the 1830 law, the missions were to "promote the propagation of the national Catholic faith and the prosperity of the State."[10]

It is remarkable that the 1830 decree, which was not superseded until 1871, contained very little regulation by the government. Although the Santa Cruz administration was eager to promote frontier development and expand into Indian territory, the missions did not figure into its strategy in an important way. Unlike in the colonial period, when the Spanish government had used the Catholic missions as an integral part of its policies to defend and expand its borders, the Bolivian state took a more laissez-faire approach. Given the political troubles any Bolivian government faced during much of the nineteenth century, the lack of administrative oversight by the state comes as no surprise. The actual administration of the missions and the conditions under which the Franciscans established new missions were not addressed in the short decree.[11]

In contrast to the benign neglect of the government, the missions received the generally enthusiastic support of the settlers in the frontier region. The few settlers who dared to live on the frontier in the early independence period found the missions vital for their survival. As chapter 1 describes, the new missions pacified indigenous populations that previously had acted autonomously and whose leaders had switched allegiances according to their perception of power relations within the Cordillera, always trying to maintain their villages' independence as much as possible. Where missions were established, the Chiriguano settlements became permanent allies of the settlers, making possible the further expansion eastward of the settlers' ranching enterprises. This was especially important during this period, since the military balance of power on the frontier was very much on the side of the Indians. The missions also served as places of refuge for settlers in the vicinity.

The Franciscans attempted to missionize the Toba peoples, who were the main consumers of the cattle that the settlers claimed to be theirs; the settlers thought of them as thieves. The establishment of the mission of San Francisco Solano on the Pilcomayo River in 1860 by Fr. Giannelli was less successful (the Tobas often used the mission as a refuge for their old and infirm people as well as women and children while continuing to raid), but a gain nevertheless. Likewise, the San Antonio de Padua mission for the Matacos, founded by Fr. Giannelli in 1863 across the Pilcomayo River from San Francisco, did not bring about the same immediate benefits for the settlers. The Matacos (now also called Weenhayek or Wichí), the most numerous ethnic group within the Gran Chaco, remained hunters, fishermen, and gatherers rather than turning to agriculture. Thus the mission was mostly empty except for the brief sowing season in the last months of the year. It was shut down briefly in 1879 because of the wildly fluctuating population, but reopened in the 1880s.[12] Despite problems, these missions served an important purpose, as they became the place of encounter between settlers and these groups. The Tobas and Matacos generally did not attack settlers living in ranches close to the missions, though they might take their cattle.[13]

Certain settlers benefited extensively from the missions. The family most favored by the missionaries were the del Castillos. In 1870 Juan Esteban del Castillo worked as a cowhand for the new mission of Machareti and brought cattle from neighboring Mission Tarairí to start a herd. The friars had hired del Castillo and two other settlers to watch over the cattle as well as help defend the mission from attacks by nonmission Indians. The friars were grateful for the services del Castillo provided the mission. In 1877 the Franciscans received permission from the national government to allot tracts of land next to the missions to ten settler families. In Machareti the friars gave away twelve tracts of half a square league (1,250 hectares for each lot). Of those, Juan Esteban del Castillo, his brothers José María and Froilan, and three others received one tract each.[14] They could now become cattle ranchers in their own right.

With the support of the missionaries the del Castillo family settled throughout the region, from Camatindi to Carandaití, far to the east into Toba territory. The relationship between the friars and the del Castillos was such that when the Franciscans traveled through the countryside far from the missions they often slept at the family homes.[15] The family maintained special privileges on the missions as well. In 1877 the mission prefect, Fr. Doroteo Giannecchini, gave permission to Juan Esteban del Castillo to build a dwelling at Macharetí: "so that he may house himself there with his respective family and other relatives, since they always pass here and to live here in times of trouble."[16] It is likely that the del Castillos had a good relationship with Mandeponay, the mburuvicha of Macharetí who was also the major intermediary between Chiriguanos and Tobas. The relationship with the Franciscans was fruitful since it permitted the del Castillos to become the most powerful family on the southern Chaco frontier.

By the 1880s the del Castillo brothers had become the commanding officers of the local militia. In 1886 Juan Esteban lived in Murucuyati and was the captain of the local militia. His brother Clodomiro was the head of the militia and quartermaster of the 1886 expedition that Arthur Thouar led into the Chaco. He later became the sergeant major and commander of the Caiza fort.[17] Their brother Manuel was the commanding officer of the fort at Crevaux, an outpost in Toba territory, in 1892.[18] In the following decades Juan Esteban's son Moisès purchased properties in the surrounding area, and by the early twentieth century was one of the largest landowners in the frontier. With his extensive grazing lands, he also turned cattle merchant, sending his cows to Argentina. With their extensive connections, Moises and his cousins became the most politically and economically powerful Creoles of the Bolivian Chaco.[19]

Unlike the Tarija missionaries, when the Potosí convent began establishing missions in 1875 the friars provided housing and small plots for Creoles on mission grounds for the missionaries' protection. In 1883 the Potosí mission prefect asked Manuel Ruiz to remain on the mission and provided a tract of one square league "under the condition that he fix his residence there or in the surrounding area, live in obedience to the missionaries, and take up arms in the defense of the same, if it were threatened by the savages." Similarly in 1889 Rafael Ríos received a square league in Boicovo next to the mission because, he said, "for the space of three years I have lived on the mission, providing all services that have been asked of me in favor of said mission, being disposed to take up arms in its defense."[20]

The missionaries were able to remain in the good graces of some of the nearby settlers by hiring their daughters as schoolteachers for the mission girls' schools; a number of female members of the del Castillo clan became teachers. In preparation for the 1898 Exposition of Catholic Missions held in Turin, Italy, Fr. Doroteo Giannecchini prepared a lengthy catalogue in which the photographs of some of the female mission teachers appear. Of the seven photos, two are of Eulogia and María Ninfa del Castillo, teachers in Santa Rosa de Cuevo, the most important mission of the Potosí convent. The captions to the photographs noted that both were members of the Tertiary Order of Franciscans, the lay organization of the sons of St. Francis.[21] By tying these women to the order and the missions, the friars could count on having the support of this important frontier family.

Not all settlers were happy to have missions as neighbors, even in this period of generally good relations between the Franciscans and the settlers. In 1854 Bayandari, a principal tubicha of the recently founded mission at Tarairí, visited Cornelio Ríos at Carapari, one of the mestizo village forts and bulwark of the Tarija frontier militia. Ríos was the head of the militia and apparently wanted the lands (and perhaps the Chiriguano workers) at Tarairí for himself. He promised Bayandari trade goods if he could persuade the rest of the Tarairí chiefs to rebel. Ríos even provided a detailed plan on how to cut off the mission's water supply as well as have independent Chiriguano villages support the rebellion. In the end the other Tarairí tubichas refused to go along, although Bayandari led a faction of the Huacaya Chiriguanos in an assault on the mission. Tarairí barely survived the attack. Ríos was discredited for some time after the missionaries denounced him to the Tarija prefect.[22]

Thereafter military relations with the friars improved and the Franciscans proved their worth to the military expeditions into the Chaco. Ríos became a supporter of the Franciscans and especially of Fr. José Giannelli, whom he accompanied as chief of the military escort on an expedition into the Chaco in 1863. Indeed, Giannelli's expedition showed the missionaries' utility to national and departmental authorities. As a result of the expedition, Ríos, by now a lieutenant colonel in the militia, established a fort in Toba territory called Bella Esperanza. Although the expedition had to turn back when the Carapari militia refused to continue, Ríos from then on proved to be a loyal friend of the missionary. As a result of the expedition, Giannelli persuaded many of the Tobas to return to the mission at San Francisco and also established the mission of San Antonio across the Pilcomayo River for the Matacos.[23] Military authorities and the missionaries worked together because both felt they could solve the problem of the unconquered Chaco peoples through the founding of missions.

When the missionaries were excluded from military projects the expeditions failed. In 1867 the Tobas, who had help from two Bolivian soldiers at Fort Bella Esperanza, overran the fort. They killed the soldiers and took some women and children prisoner. The attack doomed a planned expedition into the Chaco. The erstwhile expeditionaries, who had formed a society to explore the Pilcomayo and establish a river route to Asunción, Paraguay, had requested that the friars provide them with Chiriguanos from the missions. The friars declined because the Indians had refused to aid the expedition. The mission Indians claimed they had to attend to their fields. The expeditionaries faulted the missionaries for the Indians' refusal, but the Franciscans did not budge. Any hope of reorganizing the expedition failed a few days later, when the rest of the column was attacked by Tapietés and the soldiers had to retreat.[24]

Apogee of the Mission System

The high point of the mission system occurred around 1871. Fr. Alejandro Ercole, mission prefect of Tarija, proposed new and elaborate regulations for the missions, and the Bolivian Congress accepted his proposal without modification.[25] The Mission Code favored the Franciscans and granted them considerable autonomy and power. The missions became independent entities that did not have to answer to local authorities. The law stipulated that the missions report directly to the national government, and no other authorities could interfere in their administration, including the military. In fact, if the missionaries wanted to establish a mission, the prefects and subprefects were to "provide all resources necessary" for doing so. Any lands belonging to Creoles on the proposed mission site were to be expropriated, with the owners "having the right to solicit indemnity from the Supreme Government." The Indians were to be exclusively under the jurisdiction of the missionaries. If there was a conflict between mission Indians and individuals outside of the mission, the Indians would receive all the legal protections afforded minors. If the mission was attacked or sacked, the mission Indians had the right to defend themselves without asking permission from local authorities and keep any booty they might obtain. (Interestingly, these articles do not specify whether the aggressors are Indians or whites.) Any person from outside the mission had to request permission from the missionary to enter or remain on mission land.

Persons who wanted to contract mission Indian labor had to receive prior authorization from the missionary. No contract was valid without notifying the missionary. Finally, no taxes were to be levied on the missions or their inhabitants.

One of the only rights the government reserved for itself was that of requesting mission Indians to work on exploratory expeditions, paying salaries sufficient for their maintenance. Missions could be secularized by the national government, but only after "prior agreement with the diocesan authority." The mission prefect had the responsibility to present an annual report to the national government. The government retained the right to name mission inspectors who would report on the mission "and the means to protect them."[26]

The powers given to the missionaries in this legislation reflect the political weakness of the central state in the early 1870s. This period represented the nadir of state power in Bolivia. The country had just survived the disastrous administration of General Mariano Melgarejo, who had sold parts of the national territory to Chile and Brazil. Melgarejo and his coterie were perhaps the most corrupt of all the caudillo administrations in nineteenth-century Bolivia. Melgarejo put down numerous rebellions against his rule, decimating the Bolivian political class. He sold off vast amounts of Indian community land, destroying much of the Andean peasant mercantile economy. He was finally swept out of power by a massive rebellion of Aymara Indians in northern Bolivia that took back their lost territories. The Bolivian Constituent Assembly in 1871 acknowledged the demands of the indigenous communities by repudiating all of the Melgarejo regime's decrees and legislation. The Assembly debated vigorously whether the government should be federalist or centralist, reformed the monetary system, provided for the free export of silver ore, and tried to strengthen frontier regions. These were the actions of a desperate political class that attempted to wrest power back for the Bolivian state.[27]

Fr. Ercole's legislative proposals were an opportunity for the state to create something positive along the frontier. After the corrupt liberal experiment of the Melgarejo years, a return to the support of the Catholic Church and its strong values appealed to the legislators of 1871, especially on the undisciplined eastern frontier. There might also have been a backlash in Bolivia to the 1870 takeover of the Vatican by liberal forces in Italy, which was lamented among Catholic circles throughout the world, including in Bolivia.[28] Various legislators considered the Franciscans to be the best custodians of the frontier; one even proposed that the friars be given five thousand pesos to found and administer forts on the frontier. After some debate the assemblymen allocated the monies for forts to frontier municipalities instead.[29]

In the city of Tarija there was some opposition to the 1871 regulations, especially regarding the expropriation article that permitted the taking of private lands for the establishment of new missions. J. B. Caso wrote in the newspaper *El Río Bermejo* that the new legislation "authorized expropriation, arbitrariness, despotism, monopoly, the death of industries, slavery, and many more things."[30] Fr. Ercole responded to Caso's short piece in a seven-page letter, "to be published in some newspaper of the capital [Tarija]," defending the new regulations and accusing Caso of defaming the Catholic Church and the motives of the Franciscans.[31] Caso's complaints had no effect and the regulations remained in force. In fact, according to the historian Pilar García Jordán, the Tarija Franciscans wrote the 1871 regulations because of their problems with landlords in the region, as the purchase of lands for the Aguairenda mission and earlier problems with Francis B. O'Connor in Salinas and Itau had demonstrated.[32]

The 1871 regulations consolidated the Franciscans' power along the frontier until 1900, and the power the missionaries had for dealing with local authorities was significant. During this period the labor and market roles of the mission expanded, making the missionaries major power brokers along the frontier. For example, when Manuel Jofré, the highest government authority on the Tarija frontier, requested tools and carpenters from the missions for establishing forts in an expedition against the Tobas in 1872, the missionary of Mission San Francisco del Pilcomayo, Fr. Giannecchini, denied the request. He based his denial on the lack of resources on the mission, his "attributes from the Apostolic Chair," and the new mission Reglamento [as the mission code was known]. Giannecchini told Jofré, "[I can only] put at your disposition peons that you need, providing for their labor the accustomed salary."[33]

Although the Franciscans received support from the national government through the extremely favorable 1871 Reglamento, the local settlers began to resent the missionaries' dominance. They felt that the Indians were finally under control and that the missions were not needed anymore as defensive bulwarks against Indian attacks. The settlers saw the mission settlements as sources of labor, but the friars were not willing to provide Indians without safeguards. As the number of missions expanded, the ranchers, especially from the northern tier of the Chiriguanía, from Cordillera province (Santa Cruz), felt that they were in competition with the missionaries for choice lands. The cattle herds had destroyed much of the grazing lands to the west of the missions and the ranchers were eager to move their herds into the fertile territory that the missions had absorbed.³⁴ Two incidents, the failure to establish permanent missions in Santa Cruz frontier territories and the Indians' defeat during the Huacaya War (1874–1877), illustrate the changing realities on the ground along the frontier.

The Potosí convent entered the mission field in the 1870s and was the first to face problems with the settlers. The convent received authorization to found three missions in the departments of Santa Cruz and Chuquisaca. The lands the Potosí Franciscans selected for the missions immediately were placed under their jurisdiction.³⁵ Unlike the experienced Tarija missionaries, the Potosí Franciscans initially did not negotiate well with the local and regional politicians. In 1871 they established two missions among the Chiriguanos, San Francisco and San Antonio, on the Parapetí River in Santa Cruz department (not to be confused with the missions of the same name among the Tobas and Matacos of the Tarija convent along the Pilcomayo). The settlers from Santa Cruz did not want missions in their midst. Their method for gaining access to the natives, unlike settlers farther south in Chuquisaca and Tarija, was to ally themselves with the tubichas. They even took Chiriguano women as concubines and offered goods in return for the use of the men as laborers.

The establishment of the Parapetí missions did not go well, despite Chiriguano willingness to accept the friars. According to Fr. Angélico Martarelli, some of the old people of the Indian villages remembered the colonial period, when the Tarija Franciscans had established missions in the Santa Cruz region, and they were open to the offer of new ones. In particular, the mburuvicha Chituri, who had been baptized as a child, supported the missionary enterprise, although he refused to recognize the friars' authority over him.

The new missions of San Francisco and San Antonio de Parapetí included more than three thousand Indians, but the surrounding settlers challenged the authority of the missionaries. Since the 1850s ranchers along the Parapetí River had been busily expanding into Indian territory toward the Izozog, using the river as a source of water for their cattle.³⁶ Initially the friars enjoyed the support of the national government, despite the opposition of local authorities, made up of the rancher elite. However, the national government was weak and Santa Cruz authorities quite autonomous, rendering the government's support useless in Cordillera province. Settlers kept invading mission territories with their cattle, threatening the Indians who supported the missions and exhorting others to rebel against them. Local authorities also supported the neighboring whites in their judicial challenges of the missions in the anticlerical capital of Santa Cruz.

In 1880 the Potosí convent threw in the towel. The War of the Pacific took all the attention of the national government, providing the political space for local Santa Cruz authorities to harass the missions. The mission prefect, Fr. Estanislao Simonetti, turned over the missions to diocesan control in May of that year.[37] Thus despite the support of the national government, in the northern reaches of the Chiriguano frontier the missionaries were unable to establish their authority when presented with opposition from settlers and regional and local authorities, even with the formidable 1871 Mission Code.

Another reason the settlers began to turn against the missions was a shift in the military balance of power along the frontier, away from the Indians. The Huacaya War exploded in 1874 and tapered off by 1877 (see chapter 1). Many refugees from Huacaya settled on the new mission of Boicovo, founded in 1876. After indiscriminately distributing the lands of the defeated Indians as well as those of their own allies in the Ingre Valley, the settlers believed that they had finally defeated the Chiriguanos for good. It appeared that the struggle had moved farther east, into the Chaco itself, where conflict with the Tobas marked the rest of the 1870s and the 1880s.[38] The Potosí Franciscans founded another mission in 1887, Santa Rosa de Cuevo, just across the border from the department of Santa Cruz, where much of the remaining free indigenous population resided. The ranchers took over the rest of the land, with very few independent Indian communities remaining. In fact, many of the most important Chiriguano settlements came under the aegis of the hacienda system (such as Ingre), whereas others were able to remain nominally independent, while still providing laborers to the surrounding estates. This was the case with the settlements in the Caipipendi and Caraparirenda valleys, whose chiefs made deals with landlords such as Octavio Padilla and supplied workers to local authorities to maintain at least a façade of autonomy.[39]

In this context the settlers' primary purposes for the missions, creating permanent alliances with missionized indigenous groups and using the missions as protection for the surrounding estates, became irrelevant for the Creoles and local authorities. The deteriorating grazing lands in the hinterland of the frontier also made the underutilized range of the missions a desirable target for acquisition. The lack of good grazing lands became so problematic that ranchers began to invade mission lands with their cattle, often with local authorities refusing to punish trespassers. In 1876 the mission prefect, Fr. Marino Mariani, ordered the ranchers to round up their cattle on mission lands in Tiguipa and Macharetí within ten days, otherwise the missionaries would impound the intruding herd.[40]

More important, the settlers resented the friars' control over the mission Indian labor force, since the Franciscans would permit their charges to work only for landlords who paid fair wages, probably much higher than the wages they gave their own debt peons.[41] As examined in chapter 3, the missionaries blamed the diminution of the mission populations in large part on the settlers, who tried to seduce the Indians to move from the missions onto the haciendas. Fr. Doroteo Giannecchini explained to the archbishop of Sucre in 1883 that the principal causes of depopulation were endemic diseases and "moral" ones:

> These [moral failings] have created even greater problems these past few years than the former [diseases]; the greed of some hacienda owners within and without the republic who exploit [in] thousands of ways the ignorance of the neophytes, taking them away from the paternal care of the missionaries who extracted them from the forests, from impious doctrines, [and] principles of liberty [that are] synonymous with libertinage that some officials have predicated and taught with no shame through insults, satire, lies, and hatred towards the missionaries. . . . All this, Illustrious Sir, has influenced greatly the decrease of the population under my charge and paralyzed the beneficent work of the Apostolate.[42]

Giannecchini's desperation reflected his mounting of various expeditions into the Chaco in the early 1880s. In 1882 a French explorer, Jules Crevaux, arrived at the missions with a recommendation from the Bolivian government to explore the course of the Pilcomayo River. The missionaries accommodated Crevaux and his small party, though they warned him of hostilities with the Tobas, who at the time were on the warpath. Crevaux went ahead anyway and was killed with all but one of his party in April 1882. The trusting explorer had made camp among one of the Toba bands along the river when they murdered him and his party in their sleep.[43]

The government felt it had to retaliate and sent Colonel Andres Rivas to punish the Tobas. However, Rivas was either very unlucky or, more likely, incompetent. As soon as he moved beyond the Creole settlements some Tobas stole all of his horses. When fourteen Tobas entered the expedition's camp to parlay, his troops massacred them. After this incident the Tobas rose in revolt throughout the region and Rivas was unable to recoup his horses, much less penetrate the Chaco. There had been rumors that the missionaries had something to do with the failure of the expedition. Fr. Doroteo Giannecchini, who accompanied the troops as chaplain, had put up his tent at some distance from the soldiers' camp and some expeditionaries had seen Indians visit the friar. They conjectured that the Franciscan had given the Tobas information that made possible the theft of the horses. Fr. Doroteo later published his diary of the expedition, disavowing any involvement in its failure. Be that as it may, after these incidents the atmosphere was poisoned, and many settlers as well as local officials refused to trust the missionaries.[44]

The Campos Expedition Interlude

The Rivas expedition was the prelude to worsening relations between national government officials and the missionaries. In 1883 the national government sent Dr. Daniel Campos, an anticlerical judge of the district court of the mining town of Potosí, to investigate.[45] President Narciso Campero designated Campos national commissioner and delegate, a new kind of office that superseded the power of the missionaries. Campos was to check out the problems between missionaries and settlers along the southeastern frontier. The president also wanted Campos to find a riverine eastward route to the Atlantic Ocean through the Chaco after the loss of the Pacific coast to Chile in the War of the Pacific (1879–1884). The government placed the Tarija Battalion and the Potosí Squadron of the Bolivian Army under Campos's command. The delegate was charged with building forts east of the missions, conquering the Tobas, and finding a route along the Pilcomayo River in the Chaco to connect the country to the River Plate system that drained into the Atlantic.[46]

Campos was also named mission inspector, giving him the ability to intervene in the missions. He initially went to Aguairenda to begin the inspection. Campos was not impressed. Although the church and the missionaries' quarters were well built, he described the unconverted Indians' and neophytes' houses as huts "constructed without solidity, like birds' nests that are passing by."[47] Although he liked the girls' school and heard the boys recite a prayer in Spanish and admired their ability to shoot oranges with their arrows, he admonished the Aguairenda missionary and the girls' teacher that the Indians should speak only in Spanish in the schools, since "language is the instrument of civilization."[48] He asserted that the situation of the mission Indians was "not even moderately satisfactory."[49] He accused the missionaries of subjugating the Indians and turning them into virtual slaves who could not think for themselves. The 1871 regulations made the missions "an Asiatic cloistered petrification and nothing more."[50] In liberal fashion, his solution was to give the Indians each a piece of land for agriculture and another one for grazing, for "to make a man a landowner is to connect him to the land. Everything else is precarious."[51] According to Campos, the missionaries focused only on the soul and not the material well-being of the Indians. It was for that reason that the missions and the frontier had not flourished.[52]

The missionaries were appalled by Campos. In private they accused him of scandalizing the mission Indians and preaching insubordination. The missionaries alleged that Campos had told the Indians that the friars were despots and that they did not have to follow their orders. Other officers of the expeditionary troops also spoke poorly of the missionaries to the Indians of Aguairenda. According to the missionaries, Campos "gave them permission to celebrate their bacchanalia whenever they wanted" and promised that the Franciscans would soon be expelled from the missions.[53] Curiously, Campos recognized the brouhaha he had caused, though he tried to downplay the impressions of conflict between the missionaries and himself. In the report on his expedition, he spent five pages asserting that there had been no conflict between him and the missionaries.[54]

Campos also perceived that there was endemic conflict between local landlords and the missionaries, and he came down firmly on the side of the settlers. He believed that the 1871 regulations gave too much power to the missionaries, creating separate sovereign territories on the missions. He blamed the missions for the decay of settlements such as Caiza, which languished because of the lack of Indian labor. He accused the missions of monopolizing all the labor of the region, which threw the Bolivian property owners "into inaction and abandonment of their properties."[55]

Fortunately for the exasperated friars, Campos's inspection tour was cut short when the government told him to mount his expedition instead of dawdling at the missions. Ironically, Campos did not hesitate to use mission Indian labor for his own projects. He utilized Article 13, one of the few articles in the Reglamento of 1871 permitting the use of mission Indians in the service of national expeditions. The delegate requisitioned a hundred Indians from the Tarija missions to help build the new settlement of Colonia Crevaux along the Pilcomayo River in Toba territory,[56] and also required that the Franciscans provide mission Indians who would bring the supplies, cut new paths through the dense underbrush, do guard duty, and carry messages.[57]

The missionaries, particularly the mission prefect, Fr. Doroteo, defended the missions against Campos and the expeditionaries. He initially permitted the use of laborers for the construction of Colonia Crevaux and the other miscellaneous tasks. However, as Campos continued to demand laborers, Fr. Doroteo suggested that he stop taking neophytes from the missions and instead look for Indians who had escaped and were living among the settlers.[58] This was a dig at the delegate, since Campos refused to round up the mission Indians who had left for Yacuiba and other Creole settlements. Campos felt that the fugitives were much better off than mission Indians. His belief in individual liberty made the mission regimen loathsome to him. He recounted how the fugitive mission Indians pleaded with him: "[They were] shaking with the idea that I was to return them to the missions." He told the escapees that as long as they were working honorably, he did not feel he had the right to have them "submit to a subjection that was repugnant to them."[59] Fr. Doroteo thus backed the delegate into a corner, since Campos did not contemplate drafting the Indians he had presumably freed from the mission system.

When Campos departed for his successful expedition to Asunción in 1883 he left the missions, never to return. Despite the sympathy between the delegate and the settlers, conditions quickly returned to the status quo, and the missionaries regained the upper hand. In 1884 Gregorio Pacheco became president. Pacheco was the founder of the Democratic Party, which in the elections of that year joined with the very pro-Catholic Constitutionalist Party. Constitutionalist Mariano Baptista, Pacheco's vice president, was a vociferous defender of the Catholic Church. As a result, the anticlerical Campos interlude remained an isolated incident, as the national government returned to unconditional support of the missionary enterprise.

Tarija, the closest administrative capital and the location of the convent, also remained profoundly Catholic. The Campos report on the missions and his expedition was published in a handsome government-sponsored edition in 1888. The government presented Campos's arrival in Asunción as a great triumph of Bolivian exploration. The report had a less favorable reception in Tarija, where the Franciscan convent was the most powerful institution. One of the pro-Franciscan newspapers, *El Trabajo*, published a lengthy eighty-page pamphlet refuting Campos's claims. It was written by Luis Paz, member of one of the most prominent merchant families and an ardent defender of the friars.[60] The city of Tarija and the countryside, according to Arthur Thouar, was extremely religious as well. Virtually every house had a small altar or even a chapel. Religious celebrations, in which the Franciscans participated, dominated the city's ritual calendar. Within the city in the late nineteenth century there were few Tarijeños who dared challenge the religious establishment, dominated by the Franciscans and their huge convent that occupied several blocks in the city center.[61]

In addition to the support of the national government, the missionaries never lost the support of the powerful settler families on the frontier. Indeed, Clodomiro del Castillo, a close ally of the Franciscans, was the second in charge of the Voluntarios del Chaco militia that accompanied the Campos expedition. As Campos's and Thouar's diaries show, the Creole landowners on the frontier were essential to the success of the expedition.[62] The agents and allies of the missionaries were everywhere and thus the friars were always well informed of what the anticlerical delegate was up to. The strategy of the Franciscans of privileging some settler families favorable to the missions kept the Creoles on the frontier divided among themselves and unlikely to challenge the missionaries' predominance.

From the 1870s into the 1880s the settlers moved farther into the Chaco, into Toba and Tapieté territory. In Toba territory, especially along the Pilcomayo River, they built small adobe shacks and sent their cattle into the bush. The Tobas reacted to this invasion by taking or killing the cattle and killing the settlers and the cowhands who accompanied the livestock. Since the ranchers did not think the Tobas made good workers (except when captured young and used as slaves), they tried to exterminate them. They justified these murders by branding Tobas inveterate cattle thieves. However, subduing them was no easy matter. The Tobas were fierce warriors. Because they had adopted horse culture and were highly mobile, it was difficult to eliminate them. Fr. Giannelli had founded the mission of San Francisco on the Pilcomayo in 1863 to convert the Tobas and change their nomadic lifestyle. The mission did not accomplish this goal, for the Toba men used the mission as a place of refuge for their elderly and women with young children. The warriors visited only when there was little hunting, fishing, or gathering. The Tobas also fled at any sign that the settlers planned to massacre them, such as in 1873, when all abandoned the mission overnight.[63]

Despite all these problems, Mission San Francisco served an important purpose as the place where each side gathered information on the other and where negotiations took place. Fr. Doroteo used the mission to parlay with Toba chiefs. (An accomplished linguist, he also apparently learned Toba and provided a working vocabulary to the French explorer Jules Crevaux.)[64] The missionaries were vital to the signing of peace treaties between the Tobas and the Creoles in 1859 and 1884. They also served as the intermediaries between the Indians and whites for the return of captives.[65] Government officials on the departmental and national levels realized that the missionaries were essential to keeping the peace with the Tobas as ranchers expanded into the Chaco. The missionaries themselves did not attempt to establish more missions among the Chaco ethnic groups. The Tarija missionaries had bad experiences with the Tobas in San Francisco and the Matacos in San Antonio on the Pilcomayo River; this made them loath to try to harness seasonal nomads to missions that needed full-time agricultural laborers.[66]

In the vocabulary of the time, the friars felt that the Tobas, Matacos, and other ethnic groups could not be "civilized." The missionaries believed that these peoples could not be made into farmers nor made to stay in one place except through force. Fr. Doroteo was aware of this problem and tried to found more missions among the Chaco peoples in the 1880s, when he was the prefect of Tarija, in charge of the missionary enterprise. Instead, the national government turned the job of frontier expansion in the 1880s to private military colonies under the auspices of Manuel Mariano Gómez. The national government gave Gómez a limited number of rifles and ammunition for their defense and the right to distribute land grants among settlers. The del Castillo family was involved, receiving most of the land grants at one of the two forts, Ñaguapoa.[67] With the move toward private military colonies in the Chaco the Franciscans began to lose their position as the dominant institution along the southeastern frontier.

Relations during the 1892 Uprising

The settlers and the national government were caught unawares by the messianic movement of 1891–1892. The missionaries had worried greatly about the movement of Apiaguaiki Tumpa in 1891, before it escalated into full-scale rebellion (see chapter 5). This was the case not only because of the threat to their religious monopoly, but also because many mission Indians and even some tubichas left the missions to follow the new messiah. The missions, especially the recently founded Santa Rosa, became the bulwark against the rebels. In the end, the use of warriors from the missions against the rebels in the climactic battle of Curuyuqui in 1892 resulted in the failure of the rebellion.

The Aniceto Arce administration (1888–1892) sent a national delegate, Melchor Chavarría, to the region in 1891 to try to settle land disputes resulting from the foundation of Mission Santa Rosa. According to Fr. Martarelli, part of the reason for the revolt was that Chavarría promised the Chiriguanos at neighboring Ivo that he would try to get them authorization to establish their own mission. Chavarría returned to Sucre to forward the petition. The delegate did not return for months, and so the Ivo Chiriguanos believed that they had been cheated. Believing they had no alternative, they revolted under the banner of the messianic leader, Apiaguaiki. During the rebellion, Chavarría acted forcefully to contain the revolt and executed many Chiriguano leaders, including Apiaguaiki. After the revolt, he decreed the founding of the mission at Ivo under the control of the Potosí convent.[68]

Despite the rebellion, Arce himself was profoundly sympathetic to the missionaries, donating some of his own lands in Cuevo and Ivo for the establishment of Ivo mission in 1893.[69] Moreover, in the late 1890s he had employed Chiriguano laborers to work on one of his haciendas in the high valleys close to Sucre.[70] Arce was locked in a long political conflict with the anticlerical Liberal Party and certainly was grateful for the support of the Catholic Church.[71] In the aftermath of the 1891–1892 revolt, many settlers accused the missionaries and many of the tubichas (including Mandeponay), of having aided the rebels, despite the crucial role of the mission Indians and Santa Rosa in the defeat of the rebellion. The national government, however, remained a firm supporter of the missionary enterprise.

The 1890s was a decade of strong support for the missions on the national level. In 1892 the fervently Catholic Mariano Baptista won the presidential election and appointed as minister of colonization Luis Paz, the Tarijeño who in 1888 had written articles countering Campos's attacks on the friars.[72] In 1893 Paz sent Dr. Manuel Jofré to visit the missions of the Tarija convent and the Chaco military colonies and show support for the missions. Jofré, a friend of Paz and the son of a military man and Indian fighter from Tarija who after the War of the Pacific became a merchant on the Chaco frontier, was a profoundly religious man, a member of the Conservative Party, and an admirer of the Franciscans.[73] His 1895 report was highly sympathetic toward the missions and is one of the most detailed documents available on mission life written by an outsider.[74] In his report, Jofré explicitly took on Campos and even Chavarría, whom he accused of "erroneous concepts" and "egotistical passions." For Jofré, all that the missionaries did was good; the friars are described as "virtuous and sympathetic" and "intelligent." Jofré described in great detail the school regimen, which he considered excellent. He admired the houses of the neophytes of Aguairenda, which he described as "ample" and "comfortable," emphasizing the cleanliness of the mission. He asserted that the mission Indians lived "contented"; "They take care of their needs without scarcity, enjoying wellbeing and health," he wrote.[75]

Like Daniel Campos a decade earlier, Jofré recognized that the missions' greatest adversaries were the settlers. Unlike Campos, however, Jofré came down squarely on the side of the missionaries. He lambasted the settlers and blamed them for the problems on the missions. He singled out two areas of particular concern: the settlers' role in the depopulation of the missions and the effects of the introduction of the ranchers' cattle on mission lands. He wrote, "[The problem of the missions is that] they are surrounded by settlements and ranches of the *cristianos*, where the Indians are not just received, but attracted and seduced by any means possible, even through corruption, to occupy them in their tasks."[76] The bad influence of the settlers and their attempts to steal the mission Indians was in large part the explanation for the depopulation of the missions. (See chapter 3.)

According to Jofré, ranchers sent their own cattle onto mission lands and then used this as a pretext to steal from mission herds by branding unmarked cattle with their own brands. Some ranchers were so unscrupulous that they altered the brands on the Indians' livestock so that they could claim the cattle for their own.[77] The Franciscans had trouble getting rid of the intruding herds. One settler from Camatindi, Marcelino Rivera, went so far as to threaten the mission prefect with firearms when he was ordered to take his herds off mission property. Rivera was the local justice of the peace and tried to use his official position to defend his actions. Jofré's report shows that local officials were largely opposed to the mission enterprise by the 1890s. Since the major source of income for most of the missions was the sale of cattle, the intrusion of settlers' livestock seriously diminished the missions' earnings.[78]

The Jofré report, in conjunction with favorably disposed national administrations in Sucre, provided moral backing on the national level for the Franciscans against the settlers. Moreover, their links to the militias, through the good offices of the strategically placed del Castillo family, gave them local clout on the frontier. During the Baptista presidency another strong supporter of the Franciscans, Domingo Paz, was prefect of Tarija, shoring up support for the missions at the departmental level.[79] Problems with some neighboring settlers and local officials always existed, but in the last years of the nineteenth century the Franciscan missions enjoyed the highest level of support from outside institutions.

Decline under the Liberals

Relations between the missionaries and the government deteriorated dramatically at the turn of the century, when the anticlerical Liberal Party came to power after the Federalist War (1898–1899). This period marked the beginning of the rapid decline of the mission system as the national government redefined its relationship with the missions and allied itself with frontier settlers and local officials against the missions. In the long run, the mission system could not survive the assault from virtually all sides. The ascendance of the Liberal Party consolidated the changes that Bolivia experienced at the turn of the century. Tin replaced silver as the most important export; La Paz asserted its primacy over the southern cities of Sucre and Potosí. The Liberal Party had made its reputation in the aftermath of the War of the Pacific (1879–1883) for opposing the peace treaty that the Sucre oligarchs signed with Chile. Once they came to power, the liberals remained concerned with the peripheral territories that might be usurped by powerful neighbors. In 1900 the Liberal administration established a National Territory of Colonies in the Amazon as a means of controlling a largely ignored region. The threat turned real when in 1903 Bolivia, despite the efforts of President José Manuel Pando in putting down an insurrection, had to cede the far northern Amazon territories of Acre to Brazil.[80]

The new Liberal administration true to its anticlerical bent also wanted to break the power of the missionaries on the frontier. After only months in power, the Liberal-dominated National Convention of 1900 abrogated the 1871 mission regulations. The purpose of the abrogation became clear when a few months later the National Convention voted to have the mission Indians provide labor for building roads, an activity administered by the neighboring municipalities under the control of the settlers.[81] This followed the liberal dicta, which gave power to local elites while attacking the Catholic Church.

The next blow came in 1901 with a new Reglamento of the missions. Unlike the 1871 ordinance, the new law ended the friars' monopoly on power in the missions. For example, earlier, outsiders had to ask permission to pass through the missions; after 1901 the regulations determined that all could enter the missions at will, though living on the missions was still possible only with the Franciscans' consent. Assimilation of frontier Indians into national society was now the explicit governmental goal, and the missionaries were required to teach the mission children how to speak, read, and write in Spanish. Other rules, such as permitting the neophytes to defend themselves and keeping mission Indians as legal minors, remained the same.[82] The legal balance of power shifted toward local officials, a tendency not at all to the missionaries' liking.

As Pilar García Jordán has pointed out, despite its anticlerical bent, at least initially the new Liberal administration saw the missions as a vital part of its frontier strategy.[83] However, on the local level this lukewarm support by the national government still pushed the balance of power on the frontier toward the settlers. The liberals permitted the Potosí Franciscans to reestablish two missions, San Francisco del Parapetí (1903) and San Antonio del Parapetí (1908), and establish a new one at Nuestra Señora de Lourdes de Itatiqui (1914). Local opposition was fierce and immediate. As Fr. Bernardino de Nino's diary shows for San Francisco, local authorities constantly hindered the friars' work in the new missions. When de Nino set up a meeting with the San Francisco Indians in 1903, the local corregidor had the friar brought to his house and kept him there until it was too late to meet with the tubichas and their soldados. The following day, local landlords requisitioned most of the Chiriguanos to work in their fields so that again the meeting could not take place. A few days later the tubichas were finally able to get enough of their men to come to the meeting.[84]

In San Antonio local officials used the threat of violence. The corregidor entered the Indian village on 30 August 1903 with armed men and told the missionary that all the Chiriguanos were under his jurisdiction. He declared that he would send all the Indian men to work as peons on the neighboring haciendas. By November Fr. Bernardino had procured an order against the local corregidor and with that tried to comfort the Indians.[85] However, the Santa Cruz prefect took the side of the local settlers. Although he conceded that missions were important in subduing "barbarous peoples," he thought that the missionaries should found new missions farther into the frontier and not reestablish the old missions such as San Francisco and San Antonio. In this he reflected the settlers' complaints that the friars were monopolizing Indian labor in areas already pacified and that because of the new missions, the local hacendados were having trouble attracting Indians to work in their fields.[86]

The next nail in the coffin of the missions was the Reglamento of 1905, which was even more restrictive than the earlier one. It made the missionaries into public employees of the Ministry of Colonies and Agriculture. Local authorities were given even more explicit jurisdiction over the missionaries. The sale of any mission goods had to be approved first by the Ministry. Article 22 asserted that the missionary had no right to stop the exploitation of rubber stands or mines on mission territory. Although Articles 5 and 6 kept the missionary as the intermediary between the Indians and outsiders, Article 10 prohibited the friars from interfering in labor contracts within national boundaries. Also, for the first time the Indians were given the "enjoyment of the civil rights that the Constitution recognizes with all men," thus undercutting the absolute powers of the friars on the missions. This echoed Daniel Campos's complaints two decades earlier in privileging the individual liberty of mission Indians over maintaining the friars' rules in favor of mission discipline. In various articles the 1905 Reglamento looked to the eventual secularization of the missions, a development the anticlerical liberals desired.[87]

The 1905 regulations also changed the relationship between the national state, local authorities, and the missions. The missions now were under the jurisdiction of the Ministry of Colonization, whose authority was represented by prefects, subprefects, and national delegates. In other words, the missionaries now answered to local authorities and local settlers in the Chaco frontier. Settlers could now contract mission Indians at will as long as the contract lasted no longer than six months and they returned the Indians to their homes. The national government could secularize missions at will and only needed to inform diocesan authorities of its decision. The missionaries were now perceived to be "public functionaries" rather than religious authorities and were to be paid by the state.[88]

As García Jordán argued, the new Reglamento gave the local settlers new weapons in their struggle to gain resources, mainly Indian labor, from the missions.[89] The Franciscans ferociously opposed this new legislation, though they were unable to stop it. One friar in 1906 asked the mission prefect in frustration, "Why are we here? Perhaps to guard the buildings?" and requested that he be free to return to his home province in Italy.[90] The 1905 law showed how little leverage the friars had on the national level once the liberals came to rule and that the balance of power had definitely shifted against the missionary enterprise, at least as the missionaries conceived of it. The missionaries felt that they should control both the temporal and spiritual aspects of mission life. The troubles Tarija Franciscans encountered in 1905 with the liberal onslaught disgusted the convent's historian, Fr. Larruoa, to such an extent that he swore that he would no longer write about the missions in the convent chronicles because the government's actions had made them all but cease to exist.[91]

The settlers on the frontier, sensing the change in government policies toward the Catholic Church and the Franciscans, began to encroach on mission lands in ways they had not dared previously. In 1906 two brothers tried to usurp land from Santa Rosa. They pastured their own cattle and that of a renter on mission territory. When the missionaries objected the brothers alleged that their father had owned the land since before the 1892 insurrection. However, once the friars produced the legal title to the land, the brothers had to desist.[92] In another case, a local settler sold his interests in 1914 in Curuyuqui to a German firm, Holzer and Company. The company claimed the mission lands of Ivo as well, but a plea by Bernardino de Nino, the Potosí mission prefect, to the minister of war and colonization ended the threat.[93] The settlers were unable to grab mission land illegally. At this point, at least, the Liberal government was not willing to undermine land ownership on existing missions.

Instead of accepting the usurpation of mission land by surrounding landlords, the Bolivian government began to abolish the missions and turn them over to secular control. Immediately after the passage of the 1905 law, the Ismael Montes administration (1904–1909) secularized San Francisco and San Antonio del Pilcomayo, originally established for the Tobas and Matacos across from each other along the Pilcomayo River. The settlement was renamed Villa Montes (also spelled Villamontes), after the president, and became the administrative center of the delegation of the Gran Chaco. Although these two missions had always been troublesome (and had required the friars to move some Chiriguanos from Macharetí to control the other ethnic groups), this move undercut the state's presumed desire in expanding missions further into the frontier. With this one action the state abolished the missions farthest to the east, the ones that might have served the Franciscans as a jumping-off point to missionize the ethnic groups inhabiting the farther frontiers of the Chaco.

The Bolivian government handed over the secularized Villamontes to a

German company, Staudt y Compañía, to develop the region. Staudt was a large merchant company headquartered in Berlin with an important presence in Latin America. It had branches in Paraguay, Uruguay, and various cities in Argentina, as well as Europe and North America. In addition to Villamontes as its administrative headquarters, in 1905 the company purchased from the Bolivian government four hundred square leagues of land in the surrounding Chaco. It promised to build a dam on the Pilcomayo River, build irrigation canals, create vast fields of forage crops, and raise herds of purebred cattle for internal consumption and export to Argentina and Chile. On the San Francisco side of the river it built new houses at the mission settlement and an experimental farm to test new crops.[94]

Again the friars protested vigorously, but without effect. Fr. Santiago Romano, the Tarija mission prefect, traveled personally to the former missions to observe and protest the demarcation of the new town. He claimed that the town was being planned right on top of the old missions, depriving the neophytes of their houses. He protested to the ministers of religion and of colonies and agriculture, but all in vain. Fr. Santiago asserted that he was too old to go to La Paz and begged the Venerable Directorio, the highest council of friars of the Tarija convent, to name a vice prefect to go, but the Directorio refused. The delegate of the Gran Chaco, Dr. Leocadio Trigo, who was in charge of the conversion of the mission into a secular settlement, also refused to listen to the old friar and forged ahead with the distribution of houses and lands.[95]

The missionaries were also hampered by internal weaknesses. The first years of the twentieth century were a period of extreme drought in the region; in 1906, locusts appeared, worsening the already bad crop yields. These conditions lasted through 1907. As a result, many Indians left the missions for the countryside or migrated to the sugarcane plantations of northern Argentina. For the national government, the massive departure of the mission Indians confirmed that the missions were unable to hold the natives. The Franciscans thus had a very weak position from which to argue, though friars such as Bernardino de Nino vigorously defended the missionaries' positions in the Bolivian press.[96]

It also did not help that from 1905 to 1908 Leocadio Trigo, the delegate of the Chaco, was a rabidly anticlerical liberal from Tarija. He fervently defended the 1905 Reglamento and opposed modifications. According to rumors, in 1907 Trigo exclaimed publicly that he would send the missionaries back to Tarija in chains. The Franciscans had no love for the delegate either, calling him the "Great Beast" (*bestión*) in their private correspondence.[97] As crops continued to fail and mission Indians left for Argentina or even Villamontes in the early years of the century, the friars for the first time could not appeal to regional authorities for aid.[98] Indeed, when in late 1906 the missionaries attempted to sell some of the mission cattle to purchase goods for the mission, the delegate prohibited it.[99] According to the 1905 regulations, any mission goods sold to outsiders had first to be approved by local authorities. With a hostile delegate, the missionaries were helpless to use mission resources to counter local emergencies as they had before 1905. This, more than anything else, made their missions less viable and brought about increased outmigration. Since the success of the missions had been based on the Franciscans' power to help the Chiriguanos in preserving their livelihood, it weakened the friar's hold over the mission Indians as well.

It appears that Leocadio Trigo also had less need for the friars than the authorities before him. When in 1906 the delegate launched an expedition into the Chaco to explore the territories along the Pilcomayo River, he did not take along a missionary to serve as chaplain for his troops. Rather than relying on the missionaries for Indians, he relied on Guillermo Herrmann, the Staudt Company official in charge of the newly founded Villamontes, to hire workers. Herrmann had already been active in recruiting laborers from the Chaco, such as Tobas and Matacos, and he used the connections he had forged to cajole chiefs of the various bands to support the expedition.[100] The new anticlerical forces were able to take advantage of the institutions they had created on the frontier, making the missions less essential than they had been before.

The mission Indians were sensitive to the shifting balance of power on the frontier and many used the friars' weakness to their own advantage. Mandeponay and his son Napoleón Tacu, for example, rapidly expanded their liquor-selling enterprises and raked in more by taking money for each man they provided to the Argentine labor contractors.[101] When the friars became fed up with what they considered Mandeponay's irresponsible behavior, they tried to oust him from his position as leader of Macharetí in 1904. But unlike the friars, Mandeponay had read the cards right. Support from the local authorities and prominent settlers prevented the mburuvicha from being sidelined. In the end, the friars had to reinstate him as the leader of Macharetí. Mandeponay also realized that his behavior was counterproductive to keeping his own power base, and he made up with the friars. He continued to receive monies from Argentine labor enganchadores, but he was careful not to send too many men away.[102] But discipline problems within the missions grew more marked, as some mission Indians rejected the authority of the friars. Some appealed to secular authorities in the town of Villamontes or elsewhere if they did not like the missionaries' orders. This happened during the carnival season of either 1906 or 1907, when a drunken dispute between chiefs in Tarairí ended up being adjudicated by the mayor of Villamontes rather than by the missionary.[103]

The breakdown in discipline did not just affect the behavior of the chiefs and their sons, which in fact had always been somewhat problematic. Even common mission Indians were willing to flaunt the mission's order in ways they had been unwilling to previously. This included the Chiriguano girls, who generally had been the most docile group. The missionary of Tarairí, Gabriel Tommassini, complained that none of the men was willing to work: "It is impossible to find even one peon to sow beans, manioc or corn." Worse, many girls escaped from the school in Tiguipa. The exasperated missionary asserted, "If all the girls are able to escape, I need to tell you, Venerable Father, that I will leave Tiguipa and never return to that mission, given the great consideration my words have." Insubordination occurred elsewhere as well; one of the few girls in Tarairí who stayed ground up a toad with the coffee (presumably to poison the missionary) and then took off. Despite attempts to find the girl, Fr. Tommassini was unable to have her returned to question or punish her.[104] In his annual report to the minister of colonization, the mission prefect called the resistance to the missionary "a real revolution."[105]

The mostly Italian Franciscans who were administering the missions in Bolivia were acutely aware of what anticlericalism, so prominent in Italy at the same time, meant for the Catholic Church and the missions in particular. Although Fr. de Nino put up a good fight in the Bolivian press, it appears that many of his brethren began to despair of the anticlericalism of the Bolivian government and its effects on the missions. This was especially evident in the Tarija missions, where administrative problems abounded.

The secularization of the missions continued. In 1911 the government took over one of the oldest missions, Aguairenda. The rationale behind the secularization revealed what the Liberal administration thought of the missions: that the mission enterprise by its very nature retarded progress and modernity. In a private letter to the missionary Juan Argentini, the

Bolivian president Eliodoro Villazón explained that he had tried to protect the missions.

> [But] I have to recognize that [the missions] are destined to disappear and be reestablished as secular settlements, whatever resistance is put against this movement, one that has already begun and will present itself in the whole republic. We cannot get away from the influence of the railroads that advance, the immigration that comes through these means, the industry that by the iron law [of progress] has to develop especially in that frontier of the Republic. Innumerable foreigners will arrive, who will buy lands, [and] will establish new industries; and the missions need to cede to the impulse of this action, as has occurred in all parts of the world. The missionaries must take into account this law and administer the settlements under their administration prudently in this sense and not pretend that they remain in isolation and completely separated from universal progress. What is happening on that frontier is not exactly the work of the government, but the presence and impulse of foreign capital and populations.[106]

Villazón put his government squarely on the side of the foreigners he presumed would populate the Chaco: "It is not in the hands of the government to conserve these groups of the Indian race against European immigration, which must invade and dominate the deserted territories susceptible to industry."[107] In other words, Villazón saw the missions as retrograde, keeping the Indians away from the currents of progress and favoring a population that needed to be replaced by Europeans, who would bring economic dynamism. Given these assumptions, the Franciscans could not expect the government in La Paz to help them fend off attacks by local landlords.

Indeed, the secularization of Aguairenda greatly harmed the mission Indians. The government turned the mission settlement into the headquarters of an army regiment, turning the former residents out of their homes. The Indians did keep their grazing lands. However, instead of moving to the pastures, the Aguairenda Indians rented them out to the settlers who lived in neighboring El Palmar. Most of the Chiriguanos dispersed elsewhere, many going to Argentina or Yacuiba, an important town on the Bolivia-Argentina border.[108]

The settlers in El Palmar had set the secularization in motion with an official complaint that neighboring Mission Aguairenda stymied the economic development of their town.[109] They asserted that the mission contained only twenty neófito families but maintained possession over extensive territory that was far beyond the capacity of the Indians to utilize for themselves. Leocadio Trigo, still the national delegate of the Chaco, added a report confirming this state of affairs. The complaint used the rhetoric of economic progress. The signatories to the petition alluded to alkaline soils that could be used for making soap on an industrial scale if they were given the land. Among the petitioners were various del Castillos, probably part of this important frontier family. If this was the case, then even members of a prominent family that had been traditional allies of the friars were willing to oppose the Franciscans by the early twentieth century.[110]

The recently founded Parapetí missions, San Francisco, San Antonio, and Itaiqui, fell next in the government's secularization drive in 1915. As mentioned earlier, Fr. Bernardino de Nino founded San Francisco and San Antonio and Itaiqui in the early twentieth century as part of the last campaign by the Potosí Franciscans to expand their mission territory. The Bolivian government, after some years of tolerating the new missions, decided that they were not in the country's best interests. The official decree reflected liberal ideology and the local landlords' complaints and was devastating in its critique of the missions. According to the decree, "[The missions] have under their tutelage Indians sufficiently capable to lead independent lives and whose existence cannot be taken advantage of for agriculture or ranching because of the opposition of the missionaries." The following paragraph argued, "The mission regime, limiting itself to a labor without benefit for the worker, encourages the exodus of the Indians who leave annually in large numbers to the exterior [of the republic] in the search [for] unrestricted work that is prohibited to them in this country." The decree declared the missions "unnecessary and illegal" and secularized them.[111]

Mission secularization reflected the new relations of power along the frontier. The national government took the side of the settlers, who by this time saw no advantage to having new missions among the still independent Chiriguano communities. This was particularly the case in Cordillera province, Santa Cruz department, where the settlers had adopted a different method of colonization. Rather than conquering the Indians and taking over their lands as the Tarijeños had done, the Cordillera settlers tended to preserve the Chiriguano villages to serve as sources of labor. This was most evident in the Caipipendi valley, where the Aireyu dynasty had long controlled the Chiriguano villages and had supplied laborers to large landowners such as Octavio Padilla, the owner of the vast Incahuasi estate, also known as Caraparicito.¹¹² Even more important, the Parapetí missions Fr. Bernardino had established preempted the establishment of new missions from Santa Cruz among the numerous Guaraní-speaking Izoceño people farther downriver, a region that ranchers from Santa Cruz had begun to penetrate in the mid-nineteenth century.¹¹³ The settlers of Santa Cruz blocked the Franciscan expansion with the help of the Liberal administration in La Paz.

The Apostolic Vicariate of the Gran Chaco

In the hostile political environment and in view of the growing weakness of the Tarija convent, the Franciscans decided to consolidate forces to sustain their missionary efforts. Creating an Apostolic Vicariate in 1919 allowed the Franciscans to combine their personnel and administer the missions, previously divided among the Potosí and Tarija convents, as one administrative unit. The Vicariate combined various parishes of the small frontier towns inhabited mainly by settlers under their care. It meant that the friars could move from one place to another as needed and administer the entire region more efficiently. Rather than two mission prefects, there would be only one authority: the apostolic vicar. The Catholic Church adopted an ecclesiastical model of the government's frontier Delegation, mirroring the territorial extent of the jurisdiction of the delegate of the Gran Chaco.¹¹⁴ More important, establishing a Vicariate meant that mission possessions were to be treated the same as parish property, and so the friars would not lose their church and the missionary's quarters (converted into a parish house), as they had when the government secularized the other missions.

The idea of creating a Vicariate had come up earlier, in 1906, when the Liberal administration first attacked the missions. However, the government refused to consider this change.¹¹⁵ When Congress debated the law to create the Vicariate in 1918 and 1919, the congressional delegations from Santa Cruz and Beni opposed the proposal. However, even the delegation from Tarija, all liberals, supported the measure and it passed over the objections of the *cruceños* [people of Santa Cruz].¹¹⁶

The Apostolic Vicariate did not lead to a revitalization of the missions. The anticlerical program of the Liberal government had broken the spirit of the Franciscans, especially after the secularization of Itatiqui (1915), destroying all possibility of expanding into new regions. Despite its promise of reorganizing resources to move farther out into the Chaco, the Franciscans realized that they could not establish new missions.[117] Instead, the Vicariate proved to be defensive, preserving for a few decades a system that was already in decay.

In the aftermath of the establishment of the Vicariate, the internal administration of the missions changed. Gone were the restrictions on the use of mission lands exclusively for the Indians. Unlike in earlier times, when the missionaries encouraged the settlement of allies such as the del Castillo family, now the Franciscans permitted the rental of mission land by all non-Indians.[118] In 1921 the missionaries established a set of rules by which non-Indian renters had to live. On Mission Boicovo this included a maximum two-year contract, a yearly grazing fee for each kind of animal (cows, pigs, sheep, and goats), a strict policy of contracting mission Indian labor only with the consent of the missionary, and the obligation of the renter to send his children to the mission school. According to the contract, if the renter did not "maintain good behavior [*guardar buenas costumbres*]," the priest could force him to leave.[119] As a list of renters shows, many contracts were renewed over many years, with an average rental period of about six years. The friars kept a detailed list of each renter, noting yearly how many livestock each had, whether he occupied a hut on the mission, and how much land he cultivated.[120] It is not clear why the Franciscans permitted the entry of non-Indians onto mission lands. Presumably it was to gain allies among the frontier population and to gain income. The policy did not work very well. By 1930 even wealthy neighbors from surrounding towns wanted to rent mission lands. The friars refused the request by four wealthy merchants and landlords to rent one and a half leagues each of mission lands. This refusal created more friction with the settlers instead of creating alliances with local elites.[121]

The Bolivian military, which increased its presence in the region in the 1920s, also did not hold a good opinion of the missions. Lieutenant Colonel Angel Rodríguez, the author of a detailed study of the Chaco region in 1927, asserted, "Benefits [from the missions] are not as big as [people] suggest." The four Franciscans in Cuevo were, "according to general opinion, equal to four zeros." According to the officer, the mission Indian was "the most ignorant of all the Indians," because in the schools the friars taught the children to pray in Spanish, but by "teaching them to pronounce words like a parrot." When asked a question in Spanish, neither the adults nor the schoolchildren could answer. This was because all the missionaries spoke Guaraní and that is what they used, "especially with the numerous female servants, as among the Muslims."[122] In addition to echoes of the liberal discourse (as well as some sexual innuendo), it is possible to discern in Rodríguez's comments a sense of competition with the missions, which the military was replacing as the primary force for colonizing the southeastern frontier. If there is any truth to the lieutenant colonel's comments, the standards of the missions declined when the Franciscans established the Apostolic Vicariate.

The introduction of non-Indians worsened conditions on the missions, diluting the original religious charge of the missionaries and, by 1929, bringing conflicts over land between the mission Indians and the Creoles. Non-Indians began to take over Indian land, and sometimes the Indians fought back. This happened in Macharetí, where in 1929 the proximity of a camp of Standard Oil Company workers created problems. Creoles, attracted by the economic opportunities of the oil camp, began to settle in the mission over the objections of the friars. Various Creoles abused the Indians, building houses in the Indians' fields, planting orchards on land belonging to neófitos, and other such problems. The local corregidor, Ramón Marás, even tried to build a public road through the fields of various mission Indians without authorization by the missionaries. It is not surprising that when the Creoles went against their interests, the mission Indians, in alliance with the missionaries, resisted. This occurred in December 1929, when eight Indians armed with knives destroyed the house that Torcuato Tejerina had built. When asked why they had done it, they answered that the missionary had ordered them to do so.[123] The relationship between local settlers and authorities on the one hand and the missionaries on the other reached a new low in the late 1920s, though the Franciscans themselves had let the wolves in among the sheep.

The missionaries were fighting a rearguard action against the intruders. In 1930 one anonymous author writing in *El Antoniano*, the newspaper published in the Tarija Franciscan convent, railed against these newcomers. The article, titled "The White Savages," asked, "What do those parvenu whites pretend, those who have installed themselves on the missions with the only objective of impeding the beneficial work of the padres with the Indians? They have confessed it themselves: Destroy the missions, kick out the Indians, after having persecuted the Fathers and appropriate for themselves the lands that by natural right and sanctioned by the Supreme Government, belong exclusively to the Indians."[124] At this point most Creole inhabitants thought missions merely restricted their ability to recruit Indian workers and gain access to good lands. The threat of an Indian uprising was long gone as the frontier had moved farther into the Chaco (without the missionaries), and thus the missions were seen as anachronisms that, in the liberals' terms, were holding back the progress of the region.

By the 1920s the relationship between the missions and the national government had improved somewhat, and this is why the remaining missions were not secularized. The government saw the missions as a bulwark against the increasing migration of the Indians across the border to Argentina. With the fall from power of the Liberal Party and the victory of the Republicans in the revolution of 1920, it appeared that relations would improve considerably between the Catholic Church and the government. Initially the new Republican government saw the Vicariate as a means to create missions among the Matacos, Choretis, and Tapietès, a task the military also endorsed.[125] The Tarija prefect, Víctor Navajas Trigo, in 1923 also urged the government to undo the damage the anticlerical campaign had done, arguing, "Our effort should be to . . . maintain the conquests accomplished by the constancy and courage of the missionaries of the Christian faith, that the heavy hand of sectarianism has cruelly destroyed."[126]

In the last part of the decade, however, the pendulum had swung back toward anticlericalism, at least among local officials. From 1926 onward the delegate of the Gran Chaco was in the hands of officials who thought of the missions as retrograde institutions that should be secularized. One opponent was Julio A. Gutiérrez, who had been prefect of Santa Cruz in 1925 and was then named delegate of the Gran Chaco. He asserted, "The padres work on things that are related to the ornamentation of their temples," and he lamented their lack of enterprise in economic matters. Gutiérrez asserted that Standard Oil and migration to Argentina were creating progress but that the missionaries remained "in the mold of the eighteenth century." According to the delegate, the friars didn't even bother to teach the Indians Spanish, since, he claimed, it was easier for the former to learn Guaraní. Gutiérrez even accused the Franciscans of being "antipatriotic" because they did not let settlers live on the missions, next to the all-vital streams.[127] In 1928 the interim delegate also claimed, "[The missionaries] don't advance at all, remaining in a disquieting static state. They do not accept going with modern currents at all."[128] His report ignored aspects of modernity and progress on the missions. When he reported on the schools in his territory, Gutiérrez did not include the missions, which had the most schools in the territory.

By the 1920s the Chaco frontier had changed considerably. The delegates held the missionaries in check and promoted the colonization of the region through other means. Rather than relying on the missions, the delegates systematically promoted the presence of the Bolivian state in the interior of the Chaco. They did so through various methods. First of all, they built a series of forts deep into the Chaco, effectively militarizing the zone and wiping out the resistance of the Chaco peoples, especially the previously bellicose Tobas.[129] Militarization also promoted the use of force, which later proved disastrous during the conflict with Paraguay.

Second, the delegates promoted the creation of private development enterprises, such as the handing over of Villamontes to the Staudt Company for agricultural development. By the 1920s, however, this effort had degenerated significantly. The experimentation with different crops that Staudt started in its test gardens did not provide positive results, and the company turned its lands to ranching, like the other large landowners. The La Paz government reduced the original concession of 400 square leagues to 150 square leagues. With the First World War and subsequent inflation, the German firm gave up its Villamontes base and sold it to a Finnish company, S. A. Lanmaatschappij Pilcomayo. A German traveler, Hans Krieg, passed through Villamontes in the late 1920s and described a degenerate society in which indigenous women had turned to prostitution and the German administrators lived with native women concubines, drank warm beer brought on muleback from Tarija "like an old morphine addict presses the needle of the syringe through his skin," and were dying in the inhospitable climate.[130]

The national government tried other means to develop the region. In 1923 it authorized the settlement of twenty-five families from the United States in the former missions of Aguairenda and Itau, to be led by U.S. Colonel William Murray. The government ceded the former mission towns and promised 18,000 hectares to the American, whose colonists were to cultivate cotton. By 1925 the government ceded about half the promised territory to him, but the twenty-five families returned home almost immediately, frightened off by a plague of locusts.[131] Although the government brought in a cotton gin and the colonel and his family stayed to cultivate cotton, the experiment failed.[132]

The government also promoted the distribution of land on the frontier to private individuals for settlement. Wealthy speculators took advantage of this legislation. In 1912 the government gave out concessions for 20,000 hectares (the legal maximum) to twenty-eight individuals. Twenty of these concessions were handled not by the petitioners, but by two Germans, Otto Ratzsch and Carlos Rahm. Their clients were mainly Germans, Italians (in the case of Ratzsch), and Argentines from Buenos Aires (in the case of Rahm).[133] According to the 1905 legislation, the concessionaries were supposed to settle one family for every one thousand hectares, but this never happened. This failure was attributed to "the simple fact" that the land was "only useful for cattle raising, and . . . two families [were] sufficient to watch the cattle on 20,000 hectares." The state compounded the problem in 1925 by renting out the land that some concessionaries had abandoned. In the Chaco the forty-eight renters were all foreigners, mostly Argentines, who did not take care of the pastures and who built miserable huts made of sticks for their cowherds. Moreover, the state was so weak that it failed to check to see whether legal conditions had been fulfilled.[134]

Internal Problems in the 1930s

In the early 1930s trouble was brewing on the missions as well, especially in Machareti. Mandeponay, the most important mburuvicha of the missions and recognized as the leader of the "heathen Indians of Machareti and all the rest of the Chaco tribes" by the first apostolic vicar, Monsignor Hipólito Ulivelli, died in 1922.[135] A struggle ensued between the friars who wanted to designate their own indigenous authorities and the descendants of Mandeponay. In late 1929 the nephew of the great chief, Ubaldino Cundeye, walked from Machareti to La Paz. He visited the Ministry of War and Colonization as representative of the Machareti Indians. He also claimed, as had the missionaries, that the corregidor Ramón Marás had abused his authority by destroying mission Indians' fields to put a road through the mission.

Cundeye's complaints concerned the friars as well. He accused the missionaries of not providing instruction to the children in the mission schools and asked to be recognized as mburuvicha of all the missions.[136] The Franciscans opposed the naming of Cundeye. In a letter to the minister of colonization, the mission prefect asserted, "Up to now the indigenous authorities have always been named and put in their position by the Mission Prefects or the Apostolic Vicar," but the missionaries suppressed the naming of chiefs "because they abused their authority too much and were the first and biggest enganchadores of Indians to Argentina."[137]

Cundeye's complaints can be understood on a variety of levels. For one thing, as did other sons of the traditional chiefs, Cundeye felt an acute loss of prestige. Because he was baptized he had to follow the leadership of the friars and of the elected leaders of the neófitos rather than be accepted as a hereditary leader, a member of the most prestigious lineage in the missions. Indeed, in January 1930 the superiors of the missions suppressed the naming of grandes capitanes for the following reason: "[Although it] is a traditional thing among the Chiriguano Indian race ... they abuse too much their authority and are the first and strongest contractors [enganchadores] for the Argentine Republic, earning lucrative commissions from the owners of the sugar mills."[138] The attack on what Cundeye saw as his legitimate right—being named a gran capitán at some point—brought about his rejection of the mission system. He also wanted to eliminate the tutelage of friars, which would have strengthened his power within Machareti.

The reaction of the national government to the missionaries' recalcitrance was swift. In March 1930 President Hernando Siles decreed that the prefects and national delegates had the authority to name the grandes capitanes on the missions. Again the missionaries complained, asserting, "[This decree] perverts the liberty of the Chiriguano race, which has always freely elected its capitanes and in many communities of our Chaco, there are captainships within families, where the authority passes from father to son."[139] Fed up with the missionaries, the government responded by secularizing the missions in April 1930. Although the Church could keep all the cattle, the buildings that housed the friars, the churches, and agricultural plots to sustain the religious infrastructure, most of the land was to be turned over to the mission Indians and the rest given over to settlement by non-Indians.[140] The Siles government became more anticlerical as the president tried to harness and co-opt the new leftist (and anti-Catholic) student movements. In the end, traditional liberals took over the direction of the president's newly founded Partido de Unión Nacional. The combination of the emphasis on modernity and progress by the leftist adherents and the old anticlericalism of the Liberal Party was a lethal mix for the Franciscan mission enterprise.[141] In the end, with the fall of the Siles government, the secularization decrees were rescinded in 1931 and the missions continued, though with little support on the national level.[142]

The conflict with the descendants of Mandeponay did not stop there. Cundeye returned to La Paz, this time with two of his cousins, Teodosio Aparindo and Manuel Taco, the latter the son of José Napoleón Tacu, Mandeponay's favorite son. They caused a sensation in La Paz. Various newspapers interviewed them and put their photos on the front page. The Indians claimed that not only were merchants, such as the Italian Victorico Florense, taking their lands, but the missionaries were abusing them. They accused the Franciscans of living with the Chiriguano girls and claimed that they had to work for free for the benefit of the missionaries and that the missionaries sold goods to the Indians at high prices.[143] The Franciscans fought back in their own newspaper, *El Antoniano*. César Vigiani, the mission prefect, refuted the accusations point for point. He asserted that Cundeye didn't know much about Macharetí: "His libertine and sad life has made him pass [his time] among the gauchos of Argentina, even exercising the disreputable profession of cart driver." The friar claimed that all the children did know how to speak Spanish and read and write and that most mission Indians did appreciate the missionaries. Adolescent girls were able to go home three times a day, but if a boy wanted to marry a girl the missionaries required the bridegroom first to build a solid house where they could live.[144]

Cundeye and his companions distorted conditions on the missions. It was part of a political project to wrest control of the missions from the Franciscans. By allying themselves with the Ministry of Colonization and other national authorities, they tried to counteract the influence of the friars. The Indians were using the missionaries' nineteenth-century strategy, allying themselves with La Paz against local frontier groups. Thus they hoped to gain control over the mission community, including over their own labor, and gain access to the young women the friars had cloistered. Cundeye (and probably Taco as well) had grown up in Argentina, outside the influence of the missionaries. They felt that they had a hereditary right to rule and to change the mission regime. The anticlerical politicians in La Paz were willing to listen to them, since the young Indian leaders seemed to represent an enlightened, progressive group, in contrast to the retrograde and Church-bound Franciscans. In turn, the Franciscans saw the claims of the new generation of chiefs as part of the traditional setup, the kind of arrangement that the conversion of the mission Indians was supposed to prevent. In this new community of Catholic faith, the leader should be the Franciscan, not the descendants of the traditional chiefs.

Conclusion

Relationships with outsiders were crucial for understanding the rise and then the demise of the mission system. After all, the missions existed in different political fields, from the local to the national levels, and were embedded in larger relationships that at times had profound effects on their development. At the local level, the main outside actors were indigenous peoples, local officials, and local settlers. On the regional and national levels, the principal actors impinging upon the missions were the national government, prefects, and the occasional delegates such as Daniel Campos.

The missions thrived when the national government either neglected them or actively favored them. The apogee of the missions came about after the promulgation of the 1871 mission law, written by the friars themselves, which gave them virtual autonomy. This law kept the local and regional authorities at bay, though at least initially even the local settlers, looking for protection, favored the missions. The missionaries also created strategic alliances with prominent families, most notably the del Castillos, who had entered into a symbiotic relationship with them. It permitted the missions to thrive at the juncture of the mission cycle between the initial stage of mission foundation and the transition to the administrative stage. Only the brief interjection of representatives sent by the national government could wreak temporary havoc on the missionary's primacy during this period. The delegates, such as Daniel Campos, Manuel Othon Jofré, and later Leocadio Trigo, varied widely in their effect, depending on their ideology and personality. After the delegates left conditions returned to normal, though settler resentment began to grow in the late nineteenth century, when the local elites saw less and less personal benefit from the missions.

When the government turned decisively anticlerical at the turn of the twentieth century, the mission system began to fall apart. Internal problems were the lack of new missionaries in Tarija and the long-term effects of migration to Argentina by the mission Indians; these made the missions less useful in the continuing social and economic integration to outsiders and the neophytes. However, the most important factor was the national government, which, through the 1901 and 1905 mission Reglamentos, took control away from the missionaries and gave the regional governments and the local settlers primacy. The creation of the Delegation of the Chaco was detrimental to the missions as well, for this institution was created to replace the missions with a different model of frontier development and was staffed by authorities opposed to the missions. The tactics adopted by the Franciscans did not aid their cause either, as they rented out mission lands to outsiders and adopted a purely defensive posture with the creation of the Apostolic Vicariate. By the early 1930s, the missions were in frank decline. But the worst was still to come, as the Chaco War swept through the region and wiped out most of what was still left of the missions.

CHAPTER EIGHT

From the Chaco War to Secularization, 1932–1949

After 1900, as the Franciscan missions declined, the Chaco War (1932–1935) destroyed the rest of the missions in all but name. In 1934 and 1935 the front reached the missions and Paraguayan troops took over the most important mission sites, including Santa Rosa, Ivo, Tarairí, Tiguipa, and Machareti. When the war finally ended a few Chiriguanos straggled back to their ancestral lands. But much of the land had been taken by the surrounding settlers, and the missionaries as well as the Indians had to live with the massive presence of non-Indians on the missions. Relatively few documents survive from this final period of the missions. Either the Franciscans lost interest in preserving the documentation they had so assiduously kept for the period before the war, or the administrative quality declined dramatically and the missions generated less paperwork. Most of the information we do have relates to land tenure problems with the mestizo population rather than with the Indians who remained on the missions.[1]

On the eve of the Chaco War the Franciscan mission system had a total of 4,864 Chiriguanos living in the missions. This was about half the population in 1900 and about a third of what it had been in 1877.[2] Of these, only 696, around 14 percent, were not baptized. In Tiguipa there were only seven individuals whom the friars considered "heathen," and in Boicovo none at all remained. As always, Machareti had the largest number of unconverted, but Santa Rosa and Ivo were not far behind, all at around 20 percent of the total population. A total of 846 children attended mission schools, about 17 percent of the total population. The schools had an almost equal ratio of boys and girls, though there was some variation between missions. The less dynamic Tarija missions had a lower rate of schooling.[3] (See table 18.)

TABLE 18. Franciscan mission population in 1930

Mission	Neófitos	Unconverted	Male school-children	Female school-children
Santa Rosa de Cuevo	1,020	215	105	132
San Buenaventura de Ivo	602	113	86	75
San Pascual de Boicovo	286	0	38	42
La Inmaculada de Tarairí	330	40	33	30
La Purísima de Tiguipa	480	7	30	28
Madre de Misericordia de Macharetí	1,450	321	141	106
Totals	4,168	696	433	413

Source: "Cuadro sinóptico de las Misiones dependientes de la Prefectura de Tarija," *El Antoniano* 34, no. 1199 (20 February 1930), 2; "Informe de la Prefectura de Misiones del Colegio de Potosí," *El Antoniano* 34, no. 1199 (20 February 1930), 3.

By the late 1920s the missions were in crisis. They were undermined from the inside by the children of the traditional chiefs, who wanted to lead the missions as their fathers or uncles had. They had spent time in the plantation workers' camps in Argentina, where morals were much more lax and the prime objective was not creating a Christian community but making money or gaining access to goods not available on the Bolivian frontier. These new chiefs wanted the missionaries gone or at least their power reduced, and the Chiriguanos on the missions believed they were ready to face the larger world.

The Franciscans' reaction to the crisis did not recognize this change in attitude. The friars became stricter, trying to stop the hemorrhaging of the mission population, but accomplishing exactly the opposite. In 1930 the friars banished from the small Boicovo mission six families because the missionary "did not permit them to live in public adultery."[4] The Franciscans admitted their failure to hold onto the mission population. When Cundeye, nephew of the great Mandeponay, asserted that the abuses by the missionaries led to the migration of four thousand young neophytes to Argentina, the friars did not dispute the figures, but instead argued that they had left "because of the continuous abuses and bad treatment [they] receive[d] from the whites." Indeed, as the Creole authorities established their residence in Macharetí, one missionary wrote, "It is clear that as the whites have increased in number in Macharetí, the neófitos have diminished in number. Lately, some of those whites have gone to the extreme of seizing the fields of the neófitos."[5] Even the tight control over mission lands that the friars had maintained for a century quickly slipped away, leading to an increasing number of non-Indians settling on mission lands.

The missions were being assaulted from the outside as well. After the failure of the 1930 secularization decree the pressure on the missionaries continued. In 1931 the opposition Liberal Party raised the banner of anticlericalism in its campaign to regain the presidency.[6] In 1932, just as Bolivia was about to go to war with Paraguay, an editorial in the influential liberal newspaper *El Diario* asserted that the Franciscans were the principal reason for the backwardness of the Chaco region. The author asserted that the friars were the largest landholders on the frontier, on the same level as Staudt and Company, but with the advantage over the German firm that the missionaries had the best agricultural lands and access to as much Indian labor as they wanted. Furthermore, the reporter argued, if the lands were given over to the industrious peasants of the Bolivian highlands, they would prosper. After all, the Franciscans were almost all foreigners and were more adept at giving sermons than making the land produce.[7] Another author accused the friars in 1931 of teaching the Indians not to fight against the Paraguayans, since the Paraguayans were their brothers. According to the author, the Franciscans had become Paraguayan spies.[8] This was a new rhetorical assault on the mission system, blending the argument of economic progress with a nationalist discourse that began to reverberate in the Great Depression of the 1930s. Indeed, the Depression laid to waste the economic activity of the Chaco. It included the oil industry that had been the authorities' hope for economic revitalization of the region. In 1932 *El Diario* described the previously vibrant frontier town of Yacuiba, on the Argentine border, as "abandoned by its inhabitants": "Abandoned houses, empty streets, absent residents, that is all that remains of the beautiful capital of the Chaco that it was before."[9]

The Chaco War

From 1900 onward the anticlerical cast of the government rejected the missions as the best way to colonize the frontier and instead relied on the delegate of the Gran Chaco and also on the military. In the 1920s the military established a string of forts deep in the interior of the Chaco, attempting to set up on the ground the forces needed to back up the diplomatic efforts between Bolivia and Paraguay. Paraguayan forces also penetrated deep into Indian territory and placed troops in small forts connected by tenuous roads through the heavy scrub forest. Thus began a race between the two countries to explore and establish a presence in the interior of the Chaco through a series of tiny strongholds manned by small and ill-equipped garrisons. Conflict was virtually inevitable, since each side claimed the same territory and the civilian governments left the militaries of both countries in charge of penetrating as far as possible into this territory.[10]

The Chaco War was an unmitigated disaster for Bolivia and the missions. Although there had been isolated skirmishes in the late 1920s far into the interior of the Chaco that did not affect the missions, official hostilities began in July 1932 with the combat around Laguna Chuquisaca. Bolivian president Daniel Salamanca thought that he could easily win, since his troops had German military training and, unlike the Paraguayan Army, an air force. A successful war, Salamanca hoped, would unite the country and overcome the political problems and the economic effects of the Great Depression that had severely disrupted the Bolivian export mining economy.[11] Salamanca's calculations proved fatally wrong. After some initial success, Bolivian forces suffered defeat after defeat. Paraguayan troops reached the mission region at the foothills of the Andes. Finally Bolivian troops were able to stop the overextended Paraguayans.[12]

Virtually nothing has been written about the fate of the Indians during the Chaco War, though the effects on all indigenous groups of the region were profound. Many groups took refuge in Argentina when foreign troops invaded their territory. The soldiers of both sides kidnapped the Indian women they encountered, and there exist photographs of grinning soldiers posing with naked indigenous women in the Chaco interior.[13] The Tobas fled to the Argentine side of the Paraguay River when the Paraguayan troops advanced. The Izoceño group on the Upper Parapití River fought on the Bolivian side, though there appears to have been considerable fraternization between the Indians and the invading Paraguayan troops. The Paraguayans captured many thousands on Izoceños, including their chief, Casiano Barrientos. When his troops reached the Parapetí River near the Izozog and the Indians heard them speaking Guaraní, Marshal José Félix Estigarribia, the commander of the Paraguayan forces, noted, "[The Indians] received us like brothers." The Paraguayans even sent Barrientos to Asunción to speak to the president of Paraguay, to convince him to join their side. After gaining the confidence of the Paraguayan military, Barrientos and the bulk of his people later escaped through the Chaco back to their homeland, though only about half made it back to the Izozog. The Bolivians executed the Izoceño chief as a traitor in 1936.[14]

The Chiriguanos had a difficult time during the war. As with the Izoceños, the Chiriguanos spoke Guaraní, the national language of Paraguay. The vast majority of Bolivian soldiers came from the highlands and distrusted the Indians, who seemed to be more like their enemies than like themselves. Some Indians were recruited as guides, some handled the transport over the rivers, and others hacked at the dense underbrush and evened out terrain to create roads for the Bolivian troops.[15] Very few Chiriguanos saw combat since the military did not trust them and the missionaries tried to protect them from the draft. Despite the missionaries' protection, even when the war was far away, from 1932 to 1934, the missions experienced massive disruptions. The military turned Tarairí and Machareti into field hospitals as the front advanced toward the Andean foothills.[16] This meant that the military gained control over the missions, with all the concomitant problems of lack of discipline, danger to the women, and the takeover of mission housing for the troops.

In 1935 the war arrived at the missions' doorsteps. In February the war engulfed Cuevo, Ivo, Tarairí, Tiguipa, and Machareti as Paraguayan forces took these settlements and fought with the Bolivians over Villamontes and Charagua.[17] When the Paraguayan troops left Tarairí, they destroyed the surrounding fields and burned the houses and the mission church.[18] It is difficult to ascertain from the published literature what happened to the indigenous population in the zones of combat, though there are many clues scattered in official accounts and soldiers' memoirs. Many refer to the capture of Indians by Paraguayan troops and the imprisoning of a number of them, as in the case of the Izozog region, as well as cases of collaboration by indigenous people. However, the reports do not distinguish between different ethnic groups. The Paraguayans called all Guaraní-speaking Indians in Bolivia indistinctly "Guarayos," mixing Chiriguanos, Izoceños, and other groups. Guaraní was the lingua franca among indigenous people in the region and even the household language of many settlers. The Bolivian troops from the highlands saw all Indians from the region as "savages," and so it is impossible to distinguish Chiriguanos from the other ethnic groups in the many memoirs of Chaco War veterans.[19]

Fr. Gerardo Maldini, who worked in the region as a parish priest in the 1970s and 1980s, asserts that many of the Indians from Machareti, Tiguipa, and Tarairí were taken to Chimeo, away from the front, under the care of Brother Luis Mattioli.[20] But others assert that many Chiriguanos had not fled Macharetí when the Paraguayan troops encircled the mission, and so they were taken prisoner. Some of the captured Machareteños went to Argentina. Many remained in Salta, where the Franciscan convent there received 25,000 hectares and founded the mission of San Antonio along the Caraparí River.[21]

Even the few missions that had not been involved in the hostilities suffered. In 1935 Mission Boicovo, which had been spared the conflict because it was hidden in the foothills to the west of the conflict zone, contained seventy-three households of converted Indians and three households of unconverted. Altogether, there were 270 on the mission. However, eight households (more than 10 percent) had at least one family member missing (in five, it was the male head of household), and the mission contained sixteen orphans (including three males who were missing), eleven neófito widows, and five unconverted widows.[22] Unfortunately censuses for the other missions after the Chaco War do not exist. But Boicovo was the least affected mission; the others showed even greater damage. Some missions were completely destroyed by the war; some lost their entire indigenous population.

After the armistice in 1935 it was difficult for the Indians to return to the missions. One Bolivian colonel exclaimed that if the Chiriguanos returned to Macharetí, he would personally see that they were all sent to the firing squad.[23] Nevertheless, the mission Indians trickled back across the Argentine and Paraguayan borders or returned from their refuges in the western foothills. Ubaldino Cundeye, unlike many of his relatives, had been able to evade the Paraguayans. He first settled in Villamontes, in the Indian neighborhood of La Banda in the former San Antonio mission next to the Pilcomayo River, and was described as the "ex-capitán of the neófitos of Macharetí."[24] Cundeye was not content to remain in Villamontes and traveled to Argentina to bring back Machareteños to repopulate the mission. Overcoming all problems, Cundeye returned in 1938 with eighteen former inhabitants and proceeded to rebuild the settlement. According to one of the returnees, the mission prefect before and after the war, Fr. César Vigiani, considered selling the vacant mission territory of Macharetí to the cattle ranchers of Carandaití before the Indians returned.[25] Cundeye went to the military authorities of the region and had himself appointed "Capitán of the Guaranís coming from the Macharetí sector . . . because of his aptitude."[26] He was thus able to gain some support from the outside and provide a counterweight to the karai who had invaded the mission lands in the Indians' absence.

When the Indians returned to their homes little was left. The infrastructure had been destroyed. Macharetí, the largest mission before the war, was virtually wiped out. The church on the hill and the missionaries' complex next to it had survived more or less intact, though with a damaged roof and with the altars missing. The same could not be said for the Indian settlement on the plain below. According to one eyewitness, the neat rows of adobe houses of the neófitos were uninhabitable. The houses' tile roofs had caved in and the adobe walls were crumbling. The section of town for the unconverted, whose roofs were of straw, had been burned to the ground.[27] In addition, the cattle that had provided ready cash for emergency expenses over the years were gone despite having been herded to Boicovo before the Paraguayans invaded. In 1940 the mission records indicate that of the Macharetí herd "not one still remained."[28] Even worse, when Cundeye returned to the mission with his small band, much of the land had been occupied by non-Indians.

Santa Rosa de Cuevo, the most important of the Potosí missions, serves as an example of this devastation. In 1937 its missionary reported, "The military occupation has annulled all of the few resources that sustained the mission in its economic life." The numerous cattle had been wiped out, the agricultural fields had been turned into a landing strip for airplanes, and the military remained in possession of the orchard. The sugarcane field and all the fencing had disappeared, and the boys' school had been turned into a hospital. Fifteen houses that belonged to the mission Indians had been taken over by the hospital staff, and the owners of the houses had to find other lodging. According to Fr. Marcos Orsetti, the spiritual and moral gains the missionaries had accomplished over the years had been lost as well. Contact with the soldiers brought about disobedience to the missionaries and religious indifference, as well as "people walking down perverse paths."[29]

Just as important was that the missionaries' position of authority on the mission had eroded in the aftermath of the war. Non-Indians had taken over the mission lands. Orsetti complained that nobody respected the missionaries; people took lands, timber, and firewood as they wished. Outsiders entered the mission grounds and simply planted fields and built houses, claiming that the land belonged to the state and the missionaries had no say. Orsetti lamented that his complaints to local authorities to help the mission Indians were simply ignored.[30]

A new mission Reglamento, decreed in 1937 by the Military Socialist regime of General David Toro that had replaced President Salamanca, hammered one more nail in the coffin of what was left of the Chaco missions. It continued the anticlerical bent that arrogated more power to the state, taking away even further the missionaries' authority. The first article asserted that missions were to be established only among the "nomadic Indians that [went] from place to place in distinct zones of the country" to "prepare them for civilized life, making them useful for the colonization of the territory." In other articles, the Ministry of Colonization took charge of giving permission to establish new missions and determined when the "missionizing labor" was concluded and the missions secularized. The Ministry and its delegate determined what percentage of each mission population were "to be left for the attention of the communal necessities and the execution of works for the betterment of the missions." In accordance with the socialist model the military regime wanted to implant, the inhabitants of the missions were to create with the surrounding settlers a "system of cooperativism in . . . production and consumption."[31] The new Reglamento followed socialist doctrine, which posited that ethnicity was archaic and that creating a classless society was most important.

Despite the emphasis on modern relations, significant portions of the new regulations harked back to earlier times. They continued to emphasize the paternalistic role of the missionaries, as the friars were to "take care of the person and the goods of the *neófitos* with the energy that a good father would do." The mission Indians continued to be defined as legal minors and the missionaries were to be their legal representatives in the local courts. Each adult male Indian was to be assigned a plot of land according to the number of children he had, land that he was to tend in the cooperatives after the missions were secularized. Most important, the missionaries were to let the government know when the Indians had come of legal age to work on the roads, at the disposition of the army. They were to be trained by the military from age eighteen to twenty as road builders and then to work on the roads after age twenty.[32]

The 1937 Reglamento at first glance appears to severely restrict the authority of the missionaries, diminishing even further their role. Although it is outside the purview of this book, that was the case among the Guarayo missions, in the eastern tropical frontier region of Cochabamba department. There, the friars lost their ability to control the Indians' labor, and many mission inhabitants escaped so as not to work on the roads through the mountainous jungle terrain.[33] However, in the Chaco missions the Reglamento had a beneficial effect on the missions, because the new rules regarding the use of mission Indian labor for road building brought about an unusual alliance between the missionaries and the Bolivian military. This represented an important change from the period in the immediate aftermath of the war, when the military officers had seen the Indians as traitors. The army, whose presence remained massive along the southeastern border with Paraguay after the war, became a vital counterweight to the ambitions of the settlers. After the 1937 Reglamento the army got mission Indian labor to build roads in the trackless frontier region and the missions got protection from outside interlopers.[34] The settlers were unwilling to engage the Bolivian Army units stationed on the fortified border with Paraguay. It is also likely that the army brass in La Paz aided the missionaries and supported them.

In 1938 the missionary stationed at Santa Rosa, Fr. Marcos Orsetti, complained to the minister of colonization about a Sucre lawyer, Rómulo Corvera Centeno, who had usurped mission land. One of the Franciscan's arguments for having the army help him get the land back was that ninety mission Indians worked on the road crews for the military. Fr. Marcos argued that the Indians needed the usurped land to compensate for the orchards, fields, and buildings that the military had taken over in Santa Rosa.[35] However, the problem continued to fester, and in 1945 another missionary wrote to the military commander in Camiri to help him dispose of a Spaniard who had taken over Corvera's claim. He also had the indigenous authorities, including the tubicha of Santa Rosa, Celso Orosco, sign the document to give it more weight.[36]

Despite the protective role of the army, surrounding settlers continued to exert pressure on the missions. This was the case in both the missions reconstituted after the war as well as the ones not in the theater of operations. Missionaries constantly complained about people setting up houses in mission territory or about being unable to throw miscreants out.[37] The tone of the settlers toward the missionaries changed as well. In 1942, when the Boicovo missionary asked Manuel Gòmez for his authorization to cut wood on the mission and use mission Indian labor, Gòmez responded with a note accusing the friar of behaving like a "feudal king." He lectured the friar on how to write politely and called the friar's note an extortion attempt requiring an apology. Gòmez claimed that his parents had worked the mission land before the Chaco War and thus he had the right to work there again. A rude letter by a settler such as this was unthinkable in the nineteenth century, when the missionaries had great authority on the missions and control over the mission territory and its inhabitants.[38] It shows how far the Franciscans' local power and prestige had fallen by the 1940s.

The mixture of renters, usurpers, and only scattered Chiriguanos returning to the missions had fundamentally changed the nature of the missions after the Chaco War. The missions now included as many non-Indians as Indians. This occurred even among missions not overrun by the Paraguayans. For example, in 1949 a census of Boicovo revealed that about half of the adult male population had Spanish surnames (eleven had Guaraní names and twelve had Spanish ones). Some of the Creoles had apparently married into the mission, as only seven of twenty-nine women residents had non-Indian last names.[39]

Secularization of the Missions

In the late 1940s the government moved to abolish the remaining missions in the Chaco region. In late 1948 the Bolivian Congress passed a law that changed the status of the missions at Tarairí, Tiguipa, Macharetí, Ivo, Santa Rosa, and Boicovo to that of ordinary parishes, to be staffed by the Franciscan order. Each former mission was to set aside 1,700 hectares of land for the support of the parish, 1,250 hectares to support the schools run by the Franciscan nuns, and 1,250 hectares to fund a new seminary to be created in the adjacent town of Cuevo. Although the bishopric of the Gran Chaco was to be in charge of the education in the former missions, the minister of education and indigenous affairs was to name the teachers. The former missionaries would continue to provide religious instruction, as before.[40]

Article 8 of the law stipulated that the land not set aside for the parish and the schools was to become indivisible property (*pro indiviso*) of the farmers and ranchers who were already living on the mission lands. Another article decreed that excess land at the time of incorporation could not be sold, but instead was to be set aside to account for future population growth.[41] Following the decree secularizing the mission, now called the Macharetí Agricultural and Ranching Society of Small Producers (ARSSP),[42] all individuals over the age of fifteen who resided there were eligible for land. It is not possible to distinguish between whites and mestizos and Chiriguanos, because some Indians had taken Spanish surnames. Of the 278 individuals identified, however, fifty had Guaraní surnames and were certainly former neófitos of the mission. Among them was Ubaldino Cundeye and his wife, Octavia. The document that set up the Macharetí ARSSP also contained a list of names of 172 "absent neophytes" who maintained land rights there as well.

The 1949 title document thus institutionalized the land rights of the mestizo interlopers, though it also kept the rights of many Indians who had fled but who had not returned. Although it is not possible to know the exact proportions, at least initially the mestizo population appears to have been in the majority. Cundeye's political project, to repopulate the mission with its indigenous inhabitants, had only partially come to fruition. But he successfully staked a claim for the neophytes despite initial opposition by the military.

The new Machareti ARSSP also had a governing structure that reflected ethnic reality. The board consisted of a president, vice president, secretary, treasurer, and three other members. From the beginning the president of the board was a karai, though from 1949 to 1951 Ubaldino Cundeye served as vice president. In 1952 no Indian was elected to the board. From 1953 to 1958 there were two or more Indians on the governing board, including Cundeye's brother Gerónimo. Thus until the late 1950s neófitos were formally part of the governing structure of the ARSSP. Thereafter, however, no Indian was elected to the governing board. Although we do not have an ethnic breakdown of Machareti's population for this period, many Indians continued to live in the settlement. Nevertheless, within a decade of the secularization of the mission the neophytes were excluded from the running of the ARSSP.[43]

It is not clear what effect this had on the authority structures among the neófitos in Machareti or their relative position within the community. Did the Indians go the "ethnic route" and separate themselves from the mestizo body, keeping separate authority structures not visible in the documentation? It is curious that in 1958, when Indians were on the governing board (one committee member, Juan Dare), Ubaldino Cundeye again requested and received a paper designating him "Capitán of the Guaraní Indians of the Machareti sector." The document was signed by both the commander of the Third Division of the Bolivian Army and the civilian mayor of Villamontes.[44] There is little other information on Cundeye's activities during this period, though Fr. Gerardo Maldini remembered him as being an "instrument of the ranchers."[45]

Other former missions lacked such prestigious leaders as Cundeye, who had been a leader since the 1920s and had gone to La Paz to complain about the missionary regime in 1930. In Tarairí the vice presidential role was reserved for an Indian. In addition to the friars, the military brass at the local base in Boyuibe continued to support the former mission Indians at the expense of the local settlers. Thus Fernando Avenante, the last capitán of Tarairí, was also the first vice president of the Tarairí ARSSP when it was formed in 1949.[46] Another informant, Juan Acosta, who was an interim corregidor, the top political authority of Ivo canton, asserted that on all the former missions "vice-presidents of the ARSSP [were] always neófitos."[47] This was also still the case in Ivo, where the presidency went to a karai and the vice presidency to an Indian, though in 1990 there continued to be conflict between the whites or mestizos and the Indians.[48]

In the new governmental structure of the ARSSP, other than the role of religion teacher in the schools, there was no other for the Franciscans. However, they continued to play a vital role in the community through their moral authority from the pulpit, their connections to the ranking military officers on the frontier, and their role as educators. The vast majority of friars continued to work for the benefit of the indigenous community on the former missions. The exception was Fr. Jacinto Venturi. He became the parish priest of Macharetí, bringing his brother Poeri from Italy. Poeri was in charge of the cattle herds. In 1952 Fr. Jacinto had his brother bring Santa Rosa's herd to Macharetí, where he grazed the cattle in Timboy, land ceded for the maintenance of the parish. However, the Venturi brothers then proceeded to purchase land from the bishop, a transaction that was specifically forbidden by the titles of incorporation. Worse, they promised to pay ten thousand Bolivianos for the land, but in the end gave the parish only a load of wood worth one thousand Bolivianos and a zebu steer.[49] The Venturi brothers, however, were the exception to the rule; most Franciscans worked hard to help the Indians.

Elsewhere the Chiriguanos were not as lucky. As Kevin Healy explains, local landlords hijacked the Agrarian Reform of 1953. The landlords took over the leadership of the Movimiento Nacionalista Revolucionario throughout the region, stymieing any redistribution of land to its indigenous owners. Moreover, the agrarian reform did not distinguish between indigenous peoples and the colonists who came later, making recuperation of lands by the Chiriguano communities more difficult. The Chiriguanos were also not able to join or to form independent peasant unions. Instead, most Chiriguanos outside the former missions remained as hacienda peons and only a few lived highly marginalized lives in the independent communities that eked out an existence in the region.[50]

The agrarian reform also did not affect the former missions. Instead, the Franciscans continued to use their alliance with the military. When a cattle rancher from Ingre again tried to take over Caruruti in Santa Rosa, Fr. Gerardo Maldini, who was the parish priest, had the military dislodge the rancher when he ignored the Franciscans' entreaties.[51] No local civilian authority was willing to help the friars; none wanted to support the Indians in their struggles for land.

Despite the military's help, the alienation of former mission lands was a long process that neither the Indians nor the Franciscans could stop. At least it did not occur all at once, as did the secularization of San Francisco and San Antonio (today Villamontes) and Aguairenda at the turn of the century. But change was inevitable. By the 1960s no indigenous leader was left to defend the Chiriguanos' cause. Cundeye, who had struggled so long for his people, lost his position as leader in the late 1960s, though the story of his exploits in La Paz and his courageous return to Machareti in 1938 became popular legend. By that time he was reduced to a lowly position as the watchman of the school in Machareti. In the last years of his life he lived in a modest house under the largest tree in the former mission village, paid a small salary by the Bolivian state to watch over part of his beloved home. He died in August 1976 at the age of ninety-seven.[52]

CHAPTER NINE

Comparisons

The study of the Franciscan missions among the Chiriguanos fills an important gap in the study of missions. Most histories written on Latin American missions concern the colonial period or are anthropological studies of contemporary missions. Although many missions continued to exist at the beginning of the republican era (with the important exception of the Jesuit missions, put under secular control in the aftermath of the expulsion of the Jesuits in 1767), they tended to be much smaller in population. In many countries, such as Colombia and Mexico, anticlerical policies doomed the missions; with few exceptions, they disappeared relatively soon after independence.[1]

The new era of Latin American missions began in the mid-nineteenth century, when the Catholic Church revived its missionary enterprise in the region and Protestant missionaries began to enter Latin America.[2] They went to the cities to convert Catholics and to the frontiers to convert non-Catholic indigenous peoples. Catholic missions subsisted or restarted in certain countries soon after independence, such as Peru and Bolivia.[3] It appears that the Franciscan missions in Bolivia were the most important in Latin America during the nineteenth century and so merit special attention as a model for looking at other republican-era missions. For Latin America, missions were key to expanding the presence of the nation-state in frontier regions. On a broader scale, Christian missions were crucial for expanding "civilization" into frontier regions throughout the world, including Africa and Asia. This case study helps us understand the local and transnational processes that encouraged and hampered this institution during this period throughout the world.

All institutions reflect their times, and religious missions are no different in this respect. Republican-era missions such as the ones examined here can serve as guides with which to examine changes over time in society as a whole, on frontiers, and in the relationship between unconquered indigenous peoples and national societies. Despite the changes in context, the rich literature on colonial missions can serve to highlight these differences and similarities as well as bring into sharp relief the characteristics of republican-era missions. The vast bibliography on colonial Latin American missions in particular serves as an interesting counterpoint that reveals how societies changed from colonial to republican.

How were the missions in republican Bolivia different from the colonial missions in Latin America? How were they similar? These are questions that Robert H. Jackson and I attempted to answer a number of years ago, taking as examples the colonial Alta California missions and the republican-era missions among the Chiriguanos.[4] Comparing the California missions with the missions in Bolivia was largely a study in contrasts, but the general principles of the comparison, I think, still hold. We analyzed the missions from four perspectives: demographic factors, acculturation, the economic role of the missions, and indigenous resistance.

Demographic factors, essential for understanding virtually everything else in the missions, were in some ways similar and other ways rather different. On the one hand, all missions, whether in the colonial or the republican period, suffered from population loss over time. However, in the case of the colonial missions, most of this was due to "virgin soil" epidemics, when the missions exposed the Indians for the first time to European diseases in a sustained manner. Indians remained in constant contact with Europeans in the missions and often lived in much more crowded circumstances than they would have if they had been in their own villages. While the California example might be the extreme here—the missionaries sustained populations only by continuously importing more Indians—it was a pattern repeated throughout the colonial missions.[5] Some missions, such as the Jesuit Paraguayan missions, recouped much of their population in the late eighteenth century, but the main story was of secular decline.[6] In part, the demographic decline might have varied not just because of disease, but, as Robert Jackson has suggested, because of differing levels of social control by the missionaries. Jackson suggests that factors other than disease affected mortality and reproduction rates in Alta California; among the violently dispossessed mission Indians suicide, abortion, and psychological stress might have played a role.[7] Demographic factors played a vital role in the relative success or failure of the missions since only healthy Indians who lived long enough to be converted could make possible the religious goals of the missionaries. Even without conversion the cultural survival of the ethnic groups was at stake if not enough individuals lived long enough to pass on their customs to their descendents.[8]

The demographic decline of the Chiriguano missions in the republican period was due to a combination of disease and emigration to the Argentine sugarcane plantations or to surrounding towns. Coercion by the Franciscans was relatively minor. In fact, one of the most important reasons Indian villagers accepted the friars was to preserve their way of life. Also, according to James Saeger, by the 1760s in the Chaco indigenous groups had developed some resistance to European disease.[9] Since their ancestors had already participated in Jesuit and Franciscan mission systems during the colonial period, the Chiriguanos must have accumulated some genetic resistance. The Chiriguano frontier, as we have seen, was a place of constant interaction between Creoles, mestizos, and Indians, and people brought diseases from elsewhere constantly over centuries. A return to the more crowded and densely populated missions made possible the diffusion of disease more rapidly, but this appears to be little different from what was happening in the surrounding mestizo towns.[10] Moreover, agricultural peoples such as the Chiriguano—in contrast to hunters and gatherers—were more capable of recuperating from epidemics. This was especially the case with those Chiriguanos who hired themselves out away from the missions and mixed with the mestizo population, as also occurred among the colonial Yaqui of northwestern Mexico.[11] Although no one has done a study of race mixture of the Chiriguano with the mestizo population, it is likely that there was a considerable amount over the centuries, and this also provided some immunity.[12]

Acculturation has been a contentious issue for colonial missions, as it goes to the heart of the missionary enterprise: the adoption of new beliefs by the mission Indians. Acculturation is difficult to measure: historians need to measure what was going on in the minds of long-dead people without being able to ask them. Scholars have rightfully complicated the issue, since acculturation was not simply a one-way street in which Indians adopted new Christian beliefs wholesale without creatively integrating them with their own frames of reference.[13] It is clear, as with rates of population decline, that colonial missions varied widely in the levels of acculturation they achieved.

The colonial missionaries had their greatest successes among the Guaraní of Paraguay and the peoples of Mojos in eastern Bolivia. There are multiple reasons for this success: the Jesuits were able to adjust to indigenous society, such as learning Guaraní, and slowly teach Spanish customs on the missions. They were also well organized and co-opted the Indian caciques into the mission system despite some problems well into the eighteenth century. This meant that acculturation created dynamic mission cultures that melded missionary projects with indigenous culture into often new and original cultural forms. In Mojos and in Paraguay a new missionary indigenous elite emerged that was closely tied to the original families of the old caciques. Both the Guaraní and the multiple ethnic groups in Mojos were agriculturalists, closer to the mission model that revolved around the agricultural economy than many other missionized native groups. Demographic decline was not as marked and the missions lasted for centuries, thus providing the missionaries with many generations to transform their charges in their schools. David Block makes the case for Mojos that a new hybrid mission culture developed that was so successful it lasted many decades after the suppression of the missions themselves.[14]

There were at least three other types of acculturation experienced by colonial missions. The most frequent was that of violent change that destroyed indigenous culture because the difference between life prior to the missions and life on the missions was too great. This happened in the majority of the missions, which attempted to incorporate into the mission regime peoples who were either hunters and gatherers or swidden agriculturalists. The change from their previous way of life to the sedentary agriculture that the missionaries attempted to teach them as a means of "civilizing" them was extremely disruptive. Not only did gender roles often undergo vast alterations—agricultural labor was usually the preserve of women, whereas the missionaries required the men to work the fields—but also the change in diet, the constrained housing, and the lack of movement brought about the social and cultural death of their often millennial societies. In addition, these types of groups, by the very nature of their economic activities prior to mission establishment, had to be relatively small in number and thus were much more exposed to annihilation when members died of disease in the missions. This is not to say that the Indians did not try to accommodate their culture to that of the new missionary requirements, but that they had very little chance to do so. The classic case is the Californias, both Upper and Lower, but there are many other examples as well.[15] This process occurred in much of northern New Spain, where many of the Spanish missions were located, but also in Florida, in the Peruvian lowlands, among certain ethnic groups of the Chaco, and in

Brazil.[16] When the "reduction" of semisedentary Indians into missions—mostly by force—was combined with forced labor, such as the *aldeias* [Jesuit-led Indian villages] in Brazil or in the Californias, that accelerated the process of cultural annihilation.[17]

The third type of acculturation was one that led to only a superficial acceptance of Catholic doctrine and relatively little acculturation. There were many variations of this type of mission; some did not last very long and some were quickly eliminated by massive rebellions. This was the case in the colonial pampas of Argentina, to a certain extent among the Jesuit missions in Chile as well as the Jesuit missions in the Chiriguanía, and in the Guajira peninsula of New Granada. In none of those places did missions last very long. In the pampas close to Buenos Aires in the eighteenth century the Jesuits had to retreat after only three years among the Puelche.[18]

Closely related to these were the Indians who were able to gain some autonomy despite the presence of the missionaries. Most notable in this respect were the Franciscan missions among the Pueblo Indians in New Mexico after 1693. The Spanish took their revenge on the Pueblos for their 1680 revolt, which had eliminated the European presence in the area. Upon their return after the Spanish reconquest in 1693 the missionaries largely left the Pueblos to their own devices.[19] In other cases the power differential between the semisedentary Indians and the missionaries was so great that the missions were essentially seasonal; the Indians spent time on the missions when there was little to harvest in the forest and when there was enough food. Only invalids, some women, and small children stayed on the missions year-round. Many Chaco missions and some missions in northern Mexico, such as among the Tarahumara, followed this pattern. In the eighteenth century in the Chaco the missionaries often did not have the resources to feed all their charges or the ability to keep them on the missions. Among the Tarahumara missions in the seventeenth and eighteenth centuries labor obligations and a foraging economy provided great mobility for mission Indians despite the Spanish colonial government's concern over contamination by non-Indians and lack of social control over the Indians.[20]

Economic organization was closely related to the fate of the missions and to levels of acculturation. Most colonial missions were essential in maintaining the frontier economy through the apportionment of mission Indian labor to colonial authorities, mining concerns, or haciendas. As Susan Deeds makes clear, how Indians participated in the frontier labor economy helped determine their cultural survival.[21] During the colonial period the participation of mission Indians as laborers on the missions and outside was often obligatory. This was most pronounced and devastating in northern Mexico, but was also the case in Paraguay, where the Jesuits obligated the Guaraní to work mainly on the missions, though the Indians' roles in the mission militias, often away from the missions, must also be taken as part of the obligatory labor regime.[22] It is less clear whether on the republican Chiriguano missions Indian labor was obligatory. The Franciscans claimed that they always paid for labor on the missions. Just as on some colonial missions, they farmed out hands to neighboring settlers, though this work was presumably voluntary and the workers got to keep their wages. On the other hand, especially during the 1880s, when Bolivian authorities made a push into the Chaco, the friars were obliged to send Chiriguano workers to accompany expeditions and build forts along the frontier. In sum, in the republican period there were obligatory aspects to the mission Indian labor regime, but much less so than in the colonial period.

The issues of labor and acculturation point to the issue of power, for coercion was possible only if the missionaries wielded enough to force their charges to work against their will. In certain colonial missions, such as in California, the combination of presidios with missions meant that the missionaries had at hand, at least in theory, the guns and soldiers of secular authorities to enforce their policies on the Indians. However, even in the most extreme cases, such as the missions in Alta California, a lot of negotiation took place between the friars and their charges, as Steven Hackel has shown.[23] Rather than simply define the power debate as one between missionaries and mission Indians, it is important to take into account a group that was vital to the issue, namely, the indigenous mission authorities. As many of the most recent studies have shown, the issue of social control among mission Indians was mediated through the local indigenous leaders.[24] However, this changed over time, as the first generation of indigenous leaders died, to be replaced (where the missions had survived long enough) by authorities raised in the mission schools and often appointed by the missionaries themselves. At that point, the "first-generation revolts" that Susan Deeds describes receded, and types of resistance and the struggle for power changed to the quotidian individual acts of resistance, stealing, fugitivism, and the like.[25] In other words, power shifted as the life cycle of the mission advanced.

The calculus of power, however, was fundamentally different in the colonial and republican periods. Although there are some exceptions, such as in the Chaco and certain places in northern New Spain (especially New Mexico), one must take into account that most missionaries were embedded alone or in pairs among hundreds, if not thousands, of Indians on their missions. In the colonial period, the close relationship between the presidio and the missions made the colonial missionaries much more powerful because they were able to call on the Spanish or Portuguese military to maintain order in their settlements.

In the case of the republican-era Chiriguano missions, no such arrangement existed. Indeed, there were rarely any military forces close to the missions. Only during conflictive periods when the government launched expeditions into the frontier or during the 1892 uprising were regular troops nearby. At best, the missionaries had some ragtag militia within a day's travel to rely upon or some mestizo employees or nearby settlers, such as the del Castillo family. Instead, the missionaries used reliable Indians from other missions when they felt their safety threatened. This occurred in San Francisco del Pilcomayo, where the Franciscans settled fifty Chiriguano families to counterbalance the dangerous Tobas. This meant that the balance of power was much more in favor of the traditional chiefs, since the friars had little leverage to impose their ways. The case of mburuvicha Mandeponay, who remained unconverted until he lay on his deathbed, is a striking example of a strong indigenous leader who was able to maintain great power and relative independence throughout his life. Given the relatively short life span of the Franciscan missions of the republican period—none reached the century mark in longevity—indigenous leadership did not get much beyond the first generation.

More than colonial mission Indians, even the Guaraní of the Río de la Plata area, who left the missions for work in the towns or estancias, the republican-era mission Chiriguanos were able to leave the missions with relative ease and migrate to the sugar plantations of northern Argentina. This phenomenon starkly underlines the Franciscans' inability to control their charges, for neither they, the Bolivian state, nor the local settlers wanted the Indians to leave the area. The caciques were able to lead their people on routine migrations to the neighboring state, and no scheme by the friars or the state was able to stop them. This meant that, at times in the early twentieth century, the missions were inhabited to a large extent by women, small children, and old men, changing profoundly the dynamics of mission life and frustrating the ability of the Franciscans to convert the population.[26]

In sum, the republican-era Chiriguano missions were in many ways quite similar to the colonial-era missions. Of course, the colonial missions covered a whole range of situations and the length of the missions changed the internal and external dynamics. Nevertheless, in the large categories the basic similarities were more important than the differences. The republican-era missions remained instruments of state frontier policy, just as in colonial times. The missions helped significantly in breaking the independence of the native peoples on the frontier, as state policy makers and the missionaries themselves had hoped. The missions created permanent alliances between the settlers and the Indian groups that accepted missionaries in their settlements, permanently dividing the Chiriguanos and causing the system of shifting village alliances to break down.

The missions were also population sinks, though to a lesser extent than in some of the extreme cases, such as in the Californias. In northern Mexico, for example, many mission Indians also left to work on the outside, with or without the permission of the friars. However, unlike in the colonial period, the Chiriguanos passed international borders and went much farther than most mission Indians went in the colonial period. While in both cases mission inhabitants seasonally left and returned to the missions, the realities of work and the creation of new habitats and families in the new workplace meant that increasingly mission residents did not return to the mission but settled in their place of work. Many Chiriguanos thought that Argentina was a better place for them temporarily, without restrictive regulations and where they could make more money than in their homeland. Most returned to their homes in Bolivia, at least initially. Also, the caciques were very much involved in the labor traffic, probably more than they were able to be in the colonial period. The missionaries were unable to stop this labor migration or the involvement of the chiefs in it.

This leads to the major difference: power was distributed differently in the republican missions among the Chiriguanos than in the colonial missions. Although further study of the colonial missions has revealed a more complex play of power between the missionaries and the Indians, it is clear that the missionaries had much more power than in the republican period. This affected the rates and types of acculturation, for in the republican period the caciques were able to shield the adults from conversion and also spearheaded migrations to Argentina. They truly ruled over the many unconverted and often had considerable influence among the neophytes as well. As a result, conversion—the main goal of the missionaries—took much longer than under the more coercive colonial regimes. When this goal had been reached by the late 1920s, the sons of the caciques, such as Cundeye, spearheaded a movement to reform the missions and give themselves more power at the expense of the friars. The incomplete missionization might explain the success that Protestant missionaries had among indigenous groups during the twentieth century.[27]

Mission Indians and Citizenship

It is useful to compare colonial and republican missions, but this cannot account for one major difference: the colonial system created subjects, whereas the republican states created citizens. After all, that is what distinguishes the colonial missions most from the republican-era ones. How did the republican state build the nation-state along the frontier? What role did the missions play in the creation of the nation-state? What was the role of mission Indians in this endeavor? Given the large and growing literature on nation-state formation in Latin America and its emphasis on the way subaltern groups creatively contributed, the missions and their populations must be taken into account as well.

Three perspectives are necessary to analyze the role the missions played in the formation of the Bolivian nation-state. These have been described in the previous chapters, but it is useful to pull together this information here. First of all, consider the visions of the missionaries and the national state of the purposes of the missions for the nation-state. Second, it is necessary to take into account the perspective of local settlers and officials, who experienced the effects of the missions in concrete ways. They had a lot of say in how to integrate the mission Indians into the body politic. Last, and most important, the perspective of the mission Indians themselves has to be ascertained, for they had something to say about how they were to be integrated into the nation-state.

In an excellent work comparing the frontier policies of Peru and Bolivia in the nineteenth century and early twentieth Pilar García Jordán argues that the missionaries and national policy makers were interested in transforming the "savages" into citizens. This was to be done through converting the Indians to Christianity and "civilizing" them. In addition, the missions were to make the Indians into productive subjects and also defend the territorial claims of the country against others.[28] García Jordán's comparative history works well from the institutional viewpoint she uses, but my research at the mission sites and a close focus on the Chiriguanos reveals a more complex picture.

García Jordán is correct when she posits that the missions were seen as a means of asserting national territorial rights to frontier areas. The national government realized that it could not assert sovereignty without controlling the populations that resided on the frontier. The Franciscans, as García Jordán shows, accepted this premise, as they realized that this role permitted them to fulfill their primary function: the religious conversion of the heathen Indians to Catholicism and the creation of bulwarks against an increasingly secular and anticlerical Europe.[29]

The issue of "civilizing" the Indians and thus turning them into citizens was a more complex endeavor and related to the conversion question. By the time the missions were established in the 1840s, the concept of "the citizen" did not signify that all members of the nation-state were to be equal in political rights or economic opportunities. Rather, as had occurred in the highlands, in Bolivia (and elsewhere) there were different levels of citizenship. For example, the Sucre administration in 1827 reinstituted the colonial-era tribute payments by members of the Andean Indian communities, thus negating the idealism of Simón Bolívar, who had abolished tribute just three years previously. It also instituted, because of fiscal realities, an unequal system whereby Indians paid a poll tax while other members of society were exempt.[30] According to the various constitutions of Bolivia, Indians could vote in elections, and thus be full citizens, but in practice the literacy requirement and, after 1839, private property requirements effectively shut Indians out of direct participation in elections.[31] Only after the 1952 revolution was universal suffrage instituted in Bolivia.

Mission Indians were exempt from paying tribute, but all parties (other than perhaps the mission Indians themselves) implicitly envisioned placing native peoples in a lowly place in the country's socioracial and economic hierarchy, despite the lofty rhetoric of citizenship that García Jordán documents. The friars "civilized" the Indians to turn them into mestizos who would then become the (God-fearing) working class of the frontier regions. The economic role that the mission Indians were to play fit nicely with the Indians' role that García Jordán detected, namely, as economically productive subjects. This project also coincided with the desires of the local settlers, who came to the region to run their ranches with Indian labor. The conflicts that emerged between the missionaries and the settlers (as well as local and national authorities, such as Daniel Campos in 1883) were not about whether the Indians should work as agricultural laborers, but under what conditions, for what pay, and at what point in the conversion process. At best, certain promising young Indian men should be able to ascend slightly the social scale and become artisans, but even the Italian missionaries did not conceive of the Chiriguanos as landlords or as highly educated professionals. Indeed, other than a few Indian women who became teachers in the girls' mission schools, there was no project to provide opportunities for other than manual labor for any of the Indian men (or the vast majority of women). Only in the late twentieth century did Chiriguano men and women join the priesthood and enter the female orders.

Over time the opportunities for mission Indians in national (or frontier) society became more restricted. In the late nineteenth century the Bolivian elites believed in "scientific racism," limiting even more what people of indigenous ancestry were thought capable of achieving. Concomitantly, by the reign of Pope Leo XIII (1878–1903) the Franciscans were interested in (re)converting the laboring classes to a muscular Catholicism, in this instance creating a Catholic frontier laboring class among the mission Indians. Here the economic rationale for the missions dovetailed perfectly with the "civilizing" mission that placed the Indians into subordinate positions within the Bolivian social structure.

It is all well and good to examine the motives behind the friars', government officials', and local settlers' ideas about the integration of the Indians into the nation-state. But the copious historiography on the formation of the nation-state has shown us that the subalterns' views also matter and affect in profound ways how the state is finally constructed.[32] So, what were the apparent views of the Chiriguanos to the challenge of integrating into the Bolivian nation-state?

At first blush it appears that the Chiriguanos did not want to be integrated into the Bolivian state, as citizens or anything else. In fact, their preference was to ignore the state. After all, what had the Bolivian state done for them? It had permitted the sale of their land, had invaded their territory with forts and militia, had almost uniformly sided with the settlers, and had given them, because they were considered "savages," no legal rights whatsoever. Indirectly the state fostered the missions that had protected them from humiliating peonage. However, there their interactions with the government were mediated through the friars. Only mburuvichas such as Mandeponay and Maringay were able to negotiate directly with the (local) authorities and make themselves heard. This was different from the Quechua and Aymara Indians of the highlands, who could use the common justice system or petition the state directly.

Many Chiriguanos voted with their feet and, to the chagrin of state officials (and the friars), left for mbaporenda, the Argentine sugarcane fields, where they worked hard but were also able to do what they wanted and acquire goods not available on the Bolivian frontier. But neither did migration to a different country provide a sense of national identity. The border between Argentina and Bolivia in that region was so porous and poorly guarded that the Indians did not need any identity documents that might have signaled their national provenance. National identity was very fluid on the plantations, where Chiriguanos were not known as Bolivians, but as Chiriguanos. The term Bolivian was reserved for migrants from the highlands of Potosí or the valleys of Tarija, peasants who increasingly flocked to the plantations in the twentieth century.[33] In other words, the missionaries failed to inculcate the idea of Bolivian citizenship into their charges. On the Argentine plantations they were also not identified by nationality. For the mission Indians there seemed to be little advantage to being counted as Bolivians, even if others, such as the plantation owners of Salta and Jujuy, had wanted to do so.

Another potentially important aspect of citizenship was to participate in the administration of state justice. After all, many citizens realized that they were members of a larger community through the police and court systems. Uniform laws across the nation bound people together, even when these laws were not necessarily administered justly. Citizens presumably could also petition the courts and use them, as the Indians in the Andean highlands had done since early colonial times, to try to gain some advantage against local elites or the government itself.[34] In the case of the Franciscan missions, the Mission Reglamento of 1871 gave judicial powers to the missionaries, thus separating them from the national justice system. Of course, during much of this period, power in fact resided with the traditional Chiriguano chiefs, making the national court system moot on the missions. When in 1905 the new regulations restricted the friars' powers, the dispute between local authorities and the Franciscans, despite the complaints of the latter, still left most power in the hands of the missionaries. Thus the mission Indians were largely disconnected from the nation-state at this basic level.

Eventually the Chiriguanos began to engage with the state, but to the detriment of the mission system. The epochal journey of Cundeye and his cousins to La Paz in 1930, in which Cundeye played on his exoticism as a lowland Indian in the highland capital city but also as a citizen, was the first time that mission Indians appealed to national authorities and demanded their rights and duties as citizens.[35] If the sources the Franciscans cited are to be believed, the mission Indians in La Paz asserted that, "being Bolivians, they want[ed] to serve the Fatherland in the ranks of the Army." These rights also included not remaining under the tutelage of the missionaries, as another of the dissidents' demands was that the mission lands be distributed among the neófitos and each mission Indian receive a title to his own plot.[36]

Although this visit forms part of the second-generation revolt of the sons of caciques against the loss of their power to the missionaries, Cundeye's party insisted on the mission Indians' rights as citizens of Bolivia as no other Chiriguano leader had done. Mandeponay and the previous generation of leaders had dealt only with local authorities and had accepted the tutelage of the missionaries. Appealing directly to the national government without the mediation of the Franciscans had not occurred before. That the small group in La Paz desired the abolition of the mission system to become full citizens of the nation-state was a new development.

Ironically, when some of the mission Indians wanted to become full citizens the missionaries were unwilling to concede this. The friars argued that their tutelage shielded the Indians from abuses and usurpations, negating their own discourse about the formation of complete citizens. Perhaps institutional inertia and the fear of losing their life's work prompted this reaction. Also, a profound paternalism, which permeated the mission enterprise to its very core, impelled the friars to deny their charges full rights. To the Franciscans, the mission Indians continued to be children in their religious infancy and incapable of defending themselves against the settlers' depredations.

If the Chaco War had not intervened it is likely that Cundeye would have had his wish granted and the secularization decree of 1930 would have been made effective. Instead, after the war Cundeye became the most important figure to attempt to reclaim the missions for the Chiriguanos. In the end, he did become vice president of the Macharetí cooperative, the most important elected Chiriguano of the institution that took over from the mission when it was secularized in 1949.

On balance, the Franciscan missions among the Chiriguanos in the republican period served an important role in the integration of the Indians into the nation-state. Despite the rhetoric of fashioning citizens out of "savages," the missions aimed solely at integrating the Indians economically as the laboring classes on the frontier. This was what the settlers and local officials wanted and national authorities (as well as the friars) expected of the Indians. The preparation of Indians as political citizens, as soldiers, voters, and full actors in the complete spectrum of acts that citizens were entitled to, had not been contemplated. The inability of the Franciscans to let go of their roles as missionaries and the highly unequal power structures that placed Indians, even those converted and trained on the missions, in disadvantageous positions vis-à-vis the settlers conspired against giving the neófitos full political citizenship rights. But most of all, it was the profound purpose of the missions—for European missionaries to transform the religion, culture, and society of the Indians into a European or Creole version of themselves—that made giving mission Indians full political and social rights a contradiction in terms. In this way the mission enterprise, by its very nature, remained colonial at heart.

APPENDIX

The Inauguration of Tiguipa Church
(1902)

It was eight o'clock in the morning the third day of the month [of February] when the Reverend Father Nazareno Dimeco surprised us by announcing the coming arrival of the kind Missionary Fathers of Aguairenda, San Antonio, San Francisco Solano, and Tarairí together with 650 schoolchildren of one and the other sex with their teachers followed by about 300 neophytes of both sexes who were coming to attend the celebration of the inauguration of this new and magnificent church, erected to the worship of God by the selfless Padre Gerónimo Basili in eight years of painful tasks and sacrifices without count.

About three quarters of an hour later, the path to the south, in front of the facade of the majestic temple and lofty belltower, was occupied by more than 900 persons including schoolchildren and neophytes, with 80 violin players, holding the streaming flags that, bathed by the sun, offered an enchanting panorama.

The whole of the host so well ordered, which had walked all night to liberate itself from the hot sun had to camp there and wait for the arrival of the Fathers, the schools, violin players, and neophytes of Mission Machareti that had to come accompanied by the children's band, from Santa Rosa mission and its kind Father and Director, Fr. Antonio Chientaroli, a very meritorious member of the Apostolic Potosí convent.

Among so many people and the Reverend Father Prefect of the Missions of said convent together with six Fathers and a lay brother we were waiting for them and seeing in them as a kind of privileged being which should bring the most vibrant faith, saintly enthusiasm, and the most perfect joy.

The two settlements and their large plazas (of neophytes and heathens) were full with an immense crowd, eager to see the solemn entrance of the rhythmic music and accompanying schools, etc., and impatient at the same time to hear the admirable melodies of the wind instruments, which for the first time came to our missions to move the soul, to soften the heart, and exalt the spirit with the divine beauty of their celestial harmony.

Around 10 a.m., given the signal with rifle shots, they started to march from the northern side and from the south with regulated movements and in beautiful order an infinity of national flags, the rhythm section, with a beautiful uniform, the nine mission schools and their respective male and female teachers, the neophytes and the Missionary Fathers, the violinists playing at the same time all the selected pieces, and ringing accordingly and melodically the bells, already placed in the new and beautiful belltower.

It is impossible to describe the sweet and soft emotions in the spirits of these 1,400 individuals more or less who waved their beautiful flags, who played their stringed instruments with such skill, and who preceded with such devotion toward the new building, which the next day was to be put to use only for the worship of God three times holy, and where the divine Majesty receives the humble homage of His happy and hopeful creatures.

As the multitude advanced more from one and the other side, it softened or affected more by the profound silence, interrupted only by the melodious harmonies of the violins, delicate fibers of the heart.

The profound silence, interrupted only by the melodious harmonies of the violins, excited the soul and almost overwhelmed the senses. Even the fatigue of the large following, above all of the children, caused diverse effects of compassion and pleasure at the same time.

The Indians from Machareti finally arrived with 25 pretty flags at the grand portal of the church, which was closed. The violins went quiet, the children sang in a grave and soft tone a lovely stanza to the greatest of the ancient patriarchs the chaste Husband of the excellent Mother of God, and then they retired; providing room for the other groups which followed and that, repeating at the same time their devout chants and retiring as the first to rest and regain their energy, they prepared to receive the most welcome and rapturous impressions which they could have desired.

Already an hour had passed, though it seemed a century. . . . A young Franciscan priest of tall stature in a military uniform, of clear intelligence and with a nice physiognomy (already mentioned above) topped over a group of 32 beloved Chiriguano children, there in the back of the neophyte settlement, on the path that comes from Machareti. Thousands of eyes were turned toward him, observing at the same time his movements and admiring the very new musical instruments that the children were bringing to their mouths. A moment later they began to play a march of the famed maestro and in this way bringing to them the immense and amazed crowd.

When they arrived at the church building, they stopped like the others and while they took a rest, Viva Saint Joseph! Viva religion! Viva Jesus Christ! Viva the Fathers of Tarija! Viva the Fathers of Potosí! resounded, gladdening the people incredibly. Then they took their leave with another beating of the drums and they retired to the patio of the house to drink a small refreshment and let us enjoy other pieces, which their enthusiastic and valiant director had reserved for us.

At night there was an open-air concert. The violins and the band alternated playing, entertaining the spirit and cheering it up.

The dawn of the fourth day was saluted with gunfire and rifle shots and fireworks and new musical pieces: this was also done on the fifth and the sixth.

At 7:30 of the fourth the Reverend Father Prefect of our missions, assisted by the 15 Missionary Fathers, the lay brother, and 2,000 persons, at least, blessed solemnly the new church. Right away Fr. Bernardino de Nino, the Reverend Father Prefect of the Potosí convent and esteemed subject of thousands of titles and inspired poet, chanted the Holy Mass. Reverend Father Nazareno Dimeco served as deacon and as subdeacon the Reverend Father Gil Agostini. The Reverend Fathers Vicente Capalongo (a subject of his), Benvenuto Boccaccini, Cristobal Chiantini, and Herman Cattunar assisted the Mass with the vestment and cape of the chorus, working as Master of Ceremonies the Reverend Father Inocencio Massei and singing in the chorus the Reverend Father Alfonso María Puccetti predicated, in the Chiriguano idiom, a praiseworthy sermon for the circumstances. The musical band from Santa Rosa was the only that shone during the Mass, but the church, the most spacious one of all the ones that existed in the frontier region, could not contain all the people who came to Mass. About two thirds heard it from outside.

Before the setting of the sun of the same day the colossal statue of Saint Joseph was taken in procession, with the attendance of 3,000 persons. The seven musical bands, both rhythmic and wind, alternated, stopping only during the holy chants.

At night there was an open-air concert, fireworks, and balloons. The beautiful climate and the sonority of the instruments smiled on us in an admirable manner. The whole town jumped for joy and God was blessed and glorified by thousands of mouths.

The second day of the feast (the fifth of the month) Father Mariano Colagrossi chanted Mass with the deacon and subdeacon. Father Benvenuto Boccaccini preached the panegyric of Saint Joseph, very well written, tenderly and effectively. The Fathers Domingo and Francisco chanted a Mass of the Maestro N. Giorgi, which was a faultless work. In the afternoon there was a procession with the statue of Our Lady of the Purísima, and at night the same things happened as the one before, although the number of people had diminished somewhat because of a scarcity of food in the mission.

The third and last day there was also a solemn Mass, chanted by Father Inocencio Massei. The aforementioned Fathers in chorus executed a stupendous Mass of two voices; by the same Father Francisco Francocci, pronouncing the panegyric of Our Father Saint Francis the emphatic and correct holy orator Father Mariano Colagrossi, already mentioned. As in previous days, the Santa Rosa band had the exclusive during Mass. We had at the accustomed hour the procession of the statue of Our Seraphic Patriarch; and with bonfires and night balloons and delightful concerts, crowned by the saddest farewell which the children's band gave us, we finished our religious celebrations, for ever more a memorable occasion in the annals of Religion.

And now we have only left to thank cordially and sincerely the above-mentioned Reverend Father Prefect and his four well-loved companions and subjects, who honored us with their presence and helped us with their talents and advances; to the kind Father Gabriel Tomassini, to whom we owe the arrangement and composition of the altars and the extreme punctuality of the church functions, to the dear Father Cristobal Chiantini, professor in the art of making fireworks and balloons; and to all and every of our venerated Fathers who came with their contingents of all their forces to celebrate our feasts and honored the Brother Gerónimo Basili, who erected the beautiful but solid temple, emulating the glories of those who already preceded him in such laborious but difficult tasks; and lastly to the Corregidor of Camatindi, Don Medardo G. Garcia, who sent us the irreplaceable Don Mauricio Jurado at the head of prudent men so that in conjunction with the eight neophytes of Mission Macharetí (four of whom had very elegant uniforms) kept order, as in effect they did to the complete

satisfaction of the Fathers and of the whole town during the above processions.
Viva God!
San Francisco Solano, February 16, 1902
Fr. Gervasio Costa, OFM
Mission Prefect

Source: "El estremo de la Iglesia de Tigüipa," No. 178, Gaveta 8, AFT.

GLOSSARY

aguardiente	Sugarcane alcohol; brandy.
ahijado	Godson.
alcalde	"Mayor"; mission Indian authorities designated by the neophytes or the missionary.
ava	"Human being"; what the Chiriguanos call themselves.
bárbaro	Barbarian; term for independent Indians.
camba	A term of disrespect used by Creoles for the Chiriguanos.
cangui	Corn beer (also called *chicha*).
cantón	Territorial and administrative unit; similar to "county."
capitán	Village chief, as Creoles called them. Same as *tubicha*.
capitán grande	Maximal or prestigious chief (same as *tubicha rubicha* or *mburubicha*).
carga (of corn)	Unit of measurement, approximately 100 kgs.
catecúmeno	A mission Indian learning Catholic ritual, but unbaptized.
caudillo	Strongman, often member of the military, who dominated nineteenth-century Latin American politics.
chicha	Corn beer (also called *cangui*).
Chiriguanía	Region controlled by the Chiriguanos in the Andean foothills in southeastern Bolivia.
chola, cholo	Mestizo.
compadrazgo	Godfather relationship; important personal links between socially inferior people with elites in Hispanic society.
compadre	Godfather (literally, "co-father"); often includes relationship with biological parents.
conumi, cunumi	Child or warrior; the product of a Guaraní warrior and a Chané woman.
Cordillerano	Settler from Cordillera province (Santa Cruz).
cristiano	A Creole or mestizo settler.
enganchador	Literally "someone who hooks." Designation for labor contractors.
estancia	Cattle ranch.
frontera	"Frontier"; the area from the Andean foothills to the Chaco region.

guarapo	Sugar juice squeezed from the cane; the raw material for producing sugar.
infiel	"Infidel"; what the missionaries and settlers called the unconverted Indian.
ingenio	"Sugar refinery"; used as shorthand for sugar plantations in northern Argentina.
ipaye	Shaman.
jefe político	Important administrative position for Creoles on Bolivian frontier.
karai	"Evil or powerful godlike creature"; a term Chiriguanos used for settlers.
mbaepiro	Dry season.
mbaporenda	"The land where there is work"; the term that Chiriguanos used for the plantation complex in northern Argentina.
mburuvicha	Maximal or prestigious chief (same as *tubicha rubicha* or *capitán grande*).
neófito	Neophyte or converted mission Indian.
obraje	Primitive textile factory, often with coerced indigenous labor.
pollera	Skirt favored by *cholas*.
queremba	Chiriguano warrior.
Risorgimento	Period in mid- to late-nineteenth-century Italian history when the Italian state formed, largely at the expense of papal temporal power.
soldado	"Soldier"; a term used for a Chiriguano warrior, follower of a *capitán*. The Spanish equivalent of *queremba*.
tapuy	"Slave" in Guaraní, but used by the Chiriguanos for Indians they considered their inferiors (such as the people from the Izozog, probably of Chané origin).
Tarijeño	Settler from Tarija department.
tembeta	Chin plug worn by unconverted Chiriguanos.
tercerola	Carbine, used in frontier warfare by Creole militia up to the late nineteenth century.
tipoy	See *tiru*.
tiru	A long cloth sown together with two holes for the arms, worn by Chiriguano women.
tubicha	Village chief.
tubicha rubicha	Maximal or prestigious chief (same as *mburubicha* or *capitán grande*).
tumpa, tunpa	Chiriguano prophet, often the leader of messianic rebellions.
yerbajes	Grazing fees that the Creole landlords paid to the Chiriguanos for pasturing their cattle on what the landlords claimed was their own land.

NOTES

Introduction

1. On the Yanomami, see, for example, Tierney, *Darkness in El Dorado*.
2. Dean, *Brazil and the Struggle for Rubber* and *With Broadax and Firebrand*.
3. See Hvalkof and Aaby, *Is God an American?*; Hartch, *Missionaries of the State*; Miller, *Peoples of the Gran Chaco*.
4. I am using Bayly, *The Birth of the Modern World, 1780–1914*, as the conceptual framework.
5. This idea borrows from the influential work by Guy and Sheridan, *Contested Ground*, especially the introduction (1–15). Also see Hennessy, *The Frontier in Latin American History*.
6. Lockhart and Schwartz, *Early Latin America*, chapter 8. Hebe Clementi, using Frederick Jackson Turner's paradigm, tried to create a conceptual unity in her study of frontiers in the Americas. See her *La frontera en América*.
7. Bolton, "The Mission as a Frontier Institution." For works and critiques of this approach, see, for example, Bannon, *Bolton and the Spanish Borderlands*; Hanke, *Does the New World Have a Common History?*; and more recently, Cummins and Cummins, "Building on Bolton."
8. Ricard, *The Spiritual Conquest of Mexico*. A similar focus, in this case on the Franciscans in New Spain, is Phelan, *The Millennial Kingdom*. In the same vein, the failure of missionary endeavors in Peru is detailed in Tibesar, *Franciscan Beginnings*. A fine intellectual history of the early colonial Peruvian missionaries is MacCormack, "'The Heart Has Its Reasons.'"
9. For example, see Marchant, *From Barter to Slavery*, and Kiemen, *The Indian Policy*.
10. Cook, *The Conflict* and *The Population*; Jackson and Castillo, *Indians, Franciscans, and Spanish Colonization*. Also see Langer and Jackson, "Colonial and Republican Missions Compared."
11. This made the efforts to canonize Junípero Serra, the prime force in the missionization of the California Indians, highly controversial. See, for example, Sandos, "Junípero Serra's Canonization."
12. For some salient examples, see Clendinnen, *Ambivalent Conquests*; R.A. Gutiérrez, *When Jesus Came*; and Radding, *Wandering Peoples*.

13 Hennessy, *The Frontier in Latin American History*.
14 Robert Jackson and I did some preliminary comparisons in "Colonial and Republican Missions." Interestingly, James S. Saeger makes a similar argument for the colonial Upper Plata missions as types of refuges. See his "Another View of the Mission" and "Eighteenth-Century Guaycuruan Missions." This case, however, appears an exception for this period.
15 This is a concept that I used in "Mission Land Tenure" and "Missions and the Frontier Economy."
16 Ricard, *The Spiritual Conquest*; Hu-DeHart, *Missionaries, Miners and Indians*.
17 Jackson, "Patterns of Demographic Change."
18 Bolton, "The Mission"; Mörner, *The Expulsion of the Jesuits*. For a more recent take, see Ganson, *The Guaraní*.
19 Deeds, "Indigenous Rebellions."
20 Block, *Mission Culture*.
21 Deeds, *Defiance and Deference*.
22 Nordenskiöld, "The Guaraní Invasion"; Métraux, "Migrations historiques"; Susnik, *Dispersión Tupí-Guaraní prehistórica*; Pifarré, *Los Guaraní-Chiriguano*, 25–34.
23 Saignes and Combès, *Alter Ego*.
24 For the process of mixture between Chiriguano and Chané, see Saignes, *Ava y karai*, 21–38. For the presence of Chané in the Caipependi valley, see Fr. A. Ercole to Guardian and Venerable Discretorio del Apso, Colegio de Tarija, Aguairenda, 12 February 1872, AFT, Gaveta 8:47. In Itiyuro, see Nordenskiöld, *Indianerleben*, 148–50; for the Izozog, see Combès, *Etno-historias del Isoso*, 57–89.
25 Pifarré, *Los Guaraní-Chiriguano*, 26. Also see Meliá, *Ñande Reko*. But see Combès's critique of this idea in "Las batallas de Kuruyuki," 230.
26 See, for example, Cobo, *History of the Inca Empire*, 49–50, 154.
27 H. Clastres, *The Land-Without-Evil*; also see Métraux, "Les hommes-dieux."
28 Mather, "Along the Andean Front."
29 P. Clastres, *Society against the State*. The idea of using Clastres to understand the Chiriguanos originates from Clastres's student Thierry Saignes. See Saignes, *Historia del pueblo chiriguano*.
30 De Nino, *Etnografía chiriguana*, 163.
31 Pifarré, *Los Guaraní-Chiriguano*, 69–132. Brooks, in *Captives and Cousins*, finds very similar patterns. Indeed, the racial mixtures and boundaries on the Chiriguanía and New Mexico are as a result also very similar.
32 Saignes, *Ava y karai*, 40.
33 The change in housing style could have occurred in part also because of demographic losses. However, it is difficult to trace Chiriguano demographic patterns during the sixteenth and seventeenth centuries because the group

was still in the process of defining itself and mixing with other groups, such as the Chané (and, to a lesser extent, with Andeans and Europeans). For an attempt at Chiriguano demographics, see Pifarré, *Los Guaraní-Chiriguano*, appendix B, 426–36. Pifarré is unable to discern patterns of decline, though he posits that the epidemics of the first third of the seventeenth century must have reached the Cordillera.

34 Pifarré, *Los Guaraní-Chiriguano*, 23–28. Interestingly, one scholar has also called Spain "a society organized for war." See Lourie, "A Society Organized for War."

35 Pifarré, *Los Guaraní-Chiriguano*, 138–39; Saignes, *Ava y karai*, 49–50; de Nino, *Etnografía*, 78. For recent figures, see Secretaría Nacional de Asuntos Étnicos, Género y Generacionales, *Primer Censo indígena rural de tierras bajas*, 23. Also see Albó, *Los Guaraní-Chiriguano*.

36 Pifarré, *Los Guaraní-Chiriguano*, 137–40; Saignes, *Ava y karai*, 77–82. For the crisis in the south-central Andes at the turn of the eighteenth century, see Tandeter, "Crisis in Upper Peru." It is highly likely that these processes also affected the Cordillera.

37 Saignes, *Ava y karai*, 85–96, especially 86; Pifarré, *Los Guaraní-Chiriguano*, 171–81.

38 Saignes, *Ava y karai*, 100; Pifarré, *Los Guaraní-Chiriguano*, 182–230. These studies are based in large part on the great Franciscan missionary histories by Mingo, *Historia de las misiones franciscanas*. This history was not published until the twentieth century, as the Franciscan authorities in the late eighteenth century did not permit its publication because of the manuscript's poor organization. See del Pace, "Ambientación histórica," Mingo, v. 1, 20–25.

39 Saignes, *Ava y karai*, 87; Pifarré, *Los Guaraní-Chiriguano*, 207–9. James Saeger also argues that the Indians who desired a mission did not necessarily want to convert. See his "Another View" and "Eighteenth-Century Guaycuruan Missions" as well as *The Chaco Mission Frontier*.

40 See Mingo, *Historia de las misiones*. Throughout the text Mingo declared his doubts about the steadfastness of the Chiriguanos' faith. Also see Saignes, *Ava y karai*, 106.

41 Saignes, *Ava y karai*, 108; Pifarré, *Los Guaraní-Chiriguano*, 207, 224 n. 5.

42 Saignes, *Ava y karai*, 116–26. Francisco Pifarré also acknowledges the great difficulties that the Franciscans had with the Chiriguanos in the missions; see *Los Guaraní-Chiriguano*, 209–11.

43 Saignes, *Ava y karai*, 150–62.

44 Nordenskiöld, *Indianerleben*, 250–303. Nordenskiöld also did not discriminate between Chané and Chiriguano belief systems. And in the ethnographic present the much better studied beliefs of the Izoceños (probably of Chané

extraction) are meant to stand for those of the ava as well. See, for example, Riester, *Chiriguano*, in which peoples of the Izozog are seen as simply one version of the Chiriguanos. This is explicitly stated by Riester on 477-78. Since the Chiriguanos were missionized and the Chané were not, one cannot assume that religious beliefs were the same, though both originated in Guaraní culture.

45 That is not to say that one should not examine the evidence closely and see what ideas the observers, especially the missionaries, imposed upon the ethnographic data.
46 The most important works are Nordenskiöld, *Indianerleben*, and de Nino, *Etnografía chiriguana*.
47 Nordenskiöld, *Indianerleben*, 259; de Nino, *Etnografía chiriguana*, 131.
48 De Nino, *Etnografía chiriguana*, 137-38.
49 See especially Nordenskiöld, *Indianerleben*, 260-71.
50 One can also add *imbaekuarenta* as the malevolent medicine men, but since this information comes from the Izoceño case, it is difficult to know if this works for ava society as well. See Hirsch and Zaryzcki, "Ipayareta, imbaekuareta y evangelistas."
51 De Nino, *Etnografía chiriguana*, 146-48.
52 This tendency in the Chiriguano belief system also made the appeals by Pentecostal preachers in the late twentieth century very attractive. See, for example, Albó, "¡Ofadifa Ofaifa!"

CHAPTER ONE *The "Chiriguano Wars"*

1 Here I am building on a number of suggestive studies that have helped me redefine my ideas about the process of frontier expansion. See Stern's introduction and his own contribution to *Resistance*, 3-93. Also see Larson, who makes a similar point in "Exploitation and Moral Economy." Specifically for frontiers, see Langer, "The Eastern Andean Frontier." For the influential North American example, see White, *The Middle Ground*; A. Taylor, *The Divided Ground*; and Brooks, *Captives and Cousins*. On the instability of Latin American frontier movements, see Langfur, *The Forbidden Lands*.
2 See, for example, Stern, *Resistance*; Katz, *Riot, Rebellion and Revolution*. The possibilities of resistance and adaptation have been explored very effectively by Mayan specialists. See, for example, Farriss, *Maya Society*; Clendinnen, *Ambivalent Conquests*; G. D. Jones, *Maya Resistance*.
3 An excellent summary of this history is Klein, *A Concise History*, 89-156.
4 Notaría de Hacienda y Minas, Libro de Escrituras 1901:14, Fondo Prefectural, Biblioteca y Fondo Documental de la Universidad Mayor y Pontificia de San Francisco Xavier (Sucre). Hereinafter NHM. This type of society was quite common throughout other parts of South America as well, such as on the

Argentine pampas. See, for example, Ricardo Salvatore's masterful *Wandering Paysanos*.

5 Although we do not have population statistics for the region in the early independence period, there are other indications. For example, in the 1855 parish census of Cordillera Province the northern sector of the Chiriguanía listed a total of 1,233 men, women, and children who were Catholic (and thus presumably members of this *piquero* [small rancher] society). In 1871 the total "national" population of Salinas province, which encompassed the whole area of the Tarija Chaco and even Iguembe, part of what later was to become part of Chuquisaca, totaled 1,601 men, women, and children. For 1855, see "Padron Jeneral," Archivo Parroquial de Lagunillas; and for 1871, "Tarija: Cuadro sinóptico del censo rural del Departamto," Ministerio del Interior [hereinafter MI] 1871 t. 195 No. 93, Correspondencia Oficial, Archivo y Biblioteca Nacionales de Bolivia [hereinafter ABNB].

6 "N 100 Juicio criminal se que instruye contra Santiago Buricanambi por el delito de matanza saqueo é incendio en el pueblo de Guacaya," 1866:82, Archivo Judicial de Partido de Entre Ríos [hereinafter AJPER]. For an analysis of this case and violence on the frontier, see Langer, "A violência no cotidiano da fronteira."

7 Hilarion Terrazas al Ministro de Guerra [hereinafter MG], Sucre, 14 June 1844, p. 3, MG t. 174, no. 17, Correspondencia Oficial, ABNB. Unless otherwise noted, all correspondence is from this source.

8 "República Boliviana, Departamento de Santa Cruz, Censo jeneral que manifiesta el número de Almas que tiene el espresado correspondiente al año procsime [*sic*] pasado de 1839," MI t. 82, no. 28. This census did not include indigenous peoples outside the control of the Creole state.

9 See, for example, Calzavarini, *Nación chiriguana*. Writing in 1980, Calzavarini describes certain characteristics of the Chiriguanos but does not use the term *nación* in the eighteenth-century sense, in which it is more closely related to "ethnic group" than in a modern national sense.

10 Sanabria Fernández, *Apiaguaiqui-Tumpa*, 116–17. Sanabria's list is incomplete, since it does not include the Izozog. See Combès, *Etno-historias*, 133.

11 For warfare among the Chiriguanos, see de Nino, *Etnografía*, 272–83. For an analysis of the Chiriguano political system, see Saignes, "Guerres indiennes"; P. Clastres, *Society against the State*.

12 De Nino, *Etnografía*, 247.

13 Susnik, *Chiriguanos I*, 9–22. Also see Melià, *Ñande Reko*, 47–51.

14 Sanabria Fernández, *Apiaguaiqui-Tumpa*; Corrado, *El colegio franciscano*; and de Nino, *Etnografía*, are all examples of this perspective, though the Franciscans for somewhat different reasons than Sanabria. For a general overview of changes in indigenous policies in the early republican period, see Weber, *Bárbaros*, 257–78.

15 Only Thierry Saignes has done so, through studying Cumbay, the most important Chiriguano leader of the independence period. See his *Ava y karai*, 127–62. Saignes does not, however, show the process by which the Chiriguano regained control over their territory, nor what happened to the inhabitants of the missions.

16 Sanabria Fernández, *En busca de Eldorado*, 241–43.

17 See White, *The Middle Ground*. This pattern was typical for many "tribal zones" in which the state impinged on indigenous peoples but was unable to control them. See Ferguson and Whitehead, *War in the Tribal Zone*.

18 Santiago Roman to Gobernador de Tomina, San Juan del Piray, 27 July 1848, MG t. 213 no. 15. Also see Combès, "Nominales pero atrevidos."

19 José Flores y García to Governador de la Provincia, Sauces, 13 September 1836; Mariano Moscoso to Feliciano Echebarría, Sauces, 9 September 1836, MI t. 59 no. 33; J. Jo. Fuentes to Gobernador of Tomina, Sauces, 25 August 1840, MG 1840 Prefectura Chuquisaca, 17.

20 Luis Calvimontes to Prefect of Chuquisaca, Padilla, 10 May 1841, MI t. 86 no. 24; Santiago Roman to Gobernador of Tomina, San Juan del Piray, 27 July 1848, MG t. 213 no. 15. In fact, Aracua had become one of the tubicha rubichas of the region by 1848, undoubtedly by relying heavily on his alliance with the settlers. Was he now trying to assert his independence from white domination?

21 Jenaro Alba to Gobernador of Tomina, San Juan del Piray, 8 July 1857, MG t. 231 no. 14.

22 See Combès, *Etno-historias*, 184–255.

23 NHM 1908:5, fs. 151–95. For a longer discussion of this case, see Langer, *Economic Change*, 135–36, 154–55.

24 Manuel Fernando Bacaflor to MI, Tarija, 25 December 1834, MI t. 51 no. 28.

25 Sanabria Fernández, *Apiaquaiqui-Tumpa*, 87–89; de Nino, *Etnografía*, 274.

26 Joaquin Lemoine to Ministro del Interior, Sucre, 9 August 1841, MI t. 86 no. 24. Also see Aranzaes, *Las revoluciones en Bolivia*, 39.

27 Damian Barrios to Prefect of Chuquisaca, Sauces, 3 July 1848, MG 1848 t. 213 no. 15. See especially f. 2v.

28 José Michel to Jefe del Estado Mayor, Tomina, 9 July 1849; José Manuel Rodas to Gobernador of Tomina, Sauces, 3 July 1849, MG t. 222, no. 26.

29 Despite the view of some scholars who want to redeem the caudillo system of government and see that the various miliary men created national institutions, the turmoil on the frontier was perhaps more palpable because of the military imbalance in favor of the Indians. For a view of the caudillos as having been positive for Bolivia, see Peralta and Irurozqui, *Por la Concordia*.

30 Clemente Carso [Carrasco?] to Ministerio de Hacienda [hereinafter MH], Tarija, 6 January 1830, p. 1, MH t. 23, no. 21. As Isabelle Combès makes clear, this was a pattern that began in the colonial period. See her *Etno-historias*, 97.

31 Estevan Fernández to Prefect of Chuquisaca, Sauces, 7 June 1835, MI t. 53, no. 27.
32 Tomas Ruiz to Gobernador of Tarija, Tarija, 24 November 1836, p. 4, MG t. 90, no. 55.
33 MG to Señor Gobernador de la Provincia de Tarija, Sucre, 17 October 1836, MG t. 90, no. 55.
34 Ml Dorado to MG, Tarija, 3 December 1836 (the quote is on p. 2), MG t. 90, no. 55.
35 Manuel R. Magariños to Ministro de Hacienda, Tarija, 8 January 1843, MH t. 95, no. 37; Francisco Burdett O'Connor, "Diario, June 1849–Sept. 1850," 12–13 June 1850, 57–59, Personal Archive of Eduardo Trigo O'Connor D'Arlach. For an analysis of this tributary relationship, see Langer, "Foreign Cloth."
36 Magariños to MH, Tarija, 8 January 1843, MH t. 95, no. 37.
37 Saignes, *Historia del pueblo chiriguano*, 141–42. Gift giving by government authorities to Indian allies was a policy that had also occurred in the colonial period. According to David Weber, this policy intensified during the Bourbon period throughout Spanish America. See his *Bárbaros*, 186–220.
38 José Ml Sanchez to Sr. Jral Jefe Superior Militar del Distrito de la Prova de Tarija Franco Burdet O'Conor, Caraparí, 14 February 1839, p. 1, MG t. 12, no. 32.
39 Bernardo Trigo to MG, Tarija, 25 March 1839, pp. 1–2, MG t. 12, no. 32. The commander claimed to have captured women and children constituting about one hundred families. However, Sanabria Fernández suggests that the casualties occurred as a result not of the battle, but of a subsequent massacre. See his *Apiaguaiqui-Tumpa*, 84. Also see Corrado, *El colegio franciscano*, 340–42.
40 Trigo to MG, Tarija, 9 April 1839, p. 5, 24 May 1839, and 24 April 1839, pp. 1–2, MG t. 12, no. 32.
41 Andrés Rodríguez to Corregidor of Sauces, Muyupampa, 20 August 1840, and J. J. Fuentes to Gobernador of Tomina, Sauces, 25 August 1840, MG 1840 Chuquisaca, 17; Luis Calvimontes to Corregidor of Padilla, Sauces, 4 January 1841, pp. 1–2, Bibian Segobia to Comandante Militar Francisco Satisaval, Campo en el Naranjal, 28 January 1841, pp. 1–2, MI t. 86, no. 24.
42 Corrado, *El colegio franciscano*, 338–46. Corrado has Passani die in the Caritati massacre, but I believe that the Trigo letter written soon after the Ipaguaso battle in 1839 trumps Corrado, who does not reveal his sources. See Bernardo Trigo to MG, Tarija, 25 March 1839, pp. 1–2, MG t. 12, no. 32.
43 Calvimontes to Prefect of Chuquisaca, Padilla, 7 February 1841, MI t. 86, no. 30.
44 Calvimontes to Prefect of Chuquisaca, Padilla, 10 May 1841; Mauricio Alzenecal to Gobernador of Tomina, Sucre, 18 May 1841, MI t. 86, no. 24. From Calvimontes's communication, it is not clear who killed Chaverao. How-

ever, the prefecture's response implies strongly that soldiers were involved: "Cualesquiera que haya sido los motivos que tuvieron presentes para sacrificar esta víctima [Chaverao], no puede dejar de ser reprobado un acto que hace resentirse a la humanidad, y tanto más escandaloso, cuanto se ejecutó por individuos que pertenecen a un país civilizado" (p. 1). [Whatever have been the motives which they had in mind to sacrifice this victim can only be reprehended as an act that is against humanity; it is even more scandalous because it was executed by individuals who belong to a civilized country."]

45 Joaquín Lemoine to Minister of Interior, Sucre, 9 August 1841; Manuel Molina to Minister of Interior, Sucre, 6 May 1841, MI t. 86, no. 24.
46 Alzenecal to Gobernador of Tomina.
47 For the frontier policies of the Ballivián administration, see Greever, *José Ballivián*.
48 Manuel Carrasco to MG, Padilla, 5 August 1842; Pomabamba, 17 August 1842; Padilla, 19 September 1842; Padilla, 19 September 1842, MG t. 147, no. 85.
49 Mariano Estrada to MG, Piray, 31 December 1842, MG t. 147, no. 85.
50 "Diario de la navegación y reconocimiento del Rio Pilcomayo por el Jeneral Manuel Rodríguez Magariños," ms., no. 478, Colección Rück, ABNB. Documents relating to this expedition are also transcribed in Langer and Ruiz, eds., *Historia de Tarija*, 208-12, 257-59, 281-88. Also see Greever, *José Ballivián*, 129-65.
51 Ildefonso Sanjines to MG, Sucre, 4 October 1845, MG t. 183, no. 18.
52 For Cinti, see Francisco Carmona to Prefect of Chuquisaca, Camargo, 17 August 1846, El Palmar, 1 November 1846, MG t. 193, no. 10; Carmona to MI, Camargo, 6 July 1846, MI t. 117, no. 47. José María Dalence suggested in 1848 that at El Palmar "it would be possible to raise an immense number of cattle," but that "that region is becoming populated because of the cultivation of sugar cane." Quoted in Dalence, *Bosquejo estadístico de Bolivia*, 96.
53 J. Francisco Fuentes to Comandante Militar of Tomina, Sauces, 4 July 1849, MG 1849 t. 222, no. 26.
54 Cnl. Ignacio Villaroel to Jefe Superior Militar de los Departamentos del Sud, Sauces, 7 November 1849, MG t. 225, no. 47.
55 Trigo to MG, Tarija, 9 April 1839, p. 3, MG t. 12, no. 32.
56 Rudecindo Moscoso to Minister of War Sucre, 29 August 1840, MG Chuquisaca, 17.
57 Manuel Carrasco to Minister of War, Padilla, 5 August 1842, p. 2, MG t. 147, no. 85.
58 Luis Blacut to Prefect of Chuquisaca, Camargo, 23 February 1841, MI t. 86, no. 24.
59 Francisco Satiaval to Coronel Comte Gral de Distrito, Tomina, 20 December 1840, p. 1, MG 1840, no. 33, Varias Comandancias Militares.
60 Francisco Barrios to Gobernador de la Provincia, Sauces, 22 March 1833, MI

t. 44, no. 25. Also see Santiago Roman to Gobernador of Tomina, S. Juan del Piray, 27 July 1848, MG t. 213, no. 15; Jenaro Abasto to Coronel de Ejército i Gob. de la Provincia, San Juan [del Piray], 8 July 1857, MG 1857 t. 231, no. 14.
61 De Nino, *Etnografía*, 274–75.
62 Ignacio Villarroel to J[ene]ral Jefe Superior Militar de los Departamentos del Sud, Sauces, 7 November 1849, p. 1; Sauces, 15 October 1849, MG t. 225, no. 47. *Camba* is another term used for the Chiriguanos, which the people from Santa Cruz department have proudly taken on as a nickname. However, in the countryside this term, when used to designate Chiriguanos, has a derogatory meaning. See Saignes, *Historia del pueblo chiriguano*, 230 n. 18.
63 Bibian Segovia to Francisco Satisaval, Campo en el Naranjal, 28 January 1841, MI t. 86, no. 24.
64 Ibid., 1.
65 Trigo to MG, Tarija, 25 March 1839, MG t. 12, no. 32.
66 Luis Calvimontes to Prefect of Chuquisaca, Padilla, 10 May 1841, p. 2, MI t. 86, no. 24.
67 Trigo to MG, 25 March 1839, MG t. 12, no. 32.
68 Ibid., 1, 3–4.
69 J. Francisco Fuentes to Comandante Militar y Govierno de Tomina, Sauces, 4 July 1849, pp. 1–2, MG t. 222, no. 26.
70 Gobernador of Cinti to Prefect of Chuquisaca, Camargo, 3 February 1844, MG t. 174, no. 17. In the Cinti case, another eight "cristianos" were killed in another attack nearby. Nevertheless, the numbers killed by Indians remained much lower than those killed by the military.
71 That is not to say that some Indians also owned some cattle; the difference is that the Indians' cattle were not permitted to enter the cornfields. Moreover, as we have seen, landlords paid the Chiriguano village chiefs to permit the cattle to pasture on certain lands under indigenous control.
72 Manuel Carrasco to MG, Padilla, 5 August 1842, p. 2, MG t. 147, no. 85; de Nino, *Etnografía*, 78. Also see note 28 in the introduction.
73 Martarelli, *El Colegio Franciscano*, 303.
74 Mariano Serrudo to Corregidor, Muyupampa, 12 September 1836, MI t. 59, no. 33.
75 Trigo to Minister of War, Tarija, 9 April 1839, p. 4, MG t. 12, no. 32.
76 Calvimontes to Prefect of Chuquisaca, Sucre, 28 August 1840, MG 1840, Prefectura de Chuquisaca, no. 17.
77 Anthony King mentions that when he was held captive by Chiriguanos close to the Argentine border in Tarija in the 1820s they had sheep but did not eat them. See King, *Twenty-Four Years in the Argentine Republic*, 109.
78 Santiago Roman to Gobernador of Tomina, San Juan del Piray, 27 July 1848, MG 1848 t. 213, no. 15.
79 Sanchez de Velasco to Minister of War, Sucre, 25 July 1848, MG t. 213, no. 15.

80 Susnik, *Chiriguanos I*, 60, 214–16.
81 See Corrado, *El colegio franciscano*, 340–42.
82 Susnik, *Chiriguanos I*, 60, 63, 70.
83 For the best discussion of the nineteenth-century Bolivian silver mining economy, see Mitre, *Los patriarcas*. Also see Langer, *Economic Change*, chapters 2 and 6. For background on the economic movement of the region, see Langer, "Espacios coloniales"; Langer and Ruiz, *Historia de Tarija*, i–xxv.
84 Martarelli, *El Colegio Franciscano*, 119–21, 301–2.
85 Demelas, "Darwinismo a la criolla."
86 See, for example, Langer and Ruiz, *Historia de Tarija*, 266–72. Ironically, in northern Argentina the sugar plantations used Toba and Mataco labor for much of the nineteenth century. See Lagos, "Conformación del mercado laboral"; Carrera, "Las modalidades."
87 Bernabé Flores to Jefe Político del Distrito, Chimeo, 17 August 1859, MG t. 274, no. 25.
88 Martarelli, *El Colegio Franciscano*, 155–57; Un misionero, *Sublevación*.
89 José Fernando de Aguirre to Prefect, Tarija, 2 January 1830, MH t. 23, no. 21.
90 For Salinas, see Gonzalo Lanza to Minister of War, Tarija, 1 April 1845, MG t. 186, no. 29. For Itau, see Manuel Fernando Bacaflor to Minister of Hacienda, Tarija, 22 March 1834, MI t. 51, no. 28. O'Connor valued the Itau Chiriguano as soldiers, claiming that none deserted and they were some of the most disciplined men he had. Only six veterans made it back to Itau. See O'Connor, *Un irlandés con Bolívar*, 234–35.
91 For the land disputes, see O'Connor to Minister of War, Tarija, 22 March 1832, MG t. 56, no. 91; for Herrera's activities and the reestablishment of Itau, see Corrado, *El colegio franciscano*, 301–35.
92 See Langer and Jackson, "Colonial and Republican Missions Compared," for a detailed comparison with Alta California. Also see Jackson and Castillo, *Indians, Franciscans*.
93 Fr. A. Ercole to R. p. Guard[ia]n y Venerable Discretorio, Aguairenda, 12 February 1872, f. 1, Gaveta no. 8:47, Archivo Franciscano de Tarija [hereinafter AFT].
94 Corrado, *El colegio franciscano*, 369–78. It is likely that chiefs used missionaries to increase their power within the same settlement as well.
95 Francisco Carmona to Prefecto de Misiones, San Luis, 10 April 1858, Gaveta no. 18. For the peace treaty, see Langer and Ruiz, *Historia de Tarija*, 225–27 [Gaveta no. 8:30].
96 Doroteo Giannecchini, "Memoria 1885," 6–8, AFT; NHM 1889:54; Martarelli, *El Colegio Franciscano*, 224–38.
97 Pressure from non-Indians often spurred indigenous peoples throughout Latin America to accept missions. In the case of the Pueblos in New Mexico,

for example, raids from other indigenous groups (in this case the Apaches, Navajos, and other groups) also could lead indigenous leaders to ask for the protection of a mission.

98 See Langer, *Economic Change*, 146-55.
99 Martarelli, *El Colegio Franciscano*, 191.
100 See, for example, the numerous letters contained in Gaveta 8 (AFT), which detail the labor demands for the Crevaux, Rivas, and Campos expeditions in the 1880s.
101 Martarelli, *El Colegio Franciscano*, 271-72.
102 Bernd Hausberger makes a similar point for the Jesuit missions in northern Mexico during the colonial period. See his *Für Gott und König*.
103 Luis Aldana to Combersores de las Miciones de S. Francisco and Tarairí, Banda Oriental del Pilcomayo, 23 January 1875, Gaveta no. 8:53; Alejandro Ercole to Revdos Padres Curas Convres . . . , Aguairenda, 26 January 1875, Gaveta no. 8:38, both AFT.
104 For a detailed discussion of the 1892 rebellion, see chapter 5.
105 For the eighteenth-century messianic movements, see Pifarré, *Los Guaraní-Chiriguano*, 246-51; Saignes, *Ava y karai*, 165-74. The 1892 rebellion is treated in Sanabria Fernández, *Apiaguaiqui Tumpa*; Un misionero, *Sublevación*; Martarelli, *El Colegio Franciscano*, 260-84; and Pifarré, *Los Guaraní-Chiriguano*, 373-92. The effect of this rebellion on the missions is discussed in Langer, "Caciques y poder."
106 Ferguson and Whitehead, *War in the Tribal Zone*.
107 Corrado, *El colegio franciscano*, 369-70, 469-75.
108 Langer, *Economic Change*, 138-46.
109 For an analysis of the changing types and levels of violence along the Cordillera, see Langer, "A violência."

CHAPTER TWO *The Franciscans*

1 A good recent English-language biography of St. Francis is House, *Francis of Assisi*.
2 See Phelan, *The Millennial Kingdom*; Tibesar, *Franciscan Beginnings in Peru*; and Schwaller, *Francis in the Americas*.
3 Saiz Pérez, "El Padre Andrés Herrero"; Corrado, *El colegio franciscano*, 301-13.
4 Maldini, "Entrada y salida," unpublished manuscript, AFT. This source does not identify all Italians, so the number was probably even higher. This is especially true after the 1864 expedition, so I have not included the more recent numbers. However, the number of Italians continued to remain very high, especially in the missions.

5 Giannecchini, *Historia natural*, 154.
6 For a recent overview, see Atkin and Tallett, *Priests, Prelates and People*, 101–6.
7 Woolf, *A History of Italy*, 235–36.
8 Atkin and Tallett, *Priests, Prelates and People*, 106–8.
9 There are many versions of *Émile* available in English.
10 Calzavarini, "Introducción" to Giannecchini, *Historia natural*, 42. Also see Maldini, *Franciscanos en Tarija*, 116–24.
11 See his expedition diary, reproduced in Langer and Ruiz, *Historia de Tarija*, 289–303.
12 Maldini, "Entrada y salida," 7; Corrado, *El colegio franciscano*, 563–64.
13 On the education of children, see R. A. Gutiérrez, *When Jesus Came*, 75–81.
14 A brief overview of Cattaneo's ideas is presented in Woolf, *A History of Italy*, 331–38.
15 In Alta California, for example, the Franciscans also had Indians labor in workshops in the early eighteenth century. However, the friars did this mainly for commercial purposes as the European settlements in California became more important. For a suggestive article on this dynamic, see Farnsworth and Jackson, "Cultural, Economic, and Demographic Change."
16 Woolf, *A History of Italy*, 338–46.
17 See Martínez, *La iglesia católica*, 257–71.
18 See especially "Memoria que en ocacion de las eleccciones Capitulares del Colegio de Tarija el Prefecto de sus Misiones de Infieles Fray Doroteo Giannecchini presenta al M. R. P. Comisario General de Colegios de Propaganda Fide en Bolivia a su Venerable Discretorio y a los R.R.P.P. Conversores de los mismos," AFT, Gaveta s/n. This is reproduced in Langer and Ruiz, *Historia de Tarija*, 357–90. The quote is from f. 17. Also see O'Connor D'Arlach, *El Padre Doroteo Giannecchini*. Lorenzo Calzavarini, in Giannecchini, *Historia natural*, 44, also asserts that Giannecchini institucionalizó las misiones, whereas Giannelli's role was more charismatic as a founder of missions.
19 Campos, *De Tarija a Asunción*; Thouar, *Explorations dans l'Amerique du Sud*. For Giannecchini's views, see "Libro 20 Copia = Notas de la Prefectura de las Misiones Franciscanas del Colegio de Nra Sra de los Angeles de Tarija que comienza el dia 7 de Abril de 1883–1890 por el actual Prefecto Fr. Doroteo Giannecchini," AFT. The quote is from Giannecchini to Dr. L. Pedro Puch, Archbishop of La Plata, Aguairenda, 12 December 1883, "Libro 20," p. 61.
20 See Valda Palma, *Historia de la Iglesia*, 166–76. Also see Langer and Jackson, "Liberalism."
21 See Martínez, *La iglesia católica*, 267–77; Smith, *Modern Italy*, 89–90; Coppa, "From Cholera to Earthquake." Two excellent summaries are Traniello, "Religione, nazione e sovranità," and Viallet, "Anticléricalisme et laicité."
22 Ordained in 1860, Martarelli left Italy in 1868. He wrote *El colegio franciscano*

  de Potosí y sus Misiones. A short biography is contained in the second edition (1918) of the work, i–iv.
23 See the compendium of many of his articles in de Nino, *Prosecución*, 170–297. For a brief biography of de Nino, see Anasagasti, *Franciscanos en Bolivia*, 372–74.
24 De Nino, *Etnografía*. Also see "Los indios y su condición lamentable" in *Prosecución*, 273–85.
25 By the late nineteenth century a new realization had dawned that the Church had to work even with liberal governments. This occurred even in Italy, where Italian bishops tried to bridge the gap between Church and state. See Bellò, "Monsignor Bonomelli."
26 Phelan, *The Millennial Kingdom*; R. A. Gutiérrez, *When Jesus Came*.
27 See, for example, Carroll, *Madonnas That Maim*.
28 The standard references for the colonial Franciscan missions are Comajuncosa, *El colegio franciscano*, and Mingo, *Historia de las misiones*. The modern-day pioneer on the colonial missions was Thierry Saignes; see his "Une 'frontière fossile.'"
29 See Saignes, *Ava y karai*, 66–79.
30 "Circular i Ordenes y decretos del Comisario Prefecto de Misiones Fr. Alfonso Corsetti [1851]"; "Circulares del Comisario y Prefecto de Misiones Fr. Alejandro Ercole [1870–1873]"; and Giannecchini, "Libro 20 Copia = Notas de la Prefectura," all AFT, Gaveta s/n.
31 Corsetti, "Circular i Ordenes," Itau, 2 November 1851, No. 19.
32 Ibid., No. 8.
33 Two versions of this description have been published. See Langer and Ruiz, *Historia de Tarija*, 289–303, and Corrado, *El colegio franciscano*, 563–84. In this chapter I cite the page numbers from Langer and Ruiz.
34 Langer and Ruiz, *Historia de Tarija*, 290.
35 See "Acta puesta en el Libro de Bautismos de la estinguida mision de S. Antonio de los Noctenes en el Pilcomayo occidental," and "Copia = Cartas de la Prefectura de Misiones año de 1877," AFT.
36 Corrado, *El colegio franciscano*, 393–441, 469–503, is very eloquent in this respect. This is striking, in that missionary efforts among the Tobas and Matacos in the twentieth century were successful, at least for Protestant groups. See Miller, *Peoples of the Gran Chaco*; Gordillo, *Landscapes of Devils*; and Alvarsson, *The Mataco*, 42–47.
37 Giannecchini, *Diario*, 46. This diary is a valuable source for understanding Fr. Doroteo Giannecchini, but it must be kept in mind that the friar published it to defend his order from accusations that the missionaries helped bring about the murder of the explorer Jules Crevaux and his party by a band of Tobas in 1883. See chapter 7 for a more in-depth discussion of these issues.

38 "Memorias del P. Bernardino de Nino Prefecto de Misiones desde el año del Señor 1903," AFT.
39 "Memorias del P. Bernardino de Nino Prefecto de Misiones desde el año del Señor 1903," 25 April 1903, AFT. The emphasis is mine.
40 This is of course a typical conceit of the Romantics, beginning with Goethe. See, for example, his *Italienische Reise* (Italian Journey; 1817), many editions.
41 In 1900, whereas the largest mestizo settlement in the Chaco was Yacuiba, a town on the Argentine border with 1,388 inhabitants, the largest missions, such as Macharetí and Santa Rosa, had 2,794 and 2,196 inhabitants, respectively. The disproportion between these two settlements was even greater in the nineteenth century, when Macharetí reached a population of about 5,000 Indians. See Bolivia, *Censo de la población de la República de Bolivia*, 74, 742. This difference is also due to the mestizo cattle economy, which did not favor large settlement, in contrast to the Chiriguanos' largely agricultural economy. On mission frontiers, see Hennessy, *The Frontier in Latin American History*, 54–60.
42 The issue of control of the urban population was also an important consideration for Renaissance-era town planners.
43 Corrado, *El colegio franciscano*, 390.
44 Thouar, *Explorations*, 239.
45 On the importance of Italian piazzas, see Bell, *Fate and Honor*, 9. Of course, in many Italian communities the church loomed over the other buildings in town as well.
46 Cardús, *Las misiones franciscanas*, 42.
47 Corrado, *El colegio franciscano*, 390.
48 Martarelli, *El Colegio Franciscano*, 248.
49 Jofré, *Colonias y misiones*, 22; Corsetti, "Circular i Ordenes," Itau, 2 November, 1851, No. 9.
50 Corrado, *El colegio franciscano*, 332–333.
51 "Santas Visitas, 1877–1913," 210, AFT.
52 This mixture of religious conversion with attempts (often failed) to completely change their belief systems occurred elsewhere as well. See, for example, Vecsey, *On the Padres' Trail*, which traces the cultural implications of conversion among the indigenous peoples of the southwestern United States from the colonial period to the twentieth century.
53 This is not new. For an explication of this term and its implications for the late colonial period, see Weber, *Bárbaros*.
54 "Registro de Escrituras" 1915:4, f. 230, Notaría de Hacienda y Minas, Fondo Prefectural, Centro Bibliográfico Documental de la Universidad Real y Pontificia de San Francisco Xavier, Sucre.
55 Corsetti, "Circular i Ordenes," Itau, 2 November 1851, No. 1.

56 Ibid., No. 16.
57 For two interesting recent perspectives on cholos, see L. Gill, *Precarious Dependencies*, and Hames, "Honor, Alcohol and Sexuality."
58 I have explored the clothing preferences of Chiriguanos in Langer, "Foreign Cloth."
59 De Nino, *Etnografía*, 4–5, 78, 297. This is not say that priests were not convinced of the inferiority of Indians before scientific racism became popular. However, the way the missionaries expressed themselves changed as a result of social Darwinism. Thus the framework of discussion, and the way the missionaries thought about their charges, changed.
60 De Nino, *Etnografía*, 309.
61 This was similar in the colonial period.
62 Giannecchini, *Historia natural*, 293. Also see Martarelli, *El Colegio Franciscano*, 173.
63 See especially de Nino, *Etnografía*, 73–75.
64 Giannecchini, *Historia natural*, 293–94.
65 Ibid., 273; Martarelli, *El Colegio Franciscano*, 177; de Nino, *Etnografía*, 116, 299; Cardús, *Las misiones*, 41.
66 Martarelli, *El Colegio Franciscano*, 175.
67 See Corrado, *El colegio franciscano*, 378–81. On the establishment of Macharetí, see a similar vocabulary, 449–53.
68 De Nino, *Etnografía*, 305.
69 For similar trends in art, see Honour, *The New Golden Land*, 219–47. Also see Berkhofer, *The White Man's Indian*. While he concentrates mainly on the United States, Berkhofer reveals much about attitudes toward Indians in general.
70 Corrado, *El colegio franciscano*, 360.
71 Giannecchini, *Historia natural*, 294.
72 De Nino, *Etnografía*, 308.
73 Ibid., 70–71.
74 Ibid., 257; Martarelli, *El Colegio Franciscano*, 167; Giannecchini, *Historia natural*, 332. One might accuse the Italians of having those characteristics as well. Perhaps this similarity to the Italian laboring classes made the friars even more sensitive to this point.
75 Martarelli, *El Colegio Franciscano*, 168–69.
76 Indigenous women lived in virtually all Creole households, as seen in the 1858 census of what is now Cordillera Province. See "Padrón general (1858)," Archivo Parroquial de Lagunillas.
77 Giannecchini, *Historia natural*, 372–73.
78 De Nino, *Etnografía*, 254–55.
79 Martarelli, *El Colegio Franciscano*, 177.
80 The classic statement of this issue in slavery is Genovese, *Roll, Jordan, Roll*.

On the growing literature of subaltern studies, see the important essay by Chakrabarty, "Postcoloniality and the Artifice of History." For a provocative view of applying subaltern studies to Latin America, see Mallon, "The Promise and Dilemma of Subaltern Studies."

81 "Añadidora a los apuntes pa los anuales de 1879," Gaveta 8:77, f. 14, AFT. Although there is no author, the handwriting suggests Fr. Doroteo Giannecchini penned this document.

82 This aspect has been less studied in Latin America. For Italy, see Pociani, "Lo Statuto e il Corpus Domini." Another example is the establishment of a statue of the heretical freethinking Dominican Giordano Bruno by the Italian government, which has been intensively studied. See Rivinius, "Der Giordano-Bruno Skandal," and Rill, "Ein Höhepunkt im italienischen Kulturkampf." For a useful comparison, Richard Warren has explored the uses of public rituals in politics for early nineteenth-century Mexico City. See his *Vagrants and Citizens*.

83 I rely heavily on these notions as they have been developed by Hunt, *The New Cultural History*. Also see Kertzer, *Ritual, Politics and Power*.

84 De Nino, *Etnografía*, 254–55. Others noted the mission bands as well. In the famous novel *Tierras hechizadas*, Adolfo Costa du Rels, who had spent many years in the region prospecting for oil, featured the mission bands that played for the large landowner at his estate.

85 See, for example, Giannecchini, *Historia natural*, 332–42.

86 De Nino, *Etnografía*, 263.

87 There is a large literature on the process of conversion and its meanings. For one sophisticated approach, see MacCormack, *Religion in the Andes*.

CHAPTER THREE *Death and Migration*

1 The classic study on this phenomenon is Cook, *Population Trends*. More recent studies include Jackson, *Indian Population Decline*; Block, *Mission Culture*; and various essays in Langer and Jackson, *The New Latin American Mission History*. On the issue of flight, see Deeds, *Defiance and Deference*, and Radding, *Landscapes of Power*.

2 Langer and Jackson, "Colonial and Republican Missions."

3 Reff, "The Jesuit Mission Frontier."

4 For the 1877 figures, see "Memoria que en ocacion de las elecciones capitulares del Colegio de Tarija el Prefecto de sus Misiones de Infieles Fray Doroteo Giannecchini presenta al M. R. P. Comisario General . . ." f. 27, AFT; Martarelli, *El Colegio Franciscano*, 195. Martarelli does not give a population count, but asserts that seventy Chiriguano families settled in Boicovo at the founding of the mission. They must have comprised over two hundred individuals,

and I added this to the 12,860 figure cited for the Tarija missions. The 1900 figures are from Bolivia, *Censo de la población de la República de Bolivia según el empadronamiento de 1 de septiembre de 1900*; the 1924 figures are from Juan Manuel Sainz, *Memoria de Guerra y Colonización 1924* (La Paz: Intendencia de la Guerra, 1924), 70.

5 "Primer libro parroquial en que se sientan las partidas de bautismos, casamientos, confirmaciones y entierros de esta reducción de Nuestra Sra. la Purísima de Tarairí año 1854," 64, AVAChC.

6 This was also usually the case for colonial-era missions, though often for different reasons. In many cases the missionaries had a policy of forcing Indians living in the surrounding area to join the missions, often with the aid of Spanish soldiers from the *presidios*. See, for example, Jackson, *Indian Population Decline*. Summary information for the Chiriguano missions exists only from 1877 to 1913.

7 Martarelli, *El Colegio Franciscano*, 256–94.

8 "Santas Visitas: Ivo:" 1897, 1900, AFP.

9 "Misión de San Francisco Solano o Cantón Parapiti Grande," 1907:2; 1909:5; "Santas Visitas 1889–1912," AFP. San Francisco was unusual, of course, since it had been founded in 1871 and then abandoned by the Franciscans. Unlike in the nineteenth century, resistance from local ranchers was also much greater and the mission was resecularized in 1915. See chapter 7 for a discussion of the founding and secularization of San Francisco del Parapetí. All figures are from the visitas if not otherwise noted.

10 "Memoria que . . . Fray Doroteo Giannecchini presenta al M. R. P. Comisario General . . . ," f. 27, AFT.

11 Giannecchini to Archbishop of La Plata, Aguairenda, 12 December 1883, "Libro 2° Copia = Notas de las Misiones Franciscanas del Colegio de Nra Sra de los Angeles de Tarija que comienza el día 7 de Abril de 1883–1890 . . ." 61–62, AFT.

12 De Nino, *Etnografía*, 78.

13 For a brief discussion of ecological changes in the region, see Langer, *Economic Change*, 129–30.

14 "Libro segundo de defunciones San Pascual de Boicovo," APC.

15 "Informe del Prefecto de las Misiones de la p. F. de Potosí, Fr. Romualdo Dambrogi," in *Memoria del Ministro de Instrucción Pública y Colonización Dr, José Vicente Ochoa presentada al Congreso Nacional de 1895* (Sucre: Tipografía Excelsior, 1895), 140, ABNB.

16 "Apuntes pa los anales de 1880," No. 277, 79, AFT; Nordenskiöld, *Indianerleben*, 158–59. For 1922, see Hernando Siles, *Memoria de Guerra y Colonización* (La Paz: N.p., 1922), 70.

17 "Informe del Prefecto . . . Dambrogi," 140.

18 "Santas Visitas: Santa Rosa de Cuevo," AFT.
19 "Santas Visitas: Macharetí." The figures do not add up exactly, because apparently the dejected missionaries made only estimates in 1913, not an accurate population count as they had before.
20 If there had been an epidemic to explain the distorted pyramid, then men and women should have been absent in roughly the same numbers. See "Padron de la Misión de Macharetí Censo 1. formado por el p. Columbano Ma Puccetti 1900," APM. Unfortunately there is no indication of what month this census was taken, so it can't be known whether or not the census incorporates seasonal migration patterns.
21 Alejandro Ercole to Vicente Piccinini, Chimeo, 4 August 1873, "Copiador de cartas de Fr. Alejandro Ercole, 21 Dic. 1870–9 Feb. 1874," AFT.
22 "Santas Visitas: Macharetí" 1886:262, 1896:285, 1897:287, 1900:309, AFT.
23 For an overview that takes into account labor migration to the northern Argentine ingenios beyond that of the Chiriguano mission laborers, see Conti, Lagos, and Lagos, "Mano de obra indígena," and Lagos, "Conformación del mercado."
24 Rutledge, *Cambio agrario*, 109–10. An arroba weighs about 25 lbs.
25 Carrera, "La violencia."
26 Villafañe, *Orán y Bolivia*, 60.
27 Rutledge, *Cambio agrario*, 131, 133.
28 Ibid., 133.
29 José María Suárez to Minister of War, Tarija, 1 August 1844, MG 1844 t. 177, No. 29, CO, ANB.
30 Villafañe, *Orán y Bolivia*, 33, 36.
31 Ibid., 37–38.
32 Lagos, "Conformación del mercado."
33 Guy, *Argentine Sugar Politics*; Sánchez Román, *La dulce crisis*; Rutledge, *Cambio agrario*.
34 Lagos, "Conformación del mercado," 53–63.
35 Bialet y Massé, *El estado*, 78.
36 Lagos and Teruel de Lagos, "Trabajo y demografía," 124; Rutledge, *Cambio agrario*, 165.
37 Villafañe, *Orán y Bolivia*, 35; Bialet y Massé, *El estado*, 83.
38 Lagos and Teruel de Lagos, "Trabajo y demografía," chart 5.
39 Villafañe, *Orán y Bolivia*, 39; Nordenskiöld, *Indianerleben*, 7. For the Toba viewpoint, see Gordillo, *Landscapes of Devils*.
40 Ercole to Nicanor Echazú, S. Francisco Solano, 22 January 1871, "Copiador de cartas de Fr. Alejandro Ercole"; M. O. Jofré to Conversores de las Misiones del Distrito, Tarija, 20 May 1875, Gaveta 18; Sebastián Pifferi, "Informe del infrascrito R. p. Prefecto del as Misiones Franciscanas . . . sobre el transporte

de los Indios misioneros a la República Argentina," Aguairenda, 26 April 1886, Gaveta 8:152, all AFT.

41 Julián Campero to R. P. Prefecto de Misiones, Tarija, 17 January 1905, No. 44, Gaveta 6, AFT; Moisés Santivañez, *Informe que eleva al Supremo Gobierno, el Prefecto y Comandante General del Departamento de Tarija* (Tarija: Tipografía Guadalquivir, 1908), 9, ABNB; "Reglamento de Misiones, 1905," AFT; Langer and Ruiz, *Historia de Tarija*, 401–414; Langer, *Economic Change*, 146.

42 Santiago Romano to Minister of Colonization, Tarairí, 8 June 1907, p. 2, M-331; Romano, "Informe del segundo trieno (1911)," Gaveta s/n, AFT.

43 Víctor Navajas Trigo, *Informe presentado a la consideración del Supremo Gobierno por el ciudadano Víctor Navajas Trigo Prefecto y Comandante General del Departamento de Tarija* (Tarija: Imprenta La Velocidad, 1923), 17.

44 Jackson and Castillo, *Indians, Franciscans*, 77–80.

45 See, for example, the numerous references to this practice in the "Santas Visitas," AFT.

46 Conti, Lagos, and Lagos, "Mano de obra indígena," 19; Subprefect of Gran Chaco, *Informe anual 1912–1913* (Tarija, 1913), 13, ABNB. For a description of the final payment, the *gran arreglo*, for the Tobas, see Gordillo, *Landscapes of Devils*, 121–22.

47 See, for example, Jerónimo Miranda to Sebastián Pifferi, Tiguipa, 24 April 1886, Gaveta 3; Belisario H[evia] y Vaca to Pifferi, Yacuiba, 28 February 1888, Gaveta 8, AFT.

48 Nazareno Dimeco, "Apuntes del viaje y regreso de Sucre del Misionero Cundeye hermano del Capitán Mandeponai," Gaveta 8:147, 1; Camilo Uriburo to Dimeco, La Esperanza, 27 August 1889, Gaveta 8:170; Letter to Minister of Relaciones Exteriores y Culto, San Francisco Solano, 1 June 1904, Gaveta s/n, AFT.

49 General Carlos Villegas to Minister of War and Colonization, Caiza, 30 September 1914, "Copiador 3: Del 24 de Mayo a 4 de Novbre (1914)," 488, AC-CVM.

50 Gervacio Costa to Minister of Relaciones Exteriores y Culto, San Francisco Solano, 30 July 1902, 2, AFT.

51 Gabriel Delgado to Mission Prefect, Capitan [?], 27 February 1905, AFT. Also see Langer and Ruiz, *Historia de Tarija*, 410–12.

52 Nordenskiöld, *Indianerleben*, 6, 9.

53 Hirsch, "Mbaporenda."

54 Villegas to Minister of War and Colonization, Caiza, 30 September 1914, "Copiador 3: Del 24 de mayo a 4 de novbre (1914)," 489, ACCVM.

55 Ibid.

56 P. Clastres, *Society against the State*.

57 Nordenskiöld, *Indianerleben*, 6, 9.

58 Alejandro Ercole to Vicente Piccinini, Chimeo, 4 August 1873, "Copiador de cartas de Fr. Alejandro Ercole, 21 Dic. 1870–9 Feb. 1874," AFT.
59 Ercole to Nicanor Echazu, San Francisco Solano, 22 January 1871, "Copiador de cartas de Fr. Alejandro Ercole, 21 Dic. 1870–9 Feb. 1874," AFT.
60 See, for example, de Nino, *Etnografía*, 305.
61 For a similar treatment, see R. A. Gutiérrez, *When Jesus Came*.
62 "Informe del Prefecto . . . Dambrogi," 144, AFT.
63 See, for example, "Santas Visitas," Macharetí: 1899:289, AFT. For the importance of chicha, see de Nino, *Etnografía*, 247.
64 For cases of adultery, see Gervasio Costa to Bautista del Castillo, San Francisco, 12 November 1901, AFT; for wife beating and fighting, see de Nino, *Etnografía*, 305, and Rafael Paoli, "Informe pasado por el R.P. Guardián del Convento de San Francisco relativo a las misiones del Gran Chaco," in Manuel V. Ballivián, *Memoria que presenta el Ministro de Colonias y Agricultura á la legislatura ordinaria de 1905* (La Paz: J. M. Gamarra, 1905), 91, 93, ABNB.

CHAPTER FOUR *Daily Life, Mission Culture*

1 Doroteo Giannecchini to Eulogio Raña, Aguairenda, 13 September 1883, and Raña to Giannecchini, Caiza, 19 September 1883, "Libro 2° Copia = Notas de la Prefectura de las Misiones Franciscanas del Colegio de Nra Sra de los Angeles de Tarija que comienza el dia 7 de Abril de 1883–1890 por el actual Prefecto Fr. Doroteo Giannecchini," 47–48, AFT. We actually possess information only on the later part of the story, though Yandori's involvement in the earlier construction of Colonia Crevaux is highly likely, given his particular skills.
2 This case became a major scandal in Bolivia in 1907. The anticlerical delegate of the Gran Chaco threw the Macharetí missionary Domingo Ficosecco into jail for his mistreatment. A lengthy polemic resulted over the use of punishment in the Franciscan missions, providing fodder for both anticlerical and pro-clerical elements over the direction of state-Church relations in the wake of the Liberal Party's victory in the 1898–1899 Federalist War. (See chapter 7.) For sources on this case, consult Manuel V. Ballivián, *Memoria que presenta el Ministro de Colonización y Agricultura al Congreso Ordinario de 1908* (La Paz: Tall. Tip.-Lit. de J. Miguel Gamarra, 1908), 18–19, ANB. For the Franciscan point of view, see Santiago Romano, "Un informe desmentido," and Romano to Ballivián, n.d., No. 196 and 259, respectively, Gaveta 8, AFT.
3 For a good description of traditional houses, see Nordenskiöld, *Indianerleben*, 173–77, and de Nino, *Etnografía*, 170–78. For complaints about the poor quality of unconverted Indians' abodes, see de Nino, 303. By "traditional" I mean the houses that had evolved by the nineteenth century. In the sixteenth

century the Chiriguanos resided in large, circular houses in which a whole lineage lived. See de Nino, 174-77.
4 "Padrón de la Misión de Macharetí Censo 1. Formado por el P. Columbano Mª Puccetti 1900," APM. I used the age of the oldest member of the household to determine into which category they would fall. Of the forty-four cases, in four it was not possible to determine the ages of the couples.
5 For the nonchiefly polygynous households, see "Padrón de la Misión de Macharetí Censo 1. Formado por el P. Columbano Mª Puccetti 1900," APM, Nos. 162, 188, 279, 293, 326, 330. For Mandeponay's wives, see household numbers 68, 223, 229, 265, 391, 451. The second wives of chiefs Azucuna and Guatayu are listed in household numbers 20 and 139.
6 Jofré, Colonias y misiones, 65.
7 See the following section for a more detailed discussion of the mission schools.
8 Among the unconverted a condition of residence was to send their children to the mission school. As the other chapters show, this rule was not completely followed and depended largely on what phase of the cycle the mission was in.
9 For the quote on tembetas, see Nordenskiöld, Indianerleben, 211. European clothing is discussed on 202-3. European clothing was a high-prestige item and used frequently even before the missions among the independent villages throughout the nineteenth century. See Langer, "Foreign Cloth."
10 De Nino, Etnografía, 241. Also see Nordenskiöld, Indianerleben, 180-81.
11 Ibid., 239-25; Ibid., 183.
12 Ibid., 256-65; Ibid., 237-39.
13 Nordenskiöld, Indianerleben, 152.
14 De Nino, Etnografía, 113.
15 Ibid., 302. For the even stronger missionary view, see 304-5.
16 The best description of the way the Potosí mission schools were supposed to work is contained in Martarelli, El Colegio Franciscano, 215-22. For the Tarija missions, see Cardús, Las misiones franciscanas, 43-46. The economic implications of this vocational training is discussed in the next chapter.
17 Cardús, Las misiones franciscanas, 44-45; Martarelli, El Colegio Franciscano, 219.
18 De Nino, Etnografía, 203. The Tobas' major failing, according to missionary prejudice, was their proclivity for theft. For a similar argument that revolves around the Franciscans' control of indigenous sexuality in colonial New Mexico, see R. A. Gutiérrez, When Jesus Came. On California, the most thorough examination is Hackel, Children of Coyote, 182-227.
19 General Villegas to Ministerio de Guerra y Colonización, Caiza, 30 September 1914, "Copiador 3: Del 24 de Mayo a 4 de Novbre (1914)," 489, ACCVM.

20 Nordenskiöld, *Indianerleben*, 179, 214. Of course, Nordenskiöld had his own cultural perspective. For a brief discussion of the anthropologist's values, see Alvarsson, "El humanitarismo de Nordenskiöld."
21 Saignes, "Jesuites et Franciscains."
22 "Reglamento para la escuela de niños," APM. From the length of this document it is also possible to infer the lower levels of control by the missionaries, for the boys' regulations are a page and a half shorter than that of the girls. Unfortunately these regulations are from 1928, relatively late in the life of the missions. However, the regulations mentioned in earlier texts make these appear typical, though I suspect enforcement was much more difficult earlier in mission history. For less detailed schedules for the 1880s and 1890s, see Cardús, *Las misiones franciscanas*, 44-45; Martarelli, *El Colegio Franciscano*, 217-20; Jofré, *Colonias y misiones*, 12-14.
23 Costa du Rels, *Tierras hechizadas*.
24 Martarelli, *El Colegio Franciscano*, 218-20. Also see Sebastián Pifferi, "Informe de las misiones franciscanas," in Luis Paz, *Informe que eleva al Supremo Gobierno el Prefecto y Comandante General de Tarija sobre la administración del Departamento, año 2* (Tarija: Imprenta de El Trabajo, 1890), 30.
25 De Nino, *Etnografía*, 309. For a dissenting view from 1927, see J. A. Gutiérrez, *Delegación*, 69. However, Gutiérrez uses the Tarija-run Macharetí mission as his example and thus his tirades might not be applicable to the missions controlled by the friars from Potosí.
26 On the prohibition of wearing tembetas, see Cardús, *Las misiones franciscanas*, 41. On cholos, see Seligmann, "To Be In Between." This interstitial group was not always looked upon favorably. See Arguedas, *Pueblo enfermo*. For a larger discussion of the role of *mestizaje*, or race mixture, in the Andes, see de la Cadena, *Indigenous Mestizos*.
27 Nordenskiöld, *Indianerleben*, 202-3. On trade in textiles prior to the missions, see Langer, "Foreign Cloth," and Langer and Hames, "Commerce and Credit on the Periphery," 292-94.
28 Saignes, *Ava y karai*, 119-22.
29 An excellent discussion of this is R. A. Gutiérrez, *When Jesus Came*.
30 Corrado, *El colegio franciscano*, 387.
31 De Nino, *Etnografía*, 304; "Santas Visitas: Macharetí," 1891 and 1894, AFT. The first quote is from the 1894 *visita* [inspection], 280, and the second from 1896, 285. On Aguairenda, see "Santas Visitas: Aguairenda," 1894, 78, AFT.
32 "Santas Visitas: Aguairenda," 1894, 304.
33 Cardús, *Las misiones franciscanas*, 33; "Santas Visitas: Macharetí," 1888, 267, AFT. From 1890 onward, the number of students jumps precipitously, from an average of two hundred pupils per year to over four hundred in 1890, then to about five hundred. Only after 1904, with a large drop in total population,

does the number of schoolchildren fall to an average of a bit more than three hundred. See "Santas Visitas: Macharetí," 1890–1913, AFT.

34 We unfortunately do not have the figures for the total number of school-age children.

35 Contreras, "Reformas y desafíos," 484.

36 "Santas Visitas: Itau," 1877:1; 1886:12; 1889:18; 1892:23; 1893–1912.

37 See, for example, Doroteo Giannecchini, "Memoria que en ocasion de las elecciones capitulares . . ." (1885), 3, Gaveta s/n, AFT. Ironically, during the early nineteenth century the region was a center of a flourishing indigenous population, until the massacres of the 1840s. Possibly the massive introduction of cattle in the aftermath destroyed the quality of the water supply and brought about the proliferation of water-borne diseases.

38 "Santas Visitas: Ivo," 1912:33; "Santas Visitas: Boicovo," 1912:48; "Santas Visitas: Santa Rosa," 1913:48; "Santas Visitas: Aguairenda," 1910:60; "Santas Visitas: Tiguipa," 1913:278; "Santas Visitas: Macharetí," 1912:338; "Santas Visitas: Tarairí," 224. On the instructors of Tarairí, see Carlos M. Villegas to Ministro de Guerra y Colonización, Caiza, 30 September 1914, 487, Fondo Delegación del Gran Chaco, ACCVM.

39 Martarelli, *El Colegio Franciscano*, 218–19; Cardús, *Las misiones franciscanas*, 44.

40 "Libro de confirmaciones," Boicovo, APC; "Primer Libro Parroquial en que se sientan las Partidas de Bautismos, Casamientos, Confirmaciones y Entierros de esta Reducción de Nuestra Sra la Purisima de Tarairi. Año 1854," 13:72, APC. In 1859 Carmona became godfather to Francisco, the child of Apico and Guraimbe, who were originally from the mestizo settlement of Caiza but lived on the mission.

41 "Libro de confirmaciones," Boicovo, APC. In 1904 the Boicovo book shows that settlers also became godparents of children from Sapirangui, Tiguipa, Pipi, Cuevo, Tarairí, Santa Rosa, and Caiza.

42 Jofré, *Colonias y misiones*, 16–17.

43 Ibid., 17.

44 "Libro de Visitas: Macharetí," AFT; "Libro de Visitas: Boicovo," APT. In the case of Boicovo, one must also add the 143 schoolchildren for a total mission population of 433 souls. The number of converts was 101, and that of the catecúmenos 109.

45 "Libro Copiador de P. Alejandro Ercole (1871–1873)," 24 June 1872, AFT. Jofré in 1893 describes a more elaborate system for the neophytes of a governor, his lieutenant, two alcaldes, and two policemen, but I suspect that this was more the ideal than reality on any but the largest missions. See *Colonias y misiones*, 19.

46 See Block, *Mission Culture*, for the development of this concept.

47 "Diario del ganado—Libro 1° de Cuentas 1869" [Macharetí], 126, 102, APM. In this book, however, the friars gave the bulk of goods to chiefs such as Mandeponay and Guarangai and some alcaldes rather than ordinary Indians. They in turn presumably distributed the beef to the rest. See chapter 5 for relations with the chiefs.
48 Also see Saignes, Ava y karai, 85-126.
49 De Nino, Etnografía, 308.
50 Bolivia, Censo de la población en 1900, 12-13. On 6-7 there is a listing of individuals with or without elementary instruction. However, these figures are difficult to interpret because the census here lists only eighty-seven with such instruction in Macharetí, in clear contradiction to the previous figure in the same census and to what we know about mission schools. For Ñancaroinza, the census listed sixty individuals (out of 978 total inhabitants) with some elementary instruction. Does this mean that the census takers took into account only those who had some schooling outside the missions?
51 Nordenskiöld, Indianerleben, 198.

CHAPTER FIVE *Conversion, Chiefs, and Rebellions*

1 Cardús, Las misiones franciscanas, 41.
2 See Cardús, Las misiones franciscanas, 41-43, 54-55. Cardús mentioned that on the Potosí missions children generally asked to be baptized at age ten or twelve. Since he wrote soon after the foundation of Boicovo, the only mission the Franciscans from Potosí had in 1886, this practice almost certainly applies only to the first few years of the mission at Boicovo; later the Potosí missionaries followed the rules of the Franciscans from Tarija. See de Nino, Etnografía, 303-4.
3 De Nino, Etnografía, 116, 299. Also see Cardús, Las misiones franciscanas, 41; Martarelli, El colegio franciscano, 208. The records of Santa Rosa suggest that the friars expected to baptize only sick individuals; in the early "Visitas" the missionaries boast that they were able to get the Indians to accept baptism on their deathbed. See "Santas Visitas: Santa Rosa," 1889-92, APM.
4 See de Nino, Etnografía, 89; also see table 1.
5 "Anales de este Colegio Franciscano de Tarija desde el año de 1879: Libro primero," 8-9, AFT.
6 "Anales," 9-10.
7 Ibid., 8-9; de Nino, Etnografía, 116.
8 De Nino, Etnografía, 130 n. 1, 300. For other examples of this phenomenon, see Axtell, The Invasion Within, 123, 281.
9 Alejandro Corrado suggests this indirectly as a cause for the breakdown of resistance by the Tarairí Chiriguanos. See Corrado, El colegio franciscano, 385-88.

10 For a history of the mission, see Martarelli, *El colegio franciscano*, 224-37. Martarelli, who chronicled the Potosí missions, underplays the desire of the Cuevo Indians since they preferred to have the Tarija convent found the mission. For the Tarija perspective, see Doroteo Giannecchini, "Memoria (1885)," reproduced in Langer and Ruiz, *Historia de Tarija*, 362-64.

11 Unfortunately, whether this constituted a majority of people is not known, for after 1909 the friars listed only the number of heathen versus converted families, without breaking them down into individuals. Unconverted families tended to be larger, but by 1912 there were 194 converted families versus 160 unconverted, making it highly likely that there were more Catholics than non-Catholics.

12 De Nino, for example, described Boicovo as an unhealthy place, completely cut off by surrounding mountains and where epidemics were endemic. See *Etnografía*, 89-90.

13 See Corrado, *El colegio franciscano*, 360-68.

14 Please see chapter 1 for a description of the foundation of Chimeo and the massacre preceding it.

15 Corrado, *El colegio franciscano*, 414, 444, 469-72.

16 Spalding, "Social Climbers."

17 See, for example, Saeger, *The Chaco Mission Frontier*, 151-53; Deeds, *Defiance and Deference*, 22-27. For an excellent discussion on the struggle between missionaries and medicine men, see Axtell, *The Invasion Within*, especially the section on the French. Interestingly, conflicts between shamans and missionaries were more common among the Jesuits than the Franciscans.

18 "Anales," 8-9.

19 On Macharetí, see Corrado, *El colegio franciscano*, 446-454; on Chimeo, see 345-46.

20 Francisco Carmona, "Orden Jeneral," 14 March 1860, Gaveta 8:81, AFT. The complete document is reproduced in Langer and Ruiz, *Historia de Tarija*, 224-25.

21 Corrado, *El colegio franciscano*, 377-78.

22 See Corrado, *El colegio franciscano*, 378-82; also Gaveta 8:25, AFT. This latter paper is a legal document in which the friars call as witnesses the other tubichas to testify to this incident and the only place where Ríos is mentioned by name. Presumably the Franciscans kept this document to use against this prominent citizen and embarrass him in front of national authorities if he ever decided to cause trouble again.

23 On Chimeo, see Corrado, *El colegio franciscano*, 346. On Macharetí, see 445-49.

24 For the case of Guirasavai, see "Libro copiador de P. Alejandro Ercole (1871-1873)," 1 July 1872, AFT. For a general statement, see Martarelli, *El Colegio franciscano*, 200-201.

25 Corrado, *El colegio franciscano*, 360.
26 R. A. Gutiérrez, *When Jesus Came*.
27 Corrado, *El colegio franciscano*, 360.
28 De Nino, *Etnografía*, 247.
29 These were undoubtedly *facones*, long-handled knives common in the Argentine countryside.
30 De Nino, *Etnografía*, 305.
31 Ibid., 113.
32 For a first attempt at understanding Mandeponay's life, consult Langer, "Mandeponay," 280–95. Since this early effort, new information I uncovered has deepened my understanding of his role. Mandeponay was also spelled Mandepora in some accounts.
33 Macharetí reached a population of 4,116 inhabitants in 1882. Of that number, 116 were neófitos. See "Santas Visitas 1877–1913," Macharetí, f. 255, AFT.
34 The first reference to labor contracting comes from 1882, when a manager from a plantation called San Lorenzo appeared at Macharetí. Already at that date Mandeponay took advantage of this opportunity; whereas the missionary granted permission for the migration of seventy men, Mandeponay had the manager take many more than those the friar had authorized. See Santiago Romano to Doroteo Giannecchini, Macharetí, 7 September 1882, Gaveta 18:6, AFT.
35 Corrado, *El colegio franciscano*, 444.
36 Thouar, *Explorations*, 243. Nordenskiöld, *Indianerleben*, 228.
37 See Langer, "Mission Land Tenure," 409–10.
38 "Espendiente de menzura y amojonamiento del lugar 'Picuihua' de una legua cuadrada, en favor del Capitan 'Mandeponay' Capitan de la Micion Macharetí, Año 1891," MH 1891; "Tierras, adjudicaciones, Prov. Azero," ABNB. The quote comes from f. 3. My thanks to Isabelle Combès, who brought this document to my attention.
39 "Santas Visitas: Macharetí," 1890, 1896, AFT. Also see Nordenskiöld, *Indianerleben*, 213.
40 Camilo Uriburu to P. Nazareno, La Esperanza, 27 August 1889, Gaveta 8:170. For 1891, see "Santas Visitas: Macharetí," 1890, f. 269, 271; 1891, f. 274, all AFT.
41 The best analysis of this revolt remains Sanabria, *Apiaguaiqui-Tumpa*. Also see Pifarré, *Los Guaraní-Chiriguano*, 373–91; Saignes, *Ava y karai*, 187–98. For an analysis of the role of the missions, see Langer, "Caciques y poder." Much of the last section of this chapter is based on this article.
42 Thouar, *Explorations*, 243–44.
43 "Santas Visitas: Macharetí," 1896, f. 285.
44 See "Santas Visitas: Macharetí," 1897–1903.
45 Germán del Castillo to Corregidor of Ñancaroinza, Ñancaroinza, 21 April

1904, Gaveta 8:185; Manuel Mariano Gómez to Corregidor of La Colonia, Palmar, 21 April 1904 (copy made by Domingo Ficosecco), Gaveta 8:186; Mission Prefect to Minister of Exterior, San Francisco Solano, 1 June 1904, Gaveta s/n, all AFT. For Manuel Gómez's importance on the frontier, see Langer, *Economic Change*, 132–34.

46 "Santas Visitas: Macharetí," 1906, 1910.
47 César Vigiani to Fernando Ambrosini, Macharetí, 21 July 1911, Gaveta s/n, AFT.
48 "Macharetí: Defunciones II 1916," p. 58, APM.
49 Corrado, *El colegio franciscano*, 372–73, 379; Gaveta 8:25, AFT.
50 In an undated letter, Fr. Alejandro Corrado discussed the effects of the death of Aravayu, who became the mburuvicha of the mission after Cuarenda. He was perhaps the son of Cuarenda but did not figure in the earlier documents. Although it is not clear who was selected to replace Aravayu, it appears that Guirapane, one of the original tubichas and a great medicine man, had the inside track for the job. See Corrado to Mission Prefect, Tarairí, n.d., M-312, AFT. The letter must have been written between 1855 and 1877.
51 "Santas Visitas: Tarairí," 1884, fs. 108–9; 1885, f. 111 AFT.
52 Ibid., 1891, 1895, 1896.
53 "Apuntes de viaje, y regreso de Sucre del Misionero Cundeye, Hermano del Capitan Manteponai," Gaveta 8:147, AFT.
54 "El hecho de como murió el Misionero Mataica," Gaveta 8:76, AFT.
55 Gervasio Costa to Manuel Lauruoa, San Francisco Solano, 22 February 1902, Gaveta s/n, AFT.
56 See, for example, Costa to Ministro de Relaciones Exteriores y Culto, Tarija, 19 June 1902; Anonymous to Ministro de Relaciones Exteriroes y Culto, San Francisco Solano, 1 June 1904; José María Corchetti to Santiago Romano, Macharetí, 10 September 1907, all Gaveta s/n, AFT.
57 Nordenskiöld, *Indianerleben*, 231.
58 This might also help explain the Jesuits' failure, despite repeated efforts, to missionize the Chiriguanos in the colonial period. The Jesuits not only attacked much more directly the Chiriguanos' insistence on individual liberty (falsely believing that their Paraguayan mission experience among fellow Guaraní speakers prepared them for the Chiriguanos), but also emphasized economic profit for their missionary enterprises, an attitude that the Chiriguanos considered contemptible. After all, great chiefs always redistributed their goods and thus claimed legitimacy.
59 See Sanabria, *Apiaguaiqui-Tumpa*, 140; also see "Santas Visitas: Macharetí," 1913, AFT.
60 "Juicio Civil de diligencias de inventarios de los bienes yacientes al fallecimiento del Capitan Napoleón Taco Yaguaracu . . . ," 1915:2040, Civil, Archivo

Judicial de Monteagudo. It is possible that Tacu's illness, if that is what killed him, led to financial losses and is the reason little accumulation of goods is visible in the probate records.

61 See "Santas Visitas" for all extant missions, and Jofré, *Colonias y misiones*, appendix III. I am also including the Chiriguanos settled on San Francisco del Pilcomayo, who numbered about five hundred. On Santa Rosa, of a total of 2,137 Chiriguanos, only 243 had converted. On Macharetí, out of 2,497 Chiriguanos, 550 were Christians.

62 See Martarelli, *El colegio franciscano*, 186–95, 224–38, 243–54. For a description of hacienda labor conditions, see Langer, *Economic Change*, 146–54. Little has been written about the Caipipendi Chiriguanos.

63 The name Chapiaguasu assumed is controversial. Hernando Sanabria Fernández, in *Apaiguaiqui-Tumpa*, still the only work dedicated exclusively to the 1892 rebellion, might have misspelled Chapiaguasu's assumed name, as evident in the title of the book. It is not clear why a fluent Guaraní speaker such as Sanabria, who had close ties to the Caipipendi Chiriguanos and interviewed many of them, would have misheard his name, but subsequent investigators have mostly asserted that Chapiaguasu's assumed name was Apiaguaiki. The best summary of this debate is Saignes, *Ava y karai*, 188–93.

64 Pifarré, *Los Guaraní-Chiriguano*, 375–76; Martarelli, *El colegio franciscano*, 262. On the Caste War of Yucatán, consult Rugeley, *Yucatán's Maya Peasantry*; Reed, *The Caste War of the Yucatán*; Dummond, *The Machete and the Cross*: and Robins, *Native Insurgencies*.

65 Santiago Romano to Nazareno Dimeco, Macharetí, 16 January 1892, Gaveta s/n, AFT; Martarelli, *El colegio franciscano*, 263–65. The quote is on 264. I find it unlikely that Apiaguaiki ordered the tubichas to do anything. I suspect he suggested that they join him, but Chiriguano political culture made efforts at ordering the fiercely independent tubichas largely futile. Apiaguaiki's authoritarian tone, if indeed he utilized the words attributed to him, might explain his failure to recruit major chiefs.

66 Martarelli, *El colegio franciscano*, 263. Pifarré estimates six thousand warriors, but this appears an exaggeration (*Los Guaraní-Chiriguano*, 376). However, for a geographic distribution of Apiaguaiki's warriors, Pifarré's analysis, based on multiple primary documents, is the best. See 377.

67 Romano to Dimeco, AFT.

68 Ibid. Sanabria claims that, according to Fr. Doroteo Giannecchini, Mandeponay exclaimed, "War is not good. No good can come of it. [Then] there are no homes, there is no more chicha" (*Apaiaguaiqui-Tumpa*, 140). However, I can find no written reference in the primary sources for this statement.

69 Sanabria, *Apaiguaiqui-Tumpa*, 140.

70 A good summary of the military campaign is Pifarré, *Los Guaraní-Chiriguano*, 378–87.

71　See Martarelli, *El colegio franciscano*, 271–73.
72　The only significant force from outside the missions came from the Caipipendi valley, long-standing allies of the Santa Cruz settlers. See Martarelli, *El colegio franciscano*, 279.
73　Martarelli, *El colegio franciscano*, 279–84.
74　Ibid., 284–85.
75　Nazareno Dimeco, "Informe que, por el digno organo de S.S. Ilma y Rma. el Sor. Dr. Dn. Pedro de la Llosa, Arzobispo de la Plata, eleva al Supo. Gno. el R.P. Prefecto de las Misiones Frans. del Colegio de Tarija," Tarairí, 28 July 1892, 2–3, Gaveta s/n, AFT.
76　Tomás Frías to S. Romano, Ñancaroinza, 4 February 1892; S. Romano to Nazareno Dimeco, Machareti, 6 February 1892; Z. Dueci to Dimeco, Tarairí, 8 February 1892; all Gaveta s/n, AFT.

CHAPTER SIX　*Missions and The Frontier Economy*

1　The new historiography on the missions was inspired in large part by the demographic studies of Woodrow Borah and Sherburne Cook. See especially Cook and Borah, *Essays in Population History*. This perspective is not completely new, at least for Brazil. See, for example, Marchant, *From Barter to Slavery*. Much of the new mission history has focused on California, where an important debate over the canonization of Fr. Junípero Serra brought the demographic question into the limelight. See Sandos, "Junípero Serra's Canonization"; Jackson, *Indian Population Decline*.
2　Langer and Jackson, "Colonial and Republican Missions." However, James S. Saeger has found relatively low levels of coercion in the colonial Chaco missions because the Indians remained much more powerful in relation to Spanish society in the Chaco. See his "Eighteenth-Century Guaycuruan Missions." This came on the heels of failed attempts in the seventeenth century to coerce the Indians through constant warfare and Spanish expeditions.
3　Bolton, "The Mission." This is not to say that others, such as Marchant, have not taken this into account. These authors have simply not made the missions' economic role their primary focus. The notable exceptions are the works on the Jesuits, in particular those of Nicholas Cushner, in his trilogy on the Jesuits. See, for example, *Lords of the Land*.
4　This aspect has been developed especially for colonial Brazil. See Marchant, *From Barter to Slavery*, as well as Kiemen, *The Indian Policy*. Although not strictly a mission history, this is also the central theme in Chevalier, "Signification sociale."
5　"Santas Visitas, 1889–1912," 2–3, 6, AFP.
6　De Nino, *Etnografía*, 207–9.

7 Langer and Ruiz, *Historia de Tarija*, 224-25.
8 Cited in ibid., 264-66. Francisco Burdett O'Connor, however, claims in his memoirs that only eighty-four men were inducted into his Third Battalion. See *Un irlandés*, 234.
9 The correspondence between Mission Aguairenda and the command center in Caiza is copious. See especially Gaveta No. 8, AFT. The order to capture deserters is contained in Eulojio Rana to Fr. D. Giannecchini, Caiza, 3 August 1883, "Libro 20 Copia = Notas de la Prefectura de las Misiones Franciscanas del Colegio de Nra Sra de los Angeles de Tarija que comienza el dia 7 de Abril de 1883-1890," AFT.
10 See chapter 1.
11 De Nino, *Etnografía*, 241. Since the Potosí missions were founded in 1875, 1887, 1893, 1901, and 1903 the change from indigenous to European methods occurred within one or two generations. It is difficult to measure if and how exposure to European agricultural methods prior to missionization made the transition easier or in fact this transition had occurred in Chiriguano villages before permitting missions to be established.
12 Jofré, *Colonias y misiones*, 51.
13 Nordenskiöld, *Changes*, 201.
14 Langer and Ruiz, *Historia de Tarija*, 349.
15 "Santas Visitas," 24, AFP.
16 Langer and Ruiz, *Historia de Tarija*, 373.
17 Nordenskiöld, *Changes*, 178.
18 Settlers held similar opinions in many mission territories in the colonial era, such as in Nueva Vizcaya, Mexico, and sixteenth-century Brazil. See Deeds, *Defiance and Deference*; Marchant, *From Barter to Slavery*; and Monteiro, *Negros da terra*, 141-153.
19 Quote in Doroteo Giannecchini to Eulogio Raña, Aguairenda, 16 August 1883, "Libro 20 Copia," p. 32, AFT. For labor requests, see Eulogio Raña to R.P. Fr. Doroteo Giannecchini, Caiza, 12 August 1883. Also see Ignacio Estenssoro to R. P. Sebastian Pifferi, Caiza, 26 October 1885, both in Gaveta 3, and Andres Rivas to R.P. Frai [sic] Bernardo, Caiza, February 1886, Gaveta 8, all AFT.
20 Martarelli, *El Colegio Franciscano*, 210, 219.
21 See Langer, "Franciscan Missions," 310.
22 Bernardino de Nino, *Etnografía chiriguana* (La Paz: Tipografía Comercial de Ismael Argote, 1912), 237.
23 Santiago Romano to Minister of Colonization, Tarairí, 8 June 1907, p. 2, M-331; Romano, "Informe del segundo trieno (1911)," Gaveta s/n, AFT.
24 Susnik, *Chiriguanos I*, 60, 214-16.
25 Langer, "Franciscan Missions," 311, 316; Langer, *Economic Change*, 127-128.
26 See, for example, Fr. Marino Mariani to R.P. Conversor de Tarairí, 16 August

1876, "Libro en que se transcriven las Notas mandadas y recibidas . . . Fr. Marino Mariani, 1876," Gaveta 13, AFT.
27 "Libro 20 Copia," 7–14, AFT.
28 Jofré, *Colonias y misiones*, 26. On p. 23 Jofré asserts that on all missions the mission and the families living there had separate plots.
29 Ibid., 25–26, 51, 58.
30 Population figures are taken from "Santas Visitas," 1901, 1907, AFP; production and acreage from "Rectificación del catastro de la Provincia del Azero. Libro registro, Año 1900," and "Libro de declaraciones (1900)," Cuevo, 49–55; "Registro de la rectificación del Azero, Año 1906," and "Libro de declaraciones (1906)," Cuevo 47, 48; all in Tesoro Departamental, Fondo Prefectural, Centro Bibliográfico Documental Histórico, Universidad San Francisco Xavier de Chuquisaca (Sucre). A carga equals about 100 kilograms.
31 Jofré, *Colonias y misiones*, 28.
32 "Memoria que en ocacion de las elecciones capitulares del Colegio de Tarija el Prefecto de sus Misiones de Infieles Fray Doroteo Giannecchini presenta," fs. 28, 29, AFT. Mendieta, *Tierra rica*, 40, 48.
33 See, for example, Documents No. 102, 103, 106 in "Varios documentos 1866–1921 relacionados con las Misiones," Gaveta 8, AFT. Among the largest thefts, in 1878 Tobas robbed 150 head of cattle from Tarairí and the following year 250 more. The problem did not improve; see Fr. Gabriel Tommasini to Fr. Santiago Romano, Tarairí, 1 February 1907, 4, Gaveta 15, AFT.
34 Jofré, *Colonias y misiones*, 26, 52, 59, 67.
35 For an analysis of cattle ranching on the frontier, see Langer, *Economic Change*, 123–142.
36 Langer and Ruiz, *Historia de Tarija*, 349–53, 386; Jofre, *Colonias y misiones*, 26, 37, 45, 51, 59, 67, 81.
37 "Santa Visita 1889–1912," AFP.
38 Jofré, *Colonias y misiones*, 52; Ven. Discretorio al Prefecto de Misiones, Tarija, 7 October 1905, No. 7, Gaveta 15; "Libro de Visitas, 1900–1912," 215, 222, 224; both AFT.
39 "Santas Visitas," 1901, AFP.
40 "Santas Visitas," Boicovo, 2, 1901, AFP.
41 J. A. Gutiérrez, *Delegación*, 28, 69–70.
42 Langer, "Franciscan Missions," 307–8.
43 William E. Carter (well-known anthropologist who worked in Bolivia and later became head of the Hispanic Division of the Library of Congress), personal communication, 5 July 1982. For a more general discussion of coca consumption patterns in the Chaco area, see Carter et al., *Coca in Bolivia*, 67, 77. Carter et al. also report that much of this coca was acquired through barter; apparently the ranchers paid their workers partially in coca. This corresponded to one quarter of the Chiriguanos' total consumption (77).

44 Bolivia, *Censo general de 1900*, 12–13.
45 Martarelli, *El colegio franciscano*, 221.
46 See, for example, Giannecchini and Mascio, *Album fotográfico*.
47 Martarelli, *El colegio franciscano*, 209–10.
48 See, for example, de Nino, *Etnografía*, 305.
49 Nordenskiöld, *Changes in the Material Culture*, 59.
50 See Nordenskiöld, *Indianerleben*, 200–203. For changes in access to European cloth in the nineteenth century, see Langer, "Foreign Cloth."
51 Fr. Fernando Ambrosini a Santiago Romano, Tarairi, 28 March 1908, 2, Gaveta 15, AFT.
52 De Nino, *Etnografía*, 79 n. 1, 125.
53 Langer and Ruiz, *Historia de Tarija*, 273.
54 "Libro 60, Comisión Catastral de Salinas 1906," ct T68; "Libro de cuadros estadísticos de la rectificación del catastro del Gran Chaco Año 1906," ct T48, both in Tribunal Nacional de Cuentas, ABNB.
55 Langer, *Economic Change*, 134–135, 146–55.
56 Langer and Ruiz, *Historia de Tarija*, 282–83, 285–86.
57 Domingo Paz, *Informe que eleva al Supremo Gobierno el Prefecto y Comandante General de Tarija sobre la administración del departamento* (Tarija, Bolivia: Imprenta de El Trabajo, 1893), 25–26.
58 On the growth of towns and trade, see Mendieta, *Tierra rica*, 39–40, 57–71; Langer, *Economic Change*, 138–42.

CHAPTER SEVEN *The Decline of the Missions*

1 For economic interconnections, see the previous chapter.
2 For an excellent treatment of the Sucre administration's anticlericalism, see Lofstrom, *La presidencia*, 153–232. Also see Langer and Jackson, "Liberalism."
3 On the conditions in Cuyambuyo and Tariquea, see Clemente Carso to Ministro de Estado, Tarija, 6 January 1830, Ministerio de Hacienda, t. 23, n. 21, p. 2, ABNB. For a description of Salinas, see Francisco Burdett O'Connor to Ministro de Guerra, Tarija, 2 March 1832, p. 2, MG t. 56 n. 91, ABNB. O'Connor's version of his controversial land acquisition is detailed in his *Un irlandés*, 191. On Itau, see 227, 234–35. Also see Corrado, *El colegio franciscano*, 327.
4 Ml. Dorado to Ministro del Interior, Tarija, 20 August 1836, and Francisco de Paula Araoz to Governador de la Provincia, Tarija, 22 August 1836, MI t. 59 n. 30, ABNB.
5 See O'Connor to Ministro de Guerra, 8 November 1832, MI t. 41 n. 34, ABNB. The friars did not get their lands in Salinas back until 1834, and even then the land question remained up in the air. See Manuel Fernando Bacaflor to Ministro del Interior, Tarija, 25 October 1834, ABNB.

6 Ml. Dorado to Ministro del Interior, Tarija, 20 August 1836, ABNB; also see previous note.
7 Francisco de Paula Araoz to Governador de la Provincia, 22 August 1836, ABNB.
8 Corrado, *El colegio franciscano*, 315-18.
9 On the secularization of Salinas, see Manuel Rodríguez Magariños to Sor Govr de la Prova de Salinas, Tarija, 22 May 1844, Gaveta 8, AFT.
10 "Decree of January 22, 1830," in Bolivia, *Colección oficial*, 2:230-31.
11 On the Santa Cruz administration's focus on frontiers, see Fifer, *Bolivia*, 170-74; Langer, *Economic Change*, 125-126. This is a topic that needs to be explored more fully. Also see García Jordán, *Cruz y arado*, and "Misiones," 19-20, for a similar analysis. This contrasts sharply with the Spanish colonial regime, aptly summarized in the seminal article by Bolton, "The Mission as a Frontier Institution."
12 See Corrado, *El colegio franciscano*, 401-41, 469-502.
13 It is important to keep in mind that while the settlers saw the taking of their cattle as theft, the Indians had a different conception of ownership. For them, cattle found out in the Chaco forest could be killed just like any other wild animal. By the late nineteenth century Matacos and Tobas had begun to raise their own herds of cows, sheep, and goats, at which time the idea of domestic animals and their ownership probably changed. However, theft of non-Indian goods by Indians was not seen as evil, though among themselves people of the same village rarely took from each other. For a view of this, see Nordenskiöld, *Indianerleben*, 35-36, 55-56.
14 For reference to the 1877 law, see Notaría de Hacienda y Minas, Tierras Baldías: Registro de Escrituras (NHM) 1889:55. For the grants the del Castillos received with help from the Franciscans, see 1912:4. The three other colonists were Cipriano Mendieta, Felipe Miranda, and Miguel Gerónimo Tapia.
15 On the missionaries staying with the del Castillo brothers, see, for example, Giannecchini, *Diario*, 28-29, 131.
16 Giannecchini to Fr. Leonardo Stazi, Tarairí, 26 December 1877, "Copia—Cartas de la Prefectura provisoria de Misiones año de 1877 (Libro 1°)," AFT. However, del Castillo was not permitted to graze his own cattle on the mission.
17 Giannecchini, *Diario*, 19, 21, 28-29; Jofré, *Colonias y misiones*, 93.
18 Jofré, *Colonias y misiones*, 88.
19 NHM 1894:17; 1912:5; 1913:2, 3. For an analysis of the evolution of the frontier land tenure system, see Langer, *Economic Change*, 125-38.
20 "Contra Manuel Ruiz," Boicovo—Manuscritos Varios, p. 1, APC; NHM 1889:55, s/n.
21 Giannecchini, *Historia natural*, 233, 236. I have not been able to find information about the other women in frontier society: Agueda Figueroa, a teacher in Itau and then Chimeo, unmarried (163); Margarita López in Aguairenda,

a mestiza, born in Itau (175); María Avelina in San Antonio del Pilcomayo, a mestiza (188); Guadalupe Torres in San Francisco del Pilcomayo, a mestiza and member of the tertiary order (198); Inocencia Occandaí in Macharetí, a neophyte (219); Catalina Tejerina in Ivo, a member of the tertiary order (229).

22 "Expediente original sobre la conspiración del Capitán Bayandari de la Misión de Tarairí con Cornelio Ríos y el Capitan Arayapi de Guacaya," in Langer and Ruiz, Historia de Tarija, 309–10; Corrado, El colegio franciscano, 378–82.

23 "Relación original de las expediciones del Pilcomayo en el año 1863 y fundación de la Misión San Antonio de Padua, por el Fr. José Gianelli," in Langer and Ruiz, Historia de Tarija, 289–303.

24 Corrado, El colegio franciscano, 431–41.

25 See "Lei de 10 de setiembre" and "Resolución de 13 de septiembre," in Corrado, El colegio franciscano, 82, 83–85. Daniel Campos asserts that the Reglamento was "presented at the last hour by Father Alejandro Ercole [and] accepted in a hurried fashion by the National Assembly of [18]71." See Campos, De Tarija a la Asunción, 275.

26 "Resolución de 13 de septiembre," in Campos, De Tarija a la Asunción, 83–85. The quotes are from Articles 10, 12, 4, and 32, respectively.

27 For a summary of this period, see Klein, A Concise History of Bolivia, 132–37. Also see Irurozqui, "A bala, piedra y palo," especially 369. The 1871 Assembly was one of the most important legislative sessions in nineteenth-century Bolivian political history; see Bolivia, Redactor de la Asamblea Constituyente.

28 On the Bolivian ecclesiastical reaction to the invasion of the Vatican by Victor Manuel in 1870, see Valda, Historia de la Iglesia, 149–51. We are still lacking monographs on the history of the Catholic Church in Bolivia for the republican period that provide the details needed to better understand this period.

29 The reason the motion to provide the Franciscans with the money failed was because the legislators felt that the friars were not set up to administer state funds, not because of the idea of having the missionaries build forts. See Bolivia, Redactor, 855–61.

30 As cited in Ercole to Fr. Mamerto Esquiá, Aguairenda, 10 June 1872, "Libro copiador de P. Alejandro Ercole (1871-1873)," AFT.

31 Ercole to Fr. Mamerto Esquiá, Aguairenda, 10 June 1872. Unfortunately not many Tarija newspapers have been preserved from the nineteenth century. I have been unable to find either El Rio Bermejo or the paper where Ercole's response was published.

32 García Jordán, Cruz y arado, 292.

33 Doroteo Giannecchini to Jefe Político y Militar del Gran Chaco, San Francisco Solano, 16 August 1872, "Copiador de Cartas de Fr. Alejandro Ercole, 21 Dic 1879-9 Feb. 1874," AFT.

34 See Langer, *Economic Change*, 126–27.
35 "Resolución de 14 de abril," in Bolivia, *Anuario 1871*, 31.
36 Combès, *Etno-historias*, 166–96.
37 Martarelli, *El Colegio Franciscano*, 132–46. Also see García Jordán, *Cruz y arado*, 290.
38 Martarelli, *El Colegio Franciscano*, 128–35.
39 See Pifarré, *Los Guaraní-Chiriguano*, 364–68; Langer, *Economic Change*, 135–36, 153–55.
40 Mariani to Conversor of Tarairí, 16 August 1876, "Libro en que se trascriven las Notas mandadas y recibidas y cartas de alguna consideracion pertenecientes a las Misiones, bajo el gobierno del que firma. Fr. Marino Mariani, 1876," 3, Gaveta 13, AFT. This was a problem in the 1870s even before the Huacaya War. See Alejandro Ercole to Jefe Político y Militar de Caiza, Demetrio Trigo, San Francisco Solano, 1 October 1873, "Libro copiador de P. Alejandro Ercole (1871–1873)," AFT.
41 See Langer, "Franciscan Missions."
42 Giannecchini to Pedro Puch, Archbishop of La Plata, Aguairenda, 12 December 1883, "Libro 2° Copia—Notas de la Prefectura de las Misiones Franciscanas del Colegio de Nra Sra de los Angeles de Tarija que comienza el dia 7 de Abril de 1883–1890 por el actual Prefecto Fr. Doroteo Giannecchini," 61–62, AFT.
43 See Thouar, *A través del Gran Chaco*, 39–163.
44 See Campos, *De Tarija a la Asunción*, xii–xv; Giannecchini, *Relación*.
45 At least the missionaries thought that Campos was sent to check on the missions after the failure of the 1882 expeditions. See "Anales de este Colegio Franciscano de Tarija desde el año de 1879: Libro Primero," 14–15, AFT.
46 For Campos's orders, see his *De Tarija a la Asunción*, 9–15.
47 Campos, *De Tarija a la Asunción*, 267.
48 Ibid., 268.
49 Ibid., 271.
50 Ibid., 275.
51 Ibid., 272, 283.
52 Ibid., 272, 275.
53 "Anales," 15.
54 Campos, *De Tarija a la Asunción*, 276–81.
55 Ibid., 279.
56 Colonia Crevaux was called Teyu by the Tobas and was where the French explorer Jules Crevaux was murdered by the Tobas in 1882 with all but one of his expedition.
57 See Eulogio Raña to Giannecchini, Caiza, 4 August 1883, p. 26, "Libro 2°," AFT; No. 125, Gumdo. Arancivia to Nazareno Dimeco, Colonia Crevaux, 17

September 1883; No. 126, Raña to Aguairenda missionary, Caiza, 4 October 1883; No. 135, Raña de Fr. Bernardo, Caiza, 31 October 1883; No. 140, Silbestre Araoz to Aguairenda missionary, Caiza, 11 December 1883, "Varíos documentos 1866–1821 relacionados todos con las Misiones," Gaveta 8, AFT. Also see "Anales," 15.

58 Giannecchini to Eulojia Raña, Aguairenda, 13 September 1883, "Libro 2° Copia—Notas," 47, AFT.
59 Campos, *De Tarija a la Asunción*, 271, 273–75. The quotes are on 274.
60 Paz, *De Tarija a la Asunción*. Also see Padilla, *El Pilcomayo*. For a summary of Paz's political career, see B. Trigo, *Tarija*, 2:485–508. In 1889 Paz became prefect of the Tarija department, holding that office until 1892.
61 Thouar, *A través del Gran Chaco*, 250–52.
62 Campos, *De Tarija a la Asunción*, 544; Thouar, *A través del Gran Chaco*, 134, 151, 424.
63 Corrado, *El colegio franciscano*, 473.
64 Giannecchini, *Relación*, 22.
65 See, for example, Langer and Ruiz, *Historia de Tarija*, 225–27, 249–50, 252–54, 367–70.
66 Interestingly, the Tobas were an important labor force on the northern Argentine sugar plantations, though they did not have the same prestige as laborers as the Chiriguanos. Nevertheless, they worked hard on the plantations and often were obligated by the Argentine Army to go to the plantations. For a new view of the Tobas of this phenomenon, see Gordillo, *Landscapes of Devils*, especially 103–66.
67 See Langer, *Economic Change*, 132–37.
68 Martarelli, *El Colegio Franciscano*, 260–87.
69 See Langer, "Mission Land Tenure"; Condarco Morales, *Aniceto Arce*, 673–74. According to Condarco, his donation was not completely voluntary, but he did accept this transfer of land.
70 Archivo Judicial de Monteagudo, 1897: n.n., f. 40.
71 Condarco Morales, *Aniceto Arce*, 648–752. The liberals even mounted a coup attempt in 1888 and almost had Arce assassinated.
72 This was published in 1889 as Paz, *De Asunción*.
73 For information on Jofré's father and the merchant company he founded, Jofré é Hijos, see Langer and Hames, "Commerce and Credit." For Jofré, see B. Trigo, *Tarija*, 2:537–49.
74 Jofré, *Colonias y misiones*.
75 Ibid., 5, 24, 40, 46, 23.
76 Ibid., 24. Also see 25, 96.
77 Ibid., 52.
78 Ibid., 53, 98–99.
79 See his strong defenses of the mission system in his *Informes prefecturales*

for Tarija in 1892, 1893, and 1894, ABNB. For a brief political biography of Domingo Paz, see B. Trigo, *Tarija*, 2:509-35. Domingo Paz was the brother of Luis Paz.

80 Fifer, *Land, Location and Power in Bolivia*.
81 See Bolivia, *Anuario 1900*, 74, 559. According to the law, the municipalities set the date, but the missionaries were to "execute" the order.
82 Bolivia, *Anuario 1901*, 223-29.
83 García Jordán, *Cruz y arado*, 393-94.
84 "Memorias del p. Bernardino de Nino Prefecto de Misiones desde año del Señor 1903," 27 April 1903, AFT.
85 "Memorias del P. Bernardino de Nino," 11 September and 15 November 1903.
86 Rosendo R. Rojas, *Informe del Prefecto y Comandante General Coronel Rosendo R. Rojas. En la gestión de 1904* (Santa Cruz: Tip. de "La Ley," 1905), 21-22.
87 "Reglamento de Misiones," in Bolivia, *Anuario 1905*, 598-603.
88 Bolivia, *Anuario 1905*, 598-600.
89 García Jordán, *Cruz y arado*, 397-402.
90 Fr. Benevenuto Boccaccini to Fr. Santiago Romano, Itau, 2 March 1907, no. 20, Gaveta 15, AFT.
91 "Anales de este Colegio Franciscano de Tarija desde el año 1879. Libro Primero," p. 347, AFT.
92 "Testimonio de la demanda entablada por el R.P. Fr. Romulado Dambrogi, contra Fortunato y Porfirio Aramayo pidiendo la desocupación del terrreno de Tatúcua en favor de la Misión de Santa Rosa. Año 1906," "Títulos de la Misión de Santa Rosa," AVAChC.
93 Bernardino de Nino to Ministro de Guerra y Colonización, Santa Rosa, 27 December 1914, "Títulos," AVAChC. There were more attempts to appropriate Curuyuqui in 1921 and 1926.
94 Anonymous, *Las industrias del Gran Chaco*.
95 See Romano de Ministro de Culto, Tarairí, 14 September 1905; Romano to Ministro de Colonias y Agricultura, San Antonio, 23 December 1905; Romano to Guardián y V. Drio. del Colegio Apostólico de Tarija, 14 September 1905, all in M-329, AFT.
96 See de Nino, *Misiones Franciscanas*, 170-285.
97 Francisco Cayola to Santiago Romano, Tarija, 17 November 1907, Gaveta 15, AFT.
98 See Dionisio Polverini to Prefect of Mission, Tiguipa, 31 August 1906; Polverini to Prefect, September 1906; Polverini to Prefect, 23 November 1906; Gabriel Tommasini to Romano, Tarairí, 14 September 1906; Domingo Ficosecco to Romano, Macharetí, 22 November 1906; Ficosecco to Romano, Macharetí, 18 January 1907, all Gaveta 15, AFT.
99 Tommasini to Romano, Tarairí, 24 November 1906, p. 2, Gaveta 15, AFT.

100 L. Trigo, "Informe presentado," 5:387–444; Anonymous, *Las industrias del Gran Chaco*.

101 See, for example, Mission Prefect to Minister of Colonization, Tarairí, 3 June 1907, 10, M 331, AFT. Indeed, when Leocadio Trigo took over San Francisco and San Antonio in 1905 to found Villamontes, Mandeponay was in Argentina with his men.

102 See "Copia: Juzgado Rural del Canton Yhancaroinza, April 31, 1904"; "Deposición de Mandeponai 1904"; Néstor Gambarte, Fiscalía de Partido Provincia del Azero, to Padre German de Macharetí, Monteagudo, 12 June 1902, all in Gaveta 8; Romano to Ministro de Colonización, Tarairí, 3 June 1907, f. 11. M-331, AFT. Also see Langer, "Mandeponay."

103 The friars' complaints about the lack of discipline among the Indians multiplied after 1905. See, for example, p. Polverini to Mission Prefect [?], no. 20, and Fr. Francisco Francocci to Prefecto de Misiones, Aguairenda, 4 February 1908, Gaveta 15, AFT.

104 Tommassini to Romano, Tarairí, 1 August 1906 and 18 August 1906, Gaveta 15, AFT. The quote comes from the 1 August letter.

105 Mission Prefect to Minister of Colonization, Tarairí, 8 June 1907, 8–9, M 331, AFT. Also see *Boletín Antoniano* 12, no. 138 (30 January 1908): 2.

106 Eliodoro Villazón to Juan Argentini, La Paz, 2 January 1912, 2, Gaveta 6, AFT.

107 Ibid., 3.

108 Oscar Mariaca Pando to Minister of War, Caiza, 29 September 1920, "Copiador 6 de Julio, 1920–4 de Febrero, 1921," 122–23; Oscar Mariaca Sanz to Minister of War and Colonization, Fortín Ballivián, 21 May 1923, 119, and 4 July 1923, 222–23; Plácido Sanchez to Minister of War and Colonization, Villamontes, 10 July 1928, 12, all in ACCVM. It is not clear who received the rental income.

109 "Censo general del los habitantes existentes en 'El Palmar' (copia)," Ministerio de Colonización y Agricultura, Gaveta 8, AFT.

110 "Censo general." Four del Castillos — Pedro, Antonio, Samuel, and Octavio — signed the petition. Santos Tarupayo, a Chiriguano, was also listed among the petitioners. See fs 3–4.

111 De Nino, *Prosecución*, 171–73. The quotes are from 172.

112 For a history of the Aireyus, see Sanabria, *Apiaguaiqui-Tumpa*, 87–95. Santos Aireyu, mburuvicha of Caipipendi in the mid-twentieth century, was one of Sanabria's primary oral sources for his book. Also see Pifarré, *Los Guaraní-Chiriguano*, 295–97. For a novelistic approach to these relations based on a true story of the Padilla family, see Costa du Rels, *Tierras hechizadas*. Ironically, Padilla probably supplied Chiriguano warriors from Caipipendi as troops to fight on the karais' side in the Huacaya War (1874–1877), which

provided him with a legal basis to request land grants that ended up creating new haciendas on the lands of Huacaya and Ingre Chiriguanos. See Langer, *Economic Change*, 128–31.

113 See Combès, *Etno-historias*.

114 For the best and most elaborate discussion of the Apostolic Vicariate, see García Jordán, *Cruz y arado*, 403–10. The Franciscans created two more Vicariates in Bolivia, one in Beni (1917) and the other in Chiquitos (1927).

115 See García Jordán, *Cruz y arado*, 405 n. 305.

116 Ibid., 407. Also see Bernardino de Nino, "Libro de antecedentes y actas referentes al Vicariato del Gran Chaco," La Paz 19, 9, AVAChC.

117 "Informe de la H. Comisión de Culto al Proyecto No. 172," in de Nino, "Libro de antecedentes," 9–10, AVAChC.

118 I have found only one contract for mission lands prior to 1921, in which in 1905 Bernardino de Nino provides a hundred square meters to Rosario Gonzalez and her sons in Mission Boicovo for free "in view of her continuous service since 1886." See "No. 5 Constancia para Rosario Gonzalez y sus hijos 10 Oct. 1905," in "Boicovo—Manuscritos Varios," APC.

119 "Contrato de Arrendamiento," "Boicovo—Manuscritos Varios," APC.

120 For Mission Boicovo there were a total of thirty-five renters listed for the period 1922–1941. The shortest rental period was one year (four renters) and the longest was sixteen years (1922–1937). See "Arrenderos [Boicovo]," APC.

121 Joaquin Remedi, "Informe Prefectural de Misiones," *El Antoniano* 34, no. 1199 (20 February 1930): 1.

122 "El Teniente Coronel Angel Rodríguez comisionado para estudiar las vías de penetración al Gran Chaco, al Señor Ministro de Guerra," La Paz, 25 May 1927, Correspondencia, Fondo Prefectural, Biblioteca y Fondo Documental de la Universidad Mayor y Pontificia de San Francisco Xavier, as reproduced in Langer and Ruiz, *Historia de Tarija*, 79.

123 See F. César Vigiani, Vicario Aptco., to Sr. Oficial Mayor de Colinas, Cuevo, 20 December 1929, in *El Antoniano* 35, no. 1191 (21 January 1930): 2; "El Delegado Nacional en el Gran Chaco declara que el Corregidor Ramon Marás, de Ñancaroinza, es persona honorable," *El Diario* 26, no. 8257 (8 December 1929): 12.

124 "Los blancos salvajes," *El Antoniano* 35, no. 1191 (21 January 1930): 1.

125 Hernando Siles, *Memoria de Guerra y Colonización 1922* (La Paz: N.p., 1922), 67.

126 Víctor Navajas Trigo, *Informe presentado a la consideración del Supremo Gobierno por el ciudadano Víctor Navajas Trigo Prefecto y Comandante General del Departamento de Tarija* (Tarija: Imprenta La Velocidad, 1923), 69.

127 J. A. Gutiérrez, *Delegación del Gran Chaco*. The quotes are from 28, 69, and 70.

128 To Minister of War and Colonization, Villa Montes, 6 May 1928, "Copiador 27," 345, ACCVM. The letter is not signed but probably was written by Plácido Sánchez.

129 Indeed, by the late 1920s most of the Toba bands had moved into Argentine territory, where the Argentine military forced them to work in the sugarcane plantations of Jujuy. See Conti, Lagos, and Lagos, "Mano de obra"; Carrera, "La violencia"; Gordillo, *Landscapes of Devils*.

130 Héctor Suárez, *Memoria de Guerra y Colonizacin 1928* (La Paz: Imprenta Intendencia de Guerra, 1928), 147; Krieg, *Indianerland*, 108–12.

131 There is much written about the failure of the Murray colony. See, for example, J. A. Gutiérrez, *Delegación del Gran Chaco*, 61–62; A. Melan, *Memoria de Guerra y Colonización 1927* (La Paz: Imprenta Intendencia de Guerra, 1927), 122–126, AVAChC.

132 To Minister of War and Colonization, Villa Montes, 6 May 1928, "Copiador 27," 333–35, ACCVM.

133 *Boletín Antoniano* 16, no. 303 (7 September 1912): 1–4, and "Suplemento," 1–3.

134 Ibid., 331–33. The quote is from 331.

135 Mons. Ulivelli to Mandeponai, Capitán de los indios infieles de Macharetí y de las demás tribus del Chaco, 10 October 1920, "Macharetí Defunciones II 1916," 58.

136 Copies of telegrams from S. L. Ballesteros, Oficial Mayor de Colonias, La Paz, 2 and 4 December 1929, Ministerio de Guerra y Colonización.

137 "De misiones," César Vigiani to Minister of War and Colonization, Cuevo, 28 January 1930, in *El Antoniano* 34, no. 1204 (13 March 1930), 4:2–3.

138 Ibid., 4:2.

139 Ibid., 1:1.

140 "La secularización de las misiones," *El Antoniano* 34, no. 1216 (24 April 1930): 1. The largest missions, Macharetí and Santa Rosa, were to provide 500 hectares of agricultural land and 2,500 hectares of pasture each to the mission inhabitants. Tarairí's, Tiguipa's, and Boicovo's Indians were to keep 60 hectares of farmland and 300 hectares of pasture, and Ivo's 400 hectares of farmland and 1,600 hectares of pasture.

141 Klein, *Parties and Political Change*, 88–94.

142 See José L. Lanza, *Memoria de Guerra y Colonización, 1930–31* (La Paz: N.p., 1931), 135–40. Characteristic of this ambivalence, the minister of colonization in his report asserted, p. 136, "The missions should be secularized, but in return a new entity should be established, called to make them progress or at least conserve them in the state they are in."

143 "Tres indios chiriguanos se encuentran en La Paz," *La Razón*, 12 April 1931, 1. Also see "Los Chiriguanos de Macharetí," *Los Principios* 1, no. 59 (15 April 1931): 1.

144   César Vigiani, "La famosa misión de 3 neófitos de Macharetí a la ciudad de La Paz: Confutación y rectificaciones necesarias," *El Antoniano* 35, no. 1300 (2 June 1931): 1–2.

CHAPTER EIGHT   *From the Chaco War to Secularization*

1   Indeed, the amount of historical documentation declined precipitously for the missions with the establishment of the Apostolic Vicariate in 1919.
2   Before 1905 there were twice as many missions as in 1930.
3   Only 13 percent of the mission population was enrolled in schools on the Tarija-based missions (Tarairí, Tiguipa, and Macharetí), whereas 21 percent was enrolled in the missions run by the Potosí convent.
4   "Informe de la Prefectura de Misiones del Colegio de Potosí," *El Antoniano* 34, no. 1204 (13 March 1930), 2:2.
5   Vigiani, "La famosa misión," *El Antoniano* 35, no. 1300 (2 June 1931): 2.
6   Klein, *Parties and Political Change*, 134.
7   "La colonización efectiva del Chaco en la única solución que librará al país de transcendentales problemas," *El Diario* 28, no. 3900 (14 February 1932): 7.
8   Prudencio Bustillo, *De Sucre a Santa Cruz por Tarija y el Chaco*, 41, as cited in Pifarré, *Los Guaraní-Chiriguano*, 405.
9   "El abandono en que se halla el pueblo fronterizo de Yacuiba," *El Diario* 28, no. 3900 (14 February 1932): 12.
10 A good summary from the Bolivian side is Moscoso, *Recuerdos* 1:1–147.
11 For the best political summary of the Chaco War on the Bolivian side, see Klein, *Parties and Political Change*, 114–98.
12 Many works have been written about the Chaco War from both sides. Some important works are Querejazu Calvo, *Masamaclay*; Casabianca, *Una guerra desconocida*; and Farcau, *The Chaco War*.
13 See, for example, Campero Prudencio, *Bolivia*, 307.
14 For the quote, see Ynsfran, *The Epic of the Chaco*, 192. Also see Combès, *Etnohistorias*, 286–90; Schuchard, "La conquista de la tierra," 448–53. Also see the brief note in Querejazu, *Masamaclay*, 421–22, who accuses the Isoceños of fraternizing with the Paraguayans and giving away Bolivian positions, making possible the capture of Charagua. Some also apparently voluntarily joined in the retreat from the Parapetí region. See Ynsfran, *The Epic of the Chaco*, 206.
15 See, for example, Maldini, *Franciscanos en Tarija*, 160.
16 Vidaurre, *Los indomables*, 186. Also see Maldini, *Franciscanos en Tarija*, 162.
17 Ynsfran, *The Epic of the Chaco*, 194–96.
18 Casabianca, *Una guerra desconocida*, 6–7, 403.
19 See, for example, Arze Aguirre, *Guerra y conflictos sociales*, 182, 225.

20 Maldini, *Franciscanos en Tarija*, 162.
21 Interview with Gerónimo Cundeye, Macharetí, 21 June 1990 (Cundeye is the nephew of Ubaldino Cundeye); interview with Obedelia Pintos de Hurtado, Charagua, 16 June 1990 (Pintos lived with the sister of Napoleón Tacu before the war). Also see Maldini, *Franciscanos en Tarija*, 162–63.
22 "Padrón general de la Misión de San Pascual de Boicovo Año de 1927," 1935, APC.
23 Maldini, *Franciscanos en Tarija*, 163.
24 "Tcnl. Amadeo Ballón Jefe de los Servicios del Ejército en Villa Mnotes [sic]," personal archive of Magalí de Matsusaki, Macharetí.
25 Interview with Gerónimo Cundeye.
26 "El Teniente Coronel Arturo Mendivil M., Intendente de Colonización del Chaco," Villamontes, 30 January 1938, Archive of Magalí de Matsusaki.
27 Interview with Obedelia Pintos de Hurtado. Also see Maldini, *Franciscanos en Tarija*, 155.
28 April 1940, "Libro 1° de Hacienda 1869" [Macharetí], APM.
29 Marcos Orsetti to Mons. Federico Lunardi, Apostolic Nuncio, Santa Rosa Mission, 10 December 1937, "Misc. 1923–1949," AVACHC.
30 Ibid.
31 "Reglamento de Misiones," "Misc." 1923–1949, Articles 1–14, AVACHC.
32 Ibid., Articles 17–21.
33 See García Jordán, *Cruz y arado*, 445–46.
34 A similar argument has been made for the interest of the nineteenth-century Bolivian state in maintaining the Indian communities in the highlands, for there the communities provided the state coffers with vital tribute income and thus the state generally defended the integrity of the communities, until the silver boom in the second half of the nineteenth century obviated the need for tribute revenue. See Sánchez, *Indios y tributarios*, 187–218.
35 Marcos Orsetti to Minister of Colonization, Santa Rosa, 23 April 1938, "Misc. 1923–1949," AVACHC.
36 Ildefonso Iraseo, Carlos Chituri, Celso Orosco, and "Conversor" to Colonel Antezana, 7 March 1945, "Misc. 1923–1949," AVACHC.
37 See, for example, Gregorio Furlanetto to Ministro de Agricultura y Colonización, Santa Rosa, 5 August 1943 and May 1945; Furlanetto to Minister of Justice, Santa Rosa, 13 October 1945, all "Misc. 1923–1949," AVACHC.
38 Furlanetto to Manuel Gomez, Santa Rosa, 24 November 1942 and Gomez to Furlanetto, Cuevo, 29 November 1942, all "Misc. 1923–1949," AVACHC. Earlier, only officials such as Daniel Campos in the 1880s and Leocadio Trigo in the early twentieth century would have dared to insult the friars in this way.
39 "Nómina de los havitantes de la ex Misión San Pascual de Boicovo, mayores de 15 años que no saven firmar" (1949), AVACHC. Not all those with Spanish surnames necessarily were non-Indians, though at this time few but the

chiefs had adopted Spanish names, so it is likely that most were in fact non-Indians.
40 "Testimonio que franquea . . . ," fs. 1v–2v, AVAChC.
41 Ibid., fs. 3, 3v.
42 The original name in Spanish is Sociedad Agrícola Ganadera de Pequeños Propietarios.
43 "Libro de Minutas," 1–93, Archivo de la Sociedad de Agricultores y Ganaderos de Pequeños Propietarios de Macharetí. My thanks to José Barrancos, who as secretary of the ARSSP kindly permitted me to consult the minutes of the organization's meetings.
44 "Los suscritos Ranulfo Molloja Hoyos, Alcalde Municipal de Villa Montes y Coronel Arturo Soruco, Comandante Accidental del Comando de la Tercera División de Ejército," Villamontes, 6 June 1957, Archive of Magalí de Matsusaki, Macharetí.
45 Interview with Fr. Gerardo Maldini, Tarija, 12 July 1990.
46 Interview with Juan David Avenante, Tarairí, 21 June 1990. Juan David is the grandson of Fernando and, when I spoke to him, was also vice president of the ARSSP.
47 Interview with Juan Acosta, Ivo, 19 June 1990. Acosta was born in 1921 and lived in the region all his life.
48 Interview with Alfredo Sánchez, Ivo, 18 June 1990.
49 Interview with Gerardo Maldini, Tarija, 12 July 1990.
50 Healy, *Caciques y patrones*, 35–85.
51 Personal communication, Fr. Gerardo Maldini, Tarija, 12 July 1990. Later this rancher rented the same land and became president of the ARSSP of Santa Rosa. He then appropriated the land for himself anyway.
52 Cundeye's birth date is recorded in his identity papers as 9 November 1878.

CHAPTER NINE *Comparisons*

1 See, for example, Jackson, *From Savages to Subjects*; Rausch, *Colombia*, 9.
2 The establishment of Protestant missionaries in the late nineteenth century deeply preoccupied the Catholic Church. Its hierarchy began to revive its own missionary enterprise throughout the world partially in response to the perceived Protestant threat. Missions received a new impetus under Pope Leo XIII (1878–1903). See A. Gill, *Rendering unto Caesar*, especially chapter 4. Also see García Jordán, *Cruz y arado*, 203.
3 For the Peruvian case, see García Jordán, *Cruz y arado*.
4 See Langer and Jackson, "Colonial and Republican Missions."
5 There are a host of studies on the demographic impact of the missions on indigenous populations. See Jackson, *Indian Population Decline*; Reff, *Disease, Depopulation*.

6 See Jackson, "Demographic Patterns"; Ganson, *The Guaraní*, 52–56.
7 Jackson, *Indian Population Decline*, 125–27.
8 David Sweet makes this point in "The Ibero-American Frontier Mission," 1–48.
9 Saeger, *The Chaco Mission Frontier*, 37.
10 See Langer and Jackson, "Colonial and Republican Missions," 297–98.
11 See Hausberger, *Für Gott und König*, 70.
12 Race mixture was mainly through female Indian servitude in mestizo and Creole households, often through coercive sex by male members of the household. Also, the Chiriguanos in colonial times and perhaps in the early nineteenth century raided mestizo settlements and adopted women and children they had taken into their villages. Isabelle Combès and Thierry Saignes have asserted that the Chiriguano ethnic identity is closely tied to mestization, albeit from the initial contact of Guaraní invaders with the Chané. See Saignes and Combès, *Alter Ego*.
13 Some of the best work on this comes from the Maya field, in particular Clendinnen, *Ambivalent Conquests*, and Farriss, *Maya Society*. Thomas Abercrombie, in *Pathways of Memory and Power* on the Aymara, has also influenced my understanding of this issue.
14 See Ganson, *The Guaraní*, 52–84, for a good recent summary of the Guaraní. For Mojos, see Block, *Mission Culture*. Evelyn Hu-DeHart argues that the Yaquis also acculturated in constructive ways, creating a new hybrid culture that survived past the mission experience. See her *Missionaries, Miners, and Indians*. Interestingly, all of the most "successful" missions in these terms were Jesuit.
15 Steven Hackel argues that in Monterey mission in California there was much more give-and-take than previously recognized. See his *Children of Coyote*.
16 For a good summary of the Jesuit missions in northern New Spain, see Hausberger, *Für Gott und König*. A marvelous summary of acculturation for Mexico now under U.S. jurisdiction is Vecsey, *On the Padres' Trail*. For Florida, see Hoffman, *Florida's Frontiers*. For Peru, there has been no good "new" mission history written to include the Indians. For comments and a bibliography, see A. C. Taylor, "The Western Margins," 252–53. For the Chaco, see Saeger, *The Chaco Mission Frontier*.
17 For Brazil, see Kiemen, *The Indian Policy*; Alden, "Black Robes versus White Settlers," 19–45; Hemming, *Red Gold*, 419–26.
18 K. L. Jones, "Warfare, Reorganization," 160. For Chile, see Foerster, *Jesuitas y Mapuches*. The exception appears to have been the island of Chiloé. See Urbina Burgos, *Las misiones franciscanas*. For the Guajira Peninsula, see Grahn, "Guajiro Cultura," 130–56.
19 Vecsey, *On the Padres' Trail*, 123–206 is most eloquent on this.
20 Saeger, *The Chaco Mission Frontier*; Deeds, *Defiance and Deference*.

21 Deeds, *Defiance and Deference*.
22 There were exceptions, but Barbara Ganson shows that even when colonial authorities required large numbers of mission Indians for outside work, the Jesuits were able to control the number of men and the time spent on these projects. See Ganson, *The Guaraní*, 49, 62–65.
23 Hackel, *Children of Coyote*.
24 See, for example, Radding, *Landscapes of Power and Memory*; Hackel, *Children of Coyote*; and Galgano, *Feast of Souls*, 105.
25 Deeds, "Indigenous Rebellions." These later types of power struggles could be quite important as well, such as those analyzed by Scott, *Weapons of the Weak*.
26 In the short-lived Franciscan missions in Argentina among the Tobas and Matacos, the missionaries were much more prone to provide the plantations with mission workers. See Langer, "Liberal Policy"; Teruel, *Misiones*. In turn, the plantation owners brought in Methodist missionaries from Britain to establish missions among the Tobas in the early twentieth century in a deliberate policy of creating labor reserves for the ingenios. See Gordillo, *Landscapes of Devils*, 72–75. Marcela Mendoza reconstructs patterns of migration among one Chaco people in "The Western Toba." In the Chaco temporary missions also occurred in the colonial period, though among semisedentary peoples. See Saeger, *The Chaco Mission Frontier*.
27 See, for example, Albó, *Los Guaraní-Chiriguano*, 363–404.
28 García Jordán, *Cruz y arado*, 17.
29 See chapter 2.
30 See Lofstrom, *La presidencia de Sucre*, 371–519, and Sánchez Albornoz, *Indios y tributos*, 187–94.
31 See Irurozqui Victoriano, *A bala, piedra y palo*, 143–78, and Larson, *Trials of Nation Making*, 202–53.
32 The literature on this topic is too vast to cite completely. Influential works include Mallon, *Peasant and Nation*; Grandin, *The Blood of Guatemala*; and Méndez, *The Plebeian Republic*.
33 See Whiteford, *Workers from the North*, and Rutledge, "Plantations and Peasants."
34 The best explanation of this process is Stern, *Peru's Indian Peoples*, 114–37.
35 That is not to say that there hadn't been contacts before. Local representatives consulted with Mandeponay, such as during the 1883 expedition to Paraguay and the 1892 rebellion. Mandeponay's brother Cundeye also famously visited President Gregorio Pacheco in Sucre in the 1880s. But they did not insist on their rights as citizens, but as leaders of mission Indians under the tutelage of the friars.
36 "Remachando el clavo," *El Antoniano* 35, no. 1297 (12 May 1931): 1.

BIBLIOGRAPHY

ARCHIVAL SOURCES

Public Archives
Archivo y Biblioteca Nacionales de Bolivia (ABNB)
    Colección Rück
    Correspondencia Oficial
        Ministerio de Guerra (MG)
        Ministerio de Hacienda (MH)
        Ministerio del Interior (MI)
    Tribunal Nacional de Cuentas
Archivo de la Casa de Cultura de Villa Montes (ACCVM)
Archivo Franciscano de Potosí (AFP)
Archivo Franciscano de Tarija (AFT)
Archivo Judicial de Monteagudo
Archivo Judicial de Partido de Entre Ríos (AJPER)
Archivo Parroquial de Cuevo (APC)
Archivo Parroquial de Lagunillas
Archivo Parroquial de Macharetí (APM)
Archivo de la Sociedad de Agricultores y Ganaderos de Pequeños Propietarios de Macharetí (ARSSP)
Archivo del Vicariato Apostólico del Chaco, Camiri (AVAChC)
Biblioteca y Fondo Documental de la Universidad Mayor y Pontificia de San Francisco Xavier (Sucre)
Fondo Prefectural
Notaría de Hacienda y Minas (NHM)
Tesoro Departamental

Private Archives
Archive of Eduardo Trigo O'Connor D'Arlach, Tarija
Archive of Magalí de Matsusaki, Macharetí

INTERVIEWS

Acosta, Juan. Interview with author. Ivo, 19 June 1990.
Avenante, Juan David. Interview with author. Tarairí, 21 June 1990.
Cundeye, Gerónimo. Interview with author. Macharetí, 21 June 1990.
Hurtado, Obedelia Pintos de. Interview with author. Charagua, 16 June 1990.
Maldini, Fr. Gerardo. Interview with author. Tarija, 12 July 1990.
Sánchez, Alfredo. Interview with author. Ivo, 18 June 1990.

NEWSPAPERS

Boletín Antoniano (Tarija)
El Antoniano (Tarija)
El Diario (La Paz)
La Razón (La Paz)
Los Principios (La Paz)

BOOKS AND JOURNAL ARTICLES

Abercrombie, Thomas A. *Pathways of Memory and Power: Ethnography and History Among an Andean People*. Madison: University of Wisconsin Press, 1998.
Albó, Xavier. *Los Guaraní-Chiriguano: La comunidad hoy*. La Paz: CIPCA, 1990.
———. "¡Ofadifa Ofaifa! Un pentecostés chiriguano." In *Chiriguano: Pueblos Indígenas de las tierras bajas de Bolivia 3*. Edited by Jürgen Riester. Santa Cruz, Bolivia: APCOB, 1995.
Alden, Dauril. "Black Robes versus White Settlers: The Struggle for 'Freedom of the Indians' in Colonial Brazil." In *Attitudes of Colonial Powers toward the American Indian*. Edited by Howard Peckham and Charles Gibson. Salt Lake City: University of Utah Press, 1969.
Alvarsson, Jan-Åke. "El humanitarismo de Nordenskiöld." In *Erland Nordenskiöld: Investigador y amigo del indígena*. Edited by Jan-Åke Alvarsson and Oscar Agüero. Quito: Abya-Yala, 1997.
———. *The Mataco of the Gran Chaco: An Ethnographic Account of Change and Continuity in Mataco Socio-Economic Organization*. Uppsala, Sweden: Alqvist and Wiksell International, 1988.
Anasagasti, Pedro de. *Franciscanos en Bolivia*. La Paz: Don Bosco, 1992.
Aranzaes, Nicanor. *Las revoluciones en Bolivia*. La Paz: Editora Urquizo, 1980. (Orig. pub. 1918.)
Arguedas, Alcides. *Pueblo enfermo: Contribución a la psicología de los pueblos hispanoamericanos*. Barcelona: Vda. De Louis Tasso, 1909.
Arze Aguirre, René Danilo. *Guerra y conflictos sociales: El caso rural boliviano durante la campaña del Chaco*. La Paz: CERES, 1987.

Atkin, Nicholas, and Frank Tallett. *Priests, Prelates and People: A History of European Catholicism Since 1750*. Oxford: Oxford University Press, 2003.

Axtell, James. *The Invasion Within: The Contest of Cultures in Colonial North America*. New York: Oxford University Press, 1985.

Bannon, John F., ed. *Bolton and the Spanish Borderlands*. Norman: University of Oklahoma Press, 1964.

Bayly, Christopher Alan. *The Birth of the Modern World, 1780–1914: Global Connections and Comparisons*. Oxford: Blackwell, 2004.

Bell, Rudolph M. *Fate and Honor, Family and Village: Demographic and Cultural Change in Rural Italy Since 1800*. Chicago: University of Chicago Press, 1979.

Bellò, Carlo. "Monsignor Bonomelli e l'unità politica e religiosa degli italiani." *Civitas* 41, no. 5 (1990): 21–35.

Berkhofer, Robert F., Jr. *The White Man's Indian: Images of the American Indian from Columbus to the Present*. New York: Vintage Books, 1979.

Bialet y Massé, Juan. *El estado de las clases obreras argentinas a comienzos del siglo*. Córdoba: Universidad Nacional de Córdoba, 1968. (Orig. pub. 1904.)

Block, David. *Mission Culture on the Upper Amazon: Native Tradition, Jesuit Enterprise, and Secular Policy in Moxos, 1660–1880*. Lincoln: University of Nebraska Press, 1994.

Bolivia. *Anuario de leyes, decretos, resoluciones y ordenes supremas año 1905*. La Paz: Tipografía Artística de Castillo, 1906.

———. *Anuario de leyes, decretos, resoluciones y resoluciones supremas: Año de 1901*. La Paz: Imp. Y Lit Paceña, 1902.

———. *Anuario de supremas disposiciones de 1871*. La Paz: Imprenta de la Unión Americana, 1872.

———. *Censo de la población de la República de Bolivia según el empadronamiento de 1 de septiembre de 1900*. 2nd ed. 2 vols. Cochabamba: Editorial Inca, 1973.

———. *Colección oficial de leyes, decretos, órdenes resoluciones, &c. que se han expedido para el regimen de la República Boliviana*. Vol. 2. La Paz: Imprenta del Colegio de Artes, 1834.

———. *Redactor de la Asamblea Constituyente del año 1871*. La Paz: Litografía y Imprentas Unidas, 1927.

Bolton, Herbert E. "The Mission as a Frontier Institution in the Spanish-American Colonies." *American Historical Review* 23 (1917): 42–61.

Brooks, James. *Captives and Cousins: Slavery, Kinship, and Community in the Southwest Borderlands*. Chapel Hill: University of North Carolina Press, 2002.

Calzavarini, Lorenzo. *Nación chiriguana: Grandeza y ocaso*. Cochabamba, Bolivia: Amigos del Libro, 1980.

Campero Prudencio, Fernando, ed. *Bolivia en el siglo XX: Formación de la Bolivia contemporánea*. La Paz: Harvard Club de Bolivia, 1999.

Campos, Daniel. *De Tarija a la Asunción: Expedición boliviana de 1883. Informe del Doctor Daniel Campos*. Buenos Aires: Imprenta de J. Peuse, 1888.

Cardús, José. *Las misiones franciscanas entre los infieles de Bolivia: Descripción del estado de ellas en 1883 y 1884*. Barcelona: Librería de la Inmaculada Concepción, 1886.

Carrera, Nicolás Iñigo. "Las modalidades de la coacción en el proceso de génesis y formación del proletariado para la industria azucarera del Nordeste argentino (1870–1940)." In *Estudios sobre la historia de la industria azucarera argentina—II*. Edited by Daniel Campi. San Salvador de Jujuy, Argentina: Universidad Nacional de Jujuy and Universidad Nacional de Tucumán, 1992.

———. "La violencia como potencia económica: Chaco 1870–1930." In *Conflictos y procesos de la historia argentina contemporánea*. Buenos Aires: Centro Editor de América Latina, 1988.

Carroll, Michael P. *Madonnas That Maim: Popular Catholicism in Italy Since the Fifteenth Century*. Baltimore: Johns Hopkins University Press, 1992.

Carter, William E., Mauricio Mamani P., José V. Morales, and Philip Parkerson. *Coca in Bolivia*. La Paz: N.p., 1980.

Casabianca, Ange-François. *Una guerra desconocida: La campaña del Chaco Boreal, 1932–1935*. Asunción: Lector, 1999–2000.

Chakrabarty, Dipesh. "Postcoloniality and the Artifice of History: Who Speaks for the 'Indian' Pasts?" *Representations* 37 (1992): 1–26.

Chevalier, François. "Signification sociale de la fondation de Puebla de los Angeles." *Revista de Historia de América* 23 (1947): 105–30.

Christian, William. *Local Religion in Sixteenth-Century Spain*. Princeton, N.J.: Princeton University Press, 1989.

Clastres, Hélène. *The Land-Without-Evil: Tupí-Guaraní Prophetism*. Trans. Jacqueline Grenez Brovender. Urbana: University of Illinois Press, 1995.

Clastres, Pierre. *Society against the State: Essays in Political Anthropology*. Trans. Robert Hurely. Oxford: Mole Editions, 1977.

Clementi, Hebe. *La frontera en América*. 2 vols. Buenos Aires: Editorial Leviatan, 1985.

Clendinnen, Inga. *Ambivalent Conquests: Maya and Spaniard in Yucatan, 1517–1570*. Cambridge: Cambridge University Press, 1987.

Cobo, Bernabé. *History of the Inca Empire*. Trans. and edited by Roland Hamilton. Austin: University of Texas Press, 1979.

Comajuncosa, Antonio. *El colegio franciscano de Tarija y sus misiones*. 2nd ed. Vol. 1. Tarija, Bolivia: Editorial Offset Franciscana, 1990.

Combès, Isabelle. "Las batallas de Kuruyuki: Variaciones sobre una derrota chiriguanas." *Bulletin de l'Institut d'Études Andines* 34, no. 2 (2005): 221–33.

———. *Etno-historias del Isoso: Chané y chiriguanos en el Chaco boliviano (Siglos XVI–XX)*. La Paz: Fundación PIEB, 2005.

———. "Nominales pero atrevidos: Capitanes chiriguanos aliados en el Chaco boliviano (Siglo XIX)." *Indiana* 22 (2005): 129–45.

Condarco Morales, Ramiro. *Aniceto Arce: Artífice de la extensión de la revolución industrial en Bolivia*. La Paz: Editorial "Amerindia," 1985.

Conti, Viviana E., Ana T. Lagos, and Marcelo A. Lagos. "Mano de obra indígena en los ingenios de Jujuy a principios de siglo." In *Conflictos y procesos de la historia argentina contemporánea*. Buenos Aires: Centro Editor de América Latina, 1988.

Contreras, Manuel E. "Reformas y desafíos de la Educación." In *Bolivia en el siglo XX: La formación de la Bolivia contemporánea*. Edited by Fernando Campero Prudencio. La Paz: Harvard Club de Bolivia, 1999.

Cook, Sherburne F. *The Conflict between the California Indian and White Civilization*. Berkeley: University of California Press, 1976.

———. *The Population of the California Indians 1769–1970*. Berkeley: University of California Press, 1976.

———. *Population Trends among California Mission Indians*. Berkeley: University of California Press, 1940.

Cook, Sherburne F., and Woodrow Borah. *Essays in Population History*. 3 vols. Berkeley: University of California Press, 1971.

Coppa, Frank J. "From Cholera to Earthquake: The Transition from Destra to Sinistra Viewed from the Vatican." *Italian Quarterly* 23, no. 90 (1982): 81–90.

Corrado, Alejandro María. *El colegio franciscano de Tarija y sus misiones*. 2nd ed. Vol. 2. Tarija, Bolivia: Editorial Offset Franciscana, 1990. (Orig. pub. 1884.)

Costa du Rels, Adolfo. *Tierras hechizadas*. La Paz: Amigos del Libro, 1980.

Cummins, Victoria H., and Light T. Cummins. "Building on Bolton: The Spanish Borderlands Seventy-Five Years Later." *Latin American Research Review* 35, no. 2 (2000): 230–43.

Cushner, Nicholas. *Lords of the Land: Sugar, Wine, and Jesuit Estates of Coastal Peru, 1600–1767*. Albany: State University of New York Press, 1980.

Dalence, José María. *Bosquejo estadístico de Bolivia*. La Paz: UMSA, 1975. (Orig. pub. 1846.)

De la Cadena, Marisol. *Indigenous Mestizos: The Politics of Race and Culture in Cuzco, Peru, 1919–1991*. Durham, N.C.: Duke University Press, 2000.

De Nino, Bernardino. *Etnografía chiriguana*. La Paz: Ismael Argote, 1912.

———. *Misiones Franciscanas del Colegio de Propoganda de Potosí*. La Paz: Establecimiento Tipo-Litográfico "Marinoni," 1918.

———. *Prosecución de la Historia del Colegio de Potosí y sus Misiones*. La Paz: Talleres Gráficos Marinoni, 1918.

Dean, Warren. *Brazil and the Struggle for Rubber: A Study in Environmental History*. Cambridge: Cambridge University Press, 1987.

———. *With Broadax and Firebrand: The Destruction of the Brazilian Atlantic Forest*. Berkeley: University of California Press, 1995.

Deeds, Susan M. *Defiance and Deference in Mexico's Colonial North: Indians under Spanish Rule in Nueva Vizcaya*. Austin: University of Texas Press, 2003.

———. "Indigenous Rebellions on the Northern Mexican Mission Frontier: From First-Generation to Later Colonial Responses." In *Contested Ground: Comparative Frontiers on the Northern and Southern Edges of the Spanish Empire*. Edited by Donna Guy and Thomas Sheridan. Tucson: University of Arizona Press, 1998.

Del Pace, Bernardino. "Ambientación histórica." In *Historia de las misiones franciscanas de Tarija entre Chiriguanos*. Edited by Manuel Mingo de la Concepción. 2 vols. Tarija, Bolivia: Universidad "Juan Misael Saracho," 1981.

Demelas, Marie-Danièle. "Darwinismo a la criolla: El Darwinismo social en Bolivia, 1880-1910." *Historia Boliviana* 1, no. 2 (1981): 55–82.

Dummond, Don E. *The Machete and the Cross: Campesino Rebellion in Yucatán*. Lincoln: University of Nebraska Press, 1997.

Farcau, Bruce W. *The Chaco War: Bolivia and Paraguay, 1932–1935*. Westport, Conn.: Praeger, 1996.

Farnsworth, Paul, and Robert H. Jackson. "Cultural, Economic, and Demographic Change in the Missions in Alta California: The Case of Nuestra Señora de la Soledad." In *The New Latin American Mission History*. Edited by Erick D. Langer and Robert H. Jackson. Lincoln: University of Nebraska Press, 1995.

Farriss, Nancy M. *Maya Society under Colonial Rule: The Collective Enterprise of Survival*. Princeton, N.J.: Princeton University Press, 1984.

Ferguson, R. Brian, and Neil L. Whitehead, eds. *War in the Tribal Zone: Expanding States and Indigenous Warfare*. Santa Fe, N.M.: School of American Research Press, 1992.

Fifer, J. Valerie. *Bolivia: Land, Location and Power since 1825*. Cambridge: Cambridge University Press, 1972.

Foerster, Rolf. *Jesuitas y Mapuches 1593–1767*. Santiago: Editorial Universitaria, 1996.

Galgano, Robert C. *Feast of Souls: Indians and Spaniards in the Seventeenth-Century Missions of Florida and New Mexico*. Albuquerque: University of New Mexico Press, 2005.

Ganson, Barbara. *The Guaraní under Spanish Rule in the Río de la Plata*. Stanford, Calif.: Stanford University Press, 2003.

García Jordán, Pilar. *Cruz y arado, fusiles y discursos: La construcción de los orientes en el Perú y Bolivia 1820–1940*. Lima: Instituto Francés de Estudios Andinos and Instituto de Estudios Peruanos, 2001.

———. "Misiones, fronteras, y nacionalización en la Amazonía Andina: Perú, Ecuador y Bolivia (siglos XIX–XX)." In *La nacionalización de la Amazonía*. Coordinated by Pilar García Jordán and Nura Sala y Vila. Barcelona: Universitat de Barcelona, 1998.

Genovese, Eugene D. *Roll, Jordan, Roll: The World the Slaves Made*. New York: Vintage Books, 1972.

Giannecchini, Doroteo. *Diario de la expedición exploradora boliviana al Alto Paraguay de 1886–1887*. Assisi, Italy: Tipografía de la Porciúncula, 1896.

———. *Historia natural, etnografía, geografía, lingüistica del Chaco boliviano*. Tarija, Bolivia: Fondo de Inversión Social and Centro Eclesial de Documentación, 1996.

———. *Relación de lo obrado por los Padres Misioneros del Colegio de Tarija en las dos expediciones fluvial y terrestre al Pilcomayo*. Tarija, Bolivia: Imprenta El Trabajo, 1883.

Giannecchini, Doroteo, and Vincenzo Mascio. *Album fotográfico de las Misiones Franciscanas en la República de Bolivia a cargo de los Colegios Apostólicos de Tarija y Potosí 1898*. La Paz: Banco Central de Bolivia and Archivo y Biblioteca Nacionales de Bolivia, 1995.

Gill, Anthony. *Rendering unto Caesar: The Catholic Church and the State in Latin America*. Chicago: University of Chicago Press, 1998.

Gill, Lesley. *Precarious Dependencies: Gender, Class and Domestic Service in Bolivia*. New York: Columbia University Press, 1994.

Gordillo, Gastón R. *Landscapes of Devils: Tensions of Place and Memory in the Argentinean Chaco*. Durham, N.C.: Duke University Press, 2005.

Grahn, Lance R. "Guajiro Cultura and Capuchin Evangelization: Missionary Failure on the Riohacha Frontier." In *The New Latin American Mission History*. Edited by Erick D. Langer and Robert H. Jackson. Lincoln: University of Nebraska Press, 1995.

Grandin, Greg. *The Blood of Guatemala: A History of Race and Nation*. Durham, N.C.: Duke University Press, 2000.

Greever, Janet Groff. *José Ballivián y el oriente boliviano*. Trans. José Luis Roca. La Paz: Editorial Siglo, 1987.

Gutiérrez, Julio A. *Delegación del Gran Chaco (Previsiones para su conservación y defensa)*. Santa Cruz, Bolivia: Don Bosco, 1980.

Gutiérrez, Ramón A. *When Jesus Came, the Corn Mothers Went Away: Marriage, Sexuality and Power in New Mexico 1500–1846*. Stanford, Calif.: Stanford University Press, 1991.

Guy, Donna J. *Argentine Sugar Politics: Tucumán and the Generation of Eighty*. Tempe: Arizona State University Press, 1980.

Guy, Donna J., and Thomas Sheridan, eds., *Contested Ground: Comparative Frontiers on the Northern and Southern Edges of the Spanish Empire*. Tucson: University of Arizona Press, 1998.

Hackel, Steven W. *Children of Coyote, Missionaries of St. Francis: Indian-Spanish Relations in Colonial California, 1769–1850*. Chapel Hill: University of North Carolina Press, 2005.

Hames, Gina. "Honor, Alcohol and Sexuality: Women and the Creation of Ethnic Identity in Bolivia, 1870–1930." Ph.D. dissertation, Carnegie Mellon University, 1996.

Hanke, Lewis, ed. *Does the New World Have a Common History? A Critique of the Bolton Thesis.* New York: Knopf, 1964.

Hartch, Todd. *Missionaries of the State: The Summer Institute of Linguistics, State Formation, and Indigenous Mexico, 1935–1985.* Tuscaloosa: University of Alabama Press, 2006.

Hausberger, Bernd. *Für Gott und König: Die Mission der Jesuiten im kolonialen Mexico.* Vienna: Verlag für Geschichte und Politik, 2000.

Healy, Kevin. *Cacique y patrones: Una experiencia de desarrollo rural en el sud de Bolivia.* Cochabamba, Bolivia: El Buitre, 1982.

Hemming, John. *Red Gold: The Conquest of the Brazilian Indians, 1500–1760.* Cambridge, Mass.: Harvard University Press, 1978.

Hennessy, Alistair. *The Frontier in Latin American History.* Albuquerque: University of New Mexico Press, 1978.

Hirsch, Silvia. "Mbaporenda: El lugar donde hay trabajo. Migraciones chiriguanas al Noroeste argentino." Paper presented at the Primer Congreso de Etnohistoria, Buenos Aires, 17–21 July 1989.

Hirsch, Silvia, and Alex Zarzycki. "Ipayareta, imbaekuareta y evangelistas: Cambios y continuidades en la sociedad izoceña." In *Chiriguano: Pueblos Indígenas de las tierras bajas de Bolivia 3.* Edited by Jürgen Riester. Santa Cruz, Bolivia: APCOB, 1995.

Hoffman, Paul E. *Florida's Frontiers.* Bloomington: University of Indiana Press, 2002.

Honour, Hugh. *The New Golden Land: European Images of America from the Discoveries to the Present Time.* New York: Pantheon Books, 1975.

House, Adrian. *Francis of Assisi: A Revolutionary Life.* Mahwah, N.J.: Hidden Spring, 2001.

Hu-DeHart, Evelyn. *Missionaries, Miners and Indians: Spanish Contact with the Yaqui Nation of Northwestern New Spain, 1533–1820.* Tucson: University of Arizona Press, 1981.

Hunt, Lynn, ed., *The New Cultural History: Essays (Studies on the History of Society and Culture).* Berkeley: University of California Press, 1989.

Hvalkof, Soøren, and Peter Aaby, eds. *Is God an American? An Anthropological Perspective on the Missionary Work of the Summer Institute of Linguistics.* Copenhagen: International Work Group for Indigenous Affairs. 1981.

Industrias del Gran Chaco: La empresa colonizadora Staudt y Compañía. Tarija, Bolivia: "La Velocidad" Imprenta de J. Adolfo León, 1912.

Irurozqui Victoriano, Marta. *A bala, piedra y palo: La construcción de la ciudadanía política en Bolivia, 1826–1952.* Seville: Diputación de Sevilla, 2000.

Jackson, Robert H. "Demographic Patterns on a Contested Spanish Colonial Frontier: The Jesuit Missions of Paraguay." Unpublished manuscript, 2007.

———. *From Savages to Subjects: Missions in the History of the American Southwest.* Armonk, N.Y.: M. E. Sharpe, 2000.

———. *Indian Population Decline: The Missions of Northwestern New Spain, 1687-1840*. Albuquerque: University of New Mexico Press, 1994.

———. *Missions and the Frontiers of Spanish Empire: A Comparative Study of the Impact of Environmental, Economic, Political, and Socio-Cultural Variations on the Missions in the Rio de la Plata Region and on the Northern Frontier of New Spain*. Scottsdale, Ariz.: Pentacle Press, 2005.

———. "Patterns of Demographic Change in Northwestern New Spain." *The Americas* 41, no. 4 (1985): 462–79.

Jackson, Robert H., and Edward Castillo. *Indians, Franciscans, and Spanish Colonziation: The Impact of the Mission System on the California Indians*. Albuquerque: University of New Mexico Press, 1995.

Jofré, Manuel Othon. *Colonias y misiones: Informe de la visita practicada por el Delegado del Supremo Gobierno Doctor Manuel O. Jofré, Hijo en 1893*. Tarija, Bolivia: Imprenta de El Trabajo, 1895.

Jones, Grant D. *Maya Resistance to Spanish Rule: Time and History on a Colonial Frontier*. Albuquerque: University of New Mexico Press, 1989.

Jones, Kristine L. "Warfare, Reorganization, and Readaptation at the Margins of Spanish Rule: The Southern Margin (1573–1882)." In *The Cambridge History of the Native Peoples of the Americas: Volume 3. South America Part 2*. Edited by Frank Salomon and Stuart B. Schwartz. Cambridge: Cambridge University Press, 1999.

Katz, Friedrich, ed. *Riot, Rebellion and Revolution: Rural Social Conflict in Mexico*. Princeton, N.J.: University of Princeton Press, 1989.

Kertzer, David I. *Ritual, Politics and Power*. New Haven, Conn.: Yale University Press, 1988.

Kiemen, Mathias. *The Indian Policy of Portugal in the Amazon Region, 1614–1693*. Washington, D.C.: Catholic University of America Press, 1954.

King, J. Anthony. *Twenty-Four Years in the Argentine Republic*. London: Longman, Brown, Green and Longmans, 1846.

Klein, Herbert S. *A Concise History of Bolivia*. Cambridge: Cambridge University Press, 2001.

———. *Parties and Political Change in Bolivia 1880–1952*. Cambridge: Cambridge University Press, 1971.

Krieg, Hans. *Indianerland: Bilder aus dem Gran Chaco*. Stuttgart: Verlag von Strecker und Schröder, 1929.

Lagos, Marcelo. "Conformación del mercado laboral en la etapa de despegue de los ingenios azucareros jujeños (1880–1920)." In *Estudios sobre la historia de la industria azucarera argentina—II*. Edited by Daniel Campi. San Salvador de Jujuy, Argentina: Universidad Nacional de Jujuy and Universidad Nacional de Tucumán, 1992.

Lagos, Marcelo, and Ana Teruel de Lagos. "Trabajo y demografía. Análisis de la problemática a partir de un caso específico: La composición laboral de los ingenios de Jujuy (1870-1915)." *Data* 2 (1992): 117-34.

Langer, Erick D. "A violência no cotidiano da fronteira: Conflitos interétnicos no *Chaco* boliviano." *Estudos de História* 13, no. 2 (2006): 207-30.

———. "Caciques y poder en las misiones franciscanas entre los Chiriguanos durante la rebelión de 1892." *Siglo XIX: Revista de Historia* 15 (1994): 82-103.

———. "The Eastern Andean Frontier (Bolivia and Argentina) and Latin American Frontiers: Comparative Contexts (19th and 20th Centuries)." *The Americas* 58, no. 1 (2002): 33-63.

———. *Economic Change and Rural Resistance in Southern Bolivia*. Stanford, Calif.: Stanford University Press, 1989.

———. "Espacios coloniales y economías nacionales: Bolivia y el norte argentino, 1810-1930." *Siglo XIX* 2, no. 4 (1987): 305-22.

———. "Foreign Cloth in the Lowland Frontier: Commerce and Consumption of Textiles in Bolivia, 1830-1930." In *The Allure of the Foreign: The Role of Imports in Post-Colonial Latin America*. Edited by Benjamin S. Orlove. Ann Arbor: University of Michigan Press, 1997.

———. "Franciscan Missions and Chiriguano Workers: Colonization, Acculturation and Indian Labor in Southeastern Bolivia." *The Americas* 42, no. 1 (1987): 305-22.

———. "Liberal Policy and Frontier Missions: Bolivia and Argentina Compared." *Andes: Antropología e Historia* 9 (1998): 197-213.

———. "Mandeponay: Chiriguano Indian Chief on a Franciscan Mission." In *The Human Tradition in Latin America*. Edited by Judith Ewell and William H. Beezley. Wilmington, Del.: Scholarly Resources, 1989.

———. "Mission Land Tenure on the Southeastern Bolivian Frontier, 1845-1949." *The Americas* 50, no. 3 (1994): 399-418.

———. "Missions and the Frontier Economy: The Case of Franciscan Missions among the Chirguanos, 1845-1930." In *The New Latin American Mission History*. Edited by Erick D. Langer and Robert H. Jackson. Lincoln: University of Nebraska Press, 1995.

Langer, Erick D., and Gina Hames. "Commerce and Credit on the Periphery: Tarija Merchants, 1830-1914." *Hispanic American Historical Review* 74, no. 2 (1994): 285-316.

Langer, Erick D., and Robert H. Jackson. "Colonial and Republican Missions Compared: The Cases of Alta California and Southeastern Bolivia." *Comparative Studies in Society and History* 30, no. 2 (1988): 286-311.

———. "Liberalism and the Land Question in Bolivia, 1825-1920." In *Liberals, the Church and Indian Peasants: Corporate Lands and the Challenge of Reform in Nineteenth-Century Spanish America*. Edited by Robert H. Jackson. Albuquerque: University of New Mexico Press, 1997.

Langer, Erick D., and Robert H. Jackson, eds. *The New Latin American Mission History*. Lincoln: University of Nebraska Press, 1995.

Langer, Erick D., and Zulema Bass Werner de Ruiz, eds. *Historia de Tarija: Corpus Documental*. Vol. 5. Tarija, Bolivia: Universidad "Juan Misael Saracho," 1988.

Langfur, Hal. *The Forbidden Lands: Colonial Identity, Frontier Violence, and the Persistence of Brazil's Eastern Indians, 1750–1830*. Stanford, Calif.: Stanford University Press, 2006.

Larson, Brooke. "Exploitation and Moral Economy in the Southern Andes: A Critical Reconsideration." *Columbia-NYU Latin American, Caribbean, and Iberian Occasional Papers* No. 8. N.Y., n.d.

——— . *Trials of Nation Making: Liberalism, Race, and Ethnicity in the Andes, 1810–1910*. Cambridge: Cambridge University Press, 2004.

Leland, Charles Godfrey. *Etruscan Magic and Occult Remedies*. New Hyde Park, N.Y.: University Books, 1963.

Lockhart, James, and Stuart B. Schwartz. *Early Latin America*. Cambridge: Cambridge University Press, 1983.

Lofstrom, William L. *La presidencia de Sucre en Bolivia*. Trans. Mariano Baptista Gumucio. Caracas: Academia Nacional de Historia, 1987.

Lourie, Elena. "A Society Organized for War: Medieval Spain." *Past and Present* 35 (1966): 54–76.

MacCormack, Sabine. "'The Heart Has Its Reasons': Predicaments of Missionary Christianity in Early Colonial Peru." *Hispanic American Historical Review* 65, no. 3 (1985): 443–66.

——— . *Religion in the Andes: Vision and Imagination in Early Colonial Peru*. Princeton, N.J.: Princeton University Press, 1991.

Maldini, Gerardo. *Franciscanos en Tarija y . . . más allá*. Tarija, Bolivia: Editorial Acuario, 1988.

Mallon, Florencia. *Peasant and Nation: The Making of Postcolonial Mexico and Peru*. Berkeley: University of California Press, 1995.

——— . "The Promise and Dilemma of Subaltern Studies: Perspectives from Latin American History." *American Historical Review* 99, no. 5 (1994): 1491–1515.

Marchant, Alexander. *From Barter to Slavery: The Economic Relations of Portuguese and Indians in the Settlement of Brazil, 1500–1580*. Baltimore: Johns Hopkins University Press, 1942.

Martarelli, Angélico. *El Colegio Franciscano de Potosí y sus misiones*. 2nd ed. La Paz: Talleres Gráficos Marinoni, n.d.

Martínez, Rosa María. *La iglesia católica en la América independiente (Siglo XIX)*. Madrid: Editorial MAPFRE, 1992.

Mather, Kirtley F. "Along the Andean Front in Southeastern Bolivia." *Geographical Review* 12, no. 3 (1922): 358–74.

Melià, Bartomeu. *Ñande Reko: Nuestro modo de ser*. La Paz: CIPCA, 1988.

Méndez, Cecilia. *The Plebeian Republic: The Huanta Rebellion and the Making of the Peruvian State, 1820–1850*. Durham, N.C.: Duke University Press, 2005.

Mendieta S., Manuel. *Tierra rica, pueblo pobre: Por nuestras fronteras*. Sucre, Bolivia: Imprenta Bolívar, 1928.

Mendoza, Marcela. "The Western Toba: Family Life and Subsistence of the Former Hunter-Gatherer Society." In *Peoples of the Gran Chaco*. Ed. by Elmer S. Miller. Westport, Conn.: Bergin and Garvey, 1999.

Métraux, Alfred. "Les hommes-dieux chez les Chiriguano et dans l'Amérique du Sud." *Revista del Instituto de Etnología de la Universidad Nacional de Tucumán* 2, no. 1 (1931): 61–91.

———. "Migrations historiques des Tupí-Guaraní." *Journal de la Société des Americanistes* 19 (1927): 1–45.

Miller, Elmer S., ed. *Peoples of the Gran Chaco*. Westport, Conn.: Bergin and Garvey, 1999.

Mingo de la Concepción, Manuel. *Historia de las misiones franciscanas de Tarija entre Chiriguanos*. 2 vols. Tarija, Bolivia: Universidad "Juan Misael Saracho," 1981.

Un misionero. *Sublevación de los indios chiriguanos en las Provincias de Azero y Cordillera pertenecientes a los departamentos de Sucre y Santa Cruz de la República de Bolivia*. Potosí, Bolivia: Imprenta El Porvenir, 1892.

Mitre, Antonio. *Los patriarcas de la plata: Estructura socioeconómica de la minería boliviana en el siglo XIX*. Lima: Instituto de Estudios Peruanos, 1981.

Monteiro, John Manuel. *Negros da terra: Índios e bandeirantes nas origens de São Paulo*. São Paulo: Companhia das Letras, 1994.

Mörner, Magnus, ed. *The Expulsion of the Jesuits from Latin America*. New York: Knopf, 1965.

Moscoso, Oscar. *Recuerdos de la Guerra del Chaco*. 2nd ed. Vol. 1. La Paz: Editorial Canelas, 1976.

Nordenskiöld, Erland. *The Changes in the Material Culture of Two Indian Tribes under the Influence of New Surroundings*. New York: AMS Press, 1979. (Orig. pub. 1920.)

———. "The Guaraní Invasion of the Inca Empire in the Sixteenth Century: An Historical Migration." *Geographical Review* 4 (1917): 103–21.

———. *Indianerleben: El Gran Chaco (Südamerika)*. Leipzig: Albert Bonnier, 1912.

O'Connor, Francisco Burdett. *Un irlandés con Bolívar*. Caracas: El Cid, 1977.

O'Connor D'Arlach, Tomás. *El Padre Doroteo Giannecchini: Rasgos históricos*. Tarija, Bolivia: Editorial El Trabajo, 1900.

Padilla, Félix. *El Pilcomayo*. Tarija, Bolivia: Imprenta de "El Trabajo," 1887.

Paz, Luis. *De Tarija a la Asunción: Juicio sobre el informe del Doctor Daniel Campos Delegado del Gobierno. Estudio sobre las misiones*. Tarija, Bolivia: Imprenta de "El Trabajo," 1889.

Peralta, Víctor, and Marta Irurozqui. *Por la Concordia, la Fusión y el Unitarismo:*

Estado y caudillismo en Bolivia, 1825-1880. Madrid: Consejo Superior de Investigaciones Científicas, 2000.

Phelan, John L. *The Millennial Kingdom of the Franciscans in the New World*. 2nd rev. ed. Berkeley: University of California Press, 1970.

Pifarré, Francisco. *Los Guaraní-Chiriguano: Historia de un pueblo*. La Paz: CIPCA, 1989.

Pociani, Ilaria. "Lo Statuto e il Corpus Domini: La festa nazionale dell'Italia liberale." *Risorgimento* 47, nos. 1–2 (1995): 149–73.

Prudencio Bustillo, José. *De Sucre a Santa Cruz por Tarija y el Chaco*. Sucre, Bolivia: El País, 1931.

Querejazu Calvo, Roberto. *Masamaclay: Historia política, diplomática y militar de la Guerra del Chaco*. 3rd ed. La Paz: Los Amigos del Libro, 1975.

Radding, Cynthia. *Landscapes of Power and Memory: Comparative Histories in the Sonoran Desert and the Forests of Amazonia from Colony to Republic*. Durham, N.C.: Duke University Press, 2005.

———. *Wandering Peoples: Colonialism, Ethnic Spaces, and Ecological Frontiers in Northwestern Mexico, 1700-1850*. Durham, N.C.: Duke University Press, 1997.

Rausch, Jane M. *Colombia: Territorial Rule and the Llanos Frontier*. Gainesville: University of Florida Press, 1999.

Reed, Nelson. *The Caste War of the Yucatán*. Stanford, Calif.: Stanford University Press, 1964.

Reff, Daniel T. *Disease, Depopulation and Culture Change in Northwestern New Spain, 1518-1764*. Salt Lake City: University of Utah Press, 1991.

———. "The Jesuit Mission Frontier in Comparative Perspective: The Reductions of the Río de la Plata and the Missions of Northwestern Mexico, 1588-1700." In *Contested Ground: Comparative Frontiers on the Northern and Southern Edges of the Spanish Empire*. Edited by Donna Guy and Thomas Sheridan. Tucson: University of Arizona Press, 1998.

Ricard, Robert. *The Spiritual Conquest of Mexico*. Trans. Lesley B. Simpson. Berkeley: University of California Press, 1966.

Riester, Jürgen, ed. *Chiriguano: Pueblos Indígenas de las tierras bajas de Bolivia 3*. Santa Cruz, Bolivia: APCOB, 1995.

Rill, Robert. "Ein Höhepunkt im italienischen Kulturkampf: Die Errichtung des Giordano Bruno-Denkmals auf dem römischen Campo de Fiori in Juni 1889." *Römische Historische Mitteilungen*, nos. 34–35 (1992-1993): 233–73.

Rivinius, Karl J. "Der Giordano-Bruno Skandal von 1888/1889: Eine Episode im Konflikt zwischen Vatikan und italienischer Regierung um die Wiederherstellung de weltlichen Macht der Päpste." *Historisches Jahrbuch* 107, no. 2 (1987): 389–404.

Robins, Nicholas A. *Native Insurgencies and the Genocidal Impulse in the Americas*. Bloomington: University of Indiana Press, 2005.

Rousseau, Jean-Jacques. *Émile, or, on Education*. New York, Dutton, 1950. (Orig. pub. 1762.)

———. *The Social Contract*. New York: Basic Books, 1979. (Orig. pub. 1762.)

Rugeley, Terry. *Yucatán's Maya Peasantry and the Origins of the Caste War*. Austin: University of Texas Press, 1996.

Rutledge, Ian. *Cambio agrario é integración: El desarrollo del capitalismo en Jujuy, 1550–1960*. Tucumán, Argentina: ECIRA, 1987.

———. "Plantations and Peasants in Northern Argentina: The Sugar-Cane Industry of Salta and Jujuy, 1930-1943." In *Argentina in the Twentieth Century*. Edited by David Rock. Pittsburgh: University of Pittsburgh Press, 1975.

Saeger, James S. "Another View of the Mission as a Frontier Institution: The Guaycuruan Reductions of Santa Fe, 1743-1810." *Hispanic American Historical Review* 65, no. 3 (1985): 493-518.

———. *The Chaco Mission Frontier: The Guaycuruan Experience*. Tucson: University of Arizona Press, 2001.

———. "Eighteenth-Century Guaycuruan Missions in Paraguay." In *Indian-Religious Relations in Colonial Spanish America*. Edited by Susan E. Ramirez. Syracuse, N.Y.: Syracuse University Press, 1989.

Saignes, Thierry. *Ava y karai: Ensayos sobre la frontera chiriguano (siglos XVI-XX)*. La Paz: HISBOL, 1990.

———. "Guerres indiennes dans l'Amérique pionniere: Le dilemma de la resistance chiriguano a la colonisation européenne (XVIeme–XIXeme siècles)." *Histoire, Economie et Société* 1 (1982): 77-103.

———. *Historia del pueblo chiriguano*. Compiled by Isabelle Combès. Santa Cruz, Bolivia: IFEA, 2007.

———. "Jesuites et Franciscains Face Aux Chiriguano: Les Ambiguités de la Réduction Missionaire." In *Eglise et Politique en Amèrique Hispanique*. Bordeaux: Presses Universitaries de Bordeaux, 1984.

———. "Une 'frontière fossile': La Cordillère Chiriguano au XVIIIe siècle. Contribution à l'étude des rapports entre Indiens et Espagnols dans une bordure coloniale de l'Amérique ibérique." Thèse de 3e cycle. Paris: Ecole des Hautes Études, 1974.

Saignes, Thierry, and Isabelle Combès. *Alter Ego: Naissance de l'identité chiriguano*. Paris: EHESS and Cahiers de l'Homme, 1991.

Saiz Pérez, Odorico. "El Padre Andrés Herrero y la restauración de los colegios franciscano-misioneros del Perú y Bolivia (1834-1838)." *Archivo Ibero-Americano* 57, nos. 225-26 (1997): 541-64.

Salvatore, Ricardo D. *Wandering Paysanos: State Order and Subaltern Experience in Buenos Aires During the Rosas Era*. Durham, N.C.: Duke University Press, 2003.

Sanabria Fernández, Hernando. *Apiaguaiqui-Tumpa: Biografía del pueblo chiriguano y de su último caudillo*. La Paz: Amigos del Libro, 1972.

―――. *En busca de Eldorado: La colonización del oriente boliviano.* La Paz: Editorial Juventud, 1973.

Sánchez Albornoz, Nicolas. *Indios y tributos en el Alto Peru.* Lima: Instituto de Estudios Peruanos, 1978.

Sánchez Román, Antonio José. *La dulce crisis: Estado, empresarios e industria azucarera en Tucumán, Argentina (1853–1914).* Seville: Diputación de Sevilla, Universidad de Sevilla, Consejo Superior de Investigaciones Científicos, 2005.

Sandos, James A. "Junipero Serra's Canonization and the Historical Record." *American Historical Review* 93, no. 5 (1988): 1253–69.

Schuchard, Barbara. "La conquista de la tierra: Relatos guaraníes de Bolivia acerca de experiencias guerreras y pacíficas recientes." *Chiriguano: Pueblos indígenas de la tierras bajas de Bolivia.* Vol. 3. Edited by Jürgen Riester. Santa Cruz, Bolivia: APCOB, 1995.

Schwaller, John Frederick. *Francis in the Americas: Essays on the Franciscan Family in North and South America.* Berkeley: Academy of American Franciscan History, 2005.

Schwartz, Stuart B., and Frank Salomon. *The Cambridge History of the Native Peoples of the Americas: Volume 3. South America.* 2 vols. Cambridge: Cambridge University Press, 1999.

Schwartz, Stuart B., and Frank Salomon. "New Peoples and New Kinds of People: Adaptation, Readjustment, and Ethnogenisis in South American Indigenous Societies (Colonial Era)." In *The Cambridge History of the Native Peoples of the Americas: Volume 3. South America Part 2.* Edited by Stuart B. Schwartz and Frank Salomon. Cambridge: Cambridge University Press, 1999.

Scott, James C. *Weapons of the Weak: Everyday Forms of Peasant Resistance.* New Haven, Conn.: Yale University Press, 1987.

Secretaría Nacional de Asuntos Étnicos, Género y Generacionales—Subsecretaría de Asuntos Étnicos. *Primer Censo indígena rural de tierras bajas, Bolivia 1994: Chaco.* La Paz: Gráfica Latina, 1996.

Seligmann, Linda. "To Be In Between: The *Cholas* as Market Women." *Comparative Studies in Society and History* 31, no. 4 (1989): 694–721.

Smith, Denis Mack. *Modern Italy: A Political History.* Ann Arbor: University of Michigan Press, 1997.

Spalding, Karen. "Social Climbers: Changing Patterns of Mobility among the Indians of Colonial Peru." *Hispanic American Historical Review* 50, no. 3 (1970): 645–64.

Stern, Steve J. *Peru's Indian Peoples and the Challenge of Spanish Conquest: Huamanga to 1640.* Madison: University of Wisconsin Press, 1982.

―――, ed. *Resistance, Rebellion and Consciousness in the Andean Peasant World, 18th to 20th Centuries.* Madison: University of Wisconsin Press, 1987.

Susnik, Branislava. *Chiriguanos I: Dimensiones etnosociales.* Asunción: Museo Etnográfico "Andrés Barbero," 1968.

———. *Dispersión Tupí-Guaraní prehistórica*. Asunción: Museo Etnografico "Andrés Barbero," 1975.

Sweet, David. "The Ibero-American Frontier Mission in Native American History." In *The New Latin American Mission History*. Edited by Erick D. Langer and Robert H. Jackson. Lincoln: University of Nebraska Press, 1995.

Tandeter, Enrique. "Crisis in Upper Peru, 1800-1805." *Hispanic American Historical Review* 71, no. 1 (1991): 35-72.

Taylor, Alan. *The Divided Ground: Indians, Settlers, and the Northern Borderland of the American Revolution*. New York: Knopf, 2006.

Taylor, Anne Christine. "The Western Margins of Amazonia from the Early Sixteenth to the Early Nineteenth Century." In *The Cambridge History of the Native Peoples of the Americas: Volume 3. South America Part 2*. Edited by Frank Salomon and Stuart B. Schwartz. Cambridge: Cambridge University Press, 1999.

Teruel, Ana A. *Misiones, economía y sociedad: La frontera chaqueña del Noroeste Argentino en el siglo XIX*. Buenos Aires: Universidad Nacional de Quilmes, 2005.

Thouar, Arthur. *A través del Gran Chaco (1883-1887)*. Trans. Carmen Bedregal and Teresa Bedoga de Ursic. La Paz: Los Amigos del Libro, 1997.

———. *Explorations dans l'Amerique du Sud*. Paris: Hachette, 1891.

Tibesar, Antonine. *Franciscan Beginnings in Peru*. Washington, D.C.: Academy of Franciscan History, 1953.

Tierney, Patrick. *Darkness in El Dorado: How Scientists and Journalists Devastated the Amazon*. New York: Norton, 2001.

Traniello, Francesco. "Religione, nazione e sovranità nel Risorgimento italiano." *Mélanges de l'Ecole Française de Rome. Moyen Age-Temps Modernes* 98, no. 2 (1986): 837-62.

Trigo, Bernardo. *Tarija y sus valores humanos*. 2 vols. Tarija, Bolivia: Universidad Juan Misael Saracho, 1978.

Trigo, Leocadio. "Informe presentado al Supremo Gobierno de Bolivia por el Delegado Nacional Dr. Leocadio Trigo: Expedición al Pilcomayo. Año de 1906." In *Bolivia-Paraguay: Exposición de los títulos que consagran el derecho territorial de Bolivia sobre al zona comprendida entre los Ríos Pilcomayo y Paraguay, presentada por el Doctor Ricardo Mujía, Enviado Especial y Ministro Plenipotenciario de Bolivia en el Paraguay*. Edited by Ricardo Mujía. Vol. 5. La Paz: Empresa Editora "El Tiempo," 1914.

Urbina Burgos, Rodolfo. *Las misiones franciscanas de Chiloé a fines del siglo XVIII: 1771-1800*. Viña del Mar, Chile: Editorial L'Artolé, 1990.

Valda Palma, Roberto. *Historia de la Iglesia de Bolivia en la República*. La Paz: Imprenta Papiro, 1995.

Vecsey, Christopher. *On the Padres' Trail*. Notre Dame, Ind.: University of Notre Dame Press, 1996.

Viallet, Jean-Pierre. "Anticléricalisme et laicité en Italia." *Mélanges de l'Ecole Française de Rome: Moyen Age-Temps Modernes* 98, no. 2 (1986): 837-62.

Vidaurre, Enrique. *Los indomables (Semblanza del pueblo chiriguano)*. La Paz: Última Hora, 1977.

Villafañe, Benjamín. *Orán y Bolivia a la márgen del Bermejo*. Salta, Argentina: Imprenta del Comercio, 1857.

Warren, Richard. *Vagrants and Citizens: Politics and the Masses in Mexico City from Colony to Republic*. Wilmington, Del.: UNICODE Books, 2001.

Weber, David J. *Bárbaros: Spaniards and Their Savages in the Age of Enlightenment*. New Haven, Conn.: Yale University Press, 2005.

White, Richard. *The Middle Ground: Indians, Empires, and Republics in the Great Lakes Region, 1650–1815*. Cambridge: Cambridge University Press, 1991.

Whiteford, Scott. *Workers from the North: Plantations, Bolivian Labor, and the City in the Northwest Argentina*. Austin: University of Texas Press, 1981.

Woolf, Stuart. *A History of Italy, 1700–1860: The Social Constraints of Political Change*. London: Methuen, 1979.

Ynsfran, Pablo Max, ed., *The Epic of the Chaco: Marshal Estigarribia's Memoirs of the Chaco War 1932–1935*. Austin: University of Texas Press, 1950.

INDEX

Abatire valley, 106
abortion, 271
acculturation, 10, 272–75
Acosta, Juan, 268
Acre (Bolivia), 238
Africa, 270
Agostini, Fr. Gil, 286
Agrarian Reform of 1953, 268
Agricultural and Ranching Society of Small Producers (ARSSP). *See* agricultural cooperatives
agricultural cooperatives, 219, 266–68
Agua de Castilla (Chuquisaca), 44
Aguairenda (mission), 126, 180, 284; agriculture on, 204–5; authorization to fight Tobas, 53; burial registration on, 103; Campos and, 231–32; conversion on, 168; establishment of, 51–52, 67, 171, 221; housing on, 151–52; hunt deserters, 200; Jofré and, 237; land purchase for, 227; migration on, 108–9; Murray colony on, 251; opposition to baptism, 173; schooling on, 145, 148, 237; secularization of, 52, 102, 244–46, 269; smallpox epidemic, 108; as source of labor, 55–56, 201
Aguara tunpa, 19
aguardiente, 114, 123, 136; migration and, 174–75, 178; production on Tarairí, 207–8; Tacu and, 184–86
Aireyu dynasty, 187, 246

alcaldes, 157, 172–73, 194; as part of chiefly families, 173
alcoholism. *See aguardiente*; drinking
aldeias, 274
alliances: against Belzu, 32; between Chiriguanos and Tobas, 40; between Creoles and Indians, 21–22, 30–33, 228; between Creoles and Caiza, 30–31; between Creoles and Caraparirenda, 30–31; Cundeye with national authorities, 254; between Huacaya and Cuevo, 175; between Ingre, Huacaya, and Cuevo, 38; interethnic, 59, 171; missionaries with del Castillos, 255; missionaries with military, 265, 268–69; permanent with missions, 22, 31, 56–60, 192, 200, 222, 229, 277; between Santa Cruz settlers and Chiriguanos, 228; Sapirangui defeated, 40; against Tarairí, 171; tribute payments and, 33–35
Alta California. *See* California
Amazon basin, 1, 5, 8, 9, 13, 238. *See also* rubber boom
Amerani, 127
Añarenda, 20
Andean civilization, 12
Andes, 11, 12; climate of foothills, 13. *See also* Andean civilization
Añimbo (Chuquisaca), 37, 42
anticlericalism, 10, 78, 95, 195, 210, 238–39, 242–52, 259; abolition

anticlericalism (*continued*)
of missions because of, 71; in Bolivia, 69–70; in Colombia, 270; in Europe, 279; Franciscans combat, 71–72, 78–79, 240–41; Italian republicans as, 62; in Mexico, 270; of Mission Regulation of 1937, 263–65; of Siles administration, 253; of Sucre administration, 219. *See also* Liberals; Campos, Daniel; Mission Regulation of 1901; Mission Regulation of 1905; Mission Regulation of 1937; Siles, Hernando; Trigo, Leocadio
Apache Indians, 15
Aparindo, Teodoro, 253–54
Apiaguaiki Tumpa, 47, 57; as head of 1892 rebellion, 188–93, 235–36; Mandeponay and, 177–78
Apostolic Vicariate of the Gran Chaco, 72, 247–50, 256
Aracua, 30, 38–39
Araguiyu, 181–82
Aratico (Santa Cruz), 44
Arawak language, 11, 18
Arayápui, 90, 171, 181
Arce, Aniceto, 182, 236
arete, 133, 157
Argentina, 2, 14–15, 23, 29, 50, 92, 109, 277; Army, 118, 200; cattle trade to, 223; Chaco dependency of, 59; clothing and, 212; Cundeye and, 254; dispute over Tarija, 219; earnings from, 158; migration to, 94, 111–25, 148–49, 157, 159, 174, 178, 183, 184, 202–3, 212, 214, 242–43, 245, 250, 252–53, 255, 258, 272, 276, 281; missions in, 274; as place of wonder, 120–21; refuge from Chaco War, 260, 262; sugar plantations in, 58, 111; trade with, 58, 242. *See also* Jujuy; migration; Salta; sugar plantations
Argentini, Fr. Juan, 244
armaments. *See* weaponry; *tercerolas*; arrows
arrows: construction of, 42; during 1892 rebellion, 191; ineffectiveness against forts, 48; sign for making war, 42; superiority of, 41; use against cattle, 45
Asia, 270
Asunción (Paraguay), 225, 233, 260
Atacama (department), 23–24
Atlantic Ocean, 231
Atucuna, 178
Audiencia de Charcas, 23
Augustinian Order, 16
Austria, 65, 68, 69
ava. See Chiriguanos
Avenante, Fernando, 267–68
Ayericuay, 27, 29–30, 37–38
Aymara Indians, 24, 226, 281
Azero (province), 26, 30, 32, 179; seasonal fairs in, 211
Azucari, 190

Baca Flor, Manuel Fernando, 34
Ballivián, José, 23, 32, 39
baptism, 67, 83–86; acceptance of, 6; adult, 162; beliefs after, 167–68; as causing death, 164; of chiefly sons, 183; of children, 163–64, 173; consequences of, 161; on deathbed, 102–3, 161–65, 169, 173, 180; incompleteness of, 102; of Mandeponay, 180; parents refuse for children, 144; proportion baptized, 186–87; refusal to baptize adults, 89–90, 173; on Santa Rosa, 161–63; on Tarairí, 163–64; warfare and, 167. *See also* conversion
Baptista, Mariano, 70, 182, 233, 236, 238

Baraguari, 44
Baririqui, 190
Barrientos, Casiano, 260–61
Basili, Fr. Gerónimo, 284, 287
Bayandari, 171, 181, 224
Belgrano, Manuel, 18
Bella Esperanza (Tarija), 224–25
Belzu, Manuel Isidoro, 23, 32
Beni (department), 9, 24, 111; oppose Vicariate, 247
Berlin (Germany), 2, 242
Bermejo river, 29
Bialet y Massé, Juan, 117
Bishopric of Gran Chaco, 266
Block, David, 9, 273
Boccaccini, Fr. Benvenuto, 286
Boicovo (mission), 215, 223; accounts, 209; banishment of adulterers, 258; during Chaco War, 262; clothing consumption on, 211; conversion of, 166–67, 168, 256; diseases on, 106; establishment of, 51, 53–54, 103, 187, 229; godchildren from, 150–51; Macharetí cattle on, 263; Machirope refuse to settle on, 188; population on, 104, 152, 266; rebellion of 1892 and, 189; as refuge, 55; schooling on, 148; secularization of, 53, 266
Bolívar, Simón, 23, 67, 279
Bolivia: control of, 21–22; missions on, 270; Peruvian invasion of, 23; as powerful state, 23; weakness of, 24, 226
Bologna (Italy), 64
Bolton, Herbert E., 2–4, 7, 197
Boyuibe, 267
Brazil, 11, 12, 23, 226, 238, 273–74
Buenos Aires, 2, 17
burials, 83; incompleteness of, 102
Buricanambi, 26, 187

Caigua-mi (Chuquisaca), 180–81
Cainzo, Sebastián, 26
Caipipendi Valley (Santa Cruz), 12, 30, 49, 57, 187, 229, 246
Caitume, 173
Caiza (Tarija), 30–31, 36, 40, 56, 114, 170, 171, 232
California, 3, 7, 8, 51, 101–2, 271, 273–75
Calvimontes, Luis, 37–38
Camatindi, 171, 215, 223, 237, 287
Camiri (Santa Cruz), 265
Campero, Narciso, 181, 231
Campo Santo (Argentina), 115
Campos, Daniel, 70, 126, 181, 231–34, 236–37, 240, 255, 279
cane alcohol. See *aguardiente*
cangui: in harvest festivals, 133, 136; migration and, 123, 174–75, 178; nutritional properties of, 178; politics and, 28, 30, 174
Capalongo, F. Vicente, 286
captives, 40, 69, 235; sale of, 104. See also women
Carandaití (Chuquisaca), 127, 176, 189, 223
Caraparí (Tarija), 36, 126, 224
Caraparí River, 262
Caraparicito, 247
Caraparirenda (Chuquisaca), 30–31, 56, 229
Cardús, Fr. José, 145, 161
Carmona, Francisco, 170
Carrasco, Manuel, 39
Caruruti (Tarija), 37, 40, 268
Caso, J. B., 227
Caste War of Yucatán, 188
Castedo, Manuel Ignacio, 32
Castillo, Edward, 119
catecúmenos, 82, 168, 174
Catholic Church: adopt Delegation model, 247; Arce and, 236; Baptista

Catholic Church (*continued*)
and, 233; combat liberalism, 71–72; increasing conservatism of, 65–66, 69–71, 74, 77, 84; Constitutionalist Party and, 233; ecclesiastical control, 76; education and, 76; in Europe, 74; as fount of morality, 93, 100; French aid for, 69; Gioberti and, 68; in Italy, 62–70, 74; Linares and, 23; paternalism, 93; Republican Party and, 250; relationship with state, 5, 68, 226; revitalization of, 65–66, 71; revive missions, 270; struggle between state and, 73–74, 95; transformer of Indians, 11; weakness of, 10. *See also* anticlericalism; Apostolic Vicariate; encyclicals; mission; Papal States; pope; Risorgimento; Vatican I; Vatican II

Cattaneo, Carlo, 68, 80

cattle: Aguairenda Indians return, 53; capture by Ayericuay, 37; change in ecology and, 25, 106, 227; Chiriguano ownership and, 27; conflict between corn and, 47, 55, 203; demand for, 46–47; elimination of Indians for, 43–44; exports to Tarija and Sucre, 47; fence against in Cuevo, 54; importance on frontier, 25; as incentive to invade, 47; invade Tiguipa and Macharetí, 230; killing by Chiriguanos of, 36, 59; land grants for, 252; loss of, in 1841, 38; Macharetí and, 176, 263; on missions, 205–7, 209, 220, 237, 241; objective in war, 44; penetration into frontier, 18, 47, 203, 222, 228, 234; *piqueros* and, 25; relationship to silver economy, 47; theft, 36, 45, 209, 214, 222, 234, 237; trade to Argentina, 223; Tobas as consumers of, 222; as tribute payment, 33–34, 36; use in colonization, 45, 47, 203

Cattunar, Fr. Herman, 286

caudillos, 33

Chaco. *See* Gran Chaco

Chaco province, 119

Chaco War (1932–35), 10, 11, 22, 219, 256–57, 265, 282

Chanchi, 183–84

Chané Indians, 11; conquest of, 12; of Itiyuro, 12, 36; mixture with Chiriguanos, 12, 15, 18; offspring of, 15; as residents of Macharetí, 179; steal cattle, 36

Chapiaguasu. *See* Apiaguaiki Tumpa

Chapuai, 106

Charagua (Santa Cruz), 261

Chavarría, Melchor, 236–37

Chaverao, 38, 48

Chiantini, Fr. Cristóbal, 286–87

chicha. *See cangui*

Chientaroli, Fr. Antonio, 284

children, baptism of, 67; education of, 91; exclusive presence on missions, 102, 108; participation in Tiguipa rituals, 95–100; in schools, 137–49

Chile, 23–24, 226, 238, 242

Chimeo (mission), 37, 56, 75, 168; burials on, 103; population growth on, 104; establishment of mission, 37, 51–52, 54, 103, 170–72, 221; as refuge during Chaco War, 261; schooling on, 147; secularization of, 52, 102; urban plan of, 129

Chiquitos, 16, 73, 129

Chiriguano Indians, 1, 5, 6; alliance against Belzu, 32; alliances with settlers, 29–33, 115; alliance with Tobas, 40; Argentina and, 111, 114–25, 277; attitudes of Franciscans toward, 84–94; attitudes of

358 INDEX

settlers toward, 49; barbarism of, 90; boundaries of settlement, 14; Caiza, 30-31; Caraparirenda, 30; casualties in 1841, 38-39; cattle ownership of, 27, 45; use of cattle against, 45-47, 203; during Chaco War, 261-62; Chané, mixture with, 12, 15; change in warfare, 37-38; chiefs, 96, 100; clothing and, 212; as coca consumers, 211; during colonial period, 11-18; concept of citizenship, 280-283; conquest of Chané, 12; conquest by Franciscans, 89; contact with Incas, 12; control of missions, 17; crisis of 1839-41 and, 35-39; ethnocentrism of, 12; extinction of, 88, 105; festivals, 133, 136-37; frontier dominance of, 28-29, 59; on haciendas, 229, 236, 268; independence wars and, 17-18, 21; integration as laborers, 87, 99; invasions, 31; Ipaguazo defeat of, 36, 44; kidnapping of children, 124; labor, laziness of, 91; as labor source, 246; leadership, 13, 27; maize as staple, 13; massacre at Caruruti, 37; meaning of, 12; migration, 11-12, 108-25; military strategies, 14-15, 28, 41-43, 59; military defeat of, 28, 60; mix with settlers, 272; objectives in war, 44-45; opposition to missions, 171-72; as part of nature, 90; participation in national politics, 32-33, 59; participation in warfare, 31-33; political culture of, 11, 13, 27, 29, 87, 90, 122, 157, 178; political divisions, 27, 31-32; population size of, 15, 45, 116; protection of Caiza, 40; among Pueblos, 274; reasons for accepting missions, 17, 54-55, 161, 172; reciprocity of, 158; recruits for Army, 32; refugees during Chaco War, 261-62; rejection of Jesuits, 16; relationship with Spaniards, 11, 13-17; religion of, 19-20, 52, 92, 169-70; resist settlers on missions, 249; response to cattle invasion, 47; slaves on sugar estates, 115; as soldiers, 50; state, lack of, 13; on sugar plantations, 115-17; superiority over Bolivians, 28, 33-34, 59; tribute payments to, 33-35; wages of, 119, 230; warfare and, 14-15, 31-33; women, 37, 39, 40, 42, 91-92, 123, 199. *See also* Guaraní; maize; migration; missions; *tubicha*; *names of individual leaders, missions, settlements*

Chiriguano nation, 27

Chituri, Juan Manuel, 171, 228

cholera, 106

Choreti (Santa Cruz), 37

Choreti Indians: foundation of Tarija and, 26; Macharetí and, 176; Vicariate planned for, 250; as workers, 202

Chuquisaca (department), 25; characteristics of settlers, 26; importance of cattle, 46; neglect of frontier, 26

Cinti (province), 29, 40, 41

citizens, creation of, 10-11

citizenship, 87, 94, 278-83; economic position and, 279-80, 282-83; indigenous conceptions of, 280; rights of Indians, 279-80

civilization: Chaco tribes' inability, 235; citizenship and, 279-83; clothing and, 211-13; as concept, 75, 77, 79-80, 99, 270; control and, 182; conversion and, 84-94, 172, 278; disruptions because of, 273; drunkenness and, 174; European, 98; language and, 232; migration and, 122, 124; schools and, 137-38, 141-42;

civilization (*continued*)
  on sugar plantations, 117; in urban context, 79–80
Clastres, Pierre, 13, 27, 122
clothing, 141–44, 153–54, 211–13
coca leaf, 136, 174
Cochabamba, 81
coercion, 5
Colagrossi, Fr. Mariano, 286–87
Colombia, 270
colonists. *See* settlers
Colorado, 13
Columbus, Christopher, 12
Combès, Isabelle, 12
concubines, 129, 177, 228, 251
confession, 85
confirmation, 83–85
Conservative Party, 70
Constituent Assembly of 1871, 226
Constitutionalist Party, 233
Contreras, Manuel E., 147
conversion: by 1810, 16; of adults, 161–63, 173; on Aguairenda, 168; of children, 79, 141, 161, 163–64; citizenship and, 279; civilization and, 84–88, 93, 99; on colonial missions, lack of, 16, 90; disease and, 102, 161–63; of Mandeponay, 96; on missions, 5, 10, 17, 83–84, 167–69, 277; power and, 160–69; refusal of Chiriguanos to, 92, 169, 173, 277; on Santa Rosa, 164, 166; of Toba, 77; voluntary, 161
Cook, Sherburne F., 3
Cordillera (province), 27, 32, 227; expansion of livestock in, 47; missions obliterated in, 50; population of, 27; settler policies, 246–47
corn. *See* maize
corn beer. *See cangui*
Corrado, Fr. Alejandro, 52, 76, 81, 90–91, 93, 144, 162, 173

Corsetti, Fr. Alfonso, 75, 86, 88, 220
Corvera Centeno, Rómulo, 265
Costa, Fr. Gervacio, 120, 184, 288
Costa du Rels, Adolfo, 140
cotton, 251
cowhands, 252; del Castillos as, 222–23; early republican period, 25; as victims of Indians, 33–34, 36, 42, 44, 234
Creoles. *See* settlers
Crevaux, Jules, 230
Crevaux colony, 126, 214, 233
cristianos. *See* settlers
Cuarenda, 173, 180, 183
Cuevo (Santa Cruz), 30, 37, 40, 56, 182, 266; Arce donation of land for mission, 236; desire for mission, 69; fence against cattle, 54; Indian complaints against settlers, 49; death from smallpox, 107; defeat of ava, 32, 54; fort at, 48, 214; independence of, 187; invasion of cattle into, 47; sacking in 1892, 190. *See also* Santa Rosa de Cuevo
Cuma, 32
Cumbay, 18, 27, 30
Cundeye (uncle), 129, 182–83
Cundeye, Gerónimo, 267
Cundeye, Octavia, 266
Cundeye, Ubaldino, 252–54, 258, 262, 266–67, 269, 281
cunumi, 15
Curuyuqui, 241; battle of, 57, 236; as center of 1892 rebellion, 188–91
Cuyambuyo (Tarija), 29, 219

D'Ambrogi, Fr. Santiago
Dare, Juan, 267
Dean, Warren, 1
debt peonage, 214
Deeds, Susan M., 7, 9, 274–75

de Fuentes, Luis, 26
de Gandia, Enrique, 12
del Castillo, Clodomiro, 223, 234
del Castillo, Eulogia, 224
del Castillo, Germán, 179
del Castillo, Juan Esteban, 85–86, 222–23
del Castillo, María Ninfa, 224
del Castillo, Moisés, 223
del Castillo family, 136–37, 150–51, 176, 222–23, 235, 238, 246, 248, 255, 276
Delegation of the Gran Chaco, 241–44, 247, 250–51, 255, 259
Delfante, Fr. Leonardo, 83
Democratic Party, 233
demography: on Boicovo during Chaco War, 262; compared, 271–72; on eve of Chaco War, 257–58; implications for missions, 3–5, 8, 10, 102, 125, 271–73; incompleteness of data, 102–3; colonial Chiriguano, 15–16; colonial mission, 16, 271–72; weight of Indians, 44–45
de Nino, Fr. Bernardino, 19, 42, 71–72, 78–79, 88, 89–94, 98, 100, 105, 132, 136, 138, 158, 161, 163, 174, 200, 239, 241, 242, 244, 246, 286
de Velasco, José Miguel, 32
diarrhea, 106
Dimeco, Fr. Nazareno, 284, 286
disease: baptisms and, 162–63; California missions and, 3; exposure to on missions, 5, 17; colonial Chaco missions and, 272; importance of, 101, 108; endemic on missions, 106–8; kill off unconverted, 167; role of in mission decline, 106–9, 124, 272; role of shaman in curing,, 20, 88; smallpox, 105. *See also* demography; *individual diseases*
divorce, 84

Dominican Order, 16
drinking: effects on missions, 174–75, 178–79, 184–86; political alliances and, 28. See also *cangui*; cane alcohol
drought, 119; colonial period, 16; during 1839–41, 35–36; from 1897 to 1905, 106, 119, 179, 209, 242
dysentery, 106

Easter, 76, 132
education: Catholic Church and, 76, 88; Romanticism and, 67. *See also* children
El Palmar (Chuquisaca), 36, 40
El Palmar (Tarija), 245–46
encyclicals: *Mirari vos*, 64; *Quanta Cura*, 70–71; Syllabus of Errors, 64, 70–71
enganchadores, 115, 120, 121, 123; chiefs as, 252–53; Mandeponay as, 175, 243–44; Tacu as, 184–86, 243
epidemics: virgin soil, 271. *See also* disease; *individual diseases*
Ercole, Fr. Alejandro, 225–27
erosion: cattle and, 25, 106
eschatology, 62
estancia. See ranches
Estigarribia, José Félix, 260
Ethnohistory, 3–4
Europeans: disease contact with, 102; Catholic working class, 87; immigration and, 245; invasion of, 12; medical practices, 88; missionaries from, 10–11
expeditions. *See* Gran Chaco

famine, 16; of 1839–41, 36, 45; of 1904, 162; migration and, 108, 124–25; reasons for mission decline, 106–7. *See also* droughts; locusts
feasts, 94, 178

Federalist War, 24, 238
Ferrara (Italy), 64
fertility, 105
firearms. *See* weaponry
First World War, 117, 251
Florence (Italy), 2, 61
Florense, Victorico, 254
Florida, 273
forts, 213, 251, 259; Bolívar, 215; at Caiza, 31, 223; Chiriguano, 14, 48; near colonial missions, 17; to contain at Crevaux, 223; inability of Indians to overcome, 56; at Ingre, Iguembe, Ñancaroinza, and Cuevo, 48, 214-15; labor on, 214, 227; at La Loma and El Palmar, 40; established by Magariños, 39-40, 214; Paraguayan, 260; on Pilcomayo River, 55; private in the Chaco, 179; Sucre, 215; at Taringuite, 176. See also *individual forts*
France, 68, 69
Franciscans: absorption of Chiriguano culture, 94; adherence to doctrine, 75; affinity with Chiriguanos, 73-74; as antimodern, 250; Apiaguaiki as rival of, 188-89; as authority figures, 157, 254, 276; Bolivian Congress's attitude toward, 226-27; broken by Liberals, 247-48; captives handed over to, 49; type of Catholicism of, 62; citizenship and, 281, 282; complaints about settlers of, 249; colonial missions with Chiriguanos, 16-18, 19, 73-74; Catholic working class created by, 280; Crevaux expedition and, 231; Cundeye and, 252-54, 258; disgust with Tacu, 184; effect of Italian experience, 65-73, 160; exchanges on missions, 17; faith of, 73-79; feeling of superiority, 93-94; as foreigners, 259; generations of, 65-72; history of, 62; image of Indians, 89-94, 122-23, 279-80; initiative to establish missions, 54; as Italians, 63; Jofré's opinion of, 237; land disputes with, 219-20, 241; as landlords, 259; loss of power, 265-66, 276; Mandeponay and, 120, 170, 175-80; migration attitudes toward, 122-24; motivations for establishing missions, 62-63; mysticism of, 75; need for chiefs, 170; of New Mexico, 73, 173, 274, 276; as Paraguayan spies, 259; as power brokers, 227; as protectors of Indians, 217, 282; protest secularization, 242-43; provenance of, 10, 51; as public functionaries, 240; as reason for backwardness, 259; reciprocity of, 157-58; recruitment of, 51, 63, 219-20; rejection of noble savage, 66; relation with unconverted, 132; relation with del Castillos, 222-23; religiosity, 72-79, 84; role in ASSRPS, 268; as Spaniards, 63, 219; suppression in Italy of, 69, 71-72, 73, 76; Tertiary Order of, 224; views of ideal missions, 65, 160. See also missions; *individual convents*; *individual friars*; *individual missions*
Francis of Assisi, Saint, 62, 74
French Revolution, 65-66
friars. *See* Franciscans; *individual names of friars*
Frías, Tomás, 190-91
frontiers, 1; armaments on, 41-42, 46; Ballivián's policy, 39-40; Bolivian politics and, 22; cattle and, 18; Chuquisaca neglect of, 26; conception for missions, 21; conception of property in, 33-34; definition of,

2; economic basis for Creoles, 25; exchange of diseases on, 272; expansion, 21, 215, 234; Franciscans as power brokers on, 227; government policy of, 226, 277; history, 21; Inca, 11-12; importance of missions on, 270-83; after independence, 18; Liberal policies toward, 238-39; military balance shifts, 55; mission, 80; missions transform, 8-9; Spanish policies toward, 14-17; stability in 1850s, 40; state control of, 8; Tarija, 23; village alliances in, 59; violence, 22; warfare types along, 42; War of the Pacific's aftermath and, 24

Gamarra, Agustín, 23
García, Alejo, 11
García, Medardo G., 287
García Jordán, Pilar, 227, 239-40, 278-79
Giannecchini, Fr. Doroteo, 69-70, 77, 89-90, 94, 105, 106, 126, 144, 223, 224, 227, 230-31, 233-35
Giannelli, Fr. José, 52, 57, 67, 76, 222, 234
Gioberti, Vincenzo, 68, 98
godparentage, 150
Gómez, Manuel, 265
Gómez, Manuel Mariano, 176, 179, 235
Gorriti, Juana Manuela, 23
Gran Chaco, 13, 57, 63; Argentine, 114, 117; Campos expedition into, 70, 126, 181, 200, 231-35; colonization from 1860s, 49; colonization of 1880s, 106, 229, 234; Crevaux expedition, 230-31; dependency on Argentina, 59; expansion of livestock in, 47; expeditions, 67, 69, 70, 180, 224; expedition of 1886, 77, 223; Giannelli expedition into, 76,

224; Magariños expedition into, 39-40; militarization of, 251; mission failure in, 187, 225; missions as springboards into, 58; Mission San Francisco's importance, 235; private development of, 251; study of, 248-49; Trigo expedition into, 243. See also Chaco War
grazing fees, 33-34
Great Depression, 259-60
Guadalquivir valley, 26
Guapay river, 29
Guaraní: during Chaco War, 260-61; culture, 12; Indians, 8, 272, 275, 276; language over Arawak, 12; migrations, 11. See also militia
guarapo, 115
Guarayos (Bolivia), 264
Guarayos (Paraguay), 261
Guariju, 188
Guaripa, 170
Guariyu, 129, 172, 189
Guayupa, 35
Guiracota, 31-32
Güirangay, 129
Guirasavai, 173
guns. See weaponry
Gutiérrez (Santa Cruz), 29
Gutiérrez, Julio A., 250
Gutiérrez, Ramón, 73, 173

Hacienda Ledesma (Argentina), 114-15, 117
Hacienda Misión de Zenta (Argentina), 115
Hacienda San Lorenzo (Argentina), 115, 117
Hacienda San Pedro (Argentina), 114
Hackel, Steven, 275
Healy, Kevin, 268
Hennessy, Alistair, 4, 80

INDEX 363

Hermann, Guillermo, 243
Herrera, Fr. Andrés, 51, 63, 66, 219
Holy Alliance, 65
Holzer and Company, 241
horses, 41; Chiriguano ownership of, 27
Huacareta (Chuquisaca), 29
Huacaya (Chuquisaca), 30, 37, 39, 54–56, 106, 151, 166, 171, 188, 215; attack on Tarairí by, 90, 181, 224; invasion of cattle into, 47
Huacaya War, 47, 49, 54, 56, 166, 176, 187–89, 192–93, 214, 228, 229
Hu-DeHart, Evelyn, 6–7

Igue-catupire, 40, 42
Iguembe (Chuquisaca), 48, 215
Illimani battalion, 40, 42
immigration (European), 245. *See also* migration
Inca: empire, 11; contact with Chiriguanos, 12; frontier policies, 12, 14; history, 12
Incahuasi (Santa Cruz), 247
incivilimento, 68, 80
independence wars, 17–18, 22–23, 41, 219
Indians: autonomy on missions, 5; community land, 23, 24, 226; labor, 8–9; as protagonists, 4; as victims, 3
ingenio. *See* sugar plantations
Ingre (Chuquisaca), 18, 26, 29, 30, 33, 37, 39–40, 48, 106, 121, 139, 187, 215, 229
invasions, 26
Ipaguazo, 36–37, 40, 42, 44, 49
ipaye: Araguiyu as, 181; belief in, 92; definition, 20; Guariju as, 188; on missions, 88, 169–70
Itacua (Chuquisaca), 29
Italy, 9–10, 51, 62–72, 74, 76, 77, 80, 81–82, 84

Itatiqui (mission): establishment of, 51, 239; secularization of, 51, 53, 102, 246, 247
Itau (mission), 37, 50–51, 75, 219; donation of, 220; 1834 conversion on, 168; establishment of, 220; Murray colony on, 251; O'Connor and, 50, 219, 227; rebellion, 50, 219; reestablishment, 51–52, 54; schooling on, 147; secularization of, 52; urban plan of, 129
Itiyuro (Argentina), 12, 36
Ivo (mission): agriculture on, 205; conversion on, 168; establishment of, 51, 53–54, 103, 194, 236; failed attempts at missions, 69; Indian in government of ASSRP, 268; land usurpation of, 241; Paraguayan Army take over, 257, 261; plaza of, 82; population of, 102–4; rebellion of 1892 and, 187–88; schooling on, 148; secularization of, 53, 266; smallpox vaccinations, on, 107; unconverted on, 257; urban plan of, 129
Izozog Indians, 30, 260–61
Izozog region, 12, 228, 247

Jackson, Robert H., 101, 119, 271
Jesuits, 208, 211, 274; Beni missions, 9, 272–73; conservatism and, 74; colonial Chaco missions and, 272; conversion and disease, 102; expulsion from America, 16, 270; failure among Chiriguanos, 16, 57, 73–74, 157; in Paraguay, 272–73; religious effects on Chiriguanos, 19; revival of, 65; during Risorgimento, 74; role of shaman in revolts, 20; Yaqui missions, 7
Jofré, Manuel Othon, 118, 129, 132, 151, 204–7, 227, 236–37, 255

Joseph, Saint, 96
Jujuy, 58, 111, 114–17, 120, 123, 127, 149, 156, 174, 177, 202, 281
Jurado, Mauricio, 287

Kandire myth, 12–13, 121. *See also* messianism
Karai: definition of, 14. *See also* settlers
kidnapping, 124
Krieg, Hans, 251
kurakas, 169

La Esperanza (Argentina), 117, 120, 177
Lagos, Ana, 117
Lagos, Marcelo, 117
Laguna Chuquisaca, 260
La Laguna (Chuquisaca). *See* Padilla
La Loma (Chuquisaca), 40
lances, 41
land: 1905 land legislation, 252; for Americans, 251; for Argentines, 252; for Germans, 252; of former missions, 266; grants, 34, 47–48, 85–86, 251–52; for Italians, 252; market, 24; disputed ownership of, 33–34; refusal to measure, 34. *See also* missions; settlers
La Paz (Bolivia), 22, 185, 238, 242, 265; Chiriguanos in La Paz, 252–54, 281–82; convent, 221; regionalists, 24
Larroua, Fr. Manuel, 241
Leach Brothers, 120
Liberals (Bolivia), 236, 253; accession to power, 24; alliance with Aymara, 24; alliance with Santa Cruz settlers, 247; anticlerical, 5, 71–72, 95, 179, 238–52, 259; Campos as, 232–35; as corruptive influence, 105; fall of party and, 250; Fr. de Nino and, 71–72, 242, 244; Franciscans combat, 71–72; frontier strategy, 238–39; Melgarejo and, 23, 226; reforms by, 23, 147
Liberals (Italy), 68, 72, 244; characteristics of, 63–64; condemnation of by Church, 64, 70–71; takeover of Vatican by, 226
Lima (Peru), 50
Linares, José María, 23, 32
Lockhart, James, 2
locusts, 119, 125, 179, 251
Lombardy, 68
Lucca (Italy), 66, 67

Macharetí (mission), 120, 285–87; agriculture on, 204; as ARSSP, 266–68; as barrier, 58; cattle on, 206, 263, 268; census of, 109, 128; conversion on, 167–69; Creoles take land, 258–59; Cundeye and, 252–54, 262, 266–67, 269, 282; establishment of, 51–52, 103, 164, 170, 172, 175, 221; flight from, 144; as fort, 56; field hospital in, 261; godchildren from, 151; importance of, 175–76; J. E. del Castillo and, 222–23; labor from, 182–83; land grants next to, 86; Mandeponay and, 175–80, 243–44, 252; migration and, 109–11, 175, 243–44; other Indians as residents, 179; Paraguayan Army take over, 257, 261; polygyny on, 128–29; plazas on, 129–30, 176–77; population, 104, 152, 258; prisoners during Chaco War, 261–62; problems with Standard Oil, 249; rebellion of 1892 and, 189–95; reconstruction after Chaco War, 262–63; schooling on, 145, 269; secularization of, 52, 266–67; settlers invade cattle, 230 on, 128, 186, 257; urban plan of, 129; Zoila of, 126–27.

INDEX 365

Macharetí (mission) (*continued*)
    See also Cundeye; Mandeponay; Tacu, José Napoleón
Machirope, 188
Magariños, Manuel Rodríguez, 35, 39
maize: cycle, 132–33; feasts and, 133, 136; harvest failure of 1839–41 of, 45; political culture and, 27–28, 133; production on Santa Rosa and Ivo, 205; staple of Chiriguanos, 13, 18; vs. cattle, 46, 203
Maldini, Fr. Gerardo, 261, 267–68
Mandecui, 177
Mandeponay, 109, 258, 276, 282; in Argentina, 120; conflict with Cundeye, 182–83; deposing of, 177, 179, 243; family of, 129; as intermediary with Chaco peoples, 179; as intermediary with local government, 280; as labor contractor, 175, 179, 243–44; as linchpin for mission system, 176; as leader of Macharetí, 96, 169, 170, 175–80; polygyny of, 128–29, 175, 177; prevent division in Macharetí, 130; rebellion of 1892 and, 177–78, 236, 189–95; receives land grant, 176; relationship with del Castillos, 223; as rival to Guariyu, 172; struggle with missionaries, 120, 175–80, 187; Tacu and, 184–85, 243–44; against Tobas, 176
Marás, Ramón, 249, 252
Mariani, F. Marino, 230
Maringay, 121, 139, 280
Martarelli, Fr. Angélico, 55, 71, 90, 189, 228, 236
Masavi (Santa Cruz), 29
massacre: at Caruruti, 37; at Ipaguazo, 49; increasing number of, 49; at Yuqui, 49; at Murucuyati, 49, 187–88; during rebellion of 1892, 49, 191–92

Massai, Fr. Inocencio, 286–87
Mataco-Noctenes. *See* Matacos
Matacos, 114; as laborers on sugar plantations, 115–18; Macharetí and, 176; resistance to encroachment, 49; San Antonio mission and, 222, 224, 228, 241; Vicariate planned for, 250; as workers, 202, 243
Mather, Kirtley F., 13
Matraya y Ricci, Fr. José, 66
Mattioli, Br. Luis, 261
Mbaporenda, 121, 168, 174
mburuvicha. See *tubicha*
Mealla, Andrés, 220
measles, 106
medicine, 88
Mediterranean, 79
Melgarejo, Mariano, 23–24, 48, 226
merchants, 25, 213, 215; in Carandaití, 211; in Cuevo, 211; del Castillo as, 223; Jofré as, 236; on missions, 216; in Ñancaroinza, 211
messianism, 7, 12, 20, 47, 57, 60, 162, 235. *See also* Apiaguaiki Tumpa; *tumpa*; *Kandire*; rebellion of 1892
Mexico, 6–7, 9, 62, 169, 219, 270, 272–74, 276
migration, 10, 108–10, 112–13; to Argentina, 111, 114–25, 127, 174, 211, 214, 242–43, 245, 255, 258, 272, 276–77, 281; chiefs and, 173–74, 178, 179; effects of, 122–25, 174, 211; fairs and, 211; Mandeponay and, 175, 178–79; missions as bulwark against, 250; national identity and, 281; permission for, 118, 120; as progress, 250; prohibition of, 111, 118; push and pull, 118, 199; reasons for, 119–22; regulations to contain, 118; as resistance, 119; to Yacuiba, 245
military (Bolivian): aims in expe-

366 INDEX

dition of 1863, 76; alliance with Franciscans, 265, 268-69; attack on Ipaguazo, 36-37, 43; as bit players on frontier, 31; campaigns against Chiriguanos, 31-33; casualties, 44; colonies, 39, 235; competition with missions, 249; Cundeye and, 262; defeat Ingre-Guacaya-Cuevo alliance, 38; desertion from, 200, 214; ejected from Tarairí, 171; endorse Vicariate, 250; forts and, 214, 251; Fr. Giannecchini and, 69; German training of, 260; Illimani Battalion, 40; military socialism, 263-64; missions and, 276; opinion of missions, 248-49; Potosí Squadron, 231; retreat in 1842, 39; symbolic support of the missions, 96; support of Indians on ASSRP, 267-68; tactics, 43-44, 251; Tarija Battalion, 231; uniforms, 96; use of Chiriguanos, 57, 200, 219, 261, 282; warning to not molest Indians, 34; War of the Pacific and, 24. *See also* forts; warfare; weaponry

military (Paraguayan), 256, 260-62

militia: aid missions, 237-38, 276; attack on Ipaguazo, 36-37; authorization to make war to Aguairenda Indians, 53; Caiza, 31; call-up against 1847 revolt, 32; Carapari, 224; del Castillos as officers, 223, 238; forts and, 214-15; as junior partners of Indians, 59; Paraguayan mission, 275; payment in Indians, 44; rebellion of 1892 and, 189-92; Voluntarios del Chaco, 234. *See also* military; settlers

Mingo, Fr. Manuel, 16

Ministry of Colonies and Agriculture, 240

Ministry of Colonization, 254, 264

Ministry of War and Colonization, 107, 241

Mission Regulation of 1830, 221

Mission Regulation of 1871, 221, 225-27, 239; abrogation of, 238; opposition to, 227, 232, 255; separate justice system of, 281

Mission Regulation of 1901, 239, 255

Mission Regulation of 1905, 95, 118, 179, 240-43, 281

Mission Regulation of 1937, 263-65

missionary. *See* Franciscans; Jesuit

missions: affected by Italian circumstances, 65; agricultural practices on, 200-201; alcoholism on, 178-79; as anachronisms, 250; apologists for, 3, 196; in Argentina, 274; artisanal production on, 207; bands, 81, 284-87; as barriers, 58; California, 3, 7-8, 81, 101-2, 271; Campos and, 231-35; cattle on, 205-7, 209, 213-14; Chaco War and, 256, 259-63; chiefs' role on, 169-95, 253, 276; in Chile, 274; create citizens, 278-83; clothing, 87, 131-32, 141-43, 153-54, 157, 211-13; colonial compared with, 4-6, 10, 125, 139, 142-43, 161, 171, 202, 208, 211, 271-78; coercion on, 275; conflict with chiefly sons, 183-86, 244, 252-54, 258, 282; control on, 17, 80-81, 137, 139, 144, 175-86, 264; culture, 9, 10, 154-59, 273; decline of, 238-66; definition of, 6; demographic patterns on, 103, 257, 277; decline of, 10, 136, 148, 237; disappearance after independence, 18; diseases on, 106-8, 272; division into sections, 16, 172-73; effect of military on missions, 261, 263; emigration as cause of decline, 105; establishment of, 9, 204, 215-16; economy, 10, 58, 197-217;

missions (*continued*)
exchange with Indians, 17; as factor in loss of Chiriguano independence, 22, 50, 56–58, 277; festivals in, 133, 136–37, 174; flight from, 105, 183, 233, 244, 275; as forts, 56; Franciscan colonial, 16–18; as frontier institutions, 2–5, 55–59, 69, 196–97, 213, 226–27; government relations and, 238–56, 259; history of, 2–3, 16, 161, 241, 270; housing, 82–83, 128–29, 151–52, 198, 203, 242; hunters and gatherers and, 273; income, 208–11; independence wars and, 17–18; Jesuit, 7–9, 16, 274; labor on, 8–9, 55–56, 174, 198–203, 207, 216–17, 232, 244, 275; labor for expeditions, 70, 126, 200, 227, 232–33, 275; labor for roads, 238, 264; as labor pools, 55–56, 201, 216–17, 240, 249, 274, 275; land disputes over, 219–20, 241; life cycle, 6–9, 67, 82, 127, 170, 197–98, 200, 203, 211, 215–17, 275; as market, 211–13; as means to maintain land, 16; migration from, 108–14, 156, 255; as migration bulwark, 250; military relations, 224–25; military control over, 261; morality on, 105, 138–39, 248, 258; music on, 98–99; neophytes on, 149–54; in New Granada, 274; "new mission history," 196; opposition to, 228–29, 232–35, 259; organization, 79–84; Paraguayan, 7, 81, 271; paternalism of, 92–93, 122–23, 264, 282; permanent divisions among Chiriguanos created by, 56–58, 59–60, 277; plazas of, 81–82, 129–30, 151, 198; population change, 15–16, 102–25, 277; population on eve of Chaco War, 256–58; power on, 160–95; production on, 203–11, 215–17; reasons for acceptance, 17, 51–55, 89, 161, 172, 203; rebellion on, 7, 50–51; rebellion of 1892 and, 187–95; as refuge, 55, 119, 125, 137, 172, 222, 234; as Renaissance ideal, 79; rental of land, 210, 220, 248, 256, 266; repression on, 10, 50–51; request by Caiza for, 31; resistance to, 8, 10, 173–74, 275; schools, 17, 68–69, 77, 88, 111, 123, 124–25, 127, 130–31, 137–49, 156, 158–59, 173–74, 183, 207, 211–12, 244, 248, 257; secularization of, 266; separation between converts and unconverted, 82, 172; settler relations, 4, 6, 8, 217–56, 265, 279–80; sexual decency in, 83; social control on, 8, 136, 139, 152–53, 244, 275; source of combatants, 56; source of intelligence on Indians, 58; spiritual administration of, 83–84; strategy by weak state, 22, 226; stipends for, 221, 226–27; suppression of chiefs, 253; systems, 7–8, 272; teachers on, 137–38, 224, 280, 284; create trade route, 58–59; unconverted on, 128–37, 257; as urban centers, 80, 129; urban patterns, 79–83; vagrancy on, 111, 277; weakness of, 243; weavings, 208; women's experience on, 100, 102, 108, 125, 127, 208. See also *alcaldes*; conversion; Franciscans; secularization; *individual missions*

modernity: frontiers and, 2; Potosí vs. Tarija convents and, 88; rejection by papacy of, 90

Mojos, 16, 73, 272–73

Monteagudo, 25, 26, 29, 30, 32, 36, 37, 41, 45, 49, 179, 190

Montes, Ismael, 95, 241

Movimiento Nacionalista Revolucionario, 268

Murray, William, 251

Murucuyati, 49, 187–88, 223
Muyupampa, 30, 36

Ñacamiri (Chuquisaca), 30, 38
Ñaguapoa (Chuquisaca), 235
Ñancaroinza (Chuquisaca), 48, 179, 189, 194
Nandurai, Catalina, 103
Napoleon, Louis (Napoleon III), 69
Napoleon Bonaparte, 67
Napoleonic invasions, 65
National Convention of 1900, 238
National Territory of Colonies, 238
nationalism, 64, 68, 74, 80, 98
Navajas Trigo, Víctor, 250
neófitos, 82, 87, 92, 126, 128, 154–59; adult, 149–54; citizenship rights and, 282–83; conceptions of, 154–55; feeling of superiority, 154–55; flight of, 233; housing of, 129; lack of priests, 155; part of ARSSP government, 266–68; participation in Tiguipa rituals, 95–100; plazas for, 129–30; reserve mission land for absent, 266–67; section for, 172; use of in expeditions, 200, 202, 233; whites take land of, 258–59
neophytes. See *neófitos*
New Mexico, 13, 73, 173, 274, 276
New Spain. See Mexico
Nordenskiöld, Erland von, 19–20, 107, 121, 136, 138–39, 159, 176, 185, 201, 212
Ñumbicte, 190

O'Connor, Francis Burdett, 25, 26, 34–35, 50, 219–20, 227
officials, local: interactions with missions, 4, 6; tribute payment by, 28
O'Connor Province, 119
Ohio territory, 29
Olañeta, Pedro Antonio de, 41
Orán (Argentina), 36, 58, 114–15

Orosco, Celso, 265
Orsetti, Fr. Marcos, 263, 265

Pacheco, David, 182–83
Pacheco, Gregorio, 182, 233
Pacific coast, 23, 231; Melgarejo and, 24
Padilla (Chuquisaca), 32
Padilla, Octavio, 229, 246
Pando, José Manuel, 238
Paoli, Fr. Rafael, 105
Papacy. See Popes
Papal States, 62, 64–70
Paraguay, 2, 7–8, 12, 76, 81, 89, 200, 251, 265, 272–73; Army, 10; Chaco War and, 260–62; missions, 169, 275
Paraguay River, 260
Parapetí River, 12, 32, 45, 189, 228, 260
Partido de Unión Nacional, 253
Partiñanca (Tarija), 213
Passani, 36, 43
Paz, Domingo, 238
Paz, Luis, 234, 236
peasant unions, 268
Peru, 23–24, 63, 66, 270, 273, 278
Peru-Bolivian Confederation, 23, 50, 63
Phelan, John Leddy, 73
Piedmont state. See Savoy monarchy
Pifarré, Francisco, 14, 15
Pilaya River, 40
Pilcomayo River, 29, 34, 39, 40, 55, 76, 126, 200, 214, 222, 225, 233, 234, 241–42
piquero, 25
polygyny, 84, 128–29, 175, 177, 184–85; prohibition of, 178
Pomabamba (Chuquisaca), 41
Popes, 68, 84, 90; end of temporal power of, 71; Gregory XVI, 64–66; Leo XIII, 65, 280; Pius IX, 65, 68–71
Populism, 23

Positivism, 48–49
Potosí, 18, 24, 32, 71, 231, 238; migrants from, 281; urban grid of, 79
Potosí convent, 51, 102, 221; Apostolic Vicariate and, 72; build mission at Cuevo, 54; historian of, 71; missions of, 53; more modern than Tarija, 88; permission to establish missions, 228; vigor of, 71, 104, 187
presidio, 171
prostitution, 121–22
Protestant missions, 1, 92, 270
Prussia, 65
Puccini, Fr. Alfonso María, 286
Puelche Indians, 274

Quechua Indians, 281
queremba, 15; superiority of, 28

race mixture: between Chiriguanos and Chané, 12; between whites and Chiriguanos, 27
racism, 88. *See also* Social Darwinism
Rahm, Carlos, 251
railroads, 24, 245
ranches: economic basis of Creoles, 25; labor on, 213; profitability, 47, 213; Toba resistance to, 49; tribute payment to Chiriguanos, 33–34
Ratzsch, Otto, 252
rebellion: Acre, 238; Aymara, 24, 226; 1847 rebellion, 32; "first generation revolts," 275; on missions, 274; prevent in 1839, 36; Pueblo of 1680, 274; result of Magariños expedition, 40; repression. *See* missions, repression on
rebellion of 1892, 49, 56, 60, 104, 161, 167, 186–95, 235–38; importance of missions in, 57, 194
Reff, Daniel, 102

Regini, Fr. Domingo, 99
Renaissance, 68, 79
Republican Party, 250
Revolution of 1920, 250
Revolutions of 1848, 64, 69
Ricard, Robert, 3, 6
Río de la Plata, 276
Ríos, Cornelio, 171, 181, 224
Rios, Rafael, 150, 223
Risorgimento, 61, 63, 71, 74
rituals, 95
Rivas, Andrés, 230–31
Rivera, Marcelino, 237
Rodríguez, Angel, 248
Romano, Fr. Santiago, 119, 194, 242
Romanticism, 66–68, 72, 80, 90–91
Rome (Italy), 2, 64, 69–72, 76, 84
Rousseau, Jean-Jacques, 66–67, 90
rubber boom, 9, 24, 111
Ruiz, Manuel, 223
Russia, 65

S. A. Lanmaatschappij Pilcomayo, 251
sacraments, 84–85
Saeger, James, S., 272
Saignes, Thierry, 12, 14, 15, 17, 35, 73, 139, 142, 199
Salamanca, Daniel, 260
Saldías, Fermín, 190
Salinas (mission), 29, 36, 219; donation of, 220; O'Connor and, 219–220, 227; rebellion on, 50–51, 56; rental of land, 220
Salta convent, 262
Salta province (Argentina), 114–15, 281
San Antonio, Salta (mission), 262
San Antonio del Parapetí Grande (mission): conflict with Santa Cruz and, 228–29, 239–40; converts on, 166; establishment of, 51, 54, 78, 228–29, 239–40, 246; population increase,

103–4; secularization of, 51, 53, 102, 229, 241–42, 246
San Antonio de Padua del Pilcomayo (mission), 284; closing in 1879, 77, 235; establishment of, 51, 67, 222, 224; housing of missionaries, 83; lack of success, 51–52; secularization of, 52, 95, 102, 269; urban plan of, 129
San Francisco del Parapetí Grande (mission): conflict with Santa Cruz and, 228–29, 239–40; converts on, 166; establishment of, 51, 54, 228–29, 239–40, 246; population decrease, 104; rebellion of 1892 and, 189; secularization of, 51, 53, 102, 229, 241–42, 246
San Francisco Solano del Pilcomayo (mission), 284; abandonment of mission, 234; establishment of, 51, 222; addition of Chiriguanos, 51–52, 172, 241, 276; Giannelli and, 224, 234; labor request, 227; secularization of, 52, 95, 102, 269; as site for peace treaties, 235; smallpox epidemic on, 162; smallpox vaccinations on, 106–7
San Francisco valley (Argentina), 114
San Juan del Piray (Chuquisaca), 30, 37, 40, 42
San Lorenzo (Argentina). *See* Hacienda San Lorenzo (Argentina)
San Luis (Tarija), 26, 220
Sánchez, José Manuel, 36
Sánchez Velasco, Manuel, 46
Santa Cruz, Andrés de, 23, 50, 63, 221
Santa Cruz (department), 25, 228–29; characteristics of settlers, 26–27, 228; Chiriguano alliance with, 26–27, 30, 228; forts in, 39; missions of, 71; oppose Vicariate, 247

Santa Cruz de la Sierra, 109; Chiriguano frontier, 14; schooling in, 147; trade, 58
Santa Rosa de Cuevo (mission), 215, 268, 284; accounts, 209–10; agriculture on, 205; baptisms on, 162–63, 164, 166, 186; burials on, 103; cattle from, 268; condition after Chaco War, 263; establishment of, 51–54, 187, 229, 236; as fort, 56; labor on, 201; layout, 82, 192, 198; migration and, 109; Paraguayan Army take over, 257, 261; population decline, 102; population increase, 103–4; role in rebellion of 1892, 56, 187–94, 236; schooling on, 146; secularization of, 53, 266; settlers usurp land from, 241, 265; teachers on, 224; unconverted on, 257; urban plan of, 129. *See also* Cuevo
Sapirangui (Chuquisaca), 25, 29
Sardinia, 68
Sauces. *See* Monteagudo
Savoy monarchy, 63, 69
Schwartz, Stuart, 2
scientific racism, 49, 280
secularism, 66, 74, 93
secularization, 10, 11, 51, 52, 53, 64, 226, 229, 240, 241–42, 244–46, 250, 266–269, 270, 282; decree of 1930, 253, 259; decree of 1948, 266–67. *See also* anticlericalism; liberals; missions; *individual missions*
settlers: as actors on the frontier, 28; alliances with Chiriguanos, 29–33, 229; Aracua's alliance with, 30; attitudes toward Indians, 48–49; Ayericuay's alliance with, 30, 171; cattle and, 25, 45–46; Chiriguanos resist on missions, 249; Chuquisaca characteristics, 26; in Cinti, 40; conflict

settlers (*continued*)
    with missions, 232, 237, 279; corrupt mission Indians, 105, 230, 237; death from smallpox, 107; as defenders of Mandeponay, 243; as defenders of missions, 222-23; encroachment at Caiza, 30-31, 40; expansion in 1860s and 1870s, 55; government support, 280; improvement of tactics, 47; during early independence period, 25; inability of government to protect, 34; Indian labor for, 187, 202, 214-15, 228, 239-40; influence government, 46; influence missions, 182; interactions with missions, 4, 6, 8, 171, 217-56, 265-66; invade Tiguipa and Macharetí with cattle, 230; labor from missions, 171, 198, 201, 217, 230; land grants for, 187, 220, 222, 223; land usurpation of missions, 214, 263; liberals and, 245; missions as refuge for, 222; as mission teachers, 224; neophytes and, 150-51; numbers on missions, 266; opposition to Parapetí missions, 228-29, 239, 246; opposition to Tairarí, 171, 224; political divisions, 25-26; poverty of, 25; as reason for mission establishment, 54; request donation of Itau and Salinas, 220; resent missions, 227-30, 265; rights on ARSSP, 267-68; Santa Cruz colonization characteristics, 26-27, 246-47; support missions, 221-23; take over Macharetí, 259; threaten Caiza, 31; usurp mission lands, 259, 263, 265, 268; from Vallegrande, 30. *See also* Gran Chaco; militia; ranching; *individual names*
sex: control of on schools, 138-39; decency, 83; premarital, 84; among couples, 83, 87

shaman. See *ipaye*
Siles, Hernando, 253
silver mining, 24, 47-48, 226, 238
Simonetti, Fr. Estanislao, 229
Sioux Indians, 15
slavery: African, 114-15; conditions like, 118; Indian, 26, 44, 49, 115, 192; mission Indian, 232
smallpox, 106-7, 108; epidemic of 1894, 162; vaccinations, 106-7, 125
Social Darwinism, 48, 88
Spain, 63
Spanish: attempt to conquer Chiriguanos, 14, 89; forts, 14, 17; conquest of Chaco valleys, 114; frontier policies, 14-17, 221; Franciscans, 219; Muslims, 80; Reconquest, 79-80; spiritual conquest, 16
Standard Oil Company, 118-19, 249, 250
state: control by Bolivian, 21-22; ideas about, 22; relative strength of, 10; struggle with Catholic Church, 73-74, 95
Staudt and Company, 242-43, 251, 259
Sucre, Antonio José de, 23, 219-11, 279
Sucre (Bolivia), 22, 24, 26, 47, 81, 147, 182, 236, 237, 238, 265
suffrage, universal, 279
sugarcane plantations, 108, 114-22, 127, 149, 202-3, 276; harvest, 115-17, 212; labor on, 114-16; machinery on, 116; nationalism and, 281; purchase of clothing at, 212
suicide, 271
Summer Institute of Linguistics, 1
Susnik, Branislava, 46, 55, 203
syphilis, 106

Taco, Manuel, 254
Tacu, José Napoleón, 120, 178-80, 184-86, 189-95, 243, 254

Tapieté Indians, 234; attack on Tarairí, 90; attack on expedition of 1867, 225; foundation of Tarija, 26; Vicariate planned for, 250
tapii (slaves), 14
Tarahumara Indians, 9, 274
Tarairí (mission), 215, 284; agriculture on, 204; *aguardiente* production on, 207–8; ASSRP of, 267–68; attack on, 90, 171, 224; baptismal records of, 102–3; as barrier, 58; cattle on, 206; chiefs on, 180–82; conversion on, 167–69; field hospital in, 261; establishment of, 51–53, 67, 90, 171, 221; housing in, 81, 82; license to hunt Tobas, 170, 199; Paraguayan Army take over, 257, 261; parallel government in, 182; plazas on, 130; population, 104; retire military from, 171; schooling on, 144–46, 148; secularization of, 52, 266; succession on, 173; smallpox epidemic on, 162–63; urban plan of, 129
Tarata convent, 67, 221
Tarija (department), 25; Belzu and, 23, 32; governor of, 34; governor pay tribute, 35; limit for Chiriguano, 14; Magariños and, 39; migrants from, 281; status of, 23; support Vicariate, 247
Tarija city (Bolivia), 11; Catholicism of, 233–34; composition of, 63; foundation of, 26; Franciscan convent in, 11, 50; Indian slaves distributed in, 44; Jesuit convent in, 16; residence for landlords, 25; trade, 58; urban grid of, 79; visit by Guaypa, 35
Tarija convent, 11, 50, 83, 114; apostolic vicariate and, 72; effect of Herrera expeditions on, 63, 220; decline of, 104; establishment of missions by, 51–52; failure among Tobas, 187; history of, 219–21; inability to establish mission in Cuevo, 54; power in Tarija, 234; reestablishment of, 63; relationship with the state, 218–19; relationship with settlers, 218–56; during Sucre administration, 219; Venerable Directorio, 242; weakness of, 220, 247
Taringuite (Chuquisaca), 176
Tariquia (Tarija), 33, 50, 219
Tartagal (Argentina), 115
Taruncunti, 172, 175
Tejerina, Torcuato, 249
Terán, Juan Agustín, 25
tercerola, 41
Teyu (Tarija), 126
Thouar, Arthur, 77, 81, 176, 178, 223, 234
Tiguipa (mission), 215; agriculture on, 204; as barrier, 58; conversion on, 167–69; establishment of, 51–52, 54, 221; girls escape school, 244; inauguration of church in, 95–100, 284–88; Paraguayan Army take over, 257, 261; schooling on, 148; secularization of, 52, 266; settlers invade cattle, 230; unconverted on, 257
Timboy (Chuquisaca), 268
tin mining, 238
tiru, 132, 212
Toba Indians, 114, 223, 228; alliance with Chiriguanos, 40, 170–71; Argentine conquest of, 117; attack on Bella Esperanza, 225; Campos expedition and, 231; Chaco War and, 260; conflict with Tarairí, 52, 90, 180–81; as consumers of cattle, 222; Crevaux colony and, 233; Crevaux expedition and, 230–31; effects on, 39–40; encroachment by Caiza, 40; foundation of Tarija and, 26; Fr.

Toba Indians (*continued*)
Giannecchini and, 69, 94; Fr. Giannelli and, 67, 76–77; during Huacaya War, 56, 192; impediment to ranching, 49; interethnic alliances, 59; labor on sugar plantations, 117; lack of civilization, 235; license against, 170, 199; Macharetí and, 176; Magariños expedition and, 39–40; Mandeponay relationship with, 176; missionization of, 76–77, 222; missions as barriers for, 58; participation against Belzu, 32–33; peace treaty with Creoles, 54, 69, 235; raids on Caiza, 31, 40; rebellion, 177; in rebellion of 1892, 189–91; as residents of Macharetí, 179; resistance to settlers, 49, 234; resistance broken, 251; San Francisco mission for, 51, 172, 224, 234–35, 241, 276; at Teyu, 126; as workers, 49, 117, 202, 234–35, 243

Toledo, Francisco de, 14
Tomina (Chuquisaca), 14, 30, 39, 45
Tommassini, Fr. Gabriel, 244, 287
Toro, David, 263
trade: missions and, 58–59
tribute, 157, 279; mission Indians exempt, 279; paid by colonists and government, 28, 33–35
Trigo, Bernardo, 25, 37, 41, 45
Trigo, Leocadio, 242–43, 246, 255
Trigo Raña, Julio, 147
tubicha, 13
tumpa, 20, 188–93
Tunpaete vae, 19
Tunparenda, 20
Tupí Guaraní. *See* Guaraní
Turin (Italy): exposition in, 89, 224
Tuscany (Italy), 61
typhoid, 37–38

Ulivelli, Fr. Hipólito, 180, 252
Unction, 85
United States, 251

Vallegrande (Santa Cruz), 30
Vatican, 226
Vatican I, 65, 71, 76, 77, 93
Vatican II, 71, 84
Venerable Directorio (Tarija convent), 242
Venturi, Fr. Jacinto, 268
Venturi, Poeri, 268
Vigiani, Fr. César, 254
Villamontes (Tarija), 127, 241–42, 251, 261, 262, 267, 269. *See also* San Antonio de Padua del Parapetí; San Francisco Solano del Parapetí
Villazón, Eliodoro, 245–46
Villegas, Carlos, 121–22

War of Italian Independence, 68
War of the Pacific, 24, 28, 229, 231, 236, 238
warfare: Bolivian tactics, 43–44, 191; casualties compared, 38–39, 46; change in after Spanish, 14–15; Chiriguano objectives, 44–45; Creole objectives in, 43–44; during crisis of 1839–41, 35–39; end of Chiriguano warfare, 49; establishment of missions and, 103, 199–200; forts against Indians, 48; guerrilla, 21, 42, 46; improvement of settler tactics, 47; as labor, 199–200; of mission Indians, 58, 199–200; perception of defeat and, 31–33; as public matter, 42; of resources, 45, 46; superiority of Chiriguano, 28, 33, 38, 41–43; tactics by Chiriguanos, 40, 42–47, 191; theft of cattle as sign, 45; trench, 191; Toba methods, 40, 234; total,

37–38. *See also* military; militia; weaponry

weaponry: improvement in, 47, 50; ineffectiveness of, 41–42, 59; Indian and Creole compared, 41–42; repeating rifle, 48; repair requested, 46

Weenhayek. *See* Matacos

whooping cough, 106

women: access to men on missions, 183–84; accompany men in war, 42; agricultural labor and, 132, 201, 273; as captives, 37, 39, 40, 225; as concubines, 129, 177, 228; clothing of, 153–54; exclusive presence on missions, 102, 125, 156, 159; fertility, 105; from Itau sold as slaves, 50; households, 129; kidnapping of during Chaco War, 260; labor demands, 199; migration and, 109, 114, 121–24; on missions, 100, 108, 127, 183–84; production of *cangui*, 123, 174,-175; prostitution of, 121–22; as teachers on missions, 137–38, 224; as war booty, 44, 49, 192; as weavers, 208

Yacuiba (Tarija), 114, 213, 245, 259
Yaguaracu. *See* Tacu, José Napoleón
Yaguareca, 37
Yandori, José Manuel, 126–27, 149
Yanera, 173
Yanomami Indians, 1
Yaqui Indians, 272
Yaveao, 32
Yuqui (Chuquisaca), 49

Zapatera (Tarija), 37
Zenta valley (Argentina), 114
Zoila, 126–27, 148

Erick D. Langer is a professor of history and core faculty at the Edmund A. Walsh School of Foreign Service at Georgetown University.

Library of Congress Cataloging-in-Publication Data
Langer, Erick Detlef.
Expecting pears from an elm tree : Franciscan missions on the Chiriguano frontier in the heart of South America, 1830–1949 / Erick D. Langer.
p. cm.
Includes bibliographical references and index.
ISBN 978-0-8223-4491-9 (cloth : alk. paper) —
ISBN 978-0-8223-4504-6 (pbk. : alk. paper)
1. Chiriguano Indians — Missions — Bolivia — History — 19th century. 2. Chiriguano Indians — Missions — Bolivia — History — 20th century.
3. Franciscans — Missions — Bolivia — History — 19th century. 4. Franciscans — Missions — Bolivia — History — 20th century. 5. Indians of South America — Missions — Bolivia. 6. Bolivia — Church history. I. Title.
F3320.2.C4L36 2009
266'.284 — dc22
2009006499

www.ingramcontent.com/pod-product-compliance
Lightning Source LLC
Chambersburg PA
CBHW061342300426
44116CB00011B/1958